797,885 Books

are available to read at

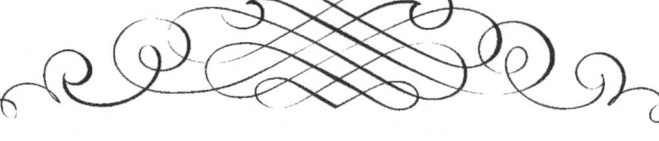

www.ForgottenBooks.com

Forgotten Books' App
Available for mobile, tablet & eReader

ISBN 978-1-333-47658-8
PIBN 10509264

This book is a reproduction of an important historical work. Forgotten Books uses state-of-the-art technology to digitally reconstruct the work, preserving the original format whilst repairing imperfections present in the aged copy. In rare cases, an imperfection in the original, such as a blemish or missing page, may be replicated in our edition. We do, however, repair the vast majority of imperfections successfully; any imperfections that remain are intentionally left to preserve the state of such historical works.

Forgotten Books is a registered trademark of FB &c Ltd.
Copyright © 2015 FB &c Ltd.
FB &c Ltd, Dalton House, 60 Windsor Avenue, London, SW19 2RR.
Company number 08720141. Registered in England and Wales.

For support please visit www.forgottenbooks.com

1 MONTH OF FREE READING

at

www.ForgottenBooks.com

By purchasing this book you are eligible for one month membership to ForgottenBooks.com, giving you unlimited access to our entire collection of over 700,000 titles via our web site and mobile apps.

To claim your free month visit: www.forgottenbooks.com/free509264

* Offer is valid for 45 days from date of purchase. Terms and conditions apply.

English
Français
Deutsche
Italiano
Español
Português

www.forgottenbooks.com

Mythology Photography **Fiction**
Fishing Christianity **Art** Cooking
Essays Buddhism Freemasonry
Medicine **Biology** Music **Ancient
Egypt** Evolution Carpentry Physics
Dance Geology **Mathematics** Fitness
Shakespeare **Folklore** Yoga Marketing
Confidence Immortality Biographies
Poetry **Psychology** Witchcraft
Electronics Chemistry History **Law**
Accounting **Philosophy** Anthropology
Alchemy Drama Quantum Mechanics
Atheism Sexual Health **Ancient History**
Entrepreneurship Languages Sport
Paleontology Needlework Islam
Metaphysics Investment Archaeology
Parenting Statistics Criminology
Motivational

A Boy Craftsman in His Workshop. *"Modern Electrics."*

Factory of the Juvenile Manufacturing Co., of Dayton, Ohio.
Fitted up in a Play-House.

(See Page 103.)

HANDICRAFT FOR HANDY BOYS

Practical Plans for Work and Play
with Many Ideas for Earning Money

By A. Neely Hall
Author of "The Boy Craftsman", Etc.

With nearly six hundred illustrations and working-drawings by the author and Norman P. Hall

BOSTON
LOTHROP, LEE & SHEPARD CO.

COPYRIGHT 1911, BY LOTHROP LEE & SHEPARD COMPANY.

Published, August, 1911.

All rights reserved.

HANDICRAFT FOR HANDY BOYS.

Norwood Press
J. S. Cushing Co. — Berwick & Smith Co.
Norwood, Mass., U.S.A.

When you *play,* play *hard;* and
when you *work,* do *not* play at all.
— THEODORE ROOSEVELT.

INTRODUCTORY NOTES

THIS is a companion volume to "The Boy Craftsman," and is intended for the same class of readers, — boys who want *the latest ideas for making things, practical plans for earning money, up-to-date suggestions for games and sports,* and *novelties for home and school entertainments.*

There are all sorts of Handicraft for Handy Boys in this new volume. Some of the ideas will appeal more directly to younger readers, while other ideas will be better suited to the older lads who have become more capable through experience with earlier ventures and advancement in school. At the time of the publication of "The Boy Craftsman," the author advanced the opinion that it is well to provide a boy with a book which contains not only a goodly measure of the simple work requiring little or no experience in the handling of tools, but also the proper instruction to help him grow more proficient, and such advanced work as he will then be prepared to undertake; and the success of this former volume has proven that such a book gets right next to a boy's heart, that it furnishes him with ideas for many years' work, and that it produces the best possible influence over him in encouraging him to be industrious. Every young fellow loves to plan and dream about what he is "going to do" some day, and in simply looking over the more advanced ideas in a book of this kind, he experiences, in his imaginative mind, much of the pleasures that his older brother or friend gets out of the actual work; for this reason, no school boy is too young to enjoy such a book, and the act of placing a copy in his hands at an early age will be the means of instilling in him an ambition to make the best possible use of his time, before he has had a chance to acquire a tendency to be an idler.

As in "The Boy Craftsman," *the author has planned the suggestions on an economical basis*, providing for the use of the materials which a boy ordinarily has at hand, — old boards, grocery boxes, cigar boxes, barrels, tin cans, worn-out pans and tins, pails, broom-handles, spools, discarded clocks, broken chairs and other furniture, old hats and clothing, stovepipe, clothes-line, screen wire, and other things too numerous to mention, — besides many things which can be purchased for a few cents. The greater part of the ideas require very little if any outlay of money, and many *suggestions for earning money* have been included to make it possible for a boy to provide himself with all the tools which he requires or wishes to own, without having to call upon the home treasurer for the means for such purchases. These features were brought together for the first time in "The Boy Craftsman," and have won the confidence of parents who realize that, in giving a book of this kind to their boys, they are providing something which will encourage self-reliance and resourcefulness rather than a dependence upon home for money for tools and working material — which is often the cause of endless worry where such cannot be furnished. The work is along such lines as will interest the boy with unlimited funds at his disposal, as well as the boy in moderate circumstances, and, inasmuch as it has been planned on a small cost basis, it should be the means of doing him more good, and help him to form a firmer foundation for later years, than something which might tend to cultivate a love for extravagance.

Much of the work is closely allied to the studies of the modern grammar and high schools, as will be seen by glancing over the table of Contents, and it is hoped and believed that

INTRODUCTORY NOTES vii

this outside instruction will be the means of helping boys to appreciate the value of close application to studies.

It is impossible to make a book of this character complete, in the sense of covering every scope of work and play in which boys are interested; for the field is practically inexhaustible, and is growing larger day by day. Every new development in the scientific world is being investigated by an eager army of boys possessing an unquenchable thirst for something new, and generally some young mechanical genius discovers how to introduce the idea into the boys' realm of work; and if costly apparatus was used in the original experiments, he "plugs away" until he finds out how this can be made, wholly or partly, with the materials boys are accustomed to work with,— the truck to be found about the house, in the shed, in alleys and in junk shops, and inexpensive stuff. This sort of original investigation should be encouraged in boys, and no better way can be found than by providing them with a book of modern and ingenious work which will appeal to their mechanical natures.

Here is an example of the pace at which boys' achievements are following the developments of the day. Every up-to-date boy is now experimenting in electrical work and wireless telegraphy, work which has put into the background experimental chemistry — not long ago one of the principal scientific pastimes, and one of the features of boys' handy books; and he is producing original forms of model aëroplanes, while aëronautics now occupies more of his attention than kite-flying, a fact which no one, a few years ago, would have believed to be possible. With the shifting of boys' interests in work and play, it is only natural for the book which contains the greatest variety of modern ideas to win the greatest amount of popularity. Whether or not this book will meet the present demands of boys, the author is willing to let his readers decide.

The manual training in the first portion of the book has been provided for the benefit of the boys who have not the advantages of such instruction at school, as well as to help those who have these advantages, in providing themselves with equipment for home use. The chapter on working-drawings has been inserted to instruct boys in enough of the principles of mechanical drawing to enable them to design and work out their own ideas accurately on paper, and the numerous plans for easily made furniture, for toys and gifts, and for such handy contrivances for the house as a fireless cooker will furnish them with a good supply of ideas to make selections from for shop work. The suggestions for fitting up a boy's room and for making box furniture and gymnasium apparatus will enable boys to provide themselves with rooms furnished to suit their convenience. The chapter on a boy's wireless telegraph outfit contains practical ideas for home-made apparatus in its simplest forms, the chapter on model aëroplanes shows some of the best model flying machines, and the "auto-airship" described is a practical scheme for a boy's airship that runs along a rope cable in which the safety of a toboggan slide is combined with some of the thrilling sensations of flying through the air.

To encourage work in the open, outdoor pastimes have been treated with as much care and consideration in the selection of material as indoor work.

Designers of home-made furniture for amateurs generally omit dimensions on their working-drawings, probably figuring that the work will thus appear less complicated to them; but designers of furniture and machines would not think of omitting these from drawings that are to be turned over to skilled workmen, so it is foolish to expect boys to get along without them. The dimensions upon the furniture-drawings in Chapter VI may make them *appear* complicated, but after studying the instructions for making working-drawings, any boy will find them clear and explicit and to contain only the necessary information.

INTRODUCTORY NOTES

All of the material in this volume has been thoroughly tested, and hundreds of thousands of boys have already had an opportunity to carry out some of the ideas which have been included in the author's articles for boys published recently in *The Ladies' Home Journal* and *Good Housekeeping*, in his "Boy Carpenter" department of *The Boys' Magazine*, and in *The American Boy*. The author wishes to extend his thanks to the editors and publishers of the above publications, for their care in preserving and returning the original drawings for the illustrations to these articles that they might be used in this book.

With a few exceptions, the photographs used were prepared by the author, either from the models he made or from the work constructed by his readers from his plans and instructions.

The author invites correspondence, and is always glad to hear how his boys succeed with their work, and pleased to receive photographs of their handicraft for his collection.

A. N. H.

CHICAGO, ILLINOIS
May 31, 1911.

PART I

AUTUMN AND WINTER HANDICRAFT

CHAPTER I

	PAGE
THE HOME WORKSHOP	1

Introduction — What a Boy should be able to Do — Selecting a Suitable Place for a Shop — Gas or Electric Light — Cabinet-made Benches — A Home-made Bench — A Solid Work Bench — The Bench-vise — An Iron Bench-screw — An Iron Vise — A Work Bench with Tool Drawers — A Tool Tray — Home-made Bench-stops — An Adjustable Bench-stop.

CHAPTER II

TOOLS AND HOME-MADE SHOP EQUIPMENT	14

Purchasing Tools — A Handy Guide for Purchasing — The Principal Tools Required — A Small Outfit and how it may be added to — Jack-knife — Hatchet — Hammer — Tack Hammer — Crate Opener — Nail-set — Wooden Mallet — Cross-cut Saw — Rip-saw — Compass-saw — Keyhole-saw — Back-saw — Coping-saw — Bracket-saw — Scroll-saw — Jack-plane — Smoothing-plane — Fore-plane — Rabbet-plane — Dado-plane — Ratchet-brace — Auger-bits — Expansive-bit — Wood Drill Bit — Brad-awls — Scratch-awl — Hand Gimlet — Rose Countersink Bit — Automatic Drill — Spiral-ratchet Screw-driver — Hand Screw-driver — Screw-driver Bit — Firmer Chisels — Framing or Mortising Chisel — Gouge — Cold-chisel — Draw-knife — Spoke-shave — Half-round Wood-file — Handiest Forms of Files — Two-foot Folding Rule — Try-square — Carpenter's Steel Square — Bevel — Marking-gauge — Wing Dividers — Level — Pocket Level — Odd-jobs — Cutting Pliers — Wrench Wood Handscrews — Cabinet-maker's Clamps — Home-made Clamps — Grindstone — Oilstone — Oiler — Grocery-box Tool-chest — Tool-cabinet — Tool-rack — Open Shelves — Material Boxes — Partitioned Nail Box — Another Box — Receptacles for Nails, Screws, and Brads — Horse — Saw-bench — Chair Saw-bench — Miter-box — Bench-hook — Shooting-board.

CHAPTER III

ELEMENTARY MANUAL TRAINING 42

Selection of Working Material — Structure of Wood — Cutting up the Log — Plain Sawing — Quarter Sawing — Knots — Cup-shakes and Heart-shakes — Checks — Seasoning — Kiln Drying — Stock or Stuff — Undressed Stuff — Dressed Stuff — Matched Stuff — Matched-and-beaded Stuff — Boards — Planks or Dimension Stuff — Timber — Stock Sizes of Lumber — Purchasing Material — A Mill List — Estimating Cost of Material — Laying out Work — Gauging — A Planing Exercise — Winding-sticks — A Sawing Exercise — Joints and Splices — Common-joint — Butt-joint — Common-splice — Fished-splice — Halved-joint — Halved-splice — Mortise-and-tenon Joint — Pins — Wedging — Rabbet — Rabbet-joint — Grooves — Housed-joint — Tongue-and-groove Joint — Mitered-joint — Mitered-splice — Dovetail-joint — Dovetail Half-lap Joint — Dowel-joint — Battens — Cleats — Taper — Bevel — Chamfer — Gluing up Work — Screws — Nails — Carriage-bolts.

CHAPTER IV

WOOD FINISHING 75

The Finishes best adapted to Boys' Work — Paint — Mixing Paints — Brushes — Painting — Staining — Water Stains — Oil Stains — Shellacking — Filling — Waxing — Varnishing — Rubbing Polishing — Oiling — Sandpapering — Puttying — A Home-made Putty-knife — Caution about Oily Rags.

CHAPTER V

WORKING-DRAWINGS 86

What a Working-drawing is and its Purpose — Why Some People have Difficulty in Reading Working-drawings — Definitions of

CONTENTS xiii

PAGE

Detail Drawings, Specifications, Plans, Elevations, Cross-sections, Longitudinal Sections, and a Perspective Drawing — Scales — A Drawing Outfit — A Drawing-board — A Drafting Table — A T-square — A 45-degree Triangle — A 60-degree Triangle — Compasses — A Ruling-pen — A Set of Instruments — A 12-inch Ruler — A Scale — Drawing Pencils — Pens — Drawing Ink — An Ink Eraser and a Pencil Eraser — An Erasing Shield — A Home-made Pencil Box and Inkstand — Thumb-tacks — Drawing-paper — Blueprints — Tracing-cloth — Tracing-paper — A Home-made Printing-frame — Preparing Working-drawings — Dimension-lines, Dot-and-dash Lines, and Dotted Lines — Titles — Marginal Lines — Lettering.

CHAPTER VI

EASILY MADE FURNITURE 103

A Good Test of a Boy's Skill — What Boys generally want to Make — Plan for Earning Money — The Juvenile Manufacturing Company — Choice of Material — A Whisk-broom Holder — A Clock-shelf — A Necktie Rack — A Towel-rack — Book-racks — An Extension Book-rack — Popularity of Tabourets and Plant Stands — A List of Material showing Exact Finished Dimensions — A Tabouret — Leveling up Uneven Legs — Another Tabouret — A Plant Stand — A Footstool — Upholstering Material and how to Upholster — A Bench — Two Magazine Racks — A Music-cabinet — An Umbrella-stand — A Roman Chair — A Mission Chair — A Mission Writing-desk — An Electric Lamp — How to wire up the Lamp with a Socket and Drop-cord — A Drafting Table — A Desk Table.

CHAPTER VII

HANDY CONTRIVANCES FOR THE HOUSE 135

Things a Boy can make and Sell — How to sell Home-made Articles — A Fireless Cooker — The Fireless Cooker used by the United States Army — A Pot-cover Rack — A Bottle-rack — How to cut Large Holes — A Flat-iron Rest — A Flat-iron Rack — A Sleeve-board — A Knife-box — A Scrub-pail Platform — A Towel-roller — An Ice-pick and Ice-chisel Rack — How to finish Household Conveniences.

CONTENTS

CHAPTER VIII

A Boy's Room in an Attic 149

A Dividing Partition — A Plumb-line — A Plumb-board — Lockers — Wainscoting — A Large Clothes Closet — Trousers Hangers Doors — The Entrance-door Transom — An Old-fashioned Cabin Latch — An Oil Heater or Stove — A Wash-stand — A Broom-handle Towel-rack — Lighting the Room — A Home-made Hanging Lamp — Furnishing the Room — Home-made Picture-frames — The Furniture — A Pirate Chest — A Window Seat — Suggestions for Boys who have no Attic.

CHAPTER IX

Box and Barrel Furniture 160

The Possibilities for Making Things out of the Materials at Hand — A Writing-desk — A Shelf for Books — An Office Chair A Waste-basket — An Arm Rocker — A Barrel Table — A Chiffonier — How to finish Box Furniture.

CHAPTER X

Home-made Gymnasium Apparatus for a Boy's Room . 170

A Chest-weight — A Striking-bag — A Striking-bag Platform — A Chinning-bar — A Hitch-and-Kick — A Wand — A Rack for Dumb-bells, Indian Clubs, and Wand.

CHAPTER XI

Cigar-box Toys and Gifts 178

Articles to give away and to Sell — Material — Finish — Cutting — An Express-wagon — A Cart — An Auto Delivery-wagon — A Jack-in-the-Box — A Round-seated Chair — A Round Center-table — A Dining-table — A Square-seated Chair — A Doll's Cradle — A Key-board — A Corner Clock-shelf — A Whisk-broom Holder — A Kitchen Match-box — A Cottage Pipe-rack and Match-box — A Cottage Match-box — Suggestions for Other Gifts.

CHAPTER XII

Clockwork Toys 189

The Necessary Materials — How to prepare the Clockwork — A Merry-go-round — The Standard — The Tent — The Tent-poles

CONTENTS

The Horses — The Sleighs — The Shafts — The Girl and Boy Riders — The Platform — How to operate the Merry-go-round — Other Animals for the Merry-go-round — A Miniature Ferris Wheel The Standard — The Station Platform — How to make the Wheel How to make the Cars — The Car Axles — How to mount the Wheel — Steps to the Platform — The "Flying Airships" — The Standard — The Mast — The Cars — How to increase the Speed of the Clockwork.

CHAPTER XIII

BRASS CRAFT 206

The Tools and Materials Required — Enlarging Designs by Squares — Piercing — Polishing the Brass — A Home-made Antique Green Lacquer — A Tea-pot Stand — A Calendar Board — A Pen Tray — A Lamp-shade — Chain Fringe — A Candle-shade — Shade-holders — A Candle-stick — A "Paul Revere" Lantern.

CHAPTER XIV

A BOY'S WIRELESS TELEGRAPH OUTFIT 219

Marconi and his Experiments — What Some Boys have Accomplished — The Chicago Wireless Club — Code Cards, Call Lists, and Aërogram Blanks — Amateur Commercial Stations — Fundamental Principles of Wireless Telegraphy — The Aërial — Masts for the Aërial — Insulating the Aërial — Grounding the Aërial — The Receiving Outfit — Telephone Receivers — Detectors — A Microphone Detector — A Razor-blade Microphone Detector — A Silicon Detector — A Tuning-coil — A Fixed Condenser — A Potentiometer — The Transmitting Outfit — An Induction-coil — A Spark-gap A Storage Battery — Dry Batteries — A Wireless Key — A Knife Switch — A Good Arrangement for the Instruments — Operation of Instruments — How to receive a Call — How to make a Call Codes — A Good Way to learn a Code — Electrical Measurements — Connection of Dry Batteries.

CHAPTER XV

STUNTS FOR A BOYS' VAUDEVILLE SHOW 256

The Best Kind of Stunts for a Boys' Show — Sam Dow, the Strong Man — Holding out a Chair upon which a Boy is Seated —

The Dumb-bell Lifting Feat — Juggling with Heavy Balls — Bonehead — The Magical Mortar — The Professor — The Wonderful Hat Trick — Other Mortar Stunts — The Professor's Final Exhibition — The Dummy Assistant — Falsetto, the Boy with a Wonderful Voice — The Ventriloquist — How to make the Ventriloquist's Doll Willie Shute, the Crack Shot of the World — The Targets — His Blunderbuss — A Program Board — Admission Tickets.

CHAPTER XVI

MOVING PICTURES 270

A Simple Moving-picture Machine — The Wooden Base — The Cylinder — The Clown and Ball Pictures — The Circus Horse and Hound Pictures — How to operate this Toy — The Automobile — The Revolving Wheels — The Boxing-match.

CHAPTER XVII

A SNOW BATTLESHIP 279

A New Idea for a Snow Fight — The Central Station — The Hull — A Torpedo Tube — The Superstructure Deck — The Conning-tower — The Forward Turret — The Midship Turret — The Mast — The Fighting-tops — Rapid-fire Guns — The Crosstree — A Coach-whip Pennant — Paper Signal Flags — A Union Jack — A National Ensign — The Funnels — The Ventilators — The Main-battery Guns — The Secondary-battery Guns — Arrangement of Ammunition Stores — Duties of the Captain — A Naval Battle Rules for the Battle — A Flag of Truce — The "Torpedo Boats" Repairing the Ships after a Battle — Marksmanship.

CHAPTER XVIII

A COASTER AND A BOB-SLED 287

A Coaster — How to lay out the Runners — Shoes for Runners — Connecting the Runners — The Seat — Sled Handles — The Foot-bar — Painting the Sled.

A Bob-sled — The Four Runners — Connecting the Runners — The Sled Seats — The Plank Seat — How to hinge the Seat to the Stern Sled — Check-chains — The Steering Foot-bar — The Steering Lines — Handle-bars — A Seat Cushion — Painting the Bob-sled.

PART II

SPRING AND SUMMER HANDICRAFT

CHAPTER XIX

MODEL AËROPLANES 297

Spring Activities — " Aëroplane Time " — Length of Model Aëroplane Flights — Junior Aëro Clubs — Model Aëroplane Meets — Types of Machines Used — Support of Aëroplane — A Cardboard Bird Glider — A Simple Monoplane Model — Center-pole — Planes — A Glider Race — An Easily Made Propeller — Shaft and Shaft Bearing — Motive Power — Winding up the Motor — A French Monoplane Model — Center-pole — Propeller — Running-gear — Skids — Planes — Adjustment of Planes — An Antoinette Monoplane Model — Center-pole — Propeller — Wings — Tail — Fin Rudder — Running-gear — A More Elaborate Monoplane Model Center-pole — Material for Binding — Running-gear — Propeller Shaft and Bearing — Motor — Planes — Bracings — Rudder Finish — Flights this Monoplane is capable of Making — Field for Experimenting.

CHAPTER XX

A BOY'S AUTO-AIRSHIP 327

A Safe and Practical " Boy-carrying " Airship — The Framework of the Balloon — Barrel-hoop Ribs — Rib-bands — Stays — The Balloon Envelope — Construction of the Car — The Propeller — A Starting Platform — A Push-off Platform — The Rope Cable — Attachment of Car — Windlass for pulling back the Airship to Starting Platform — An Auto-airship Club.

CHAPTER XXI

CAMPING EQUIPMENT 337

Prices of " A " and Wall Tents — How to make an " A " Tent — The Ridge-pole and Uprights — Tent Stakes — Pitching a Tent A Tent Ground-cloth — A Pine Twig Mattress — A Sleeping-bag — Other Equipment — An Electric Flash Lamp — Packing — A Safety Match-box — A Duffle Box — Food Supplies — If you are to be Cook — Making an Open Fire — The Backwoodsman's Camp Fireplace — Pothooks — A Sheet-iron Camp Stove — A Dutch Oven — A Camp Fireless Cooker — To build a Fire — Camp Furniture A Camp Chair — A Camp Table — A Good Table Bench — A Comfortable Box Bench — Box Cupboards

CHAPTER XXII

A HOME-MADE PUNT 351

Dimensions — Material — The Side Boards — The Stem- and Stern-pieces — The Bottom Boards — An Inner Keel Board — Seats — Rowlocks — Thole-pins — The Painter — Finishing.

CHAPTER XXIII

A HOME-MADE SHARPIE 356

Dimensions — The Side-pieces — The Stem-piece — The Stern-piece — The Stretcher — To put the Pieces Together — The Bottom Boards — The Skeg — An Inner Keel Board — Seats — Finishing the Bow — The Painter — An Easily Made Rudder — The Rowlock Blocks — Rowlocks or Thole-pins — Finishing.

CHAPTER XXIV

PUSHMOBILES AND OTHER HOME-MADE WAGONS 364

Where to get Wheels — What a Pushmobile Is — The Flushing Pushmobile Club — The Vanderbilt Cup Race — Description of a Pushmobile Race — Organizing Pushmobile Clubs — To construct a Pushmobile — The Iron Axles — The Wooden Axles — The Wagon-bed — The Steering-wheel — The Hood — The Radiator-front — The Seat — Headlights — Side Lamps — A Clock-case Side Lamp — Painting — The License Number — A Racing Pushmobile.

An Auto Wagon — The Steering-wheel — Another Steering-gear — The Seat — A Trip Gong.

A Simple Push Wagon — The Wagon-bed — The Rear Wheels The Axle for the Front Wheels.

CHAPTER XXV

BIRD-HOUSES 379

Designing the Bird-house and choosing a Location for It Materials out of which to make Bird-houses — A Box Bird-house

CONTENTS

— Another Box Bird-house — A Bird Tower — A Tin-can Bird Tower — A Bird Castle — A Bird Ark — A Wall Bracket Bird Ark — A House and Swing — A Hanging House — A Shelter.

CHAPTER XXVI

HOUSES FOR PETS 389

A Dog-house — A Rabbit-hutch — Galvanized Poultry-netting, Twist Wire Cloth, and Wire Cloth for Fronts of Hutches and Cages — A Breeding Hutch — A Two-story Rabbit-hutch — A Rabbit Yard — A Cage for White Rats — An Elevated "Race-track" Painting — Floor Covering — Drinking Receptacles — A Pigeon-cote.

CHAPTER XXVII

A CASTLE CLUB-HOUSE AND HOME-MADE ARMOR 404

Material — The Framework — The Floor Joists — The Corner Turrets — Boarding up the Walls — To cut the Openings — The Roof — If the Roof Leaks — The Battlement — Secret Treasure Vaults — The Drawbridge — To counterbalance the Drawbridge — A Windlass — A Moat.

Home-made Armor — A Helmet — A Shield — A Sword.

CHAPTER XXVIII

A BOYS' BAND OF HOME-MADE INSTRUMENTS 416

The Neighborhood Parade — Materials out of which to make the Imitation Instruments — A Cornet — A Trombone — A Bass Horn — A Fife — A Bass Drum — Cymbals — The Drum-stick — Snare-drums — The Drum Major — A Splendid "Bearskin" Cap — The Drum Major's Staff — The Major's Whistle — Uniforms — Organizing a Band — How the Band will be useful in the Home Circus, Vaudeville, and Other Shows — A Boy Scout Band.

INDEX 427

LIST OF HALF-TONE ILLUSTRATIONS

(In addition to more than five hundred text illustrations.)

PART I

A Boy Craftsman in his Workshop	*Frontispiece*
Factory of the Juvenile Manufacturing Co.	

	FACING PAGE
A Basement Workshop	2
A Corner of the Author's Home Workroom	86
Fig. 108. — Whisk-Broom Holder Fig. 109. — Clock-Shelf Figs. 110 and 111. — Necktie-Racks Figs. 112–114. — Book-Racks	104
Figs. 122 and 123. — Tabourets Fig. 124. — Plant Stand Fig. 125. — Footstool	110
Figs. 131 and 132. — Magazine-Racks Fig. 133. — Music-Cabinet Fig. 134. — Umbrella-Stand	124
Fig. 139. — A Roman Chair Fig. 140. — A Mission Chair Fig. 141. — A Mission Writing-Desk Fig. 142. — An Electric Lamp	128
Fig. 206. — Construct Your Chest-Weights First Fig. 210. — Where to Hang the Striking-Bag Fig. 215. — The Doorway Chinning-Bar is Easily Put Up	170
Fig. 223. — An Express-Wagon Fig. 224. — A Cart	178
Figs. 225 and 226. — Two Views of an "Auto Delivery-Wagon"	180
Fig. 228. — A Jack-in-the-Box Fig. 229. — The Skeleton of the Jack-in-the-Box Fig. 230. — A Round-Seated Chair Fig. 231. — A Round Center-Table Fig. 232. — A Dining-Table Fig. 233. — A Square-Seated Chair Fig. 234. — A Doll's Cradle	182–183

xxii LIST OF HALF-TONE ILLUSTRATIONS

FACING PAGE

Fig. 238. — A Key-Board
Fig. 239. — A Corner Clock-Shelf
Fig. 240. — A Whisk-Broom Holder 184
Fig. 241. — A Kitchen Match-Box
Fig. 242. — A Cottage Pipe-Rack and Match-Box
Fig. 253. — A Merry-Go-Round
Fig. 254. — A Clockwork Motor
Fig. 255. — A Ferris Wheel 190
Fig. 256. — A Flying Airship
Fig. 360. — The "Torpedo-boats" Furnish the Only Means of Attack at Close Range 280

PART II

Aëro Club of the Chicago Calumet High School
A Model Aëroplane Meet of the Calumet Aëro Club . 297
Some Good Forms of Model Aëroplanes 302
Wall Tent, Eight Feet by Ten Feet, with Fly
Flapjacks for Two 340
Some of the Competing Cars in the Flushing Pushmobile Club Races 364
Winning Car in the Vanderbilt Cup Race
At the Start Off. A Flushing Pushmobile Club Race 366
Fig. 483. — A Bird Tower
Fig. 484. — A Bird Castle
Fig. 485. — A Bird Ark 382
Fig. 486. — A House and Swing
Fig. 506. — The Castle Club-House 404
Fig. 515. — A Boy Knight with His Home-Made Armor 412
Fig. 530. — The Cornet
Fig. 531. — The Trombone 416
Fig. 532. — The Bass Horn

PART I
Autumn and Winter Handicraft

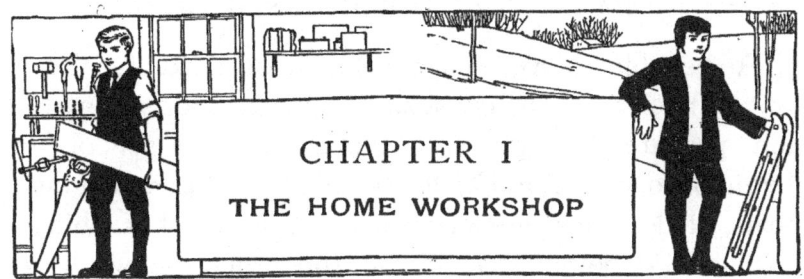

CHAPTER I
THE HOME WORKSHOP

WITH the coming of autumn and the beginning of the new school year, the majority of you boys who have enjoyed all summer the freedom of outdoor life probably pick up your books with a feeling of regret that you must knuckle down again to studies. But as soon as you meet all the boys and get to talking over last year's good times, your old school enthusiasm returns; then when some one proposes something interesting to do, you at once fall into line with the other fellows in offering suggestions, and the chances are that before the day is over you are ready to admit that school life is pretty good after all. In the course of a day or so football is under way, and possibly plans have developed for an athletic club and literary society, while all sorts of schemes have been undertaken by groups of boys who have found that they can work together congenially, and very likely each boy has mapped out a lot of individual work to do. These outside interests help probably more than anything else to keep school from becoming monotonous.

HANDICRAFT FOR HANDY BOYS

To be able to fix up a club-room or make furniture for your own room, construct apparatus for a "gym" and prepare the various "properties" for school or neighborhood "shows"; to be able to build wagons, boats, sleds, kites, model aëroplanes, and other things just a little better than those the other fellows have made; to be able to make pieces of handicraft which will be presentable as Christmas and birthday gifts to your friends and relatives; in short, to be handy about doing things in general is an accomplishment which every one of you boys should strive to attain; but before you can expect to do all of these things well it will be necessary for you to know not only how to use carpenters' tools properly, but also how to go about the work in the right way. This is the author's reason for beginning this book of handicraft for you with instructions upon manual training.

Unless you have a workshop, or at least a space large enough in which to set up a work bench, you will be handicapped for any kind of home carpentry, for to get good results it is necessary to have something strong and solid to work upon and a vise which will hold your pieces of work firmly. The basement, attic, a spare room, the wood shed, and the barn suggest possibilities for fitting up a good workshop, but in

Selecting a Suitable Place there are several important things to consider. The shop should have good light, it should be dry, to prevent your stock from getting wet

A Basement Workshop.

and your tools from rusting, and it should be located conveniently, so that material can easily be carried in and out, and far enough away from the living-room and bedrooms so that your hammering will not disturb any one. Of course, some of you will have no choice in the matter and will have to take any place you can get, but in this case make the best of the conditions for the time being and perhaps something better will turn up later on. If you locate your shop in the basement or attic, it will be a good idea to partition off a space as large as you will need and provide a door with a padlock which can be locked to keep things from being tampered with by younger hands. The building of a partition is described on page 149 and illustrated by Figs. 172 to 175. If there isn't any

Gas or Electric Light within the space partitioned off, it will also be a good plan to run a piece of rubber tubing from the nearest gas-jet, or a drop-cord from an electric fixture (see photograph opposite page 2), over to a point near the left end of your bench, so you can have light when the days are dark or whenever you wish to work in the evening.

Cabinet-made Benches can be bought at any of the large stores where tools are sold, for from $7.50 to $50, but one of these will serve your purposes no better than the old-fashioned

Home-made Bench to be found in almost every carpenter shop. One of these can be made by any boy, out of pine, cypress, or whitewood. The well-made cabinet benches have maple tops, but it is not necessary to go to the expense of buying maple for your bench, as softer material will do just as well. Dressed 1-inch, $1\frac{1}{4}$-inch, or 2-inch stock may be used for the top, 2-by-4-inch stuff for the framework, and 1-inch boards for the aprons and rails; 4-by-4-inch stock is often used for bench legs, but " 2-by-4's " are plenty heavy enough and generally easier to get.

Figure 1 shows

A Solid Work Bench, 2 feet 8 inches high, with a top 5 feet long and 24 inches wide. This is a good size to make your bench if you are crowded for room. If you would like to have it longer, it is a simple matter to add whatever you wish to the lengths given for the different pieces, and if you find that it is going to be too high for you, it is easy enough to saw off the legs before making the vise. Figure 2 shows the framework with the different members lettered. Cut the four legs *A* 2 feet 8 inches long, less the thickness of the crosspieces *B* ($1\frac{3}{4}$ inches) and the top, the 2-by-4-inch crosspieces *B* 22-inches long, the end rails *C* 22 inches long by $3\frac{3}{4}$ inches wide, and the front and back rails *D* 4 feet long by $3\frac{3}{4}$ inches wide. Spike crosspieces *B* to the tops of the legs, and rails *C* to the sides 8 inches from the lower ends; then stand the frames thus formed on end and connect them by means of rails *D*. Cut a front and a rear *apron* (*E*, Fig. 2) 5 feet long, out of 10-inch

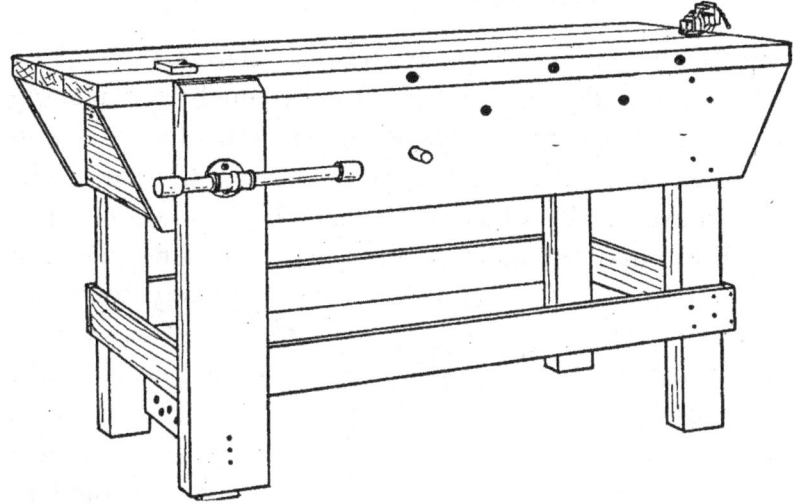

Fig. 1. — A Solid Work Bench.

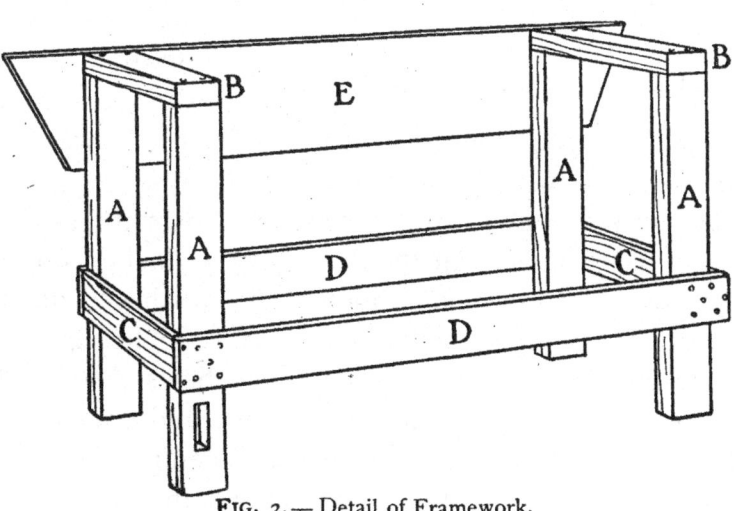

Fig. 2. — Detail of Framework.

boards, saw off the ends on the diagonal as shown, and then either nail or screw them to the bench legs, placing them with their top edges even with the top of cross-pieces *B* and with their ends projecting the same distance beyond the ends of the bench framework. The bench top may be made of three pieces 8 inches wide, or of any combination of widths that will make up a total of 24 inches, and these pieces should be fastened to cross-pieces *B* with screws. *Countersink* the screw-heads. Finish the ends of the bench by fitting pieces of 10-inch board between the aprons, as shown in Fig. 1.

SOCKET
SCREW
BLOCK OUT BACK OF LEG IF SCREW IS NOT THREADED AS FAR BACK AS SHOWN IN FIG. 4.
BLOCK
FIG. 5.
HANDLE
JAW
SLIDING-STRIP
BENCH LEG
POCKET
MORTISE
LEG
JAW
SLIDING-STRIP

FIG. 4. FIG. 3.

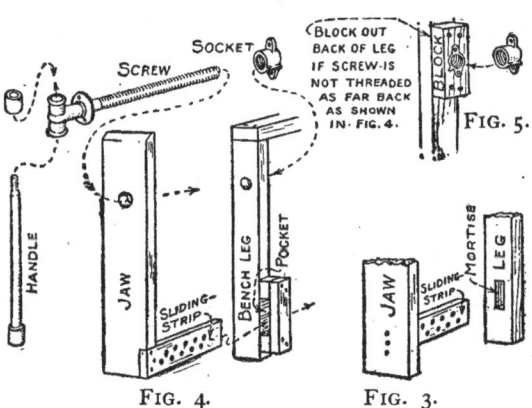

FIGS. 3–5.—Details of the Bench-vise.

Figures 3, 4, and 5 show the details for making

The Bench-vise. Cut the *jaw* about 31 inches long out of a piece of $1\frac{1}{2}$-inch or 2-inch stuff 6 inches wide, and the *sliding strip* 3 inches wide and 14 inches long out of a 1-inch board, and bore ten $\frac{1}{2}$-inch holes through the sliding strip about $\frac{3}{4}$ inch on centers and *staggered* as shown. There are several ways of fastening the sliding strip to the jaw, two of which are shown in Figs. 3 and 4.

By nailing the jaw to the end of the strip, as in Fig. 3, it is necessary to mortise the bench leg for it to slide through, while if you set the strip into the side of the jaw, as in Fig. 4, a pocket must be built on to the side of the leg. If you mortise the leg, make the mortise about $\frac{1}{4}$ inch larger all around than the strip, so there will be plenty of clearance, and locate the bottom of it 3 or 4 inches above the floor. After fastening the sliding strip to the jaw, slip the end through the mortise — or through the pocket, push the jaw up against the apron of the bench, and drive a couple of nails through it to hold it temporarily in place.

An Iron Bench-screw, socket and wooden handle (Fig. 4), can be bought at almost any hardware store for 50 cents. If this screw is $1\frac{1}{4}$ inches in diameter, describe a circle $1\frac{1}{2}$ inches in diameter on the face of the jaw, 8 inches below the bench top, and then bore a hole of the same diameter through the jaw, the apron, and the bench-leg (see "Cutting Large Holes," page 142). With a chisel enlarge the hole on the inside face of the leg (you had better turn the bench over upon its side to do this) so the iron socket will set into the leg flush with the surface; then, after screwing the socket to the leg, trim the hole in the jaw so the *collar* on the handle end of the screw will set flat against the jaw, and screw the plate in place. Some of the bench-screws are made to go through heavier stuff than we have used for the legs, and their threads stop within 3 or 4 inches of the collar plate; in this case it becomes necessary to set the socket into an extra block of wood (Fig. 5) and to spike this block to the back of the leg; otherwise, the jaw would not close entirely. Trim off the top of the jaw even with the bench top and bevel the outer edge (Figs. 1 and 4), then remove the temporary nails. Cut a peg to fit in the holes in the sliding strip, and whenever you use the vise, stick this peg into the proper hole to keep the bottom of the jaw from pushing in farther than the upper portion; the jaw must be kept vertical in order to make it grip a piece of wood squarely.

Bore several rows of $\frac{3}{4}$-inch holes through the front apron, as shown in Fig. 1, and cut a peg to fit in them. This peg may be adjusted to support the end of any length of board placed in the vise.

Never clamp screws, nails, or other pieces of metal in your vise without placing them first between blocks of wood, as they will cut up the face of the jaw and bench apron and soon make the vise unfit to hold your nice work. It is a good plan to have

An Iron Vise for metal work; one of these can be purchased for from 50 cents to $1 and may be screwed to the right end of your bench (Figs. 1 and 6).

Figure 6 shows

A Work Bench with Tool Drawers, which is almost as simple to make as the one just described. The drawers are grocery boxes and slide into the ends of the bench on the upper rails of the framework (Fig. 7). The bench

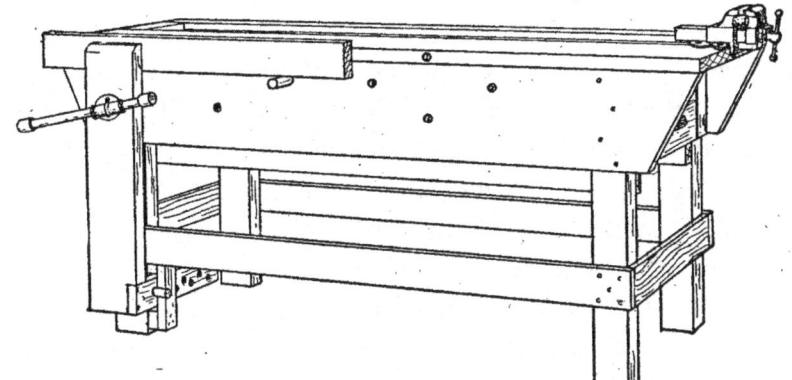

FIG. 6. — A Work Bench with Tool Drawers.

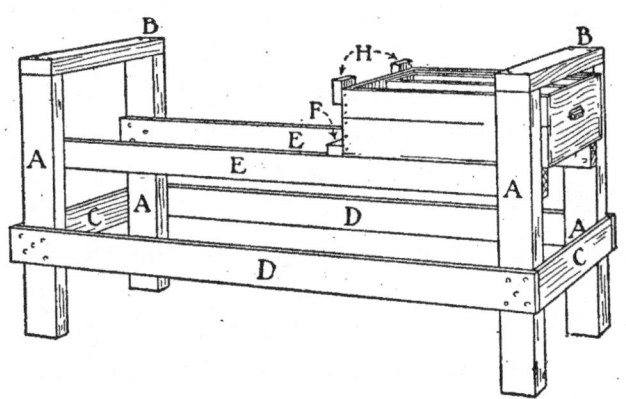

FIG. 7. — Detail of Framework.

illustrated is 6 feet long, 24 inches wide, and 2 feet 8 inches high, but as mentioned before you may change these dimensions to suit your conditions, and if you prefer to make a cabinet for your tools instead of keeping them in the bench, the drawers may be used to hold supplies. Figure 7 shows the framework of the bench. Make the end frames as described for the other bench, fasten them 4 feet 2 inches apart with the front and back rails *D*, and then cut the upper rails *E* which form the drawer slides and nail them to the legs 8 inches below crosspieces *B*. If you cannot find boxes of the proper size for

The Tool Drawers, larger boxes may be cut down, or you can build up drawers to fit. Provide the drawers with removable trays, such as are described for the tool-chest shown in Fig. 43, page 31. Nail two guide strips (*G*, Fig. 8) to the bottom of the drawers and fasten an iron drawer-pull or a wooden handle to the front. Then nail two striking blocks to the back (*H*, Fig. 7) to prevent the drawers from pulling out of the bench, and two crosspieces (*F*) in the proper places to stop the drawers when they have been pushed in flush with the ends of the bench. Figure 6 shows

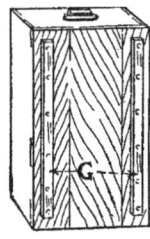

FIG. 8.— Box Tool Drawer.

A Tool Tray *recessed* in the bench top — a good arrangement, as it provides a place to lay tools while working. This top may be made by placing a 12-inch plank along the front of the top, an 8-inch board back of it, and a piece of 2-by-4 back of that again (Fig. 9), and then blocking out the ends of the board flush with the top of the planking. To finish off the ends of the bench, fit in strips around the drawers.

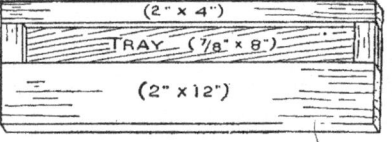

FIG. 9.— Plan for a Bench Top with Tool Tray.

Before adjustable *bench-stops* were put upon the market, a carpenter had to devise various makeshifts for shoving work against for planing and for other operations, and as many of these are still in use, I am going to show you a few of the good forms of

Home-made Bench-stops, so in case it is not convenient to buy an iron stop, you can equip your bench with one

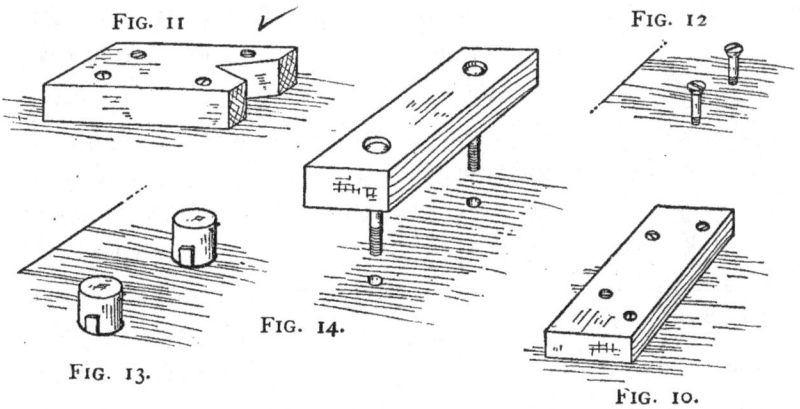

FIGS. 10–14.— Home-made Bench-stops.

of these. The stop shown in Fig. 10 consists of a short strip of wood, which is screwed in place to the bench top, and the screw-heads are *countersunk* as a protection for your edge tools. By screwing the strip in place, it is easily removed when you wish to have the bench top clear. Figure 11 shows a block with a "V" notch cut in it. This will hold the ends of narrow pieces of work. Screw stops (Fig. 12) are a favorite form, as they are easily adjusted to a required height by giving them a few turns with a screw-driver. The peg stops shown in Fig. 13 have a big advantage in the fact that they are quickly removed. Bore two $\frac{3}{4}$-inch holes through the bench, cut the pegs to fit loosely in them so they may be adjusted to the proper heights for different pieces of work, and drive in a *hammer wedge*, or a wooden wedge, at the side of the pegs to hold them in position. The stop shown in Fig. 14 is similar to that shown in Fig. 10, except that it is held in place with bolts instead of screws. Get two $\frac{3}{8}$-inch carriage-bolts about 4 inches long, and cut several strips of wood about 8 inches long and of different thicknesses. Bore two $\frac{3}{8}$-inch holes, 5 inches apart, through the bench top and through the strips for the bolts to drop through, and countersink for the bolt-heads. This stop is handy, as the strips may be interchanged to suit work of different thicknesses. Figure 15 shows

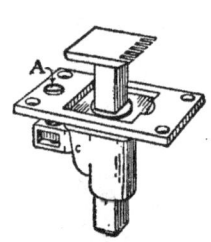

FIG. 15. — An Adjustable Bench-stop.

An Adjustable Bench-stop which retails for 50 cents. The *pin* in the center of this stop is released by giving the screw marked *A* a few turns with a screw-driver, and may be set to the proper height for your work and dropped flush with the plate when not in use. Mortise the bench top for the stop, and set the plate flush with the top.

The other shop equipment is described in the following chapter.

top, and the screw-heads are *countersunk* as a protection for your edge tools. By screwing the strip in place, it is easily removed when you wish to have the bench top clear. Figure 11 shows a block with a " V " notch cut in it. This will hold the ends of narrow pieces of work. Screw stops (Fig. 12) are a favorite form, as they are easily adjusted to a required height by giving them a few turns with a screw-driver. The peg stops shown in Fig. 13 have a big advantage in the fact that they are quickly removed. Bore two ¾-inch holes through the bench, cut the pegs to fit loosely in them so they may be adjusted to the proper heights for different pieces of work, and drive in a *hammer wedge*, or a wooden wedge, at the side of the pegs to hold them in position. The stop shown in Fig. 14 is similar to that shown in Fig. 10, except that it is held in place with bolts instead of screws. Get two ⅜-inch carriage-bolts about 4 inches long, and cut several strips of wood about 8 inches long and of different thicknesses. Bore two ⅜-inch holes, 5 inches apart, through the bench top and through the strips for the bolts to drop through, and countersink for the bolt-heads. This stop is handy, as the strips may be interchanged to suit work of different thicknesses. Figure 15 shows

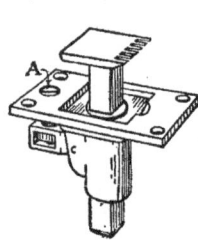

FIG. 15. — An Adjustable Bench-stop.

An Adjustable Bench-stop which retails for 50 cents. The *pin* in the center of this stop is released by giving the screw marked *A* a few turns with a screw-driver, and may be set to the proper height for your work and dropped flush with the plate when not in use. Mortise the bench top for the stop, and set the plate flush with the top.

The other shop equipment is described in the following chapter.

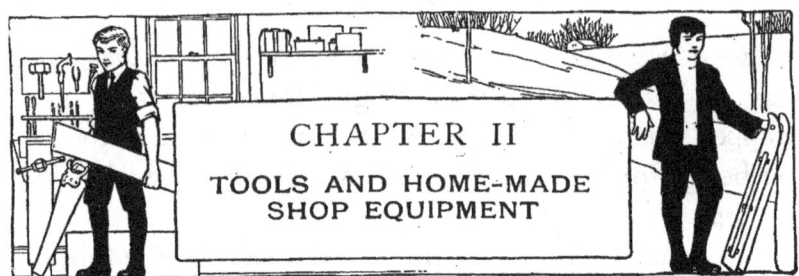

CHAPTER II
TOOLS AND HOME-MADE SHOP EQUIPMENT

BETTER results may be obtained with a few tools of the best quality than with an entire outfit of cheaper grade. Remember that, boys, when **Purchasing Tools**, and be sure that you get those made by reliable manufacturers instead of the toy variety, for though they will cost considerably more, their better wearing qualities will make them cheaper in the long run. You will find new-fangled tools for every conceivable form of work in the modern carpenter shop, but do not imagine for a minute that it is necessary to have these in order to perform the operations for which they are especially made. A good mechanic can complete almost any kind of a job with a handful of tools, but special tools do the work so very much quicker that they are adopted as time-saving devices, and usually are worth many times their cost in a large shop.

Unless you have received instruction in manual training, the variety of styles and sizes in which tools are made may make the selection of an outfit difficult; so to provide

A Handy Guide for Purchasing, the more desirable forms and sizes of all the tools which an amateur is ever likely to require have been described and illustrated upon the following pages.

A hatchet, hammer, saw, plane, chisel, jack-knife, bit and brace, screw-driver and square are mentioned in "The Boy Craftsman" as

The Principal Tools which a boy requires. If you cannot afford more at the start, add to them as soon as you can. Figure 16 shows illustrations of

A Small Outfit which a boy will find sufficient for any kind of ordinary carpentry. Every tool in this outfit is an important tool and one which you will find necessary for general use. As your money permits, you will wish to add to these tools several sizes of chisels and bits, one or two saws, and such other tools as are used in advanced work, and in this way you can increase your outfit, until before long you will have a fairly complete set of tools of which you may be proud.

First of all, you will need a good

Jack-knife. By this is not meant a four-blade pocket-knife with a polished pearl handle, but just a common knife, strongly made, and having blades of steel properly tempered so they will hold an edge. A two-blade knife with wooden handle similar to that shown in Fig. 16 is a desirable form for all-round work, and is made in a medium-priced knife with blades of a good quality of steel.

For general use

A Hatchet with a claw (Fig. 16) is to be preferred to one without, as it may be used for withdrawing nails as

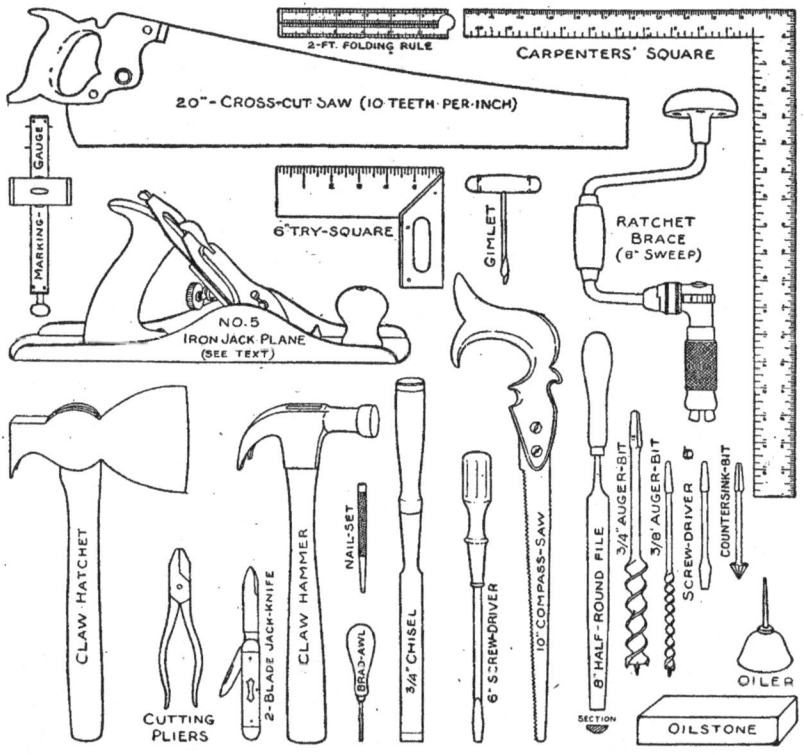

FIG. 16. — A Small Tool Outfit.

The most important tools, showing desirable forms and sizes. Additional tools may be selected from those shown and described upon the following pages, as your money permits and your work requires their use.

well as driving them. In buying a hatchet, select one of medium weight and see that it balances nicely when you swing it, for, if unevenly balanced, it is cumbersome to handle and tires out the hand and arm muscles needlessly. This is a point also to be looked out for in buying

A Hammer. Get a medium-sized claw hammer, either with a *bell* face (Fig. 16) or a *plain* face, — it does not matter which, — and if possible get one with the head fastened on with *patent-lock* wedges which make it impossible for it to loosen and fly off.

An ordinary

Tack Hammer is handy for working in small corners, but can easily be dispensed with for ordinary work. A much more useful hammer is the

Crate Opener shown in Fig. 17, which is handy not only for prying boxes apart, but also for driving and withdrawing tacks and small nails. It may be used for numerous small jobs, and its convenient size makes it possible to carry it about in one's hip pocket.

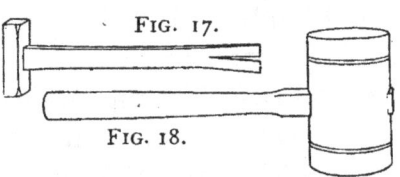

FIG. 17. — Crate Opener.
FIG. 18. — Wooden Mallet.

A Nail-set is required for driving nail-heads below the surface of work before finishing it. A *cut* iron nail may be used, but it is not as satisfactory as the regular nail-set shown in Fig. 16. You will find it handy to have two sizes, one for *finishing-nails*, the other for *common nails*.

It is advisable to have

A Wooden Mallet (Fig. 18) for mortising and cutting

where it is necessary to drive the chisel or gouge, as the use of a hammer soon splits down the end of the handle. This is also useful for knocking together the members of *halved, mortise-and-tenon*, and other joints.

The Cross-cut Saw (Fig. 16) is made to cut across the grain of wood. It will also cut with the grain, but as the teeth[1] are not properly prepared for *ripping*, the work is slower to do. When money permits, you should add a 22-inch

Rip-saw to your outfit. The

Compass-saw (Fig. 16) is made especially for cutting curves, the teeth being filed to cut with as well as across the grain, and it is handy for sawing thin wood. A finer saw which you may prefer to the compass-saw is the

Keyhole-saw, made for cutting keyholes as the name would imply, and used for various other small jobs. This is often made to fit in a handle similar to that of the compass-saw, but the more common form is the one which fits in a *pad*, as shown in Fig. 19. Other forms of saws which you will want to add to your outfit as soon as possible are the

Back-saw, shown in Fig. 59, a saw made with fine teeth (get one with fourteen teeth to the inch) and intended for very fine cutting — such as for making miter-joints, cutting tenons, etc., and either a

Coping-saw or **Bracket-saw** (Figs. 20 and 21) for saw-

---

[1] See notes regarding the teeth of the *Cross-cut Saw* and the *Rip-saw* on page 21 of "The Boy Craftsman."

TOOLS AND HOME-MADE SHOP EQUIPMENT 19

ing very thin wood, such as that of cigar boxes. If you own a

Scroll-saw, it will answer the purposes of both of the latter for shop use.

A Jack-plane (Fig. 16) fitted with a *smoothing-plane iron* is to be preferred to a smoothing-plane, if one plane must be chosen, for its long *sole* (bottom face) makes it easier to plane up a surface without hollowing it. This plane, thus equipped, may be used for both reducing thicknesses of material and removing *undressed* surfaces (the purpose of the jack-plane), as well as planing up surfaces true and smooth (the purpose of the smoothing-plane). The jack-plane iron has its cutting edge slightly rounded, instead of being ground straight across like the smoothing-plane iron, in order to make it gouge out the wood and thus reduce thicknesses quickly, so you will readily see that it cannot be expected to straighten up a surface. Of course you can buy the two irons and make the plane the equivalent of a jack- and a smoothing-plane. The Stanley "Bailey" adjustable iron plane shown in the illustration is a better form to purchase than the old-fashioned plane with a wooden stock, as it is so easily adjusted. The No. 5 size (Fig. 16) is 14 inches long

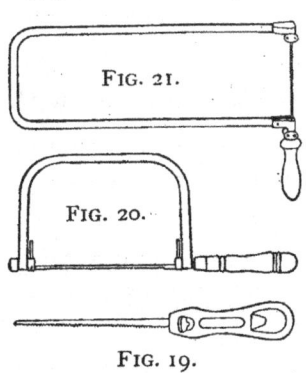

FIG. 21.

FIG. 20.

FIG. 19.

FIG. 19. — Keyhole-saw.
FIG. 20. — Coping-saw.
FIG. 21. — Bracket-saw.

and about the right length. As soon as you can do so, buy a

Smoothing-plane in addition to the jack-plane, for the two planes will save you a considerable amount of adjustment of the cutting irons. The

Fore-plane has an 18-inch sole, and is made long for the purpose of removing the high places left by the jack-plane and straightening the surface before smoothing up with the smoothing-plane, but it may easily be dispensed with by the amateur. Among the many other forms of planes upon the market, you will find a

Rabbet-plane (Fig. 22), useful in cabinet making for *rabbeting* your work (Fig. 75, page 59 — the plane-iron, or *cutter*, can be adjusted to any desired width of *rabbet* up to $1\frac{1}{2}$ inches), and the

FIG. 22. — Rabbet-plane.

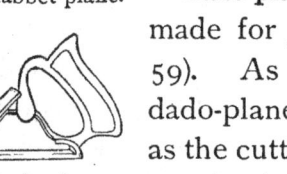

FIG. 23. — Dado-plane.

Dado-plane (Fig. 23), which is made for *grooving* (Fig. 75, page 59). As the plane-stock of the dado-plane must be of the same size as the cutter, it is necessary to select one having the width of cutter for which you will have the greatest need, for you will not likely wish to purchase more than one dado-plane. Of course, if you live near a mill, you can get all of your rabbeting and grooving done there, and it will hardly pay you to bother with it, or to purchase these tools.

TOOLS AND HOME-MADE SHOP EQUIPMENT

It is a good plan to invest in a

Ratchet-brace when buying a bit-stock, as it can be used in so many places where an ordinary brace cannot. The ratchet arrangement makes it possible to so set the brace that, when boring a hole or driving a screw in a corner or close to something which prevents a full sweep, the handle may be worked back and forth. Buy a brace with at least an 8-inch sweep; a shorter sweep than this does not give sufficient leverage.

A $\frac{3}{8}$-inch and a $\frac{3}{4}$-inch auger-bit are included among the tools shown in Fig. 16. Of course, it is often necessary to bore holes of other sizes, and

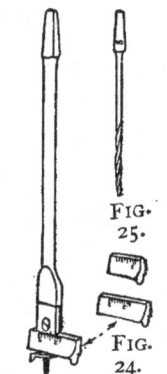

FIG. 25.

FIG. 24.

Auger-bits $\frac{1}{4}$ inch, $\frac{1}{2}$ inch, $\frac{5}{8}$ inch, and 1 inch in size should be added to these as you find need of them. Bits are made in $\frac{1}{16}$-inch sizes, and the number of sixteenths is stamped upon the shank. Figure 24 shows an

FIG. 24. — Expansive-bit.

FIG. 25. — Wood Drill Bit.

Expansive-bit, the small size of which is provided with two cutters — one adjustable to bore holes ranging from $\frac{1}{2}$ inch to $\frac{7}{8}$ inch and the other from $\frac{7}{8}$ inch to $1\frac{1}{2}$ inches; and the large size with two cutters — one boring holes from $\frac{7}{8}$ inch to $1\frac{3}{4}$ inches, the other from $1\frac{3}{4}$ inches to 3 inches. By having one of the large sizes of these bits it is not necessary to buy auger-bits larger than $\frac{3}{4}$ inch. This tool is very convenient for boring large holes, but is not required, as holes larger than 1 inch in diameter may be cut as described on page 142 and illustrated in Fig. 156. Figure 25 shows a

Wood Drill Bit. This is made in $\frac{1}{32}$-inch sizes, running from $\frac{2}{32}$ inch (No. 2) to $\frac{14}{32}$ inch (No. 14). Unless you have an automatic drill a few of these will be required for drilling holes for screws in hard wood. They are very delicate tools and "twist off" very easily, and must not be removed from a hole by reversing the brace, but by continuing to turn it in the same direction, pulling up on the head of the brace at the same time until it has loosened itself.

Brad-awls are the simplest and cheapest tools manufactured for making very small holes for nails and screws (Fig. 16). They are sold in various sizes, one or two of which will be useful. A

Scratch-awl differs from a brad-awl in the end, which is pointed instead of chisel-shaped. It is used for marking work, but a jack-knife will serve the purpose just as well. A

Hand Gimlet (Fig. 16) is also handy for boring small holes.

For countersinking screw-heads below the surface of a piece of wood you should have a

Rose Countersink Bit to fit in your brace (Fig. 16). This is used after a screw hole has been bored, and bevels off the edge of the hole enough to let the screw-head drop below the surface.

TOOLS AND HOME–MADE SHOP EQUIPMENT 23

An Automatic Drill is a great convenience and time saver (Fig. 26). It is used largely for drilling holes for screws and finishing-nails, and is especially handy for drilling in places where even a ratchet-brace cannot be used. With this tool is furnished eight drills, varying in size from $\frac{1}{16}$ inch to $\frac{11}{64}$ inch, which come either in the handle or in an extra box. A handier tool than this, though costing about twice as much, is a

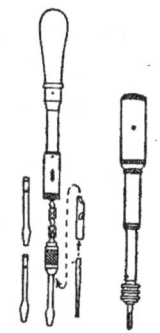

FIG. 27. Spiral-ratchet Screw-driver. FIG. 26. Automatic Drill.

Spiral-ratchet Screw-driver (Fig. 27). This may be set to drive or withdraw by moving a small *slide* to one end or the other of a slot on the side, or the spiral may be locked to make a ratchet screw-driver by giving the *milled* shell just below the slide a half turn. Three screw-drivers of different sizes are included with this tool, and a *chuck* to hold drills, together with eight sizes of drills, may be purchased for a small additional amount, which makes this tool serve the double purpose of drill and screw-driver. But the spiral-ratchet screw-driver may easily be dispensed with if you have an ordinary 6-inch

Hand Screw-driver and a medium-sized

Screw-driver Bit (Fig. 16).

A $\frac{3}{4}$-inch chisel is included in the outfit shown in Fig. 16. This size will be found best for a starter. You will soon require a smaller chisel — one about $\frac{1}{4}$ inch wide, and when you have advanced with your work you will find that at least five

Firmer Chisels, the kind made for ordinary light work, — sizes ¼ inch, ⅜ inch, ½ inch, ¾ inch, and 1 inch, — will be necessary. For any very heavy work, such as outside building, you will also require a

Framing or Mortising Chisel, which is made stronger for this purpose — 1½ inches or 1¾ inches wide. Some firmer chisels are beveled upon the face edges of the blade to make them handy for getting into corners (Fig. 28). For cutting curved grooves and curved surfaces a

Gouge is required. This is similar to a chisel except that its blade is curved instead of straight (Fig. 29). A ⅜-inch and a ¾-inch gouge will answer most purposes. Chisel and gouge handles are rounded on the ends for hand use (Fig. 29), but for heavier work, where a mallet is necessary, they should be protected by a leather cap (Fig. 16) or a metal *ferrule* (Fig. 28), to keep the wood from splitting. The chisel or gouge which fits into the handle (Fig. 29) is strong enough for hand use (*paring*), but those made with sockets for the handles to fit into (Fig. 28) are better for mortising and other work where driving is necessary. A

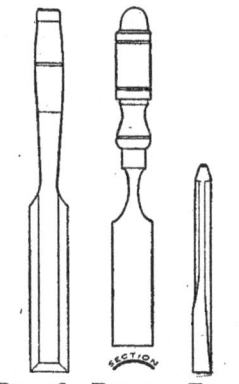

FIG. 28. Beveled Chisel.   FIG. 29. Gouge.   FIG. 30. Cold-chisel.

Cold-chisel (Fig. 30) is often needed for cutting metal and is a good tool for you to add to your outfit when you can do so.

A Draw-knife (Fig. 31) is handy for quickly reducing a narrow piece of wood in thickness and for cutting curved surfaces. It must be used carefully, however, as it will follow the grain of a piece of wood and is apt to split off more than is desired, as is the danger in *paring* with a hatchet. A

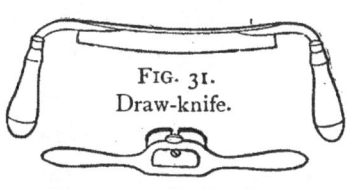

FIG. 31. Draw-knife.

FIG. 32. — Spoke-shave.

Spoke-shave (Fig. 32) is used to smooth up a curved surface after it has been roughly cut with a draw-knife, hatchet, or chisel, just as the smoothing-plane is used to smooth up a straight surface. This is not an expensive tool and will be of more use to you than a draw-knife; buy it first.

WOOD-RASP
HALF-ROUND-WOOD-FILE
FLAT-METAL-FILE
SLIM-TAPER-FILE
RAT-TAIL FILE

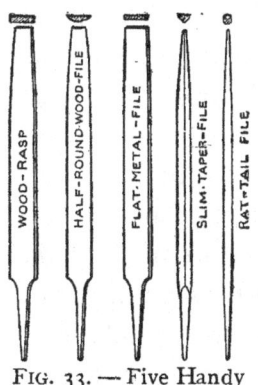

FIG. 33. — Five Handy Forms of Files.

A Half-round Wood-file (Fig. 16) may be used for smoothing up all sorts of irregular surfaces and is the best kind to purchase for a small outfit of tools. The

Handiest Forms of Files are shown in Fig. 33. The *wood-rasp* is a very coarse file for wood working, while the *rattail file*, the *slim taper file*, and the *flat metal-file* are made with finer teeth and are intended for metal work. A wood-file must not be used upon metal, as it is not made for cutting surfaces harder than wood.

For laying out work a

Two-foot Folding Rule (Fig. 16) is required, and either a *try-square* or a *carpenter's square* is necessary for laying out lines at right angles to another line or to the edge of a piece of work, for testing corners to see whether or not they are square, and for testing surfaces for irregularities. The writer prefers a

Try-square with a *mitered* handle (Fig. 16), as lines at 45 degrees may be laid out with it. The large size of

Carpenter's Steel Square has a *body* (the long end) 24 inches long and a *tongue* (the short end) 18 inches long; but a smaller size with a body 18 inches long and tongue 12 inches long (Fig. 16) will serve your purpose just as well and will be cheaper to buy and lighter to handle.

A Bevel (Fig. 34) is a handy tool for laying out angles other than 45 degrees, for laying out bevels, and for reproducing angles upon several pieces of work. It is like a try-square, only instead of being fastened rigid it is made adjustable. You can easily do without this tool for ordinary work, but it will be useful when you get into advanced work.

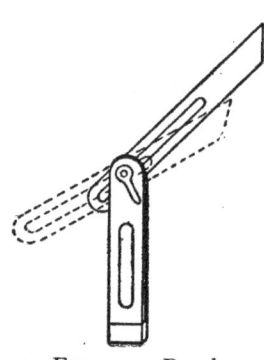

FIG. 34. — Bevel.

A Marking-gauge (Fig. 16) consists of a block of wood (the *head*) through which slides a graduated stick (the *bar*) with a point (the *spur*) near one end (see Fig. 68, page 52). The head may be set to any desired distance from the spur, then by placing the head against the edge of a piece of work and pushing the spur along the surface, a line can be scratched which will be exactly parallel to and at the required distance from the edge. The ordinary marking-gauge has only one spur; that shown in Fig. 68 has two spurs, is what is known as a *mortise-gauge* (see "Gauging," page 52), and is the better form to buy.

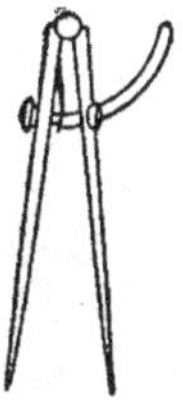
FIG. 35. Wing Dividers.

Wing Dividers (Fig. 35) come in handy for a number of operations, but are used principally for describing circles and laying off measurements. The *thumb-screws* make it possible to adjust the dividers very accurately to any desired measurement. Until you can get a pair of these you may use a stick with a couple of nails driven through it, or a piece of cardboard with a pencil and pin pushed through it, for a compass, and measurements may be laid off by means of a *rule*, a *straight-edge* (a stick with a straight edge), or a piece of paper.[1]

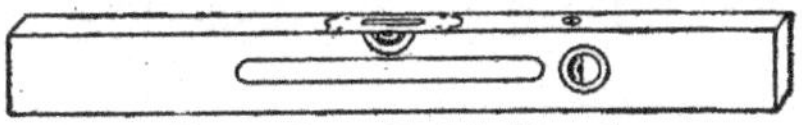
FIG. 36. — Spirit Level.

A Level (Fig. 36) is necessary in building construction to help the mechanic get his work *plumb* and

[1] A simple method for dividing a distance into a number of equal spaces by means of a rule and pencil is shown upon page 46 of "The Boy Craftsman."

level, but it is useless in the shop unless you level up whatever your piece of work rests upon before testing.[1] But a

Pocket Level (Fig. 37) is handy for getting approximate levels and is cheap enough so every boy can own one.

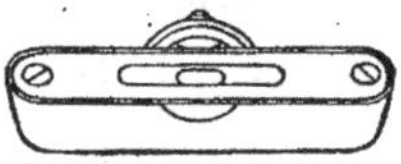

FIG. 37. — Pocket Level.

A tool with which ten different operations can be performed is the

Odd-jobs shown in Fig. 38. Besides the three operations indicated in the illustration, it may be employed as a *marking-gauge*, a *mortise-gauge*, a *depth-gauge*, a *try-square*, a *T-square*, a *scratch-awl*, and a *rule* (a 12-inch ruler comes with the tool). The many purposes for which this tool may be used make it a handy one to carry about for "odd jobs."

AS A MITRE SQUARE
AS A PLUMB
AS A LEVEL

FIG. 38. — Odd-jobs.

A Pair of Cutting Pliers (Fig. 16) will serve as pincers and nippers. Besides these you will often be in need of a

Wrench (Fig. 39) for tightening and loosening nuts, and other operations; this will be a good addition to make to your outfit when you can afford it.

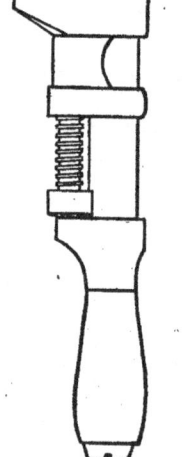

FIG. 39. — Wrench.

[1] A satisfactory home-made *plumb-board* for large work is described on page 153.

TOOLS AND HOME-MADE SHOP EQUIPMENT 29

For holding together glued-up work until the glue has *set* a pair of

Wood Handscrews (Fig. 40) are handy, as are also a pair of

Cabinet-maker's Clamps (Fig. 41) for holding wide glued-up pieces; but you can dispense with both of these by providing yourself with several

Home-made Clamps of different lengths similar to those shown in Fig. 42. These consist of two strips with two blocks of wood A and B screwed to them 4 or 5 inches farther apart than the width of the glued-up piece of work. Taper the inner edge of blocks A, but leave that of blocks B square. The work is laid upon the strips with one edge against blocks B, then a strip is placed against its other edge for a *filler*, and a pair of wedges

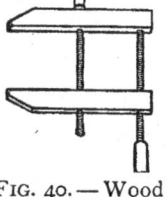

FIG. 40.—Wood Handscrews.

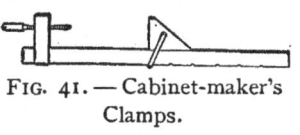

FIG. 41.—Cabinet-maker's Clamps.

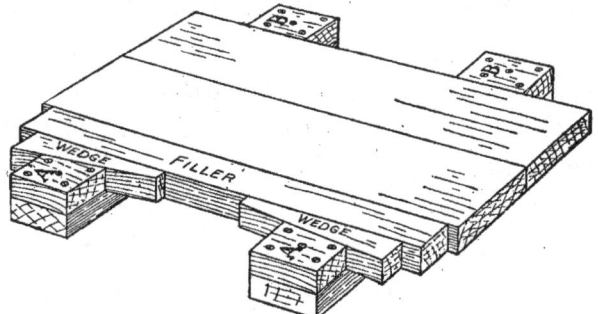

FIG. 42.—Home-made Clamps for Holding Glued-up Work.

with one edge square and the other cut to fit the taper on the edge of blocks *A* are driven in between the filler and the blocks. Care must be taken to prevent the edges or the center of the work from springing up, when "driving home" the wedges, or the surface will be *winding* when the work is removed.

A Grindstone can usually be dispensed with, as grinding is not often required if proper care is taken of the edge tools; and when it is necessary you can usually find a friendly carpenter who will allow you to use his stone. But you must have a good

Oilstone. Of the manufactured stones the India oilstone is being very extensively used, while the Lilywhite and the Rosy-red Washita oilstones are two of the best natural stones on the market. Besides an oilstone you must of course have an

Oiler and a bottle of sperm-oil — or bicycle, automobile, or sewing-machine lubricating oil.

If you have not built tool drawers in the ends of your work bench (Figs. 6 and 7), you must make a chest or cabinet as soon as possible to protect your tools from injury and from being borrowed without your permission.

When the author received his first outfit of tools when a boy, he made

A Tool-chest out of an old grocery box, this being the best material at hand; and as it was such an easy matter to turn this box into a chest and it served the purpose so well he has decided to tell you boys how to make one just like it. Figure 43 was drawn from this old chest, which the author still has in his possession. The box used was, approximately, 26 inches long, 13 inches wide, and 9 inches deep, but yours need not be of these exact

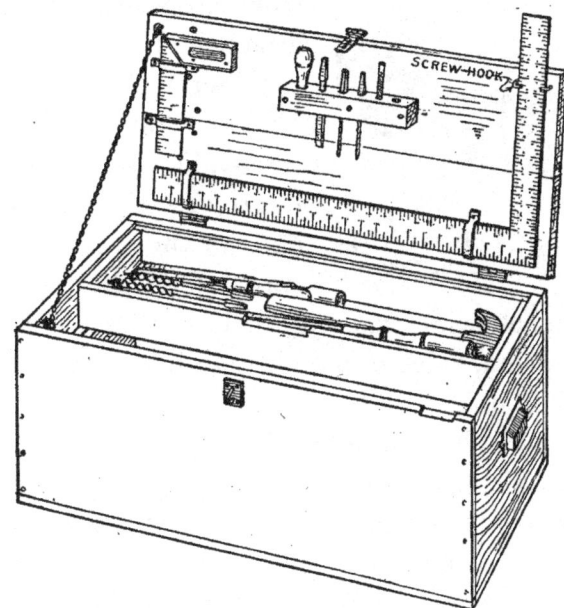

FIG. 43. — A Grocery-box Tool-chest.

dimensions, only be sure it is long enough to accommodate your large tools.

After selecting your box, renail all loose boards and replace any that happen to be split with pieces from another box. Fasten together the cover boards with a *batten* at each end (*A*, Fig. 44) and hinge to the box with a pair of strap-hinges as shown. Buy a hinge-hasp and staple (Fig. 45) and a pair of drawer-pulls at a hardware-store, screw the hasp to the box cover and the staple to the box, and screw the drawer-pulls to the ends of the box for handles. As a check to prevent the cover from dropping too far back, attach a chain to two screw-eyes screwed into the cover and the box. The tray is removable and sets upon two *cleats* or strips nailed to the ends of the box. Make this tray $\frac{1}{4}$ inch shorter than the box, 7 inches wide, and $1\frac{1}{2}$ inches deep (inside), and put the bottom, sides, and ends together in the same way that a box is made.

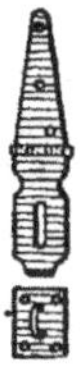

Fig. 45. Hinge-hasp and Staple.

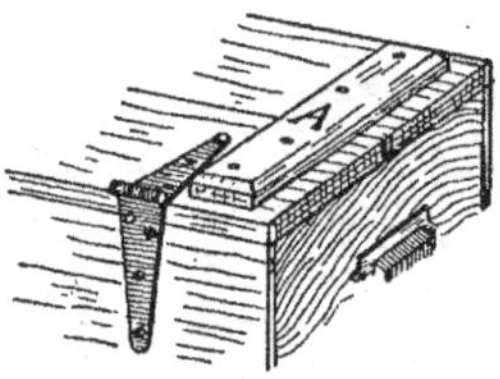
A

Fig. 44. How to hinge the Cover.

Fasten a block with holes of the proper size drilled in it to the inside of the cover, in which to stick such tools as the brad-awls, screw-driver bits, wood drills and nail-sets, and tack some loops of leather to the cover for the squares to slide in. The upper end of the carpenter's square is held by a couple of screw-hooks, and is released by giving one hook a quarter-turn. The small tools — the chisels, auger-bits, screw-driver, etc. — should be kept in the tray, and the large tools — the saw, planes, bit-brace, etc. — in the bottom of the chest. Notch the top edge of the box and tray, if necessary, to accommodate the tools on the cover.

When you have completed your chest, sandpaper it

TOOLS AND HOME-MADE SHOP EQUIPMENT   33

well, then give the inside and the tray a coat of boiled linseed-oil and the outside a coat of paint or oil stain.

A plan for an easily made

Tool Cabinet is illustrated and described in " The Boy Craftsman." This is a very simple affair made out of a box with the cover boards battened together for a door. The author has been asked for a plan for making a paneled door for a cabinet, and as others of you may also wish to panel the door, to make a neater-appearing cabinet, he suggests that you follow the directions given for making the door of the *Music Cabinet* described on page 124 (see Fig. 137), which is the simplest way for a boy to make a paneled door.

A tool cabinet is the handier receptacle for keeping tools within easy reach; but a chest is to be preferred if the tools must be carried about, which is often necessary where the shop is located in a damp place, to keep them from rusting. In case you make a chest,

A Tool-rack on the wall back of the bench is a good arrangement for holding the tools while you are

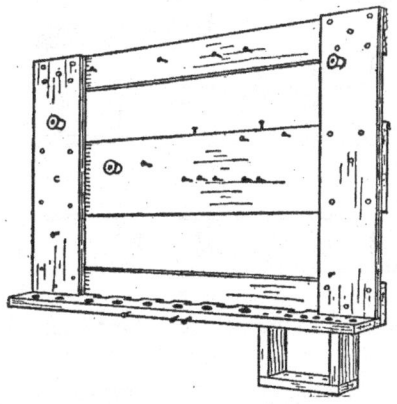

FIG. 46. — A Tool-rack.

working. In the photograph opposite page 2 is shown such a rack, and Fig. 46 shows how it may be put together. The chisels, auger-bits, wood drills, awls, and screw-driver stick into the holes bored through the bottom shelf, and the ends of the small bits are supported by a small bracket fastened below the shelf. Nails and spools hold the other tools. In the same photograph you will see how boxes may be bracketed to the wall for

Open Shelves for your paint-cans, varnishes, and other supplies, and how a shelf may be supported above the rack for miscellaneous articles; also how the under part of the work bench may be utilized for

Material Boxes by fastening boards across the rails to hold them.

Nails and screws should be kept in some kind of order, so the sizes wanted may be got quickly without unnecessary hunting, and several receptacles for these are shown in Figs. 47 to 52. The **Partitioned Nail Box** (Figs. 47–49) will hold six different lengths of nails. Cut the back and bottom (*A* and *C*, Fig. 48) 3 feet long by 8 inches wide, the front (*B*) the same length by 5 inches wide, and the partitions and end pieces (*D*, Fig.

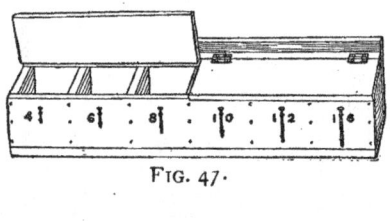

FIG. 47.

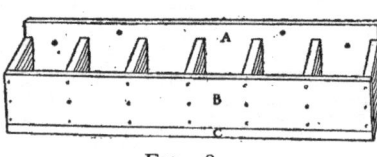

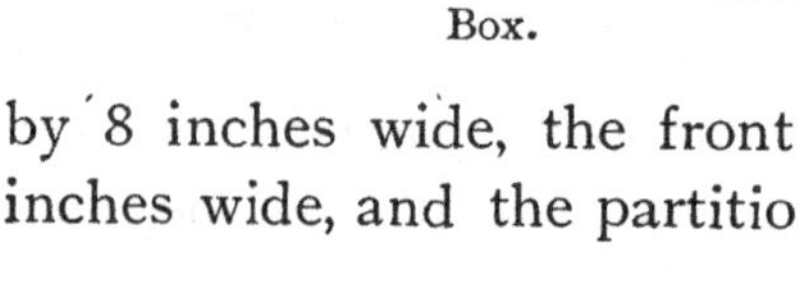

FIG. 48. 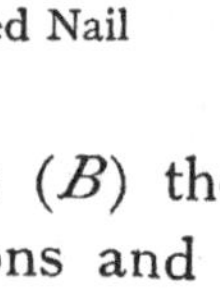   FIG. 49.
FIGS. 47–49. — Details of Partitioned Nail Box.

49) 6 inches wide by 6 inches high at the back and 5 inches high at the front. Nail together the front, back, and end pieces, then nail on the bottom and fasten the partitions in place so as to divide the box into six equal spaces. The box may either be screwed to the wall or hung upon hooks. If you screw it, do this before putting on the cover. Cut the hinge-strip (*E*, Fig. 49) 1 inch wide by the length of the box and nail it in place to the partition tops. The cover may be made in one piece, or in two as in Fig. 47; hinge it to the hinge-strip. Mark the sizes of the nails upon the front of the box, and fasten nails of corresponding sizes in front of the receptacles with small staples or bent-over brads to help you to associate the lengths with the size numbers. This box has been planned for *common nails* and to hold sizes ranging from $1\frac{1}{2}$ inches to $3\frac{1}{2}$ inches long (4-penny to 16-penny).

Another Box may be made to hold *finishing-nails*, papers of brads and tacks, and *spikes* (20-, 30-, 40-, 50-, and 60-penny nails). *Bolts* and *screws* may be kept in a third box.

Empty tin cans and cigar boxes are easy for any boy to get and make excellent

Receptacles for Nails, Screws, and Brads. There is a can with a removable lid in which molasses and sirup comes (Fig. 50) that is very handy, and baking-powder cans and even tomato cans, if the solder around the rim of their opened end is melted and the end pulled off, will serve the purpose. The cans may be hung up side by side on the wall, if mounted upon pieces of board provided with screw-eyes or holes (Figs. 50 and 51). To mount the cans, punch four holes through each and wire them to pieces of board as shown in Fig. 51. Cigar boxes may be fastened upon wooden brackets as shown in Fig. 52.

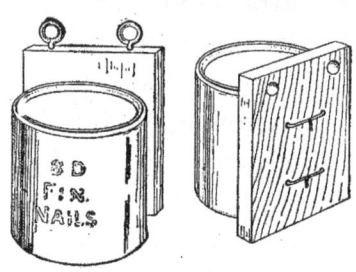

FIG. 50.   FIG. 51.
FIGS. 50 and 51. — Can Receptacles for Nails, Brads, and Screws.

After you have fitted up your workshop with a bench, shelving, racks, and receptacles, and made a chest or cabinet for your tools, there are still a number of pieces of equipment to construct before you will be ready to open up your shop for business.

Figure 53 shows

A Horse which is very much handier than the simpler forms of carpenters' horses, in so far as the board top gives a broader surface to lay work

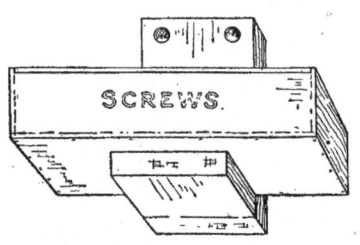

FIG. 52. — Cigar-box Receptacles for Screws, Bolts, or Miscellaneous Hardware

upon and the shelf underneath makes a convenient place to lay saws and other tools. This horse is very commonly used by carpenters. Details for its construction are shown in Figs. 54, 55, and 56. Cut the body A 3

TOOLS AND HOME-MADE SHOP EQUIPMENT

feet 10 inches long out of a piece of 2-by-4, and cut the four legs B to the dimensions shown in Fig. 55 out of 1-inch stuff, with one edge tapered ¾ inch. Trim off the upper ends of the legs as shown in Fig. 56, so when the legs are nailed to the body the lower ends will be 16 inches apart. Nail the legs in place about 5 inches from the ends of the body, then cut the end rails (C, Fig 54) and the side rails D 3 inches wide and of the required length and nail them to the legs 9 inches below the body.

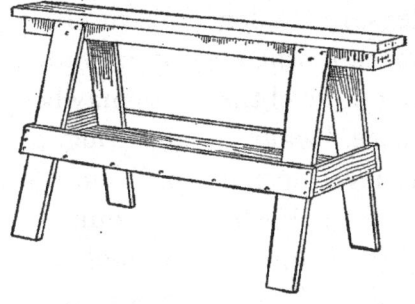

FIG. 53. — Horse.

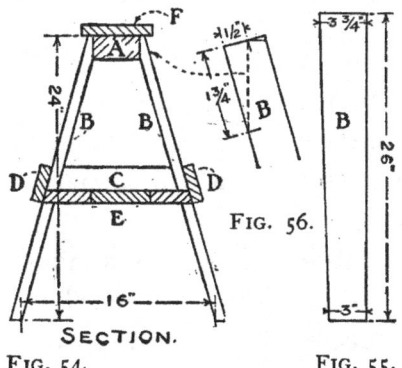

FIG. 54.   FIG. 55.
FIGS. 54–56. — Details of Horse.

Cut the tray bottom boards to fit between the rails (E, Fig. 54) and fasten them with nails driven through the rails into their edges. Cut the top board F 4 feet long out of 1-inch stuff and screw it to the body, countersinking the screw-heads as a protection to your edge tools.

When the horse has been nailed together, you will probably find that it does not stand evenly — at any rate, the legs will not be cut to the right angle on the bottom and will not rest squarely upon the floor. To allow for trimming, an extra inch was added to the length of the legs, in the leg pattern (Fig. 55). Set the horse in the place it will occupy in your shop, so in case the floor is out of level the horse may be made to stand evenly in that place, locate the short leg, and put a chip under it so as to level up the top; then take a block of wood about 1 inch thick, slide it around the bottom of each leg, and mark a line across each face even with the top of the block. Saw the legs off on these lines; and if the work has been done carefully, the horse will stand perfectly even. If you find that the horse is too high after completing it, it will be an easy enough matter to trim off the legs as much as is necessary to make it suit your height.

You should have two horses in your shop across which to lay long pieces of work for marking and sawing. Of course a couple of packing boxes may be used until you have plenty of time to make these. You will also find that a chair will serve the purpose of

A Saw-bench for small work about as well as a horse would. Such usage will be rather hard on the chair, however, unless the seat is protected in some way, so if you want

A Chair Saw-bench, prepare a wooden cover that can be placed over the seat as shown in Fig. 57. Make this cover 20 inches long and 16 inches wide; fasten the boards together at the ends with battens of just the

TOOLS AND HOME-MADE SHOP EQUIPMENT 39

thickness of the chair seat and fitted to the curve or slant of the seat (*A* and *B*, Fig. 58), and screw a wooden button to each batten. Place several thicknesses of cloth over the chair seat, then set the cover over it and turn the buttons so as to hold it in place. You may protect the back by slipping a potato sack over it.

It is necessary to have a miter-box to guide your saw in making *miters*. The adjustable iron boxes now manufactured are the most satisfactory kind, but they are rather expensive to buy and probably will not serve your purpose any better than

Fig. 57.
A Chair
Saw-bench.

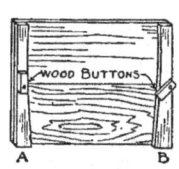

Fig. 58.
Cover to protect Chair.

A Home-made Miter-box such as the average carpenter makes for his own use (Fig. 59). This box may be made of pine. Cut the bottom piece 4 inches wide and 14 inches long out of a 1¼-inch board, and the sides 5 inches wide and 14 inches long out of 1-inch stuff, and nail the sides to the edges of the bottom. Then take the box to a carpenter and ask him to make two *miter cuts* and one 90-*degree cut* in the sides. The method of laying out and cutting the miters is described in "The Boy Craftsman"; but, unless you have had

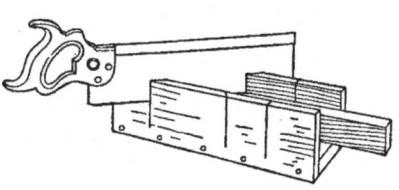

Fig. 59.—Home-made Miter-box.

enough practice in sawing so you can saw very accurately, you had better have a carpenter cut these for you.

A Bench-hook (Fig. 60) is used for a number of operations. For paring with your chisel and chopping with your hatchet it furnishes protection to the bench top, which would otherwise be cut up badly in a short time; it is handy to lay sticks and other small pieces on for sawing with the back-saw, and by making a right-angle *kerf* (slot made by a saw) and a right- and a left-hand mitered kerf in the *stop* strip it may be used for sawing small work accurately. Make the bench-hook out of a piece of board about 12 inches square, and nail the *hook cleat* to the under side of one edge and the mitered stop to the opposite edge as shown. The kerfs in the stop strip may be laid out with a mitered handle try-square (Fig. 67, page 52), but it will be easier to cut them in a miter-box.

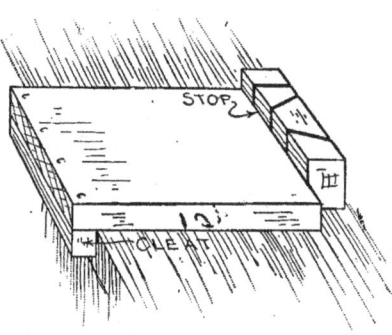

FIG. 60.— Bench-hook.

The operation of truing the edge of a board is known as *jointing* or *shooting*, and to hold the work and guide the plane while shooting short, narrow pieces of work,

A Shooting-board is generally used. Figures 61 and 62 show the construction of one of these. Cut the pieces out of 1-inch stuff, *A* 11½ inches wide by 24 inches long,

TOOLS AND HOME-MADE SHOP EQUIPMENT 41

B $7\frac{1}{2}$ inches wide by 24 inches long, C 2 inches wide by $7\frac{1}{2}$ inches long, and D 2 inches wide by 24 inches long. It is necessary to have the faces and edges straight and true in order to make it possible to true up other pieces of work by means of a shooting-board. Bevel off the lower right-hand edge of B (Fig. 62), then nail or screw it to board A with the left-hand edges flush. Nail strip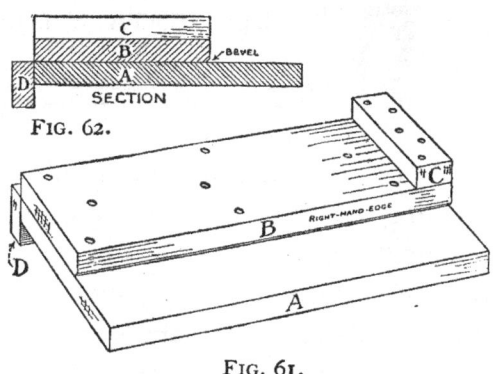

FIGS. 61–62. — Shooting-board.

C to B so that its end is exactly at right angles with the right-hand edge of board B. Nail strip D to the left-hand edge of board A.

In using the shooting-board, it is placed upon the bench with strip D close against the bench apron and the end of board A shoved against the bench-stop, then the board to be *jointed* is placed upon board B with one end against C, which forms a stop, and the edge to be planed projecting over the right-hand edge of board B; with the plane turned on its side upon board A it is then worked back and forth until the edge has been planed off accurately. The bevel on the edge of B forms a groove which keeps small shavings from getting in the way of the plane and throwing it out of line.

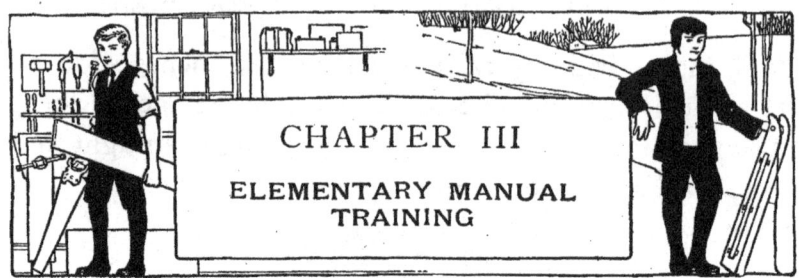

CHAPTER III
ELEMENTARY MANUAL TRAINING

MANY of you boys, no doubt, are studying manual training and learning the use of wood-working tools, how to select material, and how to lay out and carry to completion a piece of work. But the majority of schools do not provide these advantages, and many that do, furnish the course of instruction only to boys of the higher grades, so that the greater number of my readers are boys who must depend largely upon handicraft books and their own power of observation for a knowledge of how to do things.

There are all sorts of things which the average boy can construct without having had instruction in the making of wood joints, and in putting together an article and finishing it, but for any particular work, such as the making of furniture and things which you wish to sell or give away, you must understand how to proceed in order that the work may not only be substantially constructed, but be pleasing to the eye as well. The suggestions and pointers presented in this chapter are intended to help you to attain these results, and those of you who are studying manual training will do well to read over the instructions, as you will likely find something new among them which will aid you in carrying out the work described in succeeding chapters.

Every boy should, first of all, know something about the

Selection of Working Material. The softer woods are better for the beginner to use, as they are easier to work. Of these, pine, cypress, spruce, hemlock, redwood, whitewood, and basswood are probably best adapted to amateur work. The selection depends largely upon the locality, certain varieties being easier to procure in one place than another. Clear white pine is the choicest of the soft woods for cabinet making and all other nice work, but is becoming so scarce that it is now almost impossible to get in many parts of the country. Cypress is another very easily worked wood; the California redwood is also good, and can be had in very wide boards; and whitewood (from the tulip tree) and basswood (from the linden tree) furnish excellent working material. The latter two woods are close-grained, take stain exceedingly well, can be procured in boards of considerable width, and are especially good material for all sorts of amateur work, one feature in their favor being the fact that they are not easily split in nailing. The only objectionable point is their great tendency to warp, but warping may be prevented by cleating together wide pieces used in large work.

Of the hard woods, oak is best suited to the work of the amateur craftsman. It is cheap, easily worked, and easier to finish than the more expensive woods, which require very exact workmanship, the slightest defect showing through the highly polished or satin-finish surfaces customarily put upon them. Oak takes stain readily and looks best when treated in this way and then waxed — one of the finishes easiest for a boy to put on successfully. Ash, maple, cherry, birch, mahogany, and walnut are other hard woods which you will likely have occasion to use later on when you have had more experience in your work.

Many of you boys have seen how logs are cut up into boards, planks, and heavier pieces, but it will be well for all of you to know something about the

Structure of Wood and how this must be taken into consideration in converting the log into lumber, as it will enable you to select and handle your material more intelligently. Figure 63 shows a *cross-section* of a log. In the center, or generally a little to one side of the center, is a circular core known as the *pith*, then surrounding this is a series of circles known as *annual rings*, and around the outside is the *bark*. The wood between each two rings represents the amount of one year's growth, and the annual rings are produced as a result of the suspension of growth during autumn and winter. By counting the rings it is very easy to determine the age of a tree. The inner portion of the tree is known as the *heart-wood* and supplies the more solid and desirable material (unless the tree has started to decay, when the first signs are generally to be found here), while the outer wood is known as the *sap-wood*, as it contains the greater portion of the tree's juices. In the cross-sections of logs (Figs. 63 and 64) you will notice a series of lines radiating from the pith, some extending as far as the bark and others running but part way.

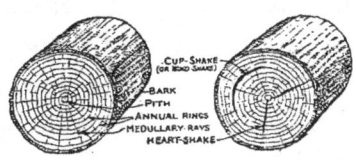

FIG. 63. FIG. 64.
Tree Structure. Cracks in Logs.

These, called the *medullary rays*, are a peculiar formation in a tree and produce what is known as *silver-grain* upon the surface of all *quarter-sawed* wood. The tree structure must be taken into consideration in

Cutting up the Log, and different methods of sawing are employed according to the purpose for which the wood is to be used. The common method of *plain sawing* is shown in Fig. 65. With this the only waste produced is in the sawdust and bark removed. But you will notice, by looking at the illustration, that with the exception of one board taken through the center of the pith, the annual rings cross the boards obliquely; this is the cause of *warping*. When wood drys out (*seasons*), the greatest amount of

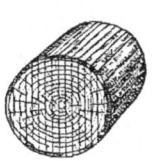
FIG. 65.
Plain-sawed.

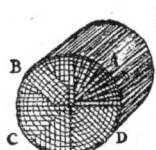
FIG. 66.
Quarter-sawed.

shrinkage occurs along the line of the annual rings, therefore the longer the arc of the ring crossing the cross-section of a board, the greater the shrinkage along that arc will be, and plain-sawed stuff, having arcs of different lengths crossing it, will shrink unequally and warp as the result. Warping is more noticeable, of course, in wide than in narrow boards and must be taken care of by *cleating* or some other method of holding the wood in position.

The board cut from the center of the log in plain sawing is the only one which will show the silver-grain to a marked degree. To get this effect upon every board

Quarter Sawing is necessary (Fig. 66). The log is first sawed into quarters, then each quarter is sawed up radially so the surface of each board will be parallel with the medullary rays. Strictly speaking, the quarter marked *A* shows the only proper method of quarter sawing, as it is the only one in which each board is parallel with the rays, but methods *B*, *C*, and *D* are also used, as they save considerable waste of material, and boards so cut are sorted into different grades. The big waste, and the fact that more time is required in the cutting, make quarter-sawed stock much more expensive than plain-sawed stuff. The irregular pieces cut from between the boards are usually utilized for moldings and other small pieces, and this reduces the amount of waste somewhat. Besides the beautiful markings, quarter-sawed boards have the advantage of uniform shrinkage and are not likely to warp.

Knots, *cup-shakes*, *heart-shakes*, and *checks* are defects occurring in logs and produce a big waste in the manufacture of lumber. The portions containing these are either cut away or, where not very marked, the boards cut from them are sorted into the poorer grades of lumber. First and second grades generally admit boards with small, sound

Knots, — pin knots and standard knots, — but if you go to a lumber yard or mill for your material, you will probably be allowed to pick out pieces from the pile which are *clear* or which have knots in places where they can easily be cut out without spoiling the boards for your purpose. Cracks, however, such as

Cup-shakes and Heart-shakes, the former being cracks between the rings and the latter cracks along the medullary rays (Fig. 64), should not appear upon any boards but those of the poorest grade of lumber, so do not let a dealer pass them off on you for first-grade stuff. Boards are likely to split at the ends through drying out unevenly, and these rifts are known as

Checks. Very long checks extending entirely through a board are not admitted in first grades, but *checking* is likely to occur even after the piece has *seasoned* for a long time and is a common fault with large timbers where the outside dries out long before the center.

After the boards have been cut, it is necessary that the

sap be evaporated before they are fit to use. The two methods employed are known as

Seasoning, which consists in piling up the boards in large piles in the open, with narrow strips of wood placed between each layer to allow a free circulation of air throughout the pile, and leaving them in this position for from two to four years, and

Kiln Drying, the best method of which consists in piling up the lumber in a similar manner in large chambers or *kilns* and passing condensed steam through and around the boards for a period of two weeks, to open up the pores and cause the water to run out, and then shutting off the steam and passing a forced circulation of heated air through them for another two weeks. The latter method is employed on lumber used for fine furniture; but as a rule material for ordinary purposes remains in the kilns not over forty-eight hours, and often a much shorter time than this. The slower the process of drying, the better it is for the wood, for the reason that rapid drying destroys much of the elasticity and toughness. On this account and for the fact that kiln-dried stock is more sensitive to atmospheric changes, weather-seasoned lumber is much to be preferred.

Lumber is spoken of as

Stock or Stuff. As produced from a log, it is known as

Undressed Stuff, and when the roughness left by the saw has been removed by the planer, it is called

Dressed Stuff (specified *D* upon material bills). If only one side is smoothed, it is said to be *surfaced-one-*

side (marked *S-1-S*); if two sides and one edge, *surfaced-two-sides-and-one-edge* (marked *S-2-S-&-1-E*), etc.

Tongued-and-grooved boards (Fig. 75) are known as

Matched Stuff (specified *M*), and when they are also beaded, they are said to be

Matched-and-Beaded (specified *M-&-B*). The beaded material is called *ceiling*, and is used for porch ceilings, backs of pantry cases, wainscotings, etc.

Lumber up to 2 inches thick (undressed) is known as

Boards, when 2 inches or more in thickness as

Planks or Dimension Stuff, and when four inches or more, it is called

Timber

Stock Sizes of Lumber. Boards are reduced $\frac{1}{8}$ inch in thickness and $\frac{1}{4}$ inch in width from the original dimensions in the process of dressing, which must be taken into consideration in laying out work. In some localities this is allowed for in cutting up the log, but as a rule it is not. Thus, a board 1 inch thick and 12 inches wide, in the rough, would be $\frac{7}{8}$ inch thick and $11\frac{3}{4}$ inches wide when dressed, but as a matter of fact all 1-inch stock is now being sawed about $\frac{1}{16}$ inch under 1 inch, and as a result is only $\frac{13}{16}$ inch thick when dressed. Stock 2 inches or more in thickness is reduced $\frac{1}{4}$ inch in dressing. Thus, a 2-inch by 4-inch piece is only $1\frac{3}{4}$ inches thick and $3\frac{3}{4}$ inches wide when dressed.

To avoid the use of fractions as much as possible, stock is generally known by its undressed dimensions, as follows:

1-by-12-inch stuff, 2-by-4-inch stuff (or simply 2-by-4's), 1-inch stock (generally spoken of as $\frac{7}{8}$-inch stock, which originally was the dressed thickness), etc. The regular thicknesses of dressed lumber are: $\frac{3}{8}$ inch ($\frac{1}{2}$-inch stock), $\frac{5}{8}$ inch ($\frac{3}{4}$-inch stock), $\frac{13}{16}$ inch (1-inch stock), $1\frac{1}{8}$ inches ($1\frac{1}{4}$-inch stock), $1\frac{3}{8}$ inches ($1\frac{1}{2}$-inch stock), $1\frac{3}{4}$ inches (2-inch stock), etc., the widths are $1\frac{3}{4}$ inches (2-inch), $3\frac{3}{4}$ inches (4-inch), $5\frac{3}{4}$ inches (6-inch), $7\frac{3}{4}$ inches (8-inch), etc., each succeeding width increasing 2 inches, and the standard lengths run from 10 feet to 20 feet in even numbers.

In Purchasing Material, if there is not a mill or lumber yard near by where you can go and place your order direct, you can probably arrange with a friendly carpenter to buy your stock for you when he is purchasing some for himself. Make out

A Mill List with the number of pieces of each size desired, the kind of wood, the dimensions (place the thickness first, then the width, and last the length) and the directions for *dressing, matching, beading,* etc., in the following order: —

PIECES	MATERIAL	DIMENSIONS	REMARKS
12	Red Oak	$\frac{1}{2}'' \times 3'' \times 12'\ 0''$	M-&-B Ceiling
4	,, ,,	$1'' \times 10'' \times 12'\ 0''$	S-2-S
4	,, ,,	$1\frac{1}{4}'' \times 12'' \times 10'\ 0''$	S-2-S-&-1-E
4	Whitewood	$1'' \times 12'' \times 16'\ 0''$	S-2-S
10	Cypress	$1'' \times 10'' \times 12'\ 0''$	S-2-S
2	Yellow Pine	$2'' \times 4'' \times 16'\ 0''$	S-4-S
	,, ,,	$2'' \times 10'' \times 18'\ 0''$	S-4-S

Lumber is sold by the thousand feet (per M), so after finding the existing retail price it is an easy matter

To Estimate the Cost of your material. A piece of board 1 inch thick, 12 inches wide, and 12 inches long is figured as a *board foot*. Upon this basis a piece 1 inch by 4 inches by 12 feet would contain 4 board feet, and a piece 2 inches by 4 inches by 12 feet would contain 8 board feet. Any thickness under 1 inch is figured the same as 1-inch stuff. The retail price ordinarily covers *dressing*, but *matching, grooving, rabbeting, beading*, and other machine work is extra.

Before attempting any shop cabinet making, a boy should spend some time in getting accustomed to handling his tools properly, so as to be able to lay out work accurately, plane up a surface true and smooth, and saw to a line. "The Proper Handling of Tools" is described in "The Boy Craftsman," and it is not my intention to repeat these instructions here, only so far as it is necessary to show the right way to lay out a piece of work, to cut and join its various parts, and to finish its surface.

Laying Out Work. Unless you lay out a piece of work accurately, you cannot expect to turn out a satisfactory job, because nothing will fit, and if you are careless at the start, you will likely be careless in the other operations as well. To guard against mistakes, it is always best to check up measurements as you go along. Use a 2-foot rule or a carpenter's square with which to lay off measurements, and a carpenter's square or try-square for *scrib-*

ing lines between points and carrying them around the four sides of a piece of work. (See Fig. 67; also *Planing Exercise* on page 54.) A sharp lead-pencil may be used for scribing, but the work can be done more accurately with a jack-knife; however, a knife line can be made only upon surfaces where it will be removed by cutting or concealed by another piece of wood.

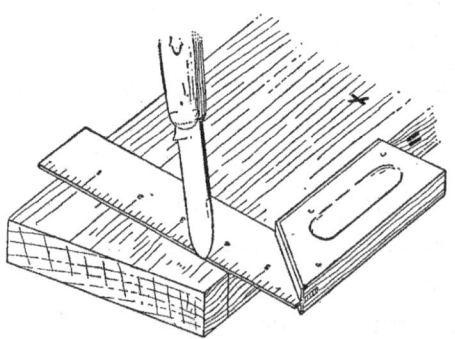

FIG. 67. — Scribing with Knife and Try-square.

When you wish to scribe a line parallel to an edge of a piece of work, the operation is known as

Gauging. Figures 68 and 76 show how to gauge with a marking-gauge. Suppose you wish to cut a piece 3 inches wide from a 4-inch board. You must first test one edge and true it up, if necessary, to make it straight for a *working edge* (see *Planing Exercise*), then place the *head* of the gauge against this edge of the board, and with

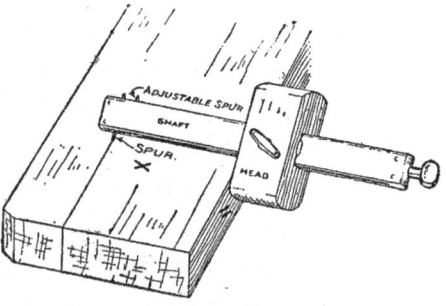

FIG. 68. — Gauging with a Marking-gauge (a Mortise-gauge).

the *spur* in the *shaft* pressed into the surface of the wood (Fig. 68), scratch a line along the board for a distance equal to the length of the piece to be removed; also scribe the line upon the opposite face and you will then have a guide-line upon both faces to saw and plane to, which is exactly parallel to and at a distance of 3 inches from the *working edge*. The gauge is also used for laying out various forms of wood joints. The *double-spur* upon the shaft of the mortise-gauge is provided for laying out the two sides of a *mortise* or *groove* in one operation (Fig. 76), the outer spur being fixed and the inner one made adjustable by means of a thumb-screw in the end of the shaft. This form of gauge saves lots of time, especially when you have a number of mortises or grooves of one size to lay out.

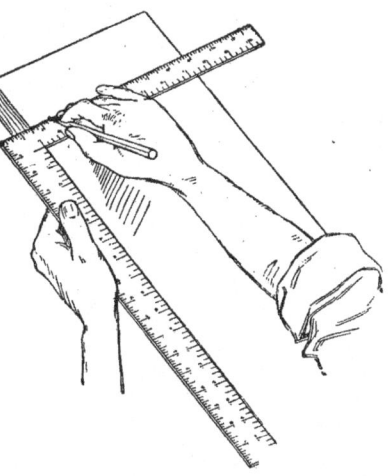

FIG. 69. — Gauging with Pencil and Carpenter's Square.

Figure 69 shows how gauging may be done with a pencil and carpenter's square. Hold the *body* of the square against the edge of the work, with the *tongue* extended across the face upon which the line is to be scribed and the pencil held against the edge at the desired point, and then, with the fingers braced as shown to hold the pencil steady, move the square toward you with your left hand. The same operation may be performed with a try-square and pencil. You will require some practice before you will be able to gauge successfully in this manner, but it is easy when you get the knack of doing it. A rule and pencil may also be used for gauging, as is shown in "The Boy Craftsman."[1] While these methods will answer the purpose for rough work, a marking-gauge is to be preferred for great accuracy.

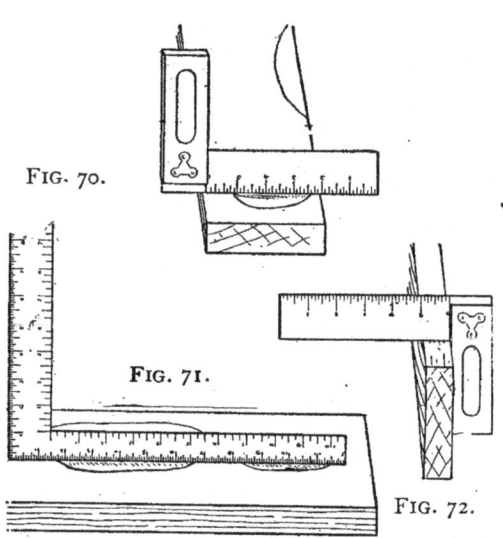

FIG. 70.
FIG. 71.
FIG. 72.

FIG. 70. — Testing with a Try-square.
FIG. 71. — Testing with a Carpenter's Square.
FIG. 72. — Testing an Edge from the Working Face.

For a Planing Exercise take a piece of board about 12 inches long. First, test one side, holding the board on a level with your eyes and sighting across it while you move the edge of the try-square along the entire length (Fig. 70). The square will strike the high places and you will be able to distinguish them as the light will show beneath the edge of the square, in the hollows. Locate

[1] Page 43.

the high portions as you pass over them, by drawing a line around them as shown in Fig. 70, so you will know where the places are which require the most planing. Also test the board lengthwise with the carpenter's square (Fig. 71).

A good way to test a board for *winding* (twisting in the length) is by means of

Winding-sticks (Fig. 73). Get two pieces of square molding of exactly the same size for the sticks. To make the test, place both sticks across the board, one at the farther end and the other at the near end, and hold the board level and at the proper height to make the tops of the sticks upon a level with your eyes; sight across the

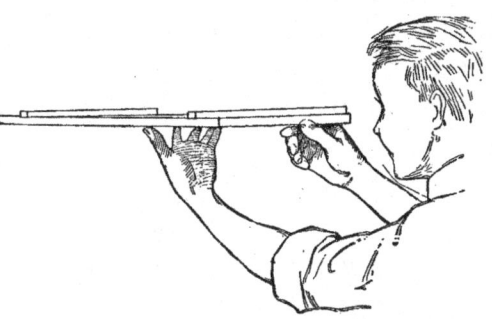

FIG. 73. — Testing with Winding-sticks.

sticks, and if their tops appear to be exactly on a line, you may know that there is no *wind* to the board; if one end of one stick appears above the corresponding end of the other stick, you can easily determine where and how much the wind is.

After determining where planing is necessary, place the board in your bench-vise and plane up the face, testing it again and again until you find it to be perfectly true. This first trued surface is called the *working face* and should be marked with a cross (Fig. 67). With the *handle* of the try-square held firmly against this working face and the *blade* extending across an edge (Fig. 72), move it along the surface, locate the high places, and plane it up and test it as you did the working face. Mark this edge, which now becomes the *working edge*, with two short parallel lines (Fig. 68). Next, set the marking-gauge to any thickness desired for the board and, with the *head* of the gauge pressed firmly against the working face, gauge a line along each edge. Plane up the second face to the gauge lines, test and true up. The ends of the board should be trimmed off next. With the handle of the try-square pressed firmly against the working face, first scribe a line across the working edge, then, with the handle of the square against the working edge, continue this line across the working face and the opposite face. From the working face carry the line across the unfinished edge. Then, from the scribed line, lay off the length to which you wish to cut the piece and scribe another line around the four sides at that distance. Saw off the ends of the board about $\frac{1}{8}$ inch outside of the lines, to allow for planing them up smooth. In planing across *end grain*, the farther edge will split down unless protected. This difficulty may be overcome by placing another piece of wood in front of it when you clamp it in the vise, but it is better to *chamfer* the unfinished edge (see Fig. 90), which is the only reason for not finishing this before the ends. After planing off both ends square, set the gauge to the width you wish to make the board and gauge a line along the faces and across the ends, sliding the head of the gauge along the working edge (Fig. 68); then saw off the edge to within about ⅛ inch of the lines with a rip-saw and finish the edge with the plane

For a Sawing Exercise, scribe a series of lines around a trued-up block of wood with your try-square, then place the block in your vise and see how well you can keep to the line while sawing through the block. Stick to this exercise until you can saw the block through exactly on the line, without running off at any point. Guide the saw with your left thumb until it has cut into the wood a little way, hold the saw exactly at right angles to the line, and use long, steady strokes.

No better exercises in laying out work, planing, and sawing can be found than the making of the

Joints and Splices used for joining together pieces of wood, and it is important to practice upon such joinings before attempting to use them upon a nice piece of work, in order that you may not run the risk of spoiling material. Any odd-sized pieces of wood which you have on hand may be used for these exercises as the proportions of the joints may be worked out to suit the size of the piece. The most important joints and splices are shown in Figs. 74 and 75 (pages 58 and 59). By a *joint* is meant any kind of a connection between two pieces placed at an angle to one another, while a *splice* is a connection between two pieces placed in a straight line.

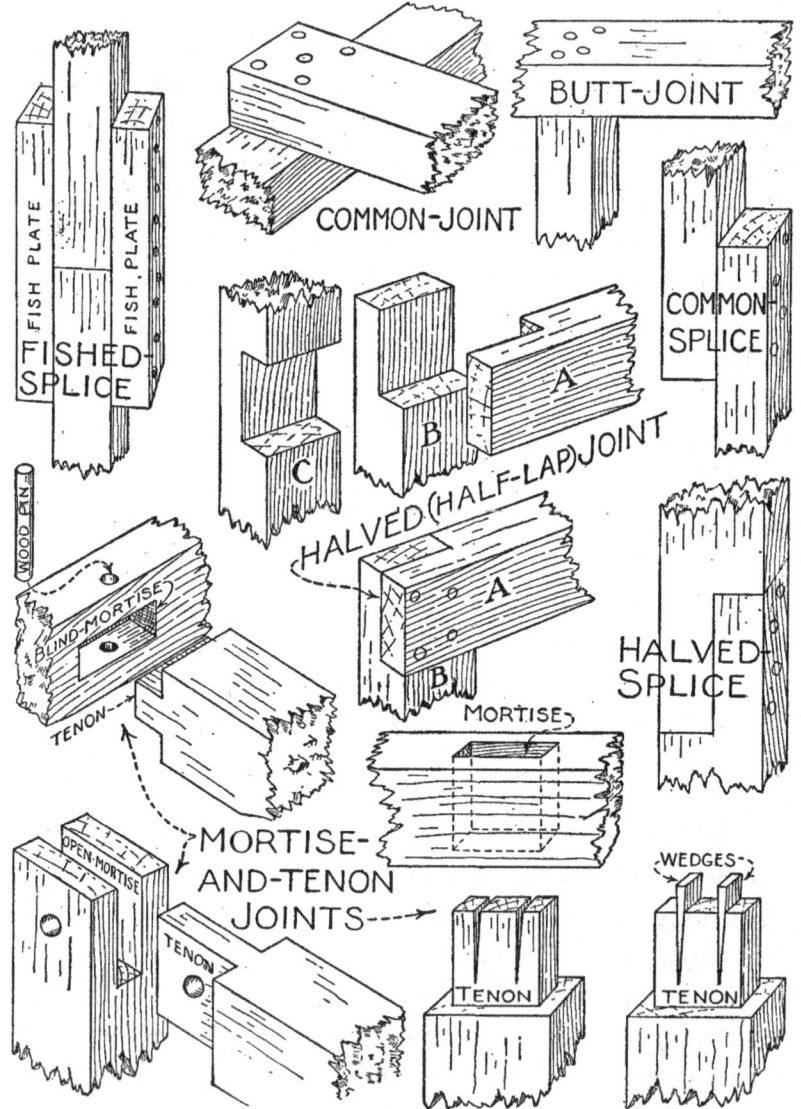

Fig. 74. — Common Forms of Joints and Splices.

Fig. 75. — Common Forms of Joints and Splices.

You are familiar, of course, with the

Common-joint and the Butt-joint, though perhaps you do not know them by name, and no doubt you have used the **Common-splice** and the **Fished-splice** — a better form of splice — in joining together pieces which have been too short in putting up the frameworks for your club-house, tree huts, and other work. You will possibly have to use one of these in constructing the partition for a basement workshop, or an attic room such as is described in Chapter VIII. The above joints and splices are shown clearly in the illustrations and require no explanation.

In the preparation of

A Halved-joint, or *Half lap joint*, as it is sometimes called, a piece equal to the width and one half of the thickness is cut away from each member so the pieces will fit together with their surfaces even or *flush*. The cutting may be done at the ends of the pieces as at *A* and *B*, or away from the end of one piece as at *C*, or in the center of both pieces as shown in Fig. 126 (page 113). Use a square and marking-gauge for laying out the lines for the *halving*. The wood should be removed with a fine saw if the ends of the pieces are *halved*, or with a saw and chisel if the lap is made at the center of the pieces. The *end halved-joint* must be fastened together with nails or screws, but the *center halved-joint* may sometimes be fastened with glue alone.

By joining two pieces lengthwise with a halved-joint

A Halved-splice is obtained (Fig. 74).

ELEMENTARY MANUAL TRAINING

The Mortise-and-Tenon Joint is one of the most important of cabinet-makers' joints, and you will have occasion to employ it in joining together work when it is necessary to make strong connections. Several forms of this joint are shown in Fig. 74, and the method of laying out the *mortise* and the *tenon* is shown in Figs. 76 and 77. Both members of the joint should first be finished up to the proper size, except that additional length must be left on the tenon piece to allow for the cutting of the tenon, and the mortise piece should also be a little longer if the cutting is to be done near the end, to prevent the end from splitting.

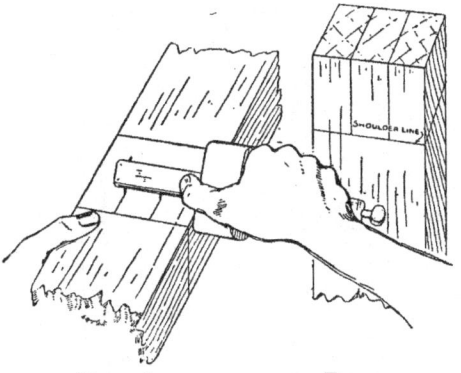

FIG. 76. Laying out a Mortise with the Mortise-gauge.

FIG. 77. Tenon Piece laid out ready to be Cut.

Ordinarily the mortise should not be more than one third of the width of the piece it is cut through, and the tenon not less then one third of the width of the piece it is cut on, in order that neither piece will be weakened by the cutting.

I shall explain, first, the making of the mortise-and-tenon joint, in which the mortise is cut entirely through the piece. Lay off the length of the mortise equal to the width of the tenon piece and scribe lines around the four sides of the block to determine the ends

(Fig. 76), then set your mortise-gauge to the width of the mortise and scribe the two side lines (Fig. 76) on both faces of the piece. The width of the mortise should be made the exact width of one of your chisels, if possible, so that the cutting of the entire width may be done in one operation (Figs. 78 and 79); this will leave little or no trimming to do on the sides.

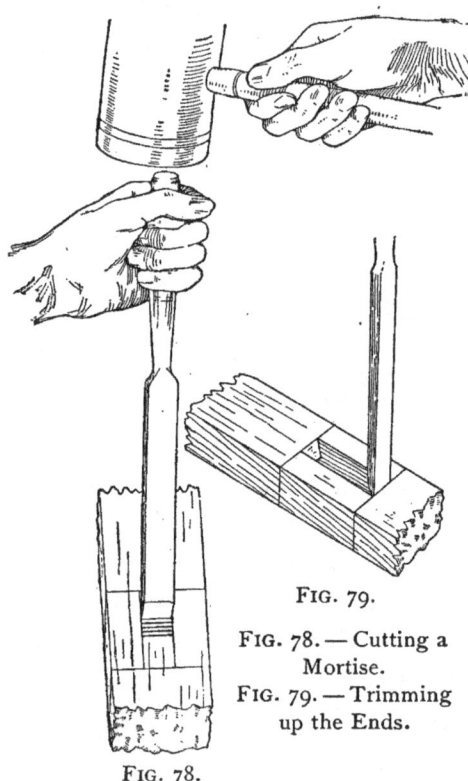

FIG. 79.

FIG. 78. — Cutting a Mortise.
FIG. 79. — Trimming up the Ends.

FIG. 78.

To cut the mortise, place the piece of work upon the bench with one end toward you, then with the chisel held as shown in Fig. 78, with the beveled side facing you, start at the middle of the space marked out and drive the chisel into the wood, then withdraw the chisel, set its edge about $\frac{1}{8}$ inch back of this first cut and drive it into the wood again; continue cutting in this manner, now and then prying out the pieces between the cuts until the farther guide-line has been reached, then reverse the position of the piece of work and, starting at the center again, cut from there back to the other end of the space. The mortise should be cut through one half the thickness of the piece, then the piece should be turned over and the remaining one half cut through from that face. The ends of the mortise must then be trimmed up, and for this part of the work the flat side of the chisel must be held toward the line as in Fig. 79. This trimming, or *paring*, should be done without the use of a mallet. A mortise is very often made by boring a number of holes and then trimming up to the guide-line with a chisel, in the same manner as is described for cutting large, round holes on page 142 (see Fig. 156).

Lay off the length of the tenon with enough allowance for trimming the end later, then scribe a line around the four sides of the piece to locate the *shoulder* of the tenon (Fig. 77). Set the spurs of the mortise-gauge a trifle farther apart than the width of the mortise, to allow for the thickness of the saw in cutting, and scribe the side lines of the tenon from the shoulder line to the end, across the end, and down the other side to the shoulder line. With a back-saw cut the shoulders along the shoulder line, being very careful to saw exactly on the line, then place the piece in the bench-vise as shown in Fig. 80 and cut down the sides of the tenon to the shoulder. The tenon should fit fairly tight in the mortise, but not so tight that it will not drive easily when coated with glue. If a little too large for the mortise, trim the tenon with a chisel. Short tenons may be cut entirely with the chisel. After fitting the pieces together, trim off the end of the tenon flush with the face of the mortise. One of the tenon pieces shown in the illustration has a shoulder cut upon all four sides, which is commonly done to conceal the edges of the mortise, while one of the mortises is shown cut but part way through the piece (a *blind* mortise); the tenon for the latter mortise must be made $\frac{1}{8}$ inch shorter than the depth of the mortise to allow plenty of clearance for the end. The *open mortise-and-tenon joint* illustrated is a common form and simpler to make than the *closed* joint, as the mortise may be cut with a saw and chisel.

FIG. 80. — Cutting the Sides of a Tenon.

In making the furniture detailed in Chapter VI you will use the full-depth mortise only on pieces through which the tenon projects, and for *pins*, as you will see by looking at the working-drawings, the blind mortise being made in all other cases.

Tenons may be fastened in place with *glue, nails, screws, pins,* or *wedges.* For gluing see page 72, for nailing see page 74, and for screwing see page 72. The form of

Pins which you will use most are those described for the construction of the furniture in Chapter VI. In Fig. 74 you will see another common way of pinning together the members of a mortise-and-tenon joint. First of all, a small hole is bored through the sides of the mortise, then the tenon is slipped into place and the position of the hole marked upon it, and then the hole is bored through the tenon about $\frac{1}{16}$ inch nearer to the shoulder than where located. By changing the position of the hole you will see that the pin will draw the shoulder on the tenon piece tight against the mortise piece, when driven into place. For

Wedging the tenon (Fig. 74), one or more *kerfs* are sawed in the end of the tenon, and after the tenon has been slipped through the mortise, wood wedges are coated with glue and driven into the kerfs, thus spreading the end of the tenon in the same way in which the handle of a hammer is fastened in the head.

A Rabbet is a square-corner *groove* cut in the edge of a board (Fig. 75), and

A Rabbet-joint may be made by fitting a square-edge piece into a *rabbeted* piece, by fitting together two pieces with rabbeted edges, and by fitting a rabbeted piece into a *grooved* piece. A rabbet may be cut with a chisel after the manner described for cutting a mortise (Fig. 78), or if it extends along the full length of a short piece, it may be cut with a saw; but if you have much rabbeting to do, it will be well to have a *rabbet-plane* (Fig. 22) for the purpose, or have your work done at a mill.

Grooves may be cut with a chisel in the same way that mortises are cut, but this work is also simplified by using a *dado-plane* (Fig. 23).

The similarity between a rabbet-joint and

A Housed-joint often causes a confusion of the two. But there is no rabbeting in the housed-joint, the entire edge of one piece being fitted, or *housed*, into a groove cut in the other; so if you will remember this, you will have no trouble in distinguishing one from the other.

The Tongue-and-Groove Joint is one which you will probably never have occasion to make, and if you ever do, it will be best to take your work to a mill and have it done by machines especially made for the purpose. You will, however, have need of tongued-and-grooved boards for work requiring tight joints, and these, of course, are stock stuff.

The Mitered-joint will be used a great deal in making picture-frames and other cabinet work. It is always a 45-degree cut and should be made in a miter-box (Fig. 59, page 39) to insure accuracy. The illustrations show

A Mitered-splice, or *beveled-lap splice*, used a good deal in splicing long stretches of interior woodwork.

The Dovetail-joint is a joint you will never need to

apply to your work, in all probability, but a great degree of accuracy is required in making it to secure a neat job, and for this reason it furnishes a splendid exercise for a beginner. The dovetail in modified forms is used in the manufacture of small boxes, and in the joining of the front and sides of drawers, in which case it is all done by a machine.

Figures 81 to 84 show the necessary steps for dovetailing the ends of two pieces by hand. First, plane up the pieces true and to the same width and thickness, then taking the piece upon which the dovetail mortises are to be cut (Fig. 81), scribe the line AB around the two faces and edges at a distance from the end equal to the exact thickness of the tenon piece.

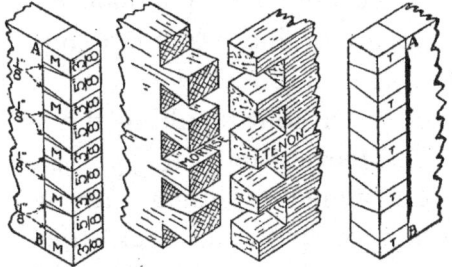

FIG. 81.   FIG. 82.   FIG. 84.   FIG. 83.
FIGS. 81–84. — Details of the Dovetail-joint.

Lay off spaces of $\frac{3}{8}$ inch and $\frac{5}{8}$ inch, alternately, upon this line and scribe lines parallel to the edges of the piece from these points to the end, around the end, and back to line AB on the other face. Next, lay off the oblique side lines of the mortises on both faces, then place the piece in the bench-vise, end up, and saw down along these lines as far as line AB, using a fine saw for the purpose, after which cut out the wood between, marked M, with a chisel (Fig. 82). Place the finished mortise piece upon the end of the tenon piece and mark off the tenons, then, to allow for cutting, move the lines over about $\frac{1}{16}$ inch each side of the tenons and, after this has been done, scribe their ends across to line *AB*, which should be scribed around this piece at a distance from the end equal to the thickness of the mortise piece (Fig. 83). The last step consists in sawing down along the side lines of the tenons and cutting out the wood between, marked *T* (Fig. 84).

A Dovetail Half-lap Joint (Fig. 75) has the advantage over an ordinary half-lap joint of so locking the pieces that it is impossible to pull it apart, lengthwise of the pieces, without breaking the tenon.

The Dowel-joint (Fig. 75) is a *butt-joint*, but the members are fastened together with wooden pins called *dowels*. The form at the left lacks the strength and neatness of a mortise-and-tenon joint, but is often used in cheap work. At the right is shown how two or more boards may be *doweled* together to form a wide piece. *Dowel sticks* of all diameters are made for *doweling*, and you can get what you need at any furniture shop, which will be more satisfactory than to cut them out yourself. The boring of the holes in the proper positions and at right angles to the edges, so the pieces will fit together *flush* and *flat*, requires some practice. After you have *jointed* the edges of the pieces (see page 40), set your marking-gauge to a measurement equal to one half their thickness, and, from the *working face* of each board, gauge a line along the entire length of the edge for a center-line. Then place the boards back to back in your bench-vise, with the edges even, locate the centers of the holes along one center-line and scribe lines from these points across to the other center-line. If the boards are perfectly straight and the holes are bored carefully, the dowels will bring the pieces together exactly right, but in case you find they do not fit, it is easy enough to adjust the trouble by boring extra pairs of holes at the points where the boards are out of line, shifting the centers just as much as is necessary. Bevel the edges of the holes with a knife or a *countersink* to form pockets around the dowels for glue. To allow plenty of clearance, cut the dowels about $\frac{1}{4}$ inch shorter than the combined depths of the holes, then, after you have found that the boards fit together perfectly, coat one half of the length of the dowels with glue and stick them into the holes in one of the edges. Allow the glue to *set*, then coat the edge of each board and the other half of each dowel with glue, put the pieces together and clamp them tightly. Allow the glue to set for about a day before releasing the work.

Battens are strips fastened across two or more pieces of wood for the purpose of holding them together (*A*, Fig. 44, page 32), while

Cleats are strips often used for the same purpose, but generally so secured that the pieces will have a chance to *swell* and *shrink*. It is well enough to nail battens across boards in rough work where it is not important whether the joints remain closed or not, but it will not do for cabinet work. All woodwork expands and contracts to a certain extent with changes in the temperature, and when battens are securely fastened across glued-up work they do not check this movement, nor do the nails or screws *give* enough to take care of it, so the only other thing possible takes place — the wood breaks away from the fastenings and possibly splits from end to end. Figure 85 shows how the movement may be taken care of by attaching cleats to the work. These cleats are held in place with screws, but the screw holes are bored about twice the size of the screws, and washers large enough to cover the holes are used to support the screw-heads. By placing the screws in the exact center of the holes, the ends are free to work back and forth with the movement of the wood. Cleats are attached to the back of single boards and glued-up work in the same way, to prevent warping, and sometimes they are grooved on to the ends of work. A strip fastened up for a shelf or drawer support is also known as a cleat.

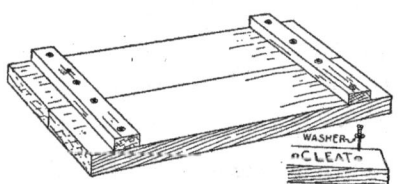

FIG. 85. — The Proper Way to cleat Boards.

You have now learned the difference between a *rabbet*, *groove*, *bead*, *mortise*, *tongue*, *tenon*, *dovetail*, and *miter*, used in making joints and splices, but there are several other *cuts* which you should know. When you read about the

Taper on a piece of work, you must understand this to refer to a gradual decrease in the thickness of the material, forming a slanted surface or edge (Fig. 86). Then there is the

Bevel, a flat surface cut obliquely to its adjoining surfaces (Fig. 87), and a

Chamfer, three forms of which are shown in Figs. 88, 89, and 90. The *bevel* and the *chamfer bevel* are similar, but the latter is usually used only on end grain for the purpose of preventing the wood from splitting down when planing against it. Use a marking-gauge with which to lay out these cuts, and make the bevel and the chamfer bevel with a plane or chisel, the *stop chamfer* with a chisel or spoke-shave, and the *chamfer groove* with a gouge.

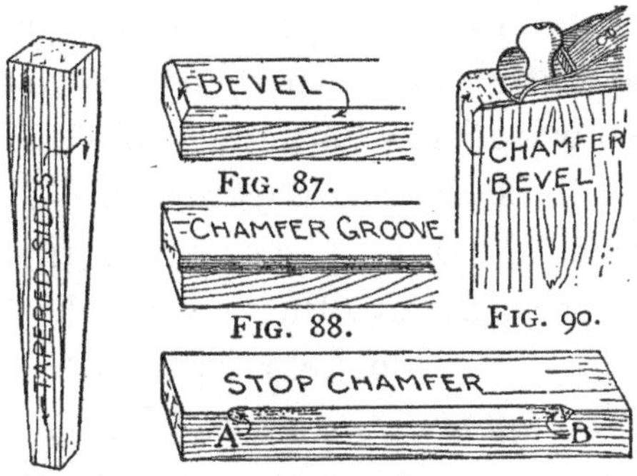
TAPERED SIDES
BEVEL
CHAMFER GROOVE
CHAMFER BEVEL
STOP CHAMFER
A
B

FIG. 86. FIG. 87. FIG. 88. FIG. 89. FIG. 90.

FIG. 86. — Tapered Surface.
FIG. 87. — Bevel.
FIGS. 88–90. — Three Forms of Chamfers.

Woodwork is usually fastened together by means of *glue*, *pins*, *dowels*, *wedges*, *screws*, *nails*, or *bolts*. The use of pins, dowels, and wedges has been discussed. The best glue for you to use for

Gluing up Work is the liquid glue such as you can buy in bottles at the drug store, or in one half pint and larger cans at a hardware store or paint shop. The can form is preferable to the bottle glue as the screw cover seals it up tighter; but when the glue thickens, it is easily thinned by adding a few drops of vinegar and setting the can or bottle for a few minutes in some boiling water. Glue must be thin to work well. Use a brush similar to that shown in Fig. 91 (page 77) with which to apply it.

Before gluing any work, fit every part together and make sure that no further trimming of the joints is necessary; then wipe the portions to be glued with a cloth to remove all sawdust, and apply the glue thoroughly, but not too thick, to one part at a time. After the pieces have been glued in place, unless the joints are mortise-and-tenon joints or other joints which will drive together, the work must be held by *handscrews* (Fig. 40, page 29), *cabinet-maker's clamps* (Fig. 41), or *home-made clamps* (Fig. 42), until the glue has thoroughly *set*, for which about a day's time should be allowed. All surplus glue which has oozed out of joints should be scraped off and the surface sandpapered clean and smooth before any *finish* is applied.

Screws will hold work together better than nails, in places where the latter cannot be *clinched*, and are to be preferred wherever it is possible to use them. The principal forms of wood-screws are the *flat-head*, the *round-head* or *finishing-screw*, and the *square-head* or *lag-screw*.

The last form is used for large, rough work, the heads being made like bolt-heads so they may be turned with a wrench.

In fastening together two pieces of hard wood, or very thin wood, it is necessary to drill holes for the screws before driving them, in the first case to make the driving easier, and in the second case to prevent the wood from splitting. The hole in the upper piece should be made a trifle larger than the diameter of the stem of the screw, so the screw will slip through it without binding, while the hole in the lower piece must of course be enough smaller than the screw so it will thread its way into the wood and take a good hold. In some cases it is necessary to bore the hole in the upper piece a good deal larger than the stem, as in the case of *cleating* (see *Cleats*, page 69). In rough work, or in unexposed places, the screw-heads may be driven in flush with the surface, but on particular work the heads must be *countersunk* (driven below the surface) far enough so the heads may be concealed with putty and whatever finish is placed upon the wood. Countersinking is done with the *countersink* (Fig. 16, page 16), which bevels off the top edge of the screw hole enough to allow the head to drop below the surface. Screws will *drive* into hard wood easier if soaped, that is, rubbed over a piece of soap until the threads are coated. This also prevents the possibility of slender screws twisting off, which they are likely to do when forced very hard.

Nails are made of wrought-iron, wire (bright and galvanized), brass, and copper. Of these you will seldom use others than the *common wire nail* for rough work, the *brad* and *finishing-nail* for work where it is necessary to drive the heads below the surface of the wood, and in so doing to make as small a hole as possible, and *copper* or *galvanized wire nails* for boat building and other outside work where nails are exposed to rust.

Holes should always be started in very thin wood to prevent splitting, and it is necessary to do the same in hard wood to prevent the nails from bending. The holes must be a trifle smaller than the nails and may be made with a brad-awl (Fig. 16, page 16), or a small drill (Fig. 26, page 23). In all work but of the roughest kind, the nail-heads should be *set* low enough so they may be concealed with putty before the wood is finished. The setting is done by means of a *nail-set* (Fig. 16, page 16).

Carriage-bolts are used more or less frequently in carpentry with which to pivot one piece to another, or to hold several pieces together (generally in large work) where they are likely to be subjected to a strain that nails or screws would not stand. You will use these as *king-bolts* in making your bob-sleds (Chap. XVIII) and your wagons (Chap. XXIV), and for securing in place the *rowlock blocks* of your boats (Chaps. XXII and XXIII).

CHAPTER IV
WOOD FINISHING

THE finishing of work is equally as important as the constructive part because the final appearance of the article depends upon the care with which it is done. Many a well-made piece of furniture has been ruined by poor taste in the selection of finish, or as a result of carelessness or inexperience on the part of the amateur craftsman applying it. With practice, however, any boy can master the common forms of finishes, such as *painting*, *staining*, *shellacking*, *waxing*, *varnishing*, and *oiling*, so as to be able to turn out a satisfactory job.

The kind of finish to be selected for a piece of work depends, of course, upon the variety of wood used, the nature of the article and the wear to which it will be subjected. For your sleds, wagons, boats, club-houses, and most of your home-made outdoor equipment, as well as much of that made for indoors,

Paint makes the most durable finish. Ready-mixed paints may be obtained in various colors, and this is probably the most satisfactory way for a boy to purchase paint if he wants a large quantity, but for small work where only a small amount of one color is required it is best to buy the *lead ground in oil*, of the color desired, and thin down with turpentine as much as is needed for the job; paint may be bought in this form in 1-pound cans. The balance of the paint in the can may be kept soft by pouring in enough water or linseed-oil to cover the surface; this may be poured off again when you wish to use more paint.

As most of you boys probably know, the combination of red and yellow makes orange, yellow and blue makes green, blue and red makes purple, green and red makes brown, and black and white makes gray. Different shades may be obtained by using a larger proportion of one or the other color, and black and white will darken or lighten the color. By purchasing *Venetian red*, *chrome-yellow*, *Prussian blue*, *lampblack*, and *white lead* (or *zinc-white*), you will be able to mix up almost every shade of any color you wish to use, but you will probably find in *burnt umber* or *burnt sienna* just the shade of brown you want, and in *chrome-green* or *olive-green* the right shade of green, in which case it will pay you to buy a can of each.

In Mixing Paints, mix up at one time as much as will be necessary to complete a job, as it is usually difficult to match a color exactly, and a slight change in the shade will spoil the appearance of the work you are finishing. Try the color upon a piece of wood of the same kind as that of the article to be painted, before you go ahead with

WOOD FINISHING 77

the painting, and allow it to dry so you can see whether or not it is going to look right.

Brushes. Figure 91 shows a number of brushes which will generally answer every purpose of the amateur. The two large brushes will be needed for general painting, the two sash-tools for small work and for getting into corners, and the smallest brush for striping, marking, and lettering. Then there is the medium-sized varnish brush which must be used only for varnishing and shellacking, and the glue brush mentioned in Chapter III. When you are through painting, staining, or varnishing, wash out your brushes in turpentine, or if you expect to use them in the same material within a day or so you may place them in water, which will keep the paint from hardening without injuring the bristles if the brushes are prevented from resting upon the bottom of the receptacle. To support the brushes, bore holes through the handles in the proper places so that when run upon a piece of wire and the wire is laid across the rim of the can or other receptacle, the ends of the bristles will not touch the bottom.

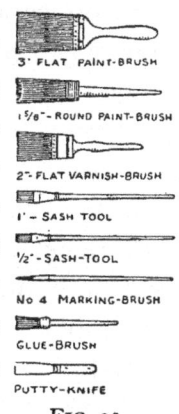

FIG. 91. Brushes and Putty-knife.

In Painting wipe off your brush upon the edge of the paint can after dipping it into the paint, so it will not drip and spatter over everything. Apply the paint thinly and always start at one end of a surface and work toward the other. If there are any *resinous* knots in the wood, first give them a coat of shellac to *set* the resin so there will be no danger of it oozing through the surface after it has been painted. The first coat is known as the *priming coat*. After it has dried, the work should be gone over carefully and all nail holes, and cracks and other defects puttied up (see *Puttying*, page 84). After puttying, sandpaper all rough places (see *Sandpapering*, page 84) before applying a second coat. Two coats will be sufficient for all ordinary work, but three coats are better for particular work. In three-coat work the priming coat may be of white or any light color, as the other coats will cover it.

Staining. For the finishing of furniture and other nice work, the modern method of treatment is to stain the wood, fill it, and then apply *wax* or a *flat varnish* (dull varnish). Any of the soft woods and a number of the hard woods take stain exceedingly well; oak is now finished in this way more generally than any other wood. The purpose of staining should be, not to imitate a more expensive wood, as is frequently done, but instead to bring out the beauty of the grain, if it has a decided grain, or at least to give it a beautiful soft tone.

There are many prepared stains upon the market which may be had at a small cost, and any paint store handling these will have a color card from which you may select the color you wish to use. These stains are made in *water stains*, which are dyes mixed in water, and *oil stains*, which are pigments mixed in linseed-oil or spirits.

Water stains roughen the grain of wood, making it necessary to sandpaper the surface after an application has dried, but they have an advantage over the oil stains in the fact that they bring out much stronger the lines of the grain, the oil stains being less transparent and concealing, somewhat, the delicate lines and pores. But for the fine-grained woods, oil stains are easier to apply, and produce better results.

Oil Stains are easy to mix, and the author advises his readers to do some experimenting along this line. With the colors mentioned under *Paint*, any of the standard shades of green, gray, and brown may be made, and with a stain manufacturer's sample color card to work from, you will be able to get pretty close to any of the shades shown, although they will look a little different when applied to the wood than they do on the card, on account of the difference in material. Always use the same kind of wood as your work is made of, upon which to try out a stain before deciding on it. The prepared stains are accompanied with full instructions for application. Before using your home-made stain, sandpaper the surface of your work thoroughly, then apply the stain with a brush or piece of cloth, and rub it in vigorously with a piece of soft muslin or cheese-cloth. Allow the work to dry for a day, then go over it and fill up all nail holes with putty colored with the stain;

clean off the putty crumbs and apply a second coat of the stain. The surface may be left without further treatment, but it is advisable to put a coat of *white shellac* over the oil, and when this has dried to wax it, in order to produce a hard finish. Unless you protect the surface in some such way, it will become spotted, as the oil in the stain never entirely dries, and rubs off.

Some very pleasing effects upon oak have been obtamed by the author by applying the two coats of stain in two different colors, instead of mixing them together and putting them on as one color. For instance, to produce a green finish, a thin coat of Venetian red was first rubbed well into the grain, then on top of this a coat of chrome-green was applied (chrome-green may be made by mixing together chrome-yellow and Prussian blue, if you do not wish to buy a can of it). The result was a pretty green with just a slight suggestion of a reddish tinge to the grain. The *Drafting Table* and *Bench* shown in the photograph opposite page 86 were finished in this way. By applying a thinner coat of the green than of the red, and wiping it off a little more, a pretty dark brown having a tinge of red showing through it may be obtained. The only difficulty an amateur will experience in putting on a stain in this manner will be in using the same amount of stain upon the work that he has used upon his sample, and in rubbing it down to the same tone; but with a little experience he will be able to obtain excellent results.

White shellac must be used for
Shellacking stained woodwork, as the commoner kind — *orange shellac* — will alter the tone of the stain and probably ruin the work. It is better to buy the white shellac already prepared. Use a 2-inch varnish brush such as is shown in Fig. 91, and if the shellac is thick, dilute it with alcohol just before using it, as it must be thin enough to flow freely over the work. Start at one end of the surface to be covered and work toward the other end, using long, even strokes and being careful not to skip any places and not to go over the same part of the surface twice; uncovered portions and *laps* will show through the finish and give it an uneven appearance.

Shellac alone makes a splendid finish for articles made of soft wood, — such as kitchen and pantry conveniences, etc., — and is quickly put on. The orange shellac is better than the white for this purpose, as it gives the wood a richer tone. You can buy the orange shellac chips and *cut* (dissolve) them by placing them in a glass preserve-jar, or empty varnish can, and covering them with wood alcohol. Dilute the shellac with alcohol as much as is necessary to make it thin, when you are ready to use it. Three coats of shellac are sufficient for an ordinary piece of work. Allow each coat to dry for at least a day before applying another, and sandpaper the surface after each coat has dried, to remove all roughness. After the final coat, instead of sandpapering it, a better finish may be obtained by rubbing the surface with a piece of flannel, or other soft cloth, dipped in powdered pumice-stone moistened with linseed-oil. Besides smoothing the surface, this rubbing *cuts* the gloss and produces an even, soft tone. All nail holes should be puttied up after the first coat has dried.

Filling is necessary in preparing a surface for varnishing, to fill out the grain and make a smooth, level surface, especially on wood having a coarse grain, such as oak. Factory furniture, finished in Flemish-oak, weathered-oak, or any of the other modern stain finishes, is filled after the staining has been done; but you will secure richer effects by omitting this from such work, as it conceals much of the beauty of the grain, especially in the open-grained woods.

Filling is best done by the amateur with a

Paste Filler, which can be purchased at any paint store. The filler must be thinned with turpentine to the consistency of cream and then be spread evenly over the wood with a brush or cloth, allowed to *set* for ten or fifteen minutes, and then rubbed off across the grain so as to fill all of the pores; do the rubbing with excelsior or a piece of burlap. The filler must be allowed to dry for about twelve hours before the shellacking is done. Filler may be bought in the *natural* and colored to suit the finish to be applied to the wood, or it may be obtained already prepared in the color of one of a number of standard wood finishes.

WOOD FINISHING

Waxing gives a stained surface a much richer tone than varnish, and is easier to apply. Prepared wax can be purchased at a paint store. It should be rubbed on with a cloth, allowed to stand ten or fifteen minutes, and then rubbed vigorously with a soft cloth until a polish is obtained. Waxed surfaces must not come in contact with water, for they will become spotted if they do and require rewaxing.

Varnishing is seldom done nowadays by amateur craftsmen in finishing woodwork, but it is necessary as a protection upon surfaces which are subjected to water, so a few pointers are given here. If the wood has an *open* grain, it must first be filled, then given a coat of shellac to form a body for the varnish. Flow the varnish over the surface with a varnish brush such as is shown in Fig. 91, then brush it crosswise of the grain and finish by brushing it lengthwise of the grain. One coat will be sufficient for all ordinary work, but two coats will produce a finer finish. Several days' time should be allowed to elapse between coats. The glossy surface may be cut by

Rubbing it down with a soft cloth dipped in powdered pumice-stone wet with linseed-oil or water. After the surface has been rubbed and the pumice-stone thoroughly cleaned off, it may be improved by

Polishing with *rottenstone* and linseed-oil, rubbed on with a piece of cotton-flannel.

In buying varnish it pays to get a good grade, as its

better wearing qualities will make it cheaper in the long run than the low-priced varnishes, which are usually very unsatisfactory.

Oiling the surface of a piece of work accentuates the markings of the grain and gives to the wood a beautiful rich tone. This is an especially good finish for articles made out of cigar boxes (see Chap. XI). Apply the oil with a brush or rag, then rub it vigorously with a soft cloth, until you have worked into the grain as much as it will take, and wipe off the superfluous oil.

Sandpapering. You will have occasion to use about four grades of sandpaper — No. $1\frac{1}{2}$ for coarse work, Nos. $\frac{1}{2}$ and 0 for medium work, and Nos. 0 and 00 for fine work. Nos. 0 and 00 are of the proper degree of fineness for sandpapering painted, stained, and shellacked surfaces. To avoid scratching a surface always sandpaper lengthwise of the grain. For sandpapering flat surfaces, the paper should be attached to a block of wood. (On page 11 of "The Boy Craftsman" is shown a specially formed block for this purpose.)

Puttying. Putty can be purchased at the paint stores now in sealed one-pound cans, at about five cents a can. A small quantity will go a long way, and it is best to buy a small amount at a time, as it hardens very quickly when exposed to the air. Putty may be kept soft, however, by placing it in a can of water.

Before using putty, knead it in your hand to *work* back into it the oil which rises to the surface, and if the article upon which it is to be used is stained, work enough of the stain into it to make it of the right color. It is always best to putty after the priming coat has been applied, in painting, and after the first coat of stain has been put on, in oil staining, as the oil soaks into the holes and cracks and the putty sticks better as a result.

Painters use a putty-knife (Fig. 91) with which to press putty into the crevices of work, but you can use the blade of your jack-knife for the purpose, or a fairly good

Home-made Putty-knife may be obtained by cutting off square the end of a five-cent potato knife.

As a final word upon the subject of wood finishing, the author wishes to caution you boys to

Be Careful of Oily Rags and waste and not allow them to lie around, for they are very likely to catch fire through *spontaneous combustion*. Burn up everything of this nature as soon as you are through with it.

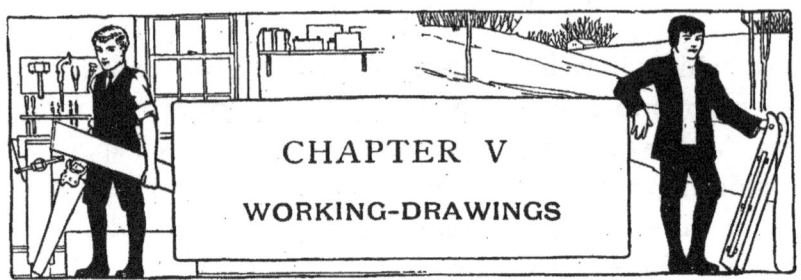

CHAPTER V
WORKING-DRAWINGS

By a working-drawing is meant a mechanical representation of an object, either drawn accurately to measurements or laid out roughly with dimensions marked upon it, with which a mechanic can get to work and make the entire object complete. Sometimes, every part of the work can be so shown upon a single sheet that no other word of explanation is required by the mechanic; again, on more complicated work, general working-drawings showing the main portions of the structure or machine must be prepared, and then all the minor parts taken up singly and worked out (*detailed*) on other sheets, forming what are known as *detail drawings*. In very complex work hundreds of these drawings are often necessary in order that the *designer* or *draftsman* may make certain that every part of the construction will work out properly and that the workmen will understand his intentions, and in many kinds of work it is necessary to furnish in addition to all these details printed or typewritten instructions, known as *specifications*, to explain the kinds, grades, and sizes of materials, and complicated

A Corner of the Author's Home Workroom.
(For Working Drawings of the Table and Bench see Figs. 147 and 180, Chapter VI.)

portions which cannot be covered by notes upon the drawings.

The average person usually has difficulty in reading a working-drawing, for the fact that he looks at it as he does a picture, expecting to see everything standing out in a photographic form. And until the beginner understands what a *plan*, *elevation*, and *section* are he will continue to have this difficulty. To make the explanation as simple as possible, the working-drawings for a dog-house are shown in Fig. 92. The *plan* shows a view of the floor of the house as you would see it if you sawed through the walls and removed the upper portion, and then could look down squarely upon every part at the same time. A view looking down upon the roof in the same way would be a *roof plan*, and a top view of any object is also known as a *plan*. A view of the front of the dog-house, which you would see if you could look squarely at every portion of the front at the same time, is called a *front elevation*, and the same kind of a view of the side is called a *side elevation*, while if a rear view had been necessary to show special work it would be known as a *rear elevation*, and in case there were two side elevations they would be named *left elevation* and *right elevation* to distinguish one from the other, or in the case of a building or any stationary work the elevations would be designated by the *points of the compass*. By sawing the dog-house in two, crosswise, from the peak down through the base, removing the front portion and then looking toward the rear, you would see a sectional view of the house, and a true drawing showing this view would be called a *section* (see Fig. 92). A section may be taken through an object either horizontally or vertically (a plan taken through an object is in reality a horizontal section), and a section through the short way of an object is known as a *cross-section*, and one through the long way as a *longitudinal section*. A *perspective* drawing shows the object as you would actually see it when viewing it from one point, which is more or less similar to the view a camera would show. In this drawing the horizontal lines *converge* (approach one another) as they recede from the eye, which produces the same effect that is obtained when looking down a railroad track — the coming together of telegraph wires and tracks at a point on the horizon. A perspective of the dog-house is shown in Fig. 495, page 390.

Working-drawings are made to different

Scales, determined largely by the size and construction of the work. A very small object may be detailed *full-size*, while a building or a large piece of machinery would be shown at a small scale with $\frac{1}{8}$ inch or $\frac{1}{4}$ inch upon the drawing representing 12 inches on the object to be constructed, and different portions which are more or less complicated would be redrawn at a larger scale to make them clear. The drawings of the dog-house (Fig. 92) were made to a scale of $1\frac{1}{2}$ inches to the foot; that is, $1\frac{1}{2}$ inches on the drawing represents 12 inches

Trimming Line
A NEELY HALL-1910
DETAILS FOR A DOG-HOUSE
PREPARED BY
ROBERT BLANK
SCALE 1½"=1'-0"
JULY 16 1911
1-FOOT
1-INCH
CENTER-LINE
BATTENS
ENDS
PLAN
SIDES
BATTEN
SHINGLES
RIDGE-BOARD
SHINGLES
ROOF BOARDS
4-¾" VENTS
4-¾" VENTS 6" ON CENTERS
6-¾" VENTS 6" ON CENTERS
FRONT ELEVATION
CROSS-SECTION AT A-A
SIDE ELEVATION

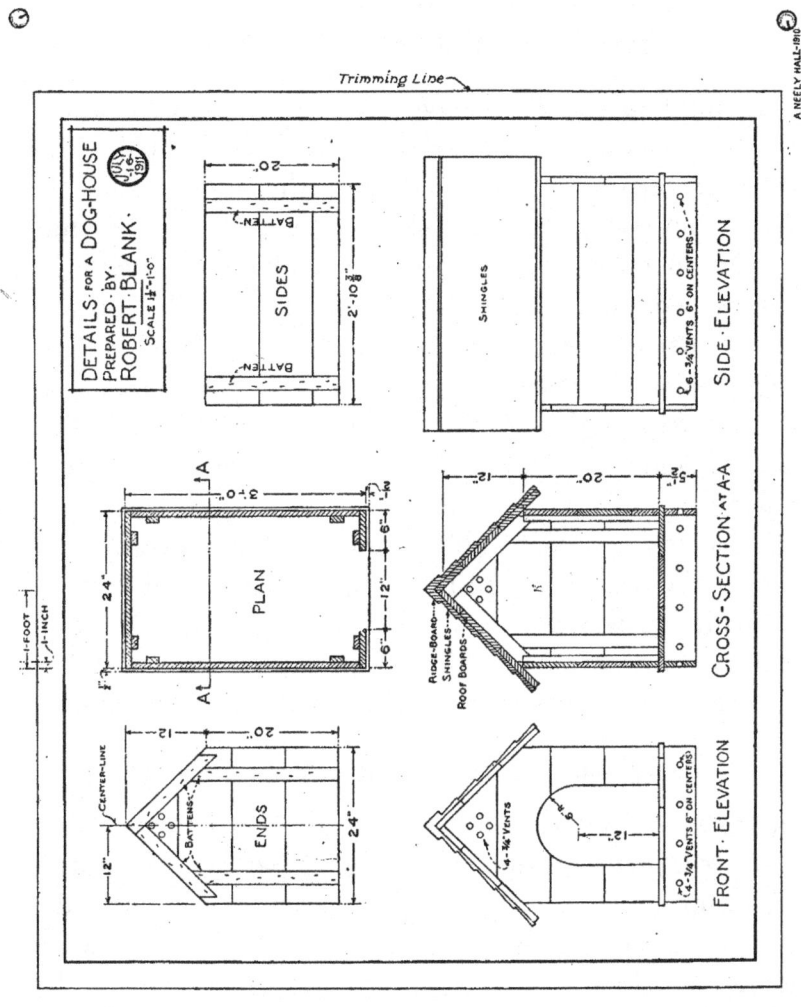

of the dog-house. They have been reduced considerably from this size in order to show them upon the page, but the ruler across the top indicates the original size to which they were drawn. Maps and printed drawings reduced to odd sizes, as in this case, have a graduated scale placed upon them, but the scale of working-drawings is usually expressed in this form: Scale 12″ = 1′-0″ (*full size*); Scale 6″ = 1′-0″ (*half size*); Scale 3″ = 1′-0″; Scale ¼″ = 1′-0″; Scale ⅛″ = 1′-0″, etc. The mark ″ stands for *inch* or *inches* and the mark ′ for *foot* or *feet*.

Every boy should be able to prepare his own working-drawings in order that he may work out his own designs for furniture, wagons, boats, kites, aëroplanes, etc., and no important work should be attempted before it has been carefully drawn out upon paper, for, as the maxim goes,

"Working without a plan is sailing without a compass,"

and work so constructed is bound to show defects either in the design or in the misfitting of parts. The furniture described in the following chapter is completely detailed and will give you a good idea of how such work should be laid out, but many of the other articles described in this book are illustrated only by sketches or perspective drawings, and before making these you should prepare drawings showing the work as you have determined to make it.

A Drawing Outfit does not need to be an expensive

WORKING-DRAWINGS

one, but as in the purchase of any kind of tools it pays in the end to buy only the best of materials; these are usually to be found in the medium-priced equipment.

A Drawing-board may be made by cleating together several boards as described on page 70 and illustrated in Fig. 85, but you can buy one so cheaply that it hardly pays to try to make one. The board must be absolutely true upon the left-hand edge, and the wood must be well-seasoned and free from *winding*, *knots* and other defects, which points are taken care of in the boards you buy. A good size for small drawings is a student's board, size 16 inches by 22 inches (Fig. 93). The board may be placed upon your desk while you work, or you may make

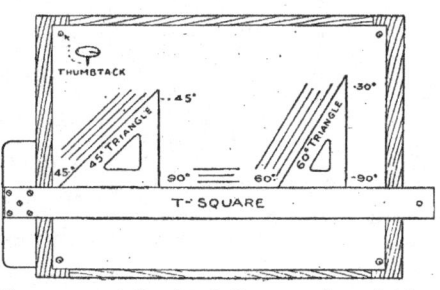

FIG. 93. — A Student's Drawing-board (size 16" × 22") and T-square and Triangles.

A Drafting Table such as is shown opposite page 86, if you wish. This table has a large drawing-board for a top, but an ordinary table top may be constructed instead if you have a small drawing-board to use on it. Working-drawings for the construction of the table are given in Fig. 147, page 132.

A T-square is used as a guide for the pencil in drawing horizontal lines, and a guide for the *triangles* for oblique lines. The crosspiece upon the end slides along the left edge of the drawing-board and is moved with the left hand. A

45-degree Triangle is required for drawing oblique lines at an angle of 45 degrees, and a **60-degree Triangle** for drawing oblique lines at angles of 60 and 30 degrees (Fig. 93). With the addition of a *ruler*, a couple of *pencils*, an *eraser*, and

Compasses, a boy will have as large an outfit as he probably will require for making drawings for shop use. Figure 94 shows a cheap pencil-compass which will serve the purpose, but if you can afford a pair such as is shown in Fig. 95, you will be better equipped for a greater variety of work. In the illustration of the latter pair, *A* represents the *body* of the compass, *B* the *needle point* which fits into one leg, and *C* the *pencil point* which fits into the other leg, while *D* and *E* are *divider points* which may be substituted in place of the needle and pencil points to form a pair of *dividers*. *F* is the *pen point* which is used in place of the pencil point for drawing in ink, and *G* is the *extension bar* with which either leg of the compass or divider may be extended.

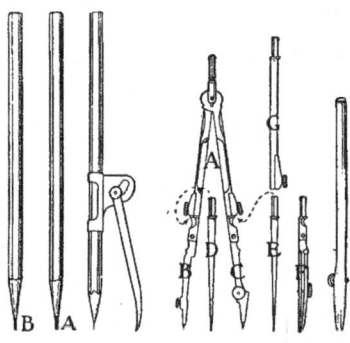

FIG. 97. FIG. 94. FIG. 95. FIG. 96.
FIG. 94.— A Cheap Pencil-compass.
FIG. 95. — Compass with Pen, Pencil, and Divider Points.
FIG. 96. — Ruling-pen.
FIG. 97. — Chisel-shaped and Pointed Pencil Ends.

WORKING-DRAWINGS

Swing the compass with one hand, as shown in Fig. 98. For drawing ink lines other than arcs of circles, a

Ruling-pen is necessary (Fig. 96). The ruling-pen must be held in a perpendicular position, with the ends of the fingers resting upon the T-square as shown in Fig. 99, so they will slide along the T-square easily. The thickness of the lines is governed by turning the screw upon the pen, which draws together or spreads apart the two blades.

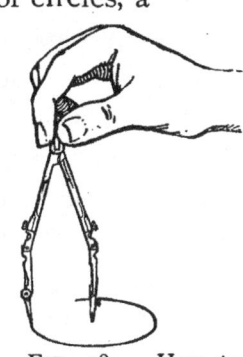

FIG. 98. — How to swing a Compass.

The ink is dropped between the blades by means of the quill upon the end of the cork furnished with the bottles of drawing ink (Fig. 102). Figure 100 shows

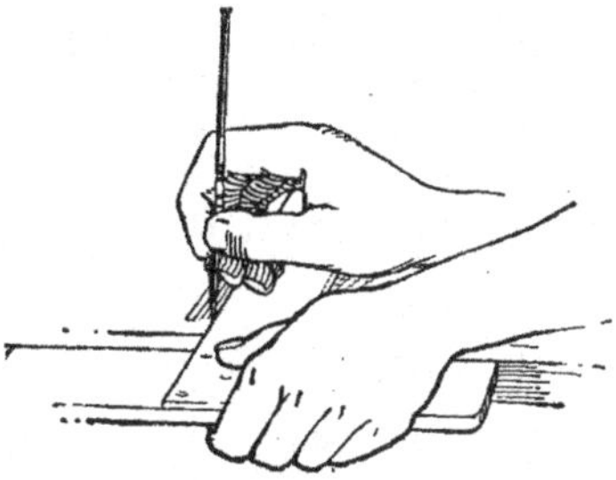

A Set of Instruments which, in addition to the compass A, compass adjusting key B, pen point C, extension bar D, and ruling-pen E, has a pair of dividers F, a small sized ruling-pen G, a small pair of dividers H (*bow-dividers*), a small pencil-compass I (*bow-pencil*), a small pen-compass J (*bow-pen*), and a box of *leads* K. A moderate priced set of these instruments will cost about $6.50.

FIG. 99. — How to hold a Ruling-pencil.

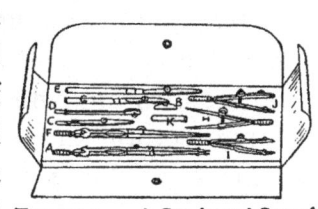

FIG. 100. — A Students' Set of Drawing Instruments.

For laying off measurements, an ordinary
12-inch Ruler (Fig. 92) will do, but at a slight additional cost a specially prepared
Scale may be purchased. One of these is a time saver in making scale drawings. Some scales are made flat like a ruler, while others are triangular in shape as shown in Fig. 101. Upon the triangular scales eleven sets of graduations are provided — $12''$ (full size), $3''$, $1\frac{1}{2}''$, $1''$, $\frac{3}{4}''$, $\frac{1}{2}''$, $\frac{3}{8}''$, $\frac{1}{4}''$, $\frac{3}{16}''$, $\frac{1}{8}''$, and $\frac{3}{32}''$. In the illustration the $\frac{3}{8}''$ and $\frac{3}{4}''$ graduations are shown along one edge and $3''$ and $1\frac{1}{2}''$ divisions along the other. Each end division

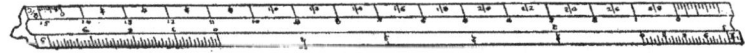

FIG. 101. — A Triangular Scale.

of these is also divided into twelve parts, each of which for that particular scale represents 1 inch. Flat scales are made with four or eight different kinds of divisions according to whether one side or both sides are graduated.

Drawing Pencils are made in various grades designated by letters, ranging from 9H, which is very hard, down to 6B, which is very soft. A 6H pencil is usually used in machine drawing, while a 3H is about the hardest used in architectural drawing. If you wish to use ordinary pencils, get a No. 4 or No. 5 (equivalent to 2H and 3H drawing pencils) for drawing upon hard paper, a No. 2 (equivalent to a B) for a medium soft pencil, and a No. 1 (equivalent to a 3B) for a very soft pencil. For drawing straight lines, a pencil should be sharpened *chisel-shape* (*A*, Fig. 97), which may be done by rubbing it upon a piece of No. 00 sandpaper, and for lettering and drawing curved lines it should be rubbed to a point (*B*, Fig. 97). For ordinary lettering in ink, Gillott's Nos. 303 and 170

Pens are most satisfactory, while a No. 659 should be used for very fine work.

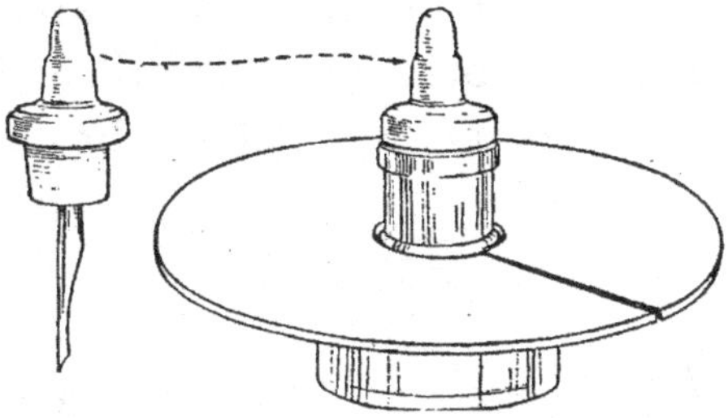

Drawing Ink. Specially prepared India ink (Higgins' Waterproof India Ink is almost universally used) should be bought for use in preparing ink drawings. This comes in small bottles with a quill upon the end of the cork with which to fill the ruling-pen (Fig. 102). Drawing inks may also be had in colors.

FIG. 102. — Drawing-ink Bottle with Cardboard Collar to prevent Upsetting.

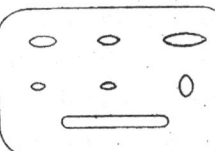

FIG. 103. — Erasing Shield.

An Ink Eraser and a Pencil Eraser are also required, and an **Erasing Shield** (Fig. 103) is a great convenience as a protection to the lines close to those which you wish to erase, as an opening of the proper size may be placed over that portion, and the surrounding lines will be covered. One of these shields can easily be prepared out of a piece of thin brass.

About the most unfortunate thing which a young

draftsman experiences is the upsetting of his ink-bottle on a drawing after working perhaps three or four days upon it. This is certain to happen sooner or later, if the bottle is set without a holder upon the table, and frequently when the boy is careless. Figure 102 shows a simple protection, consisting of a cardboard collar cut to fit over the neck of the bottle and of a large enough diameter to make it impossible to upset the ink.

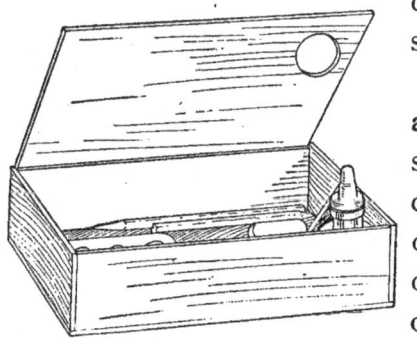

FIG. 104. — Cigar-box Pencil Box and Inkstand.

A Home-made Pencil Box and Inkstand such as is shown in Fig. 104 is very convenient. It is made out of a cigar box. One corner of the box is partitioned off to hold the ink-bottle, and the cover has a hole cut through it so it will fit over the top of the cork when closed. The box will serve the purpose of a receptacle not only for pencils, but for your pens, thumb-tacks, erasers, and erasing shield as well.

You may use small 1-ounce flat-head tacks for holding down drawing-paper, but these are not as easily removed as regular

Thumb-tacks, the best form of which is shown in Fig. 93.

Drawing-paper specially prepared for pencil or ink may be purchased in sheets or rolls. For common use, however, butchers' Manila wrapping paper will serve the purpose, and the back of smooth medium-weight wallpaper has a good surface. Out-of-date stock of wallpaper can be purchased for a few cents a roll. The chief trouble with the common paper is that it roughens up when erased, but this will not be a serious objection for your shop drawings, and when you wish to prepare better appearing drawings, you may copy them upon better paper.

The white-lined drawings which you have seen upon blue paper are known as

Blueprints and are printed upon sensitized paper in the same way that a photograph blueprint is made from a plate or film. The negative in this case is prepared upon

Tracing-cloth, which is a linen specially prepared so as to be very transparent, or upon

Tracing-paper, which is a very transparent paper. The cloth or paper is tacked down over the drawing, and then everything is traced off upon it with ink exactly as it is upon the drawing below. The cloth has a glazed and a dull side, the former the right side, but the latter the one generally preferred by draftsmen as the better working surface. To make the ink flow smoothly, *talcum powder* is dusted upon the cloth and rubbed over it with a rag to cut any oil which may have collected upon the surface. Ink lines erase very easily from the cloth, and all pencil lines and dirt may be cleaned off after the tracing has

98   HANDICRAFT FOR HANDY BOYS

been finished by wiping with a rag wet in benzine (*do not use water*, for it will ruin the finish surface on the cloth), which makes the use of the cloth for ink tracings almost universal. Tracing-paper is used, generally, for making pencil copies of drawings, and for making one drawing over another when the same measurements are to be used in both, as will be explained later.

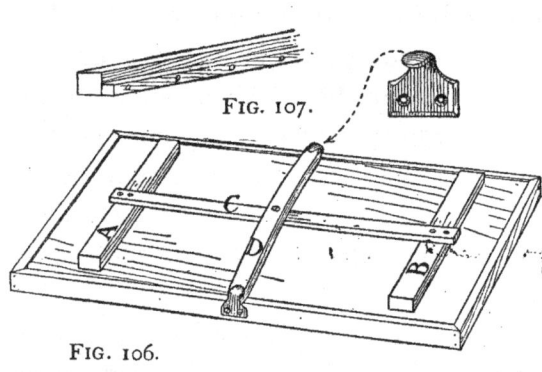

FIG. 107.

FIG. 106.

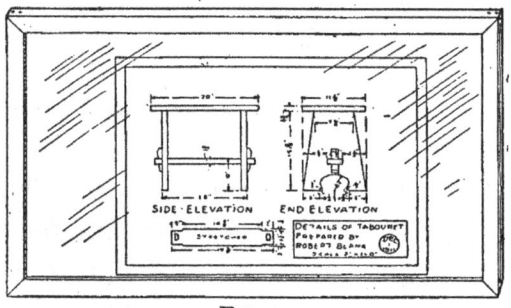

FIG. 105.

FIGS. 105–107.—Details of Home-made Blueprint frame.

After a tracing has been prepared it is placed in the printing-frame upon a piece of clear glass and a piece of blueprint paper is placed over it, then the paper is exposed and washed in the same way that an ordinary blueprint is made. If you own a photograph printing-frame, you can make your drawings to a small enough scale to fit it, but it is a simple matter to construct

WORKING-DRAWINGS

A Home-made Printing-frame. A good scheme is shown in Fig. 105. This may be made out of a picture-frame, or a similar frame can be made with the corners mitered and a rabbet formed on the inside by tacking narrow strips to the frame strips, as shown in Fig. 107. The wooden back must be provided with a spring attachment to make an equal pressure upon all parts, so there will be perfect contact between the paper and tracing at all points (Fig. 106). Make this back out of $\frac{1}{2}$-inch stuff, in one piece if possible, and fasten a cleat across it near each end to keep it from warping (*A* and *B*, Fig. 106), then cut strip *C* of the proper length to reach from *A* to *B* and strip *D* to reach from side to side of the frame. Screw *C* and *D* together at their centers, boring a hole through *D* for the screw to run through so this strip will turn easily, and screw the ends of *C* to *A* and *B*. Fasten a metal sash-lift in the proper place upon each side of the frame, and bevel off the ends of strip *D* enough so they will slip under them. The strips must be cut to the proper thickness so that strip *D* will have to be bent in the shape of a bow to slip its ends under the sash-lifts; this places a pressure upon strip *C*, which transfers it to strips *A* and *B*, and the latter distribute it over the back of the frame. The back of the frame should be covered with a piece of thin cotton-flannel; this must be glued in place and smoothed out carefully so there will be no wrinkles. A cheaper grade of paper than that used for photographic work is manufactured for blueprinting, and this can be purchased in rolls put up in sealed tubes. Use a small piece of paper to make a test print upon, to determine the proper length of time for exposure.

Preparing Working-drawings. Before laying out a set of working-drawings, the general plan of the piece of work must be sketched out, and the various dimensions and the method of construction determined upon. All this preliminary work may be done very roughly.

The first part to lay out is the plan, then the elevations and sections. It is often necessary to work out a section before the elevations, or at the same time, as in the case of a house where the heights of the exterior features are determined by the wall and floor construction. By placing the drawings as shown in Fig. 92, the lines of the plan may be continued down (*projected*) for the cross-section, and the heights may be projected horizontally to the left for the front elevation and to the right for the side elevation, while the corner spaces may be filled with detail drawings. In the details of the dog-house, the side lines of the ends were projected up from the front elevation, and those of the sides were carried up from the side elevation. Although there are many other schemes for laying out a set of drawings, this is about the simplest method for you to use in your work, which will be more or less simple. In more complicated work it is general practice, especially in the planning of buildings, to place a piece of tracing-paper over the plan after that has been laid out, and to lay out the section upon this, then to place another piece of tracing-paper over the section and lay out a front elevation upon this. The transparency of the paper makes it possible for the draftsman to see through the sheets and, without having to lay out the main widths and the heights again, to mark them off upon the top sheet just as they are located upon the plan and section sheets below. After the front elevation has been laid out, one of the side elevations is prepared in the same way, from the plan and either the front elevation or section; the opposite side elevation and the rear elevation are made by reversing the side elevation and front elevation sheets and tracing off the similar portions and changing the rest to suit the plan.

Lay out your drawings with a light line first, then check up your measurements, and if everything appears, all right, go over the work and make all the *outlines* heavy. *Cross-hatch* (shade with diagonal lines placed at equal distances apart) all portions of the plan and section which are "cut through," in order to show which is in section and which in elevation, and change the direction of the cross-hatching upon adjoining pieces to accent the point where one piece ends and another begins. After the drawing has been completed,

Draw Dimension-lines upon the plan, section, elevations, and details wherever measurements are necessary (these should be broken lines and be lighter than the outlines); then fill in the dimensions in feet and inches.

Besides the heavy and light full lines, and the broken

dimension-lines, you will have occasion to use a *dot-and-dash* line for *center-lines* and to indicate upon the plan where sections have been made (Fig. 92), and the *dotted* line to indicate upon plan, sections, elevations, and details the work concealed and that which is above or upon the opposite side (see *Furniture Working-drawings*, Chap. VI), and to show where material is to be cut or folded (see Fig. 262, page 194).

Always leave a space in one corner of the sheet, preferably the upper or lower right-hand corner, in which to

Letter the Title of your Drawing, your *name*, the *scale* of the drawing, and the *date* upon which it is finished (Fig. 92). This lettering may be separated from the drawing by heavy lines. Draw

Marginal Lines around the outside of the drawing, and leave a margin of about ½ inch upon the sheet outside of this line. Plain

Gothic Letters look best for titles and notes, when well made. Always rule two light horizontal guide-lines between which to letter, so that it will be easy to keep the tops and bottoms of the letters on a line, and if you have trouble in making vertical lines, you may use a triangle with which to straighten them.

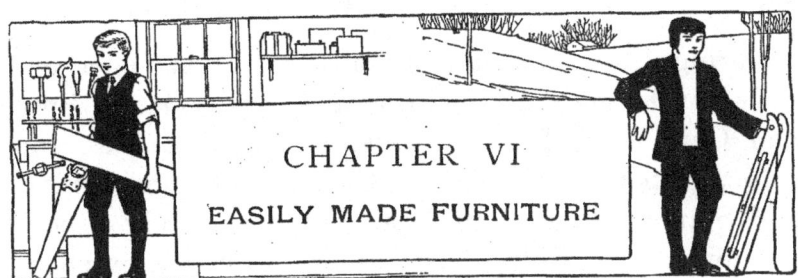

CHAPTER VI
EASILY MADE FURNITURE

IF you have carried out the exercises of the preceding chapters and studied carefully all instructions, there is no reason why you should not be prepared to undertake some simple cabinet making. This work will be a better test of your skill as a craftsman than would any other kind of carpentry.

If I am not mistaken, what you boys want to make in furniture are things which will be of practical use for your own room and for other parts of the house, and things which will be suitable to give away and to sell. The articles described upon the following pages have been selected with these points in mind. After you have turned out a few well-made pieces so you will have some good samples to show, you should have no difficulty in securing enough orders at fairs, and from friends and relatives, to enable you to work up a profitable little business, especially a month or so before the holidays, when practical gifts are much in demand.

Many boys are earning money in this way. The frontispiece shows the factory of " The Juvenile Manufacturing Company," an organization of six energetic boys of Dayton, Ohio — Masters Charles Deeds, Pres. and Gen. Mgr., Fulton Davisson, Jr., Vice Pres. and Supt., Robert Canby, Secy., Charles Whidden, Treas., and Stanley Raugh and Evan Whidden. These boys are doing a flourishing business, and from the excellent work they are turning out it is no wonder that they are succeeding so well. The firm has issued an attractive catalogue of 8 pages containing illustrations of their line of goods, a group photograph of the officers and Board of Directors, an exterior view of the office and factory, — which is fitted up in a playhouse belonging to one of the boys, — and two views of completed orders loaded on to automobiles ready for local delivery and shipment to out-of-town customers. The catalogue states, in part, the following: —

"The plant is running Mondays, Thursdays, and Fridays after school, and all day Saturdays. Visitors are welcome on Saturdays.

"Only the best materials are used, and no cheap laborers are employed; the officers and Board of Directors do the work themselves.

"The purchaser of any article produced by this Company is not only getting more value for the money paid than he could get at any store, but at the same time is encouraging a Company of energetic little business men to get a training which is most practical.

"Our business is meeting with great success. We are always behind with our orders. Our customers are our best advertisers because we give them more for their money than they can get anywhere else."

You will have to hustle some, boys, to accomplish what these lads have, but there is no reason why you

FIG. 111.

FIG. 110.

FIG. 108.

FIG. 114.

FIG. 109.

FIG. 113.

FIG. 112.

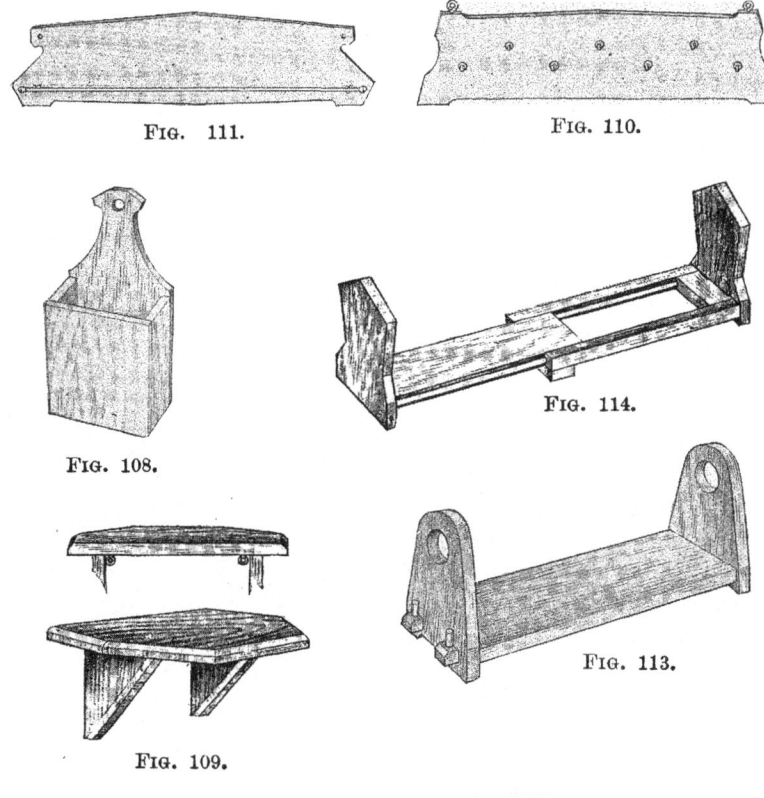

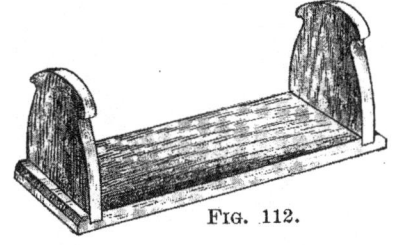

FIG. 108. WHISK-BROOM HOLDER.
FIG. 109. CLOCK-SHELF.
FIGS. 110 AND 111. NECKTIE-RACKS.
FIGS. 112, 113 AND 114. BOOK-RACKS.

cannot make a success of a similar enterprise in your own home town if you know of a number of fellows who would be good workers and would have enough stick-to-it-iveness in them to keep up an interest in the work.

The articles shown opposite page 104 are especially good material for the beginner to start upon on account of the simplicity of their construction.

Choice of Material. There are a number of varieties of wood well adapted to amateur furniture making, and these are mentioned in Chapter III, while the matter of finish is discussed in Chapter IV.

A Whisk-broom Holder such as is shown in Fig. 108 is a handy article for a bedroom. It should be made out of $\frac{1}{2}$-inch stuff (which is $\frac{3}{8}$ inch thick *dressed*) with the different parts cut as shown in the working-drawings (Fig. 115). In order to get the two side edges of the back piece alike, first draw a center-line upon the piece of wood as shown, then lay off the dimensions each side of this. Draw the curve upon one side, then reproduce it upon the other side at an equal distance from the center-line, tracing it off with a piece of tracing-paper to get the curves alike. Lay off the tapered edges of the front piece each side of a center-line in the same way. With the front, back, and side pieces prepared, nail them together with 1-inch brads, set the brad-heads, then sandpaper, putty, and finish.

A Clock-shelf is a neat gift, and Fig. 109 shows one which is easily constructed. Make this out of 1-inch stuff ($\frac{13}{16}$ inch thick *dressed*). After cutting the top and two brackets as shown in Fig. 116, bevel the upper front and end edges of the top piece and the two diagonal edges of each bracket piece, gauging the width and

CENTER-LINE

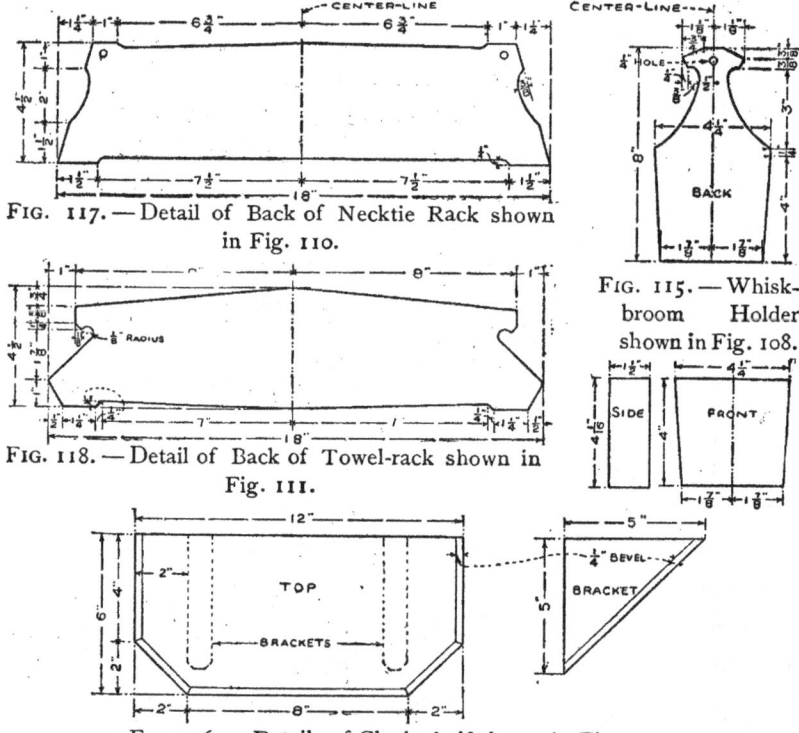

FIG. 117.—Detail of Back of Necktie Rack shown in Fig. 110.

CENTER-LINE
HOLE
BACK

FIG. 115.—Whisk-broom Holder shown in Fig. 108.

SIDE
FRONT

RADIUS

FIG. 118.—Detail of Back of Towel-rack shown in Fig. 111.

TOP
BRACKETS
BEVEL
BRACKET

FIG. 116.—Details of Clock-shelf shown in Fig. 109.

depth of the bevels and cutting them as described on page 71 (see *Bevel*). Fasten the brackets to the top piece with $1\frac{1}{2}$-inch finishing-nails in the positions indicated by dotted lines in the drawing. In the back view of the completed shelf (Fig. 109) is shown the method of fastening it to a wall. A screw-eye is screwed into the under side of the shelf top, just inside of each bracket, and these eyes slip over a couple of nails or screws driven into the wall in corresponding positions.

The Necktie Rack shown in Fig. 110 has a back cut out of $\frac{1}{2}$-inch stuff (see working-drawing for back in Fig. 117) with seven brass screw-hooks screwed into it in two rows. Scribe two pencil lines across the center of the board about 1 inch apart, then starting at the center of the length of the board, mark the location of the center hook, and each side of this locate the other hooks 2 inches apart, alternating them on the two lines as shown. Fasten two screw-eyes in the top of the board, one at each end, by means of which to hang the rack upon the wall.

In Fig. 111 is shown a rack which may be used either for a necktie rack or

A Towel-rack. Cut the back board out of $\frac{1}{2}$-inch stuff, laying it out according to the working-drawing (Fig. 118), and procure a short brass extension curtain-rod for the front. The rod will be furnished with screw-hooks with which to fasten it to the board; these should be screwed in so the rod will set 1 inch away for a necktie rack or 3 inches away for a towel-rack.

Book-racks of three forms have been designed, for they are so commonly used upon the library table of the home to keep in order the books in immediate use, that you will probably wish to make more than one kind. In the rack shown in Fig. 112 the base piece is grooved near each end for the end pieces to fit in (Fig. 119), while in the rack shown in Fig. 113 tenons are cut on the ends of the base pieces to fit mortises made in the end pieces, and these tenons are held in place by means of pins driven into holes bored through them (Fig. 120). The latter rack possesses one advantage over the former, and that lies in the fact that its pins may be withdrawn at any time and its pieces pulled apart and put away in a compact form. To prevent splitting, do the cutting of the grooves and mortises in the members of the racks before trimming off their ends, so there will be as much wood as possible outside of the portions cut. (For making mortise-and-tenon joints, see page 61.) After the racks have been put together and finished, glue strips of felt to the bottoms to prevent them from scratching any surface upon which they stand.

An Extension Book-rack is a little more complicated to make than the above two, but the work is not difficult. The rack shown in Fig. 114 is 16 inches long between the ends when pushed together and $28\frac{3}{4}$ inches long when extended. Figure 121 shows the details for this rack. The base is made out of a 1-by-4-inch tongued-and-grooved board, a piece about 3 feet long being required, while the end pieces are cut out of 1-inch stock. The idea of using the tongued-and-grooved board for the base is that the tongues and grooves for the slides are

CENTER LINE
BEVEL
SECTION THROUGH BASE
END
PLAN OF BASE
16"
5½"

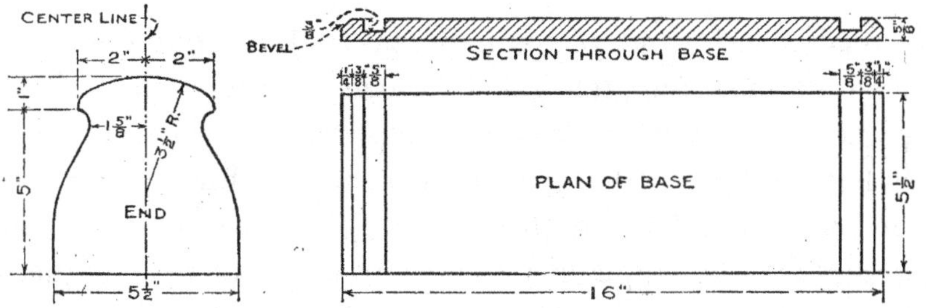

FIG. 119. — Details of Book-rack shown in Fig. 112.

16"
END
MORTISES
¾" HOLE FOR PIN
BEVEL
PLAN·OF·BASE

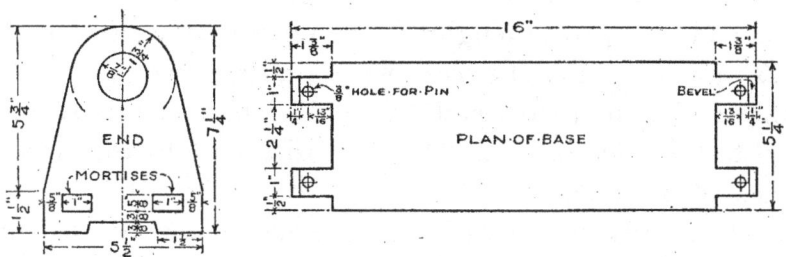

FIG. 120. — Details of Book-rack shown in Fig. 113.

END
16"
A
TONGUE
E
GROOVE
C
FOR HINGES
PLAN OF BASE PIECES
D
STRIP "E" IS FASTENED TO ENDS OF "A" AND "B"
TONGUE
14"
GROOVE
B
16"

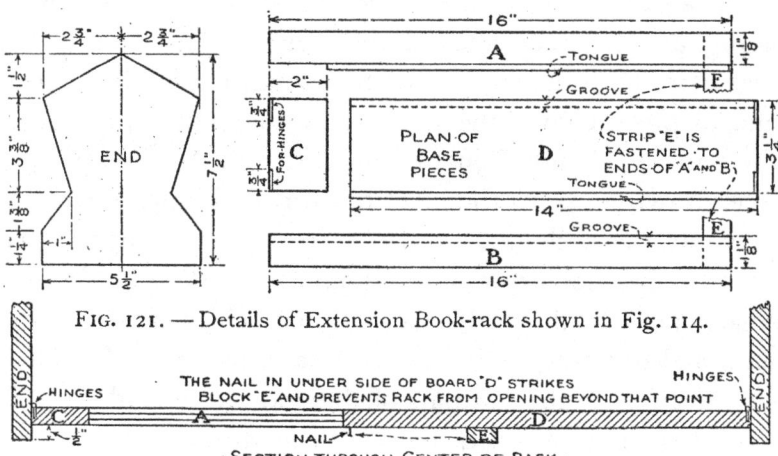

FIG. 121. — Details of Extension Book-rack shown in Fig. 114.

END
HINGES
THE NAIL IN UNDER SIDE OF BOARD "D" STRIKES
BLOCK "E" AND PREVENTS RACK FROM OPENING BEYOND THAT POINT
HINGES
END
C
A
D
NAIL
E
·SECTION THROUGH CENTER OF RACK·

FIGS. 119–121. — Working-drawings for Book-racks.

already made, and you will be saved the trouble of cutting them. The tongue on piece *A* (see plan of base pieces, Fig. 121), with the exception of a 2-inch piece, is left to slide in the groove in piece *D*, while the groove on piece *B* is left for the tongue on *D* to slide in. *A* and *B* may be ripped from opposite edges of the tongued-and-grooved board. Piece *C* should be cut to the exact width of *D* (without tongue or groove), while strip *E* should be equal in length to the combined widths of *A*, *B*, and *D*. After the base pieces and the two end pieces have been prepared, nail one end of base pieces *A* and *B* to the ends of *C* and the opposite end to the upper face of piece *E*.

The ends of the rack may be nailed directly to the ends of the base pieces, but it is better to hinge them in place, as the ends may be folded flat at any time by so doing, and the rack packed away in a small space. Buy two pairs of ¾-inch by 1-inch brass hinges, and hinge one end to piece *C* and the other end to piece *D*, notching the ends of *C* and *D* just enough to receive the hinges. The drawings show the locations for the hinges. Strip *E* prevents the ends of *A* and *B* from springing apart. To prevent the rack from pulling apart lengthwise, drive a small nail into the under side of piece *D*, as shown in the sectional drawing, so it will strike against strip *E*. Glue strips of felt to the bottoms of the end pieces and strip *E*.

Of the medium-sized pieces of furniture,

Tabourets and Plant Stands are probably most in demand, for the living-room or library is not complete nowadays without one or two of these to hold fancy vases, jardiniers, fern dishes, and potted plants. There is no limit to the number of shapes which could be devised for them, but you will probably find the three designs shown opposite page 110 of varied enough character to make the construction of one of each worth while. In presenting the working-drawings for the tabourets and plant stands, as well as those for the other pieces of furniture of an equal or a larger size,

A List of Material showing the exact finished dimensions of each part of the work, and the number of pieces of like size required, has been placed alongside or above the details. These lists will help you in figuring up the amount of material necessary for each piece of work, but they are not in proper shape to take to the mill or lumber yard from which to order, for it will be cheaper to combine pieces which can be cut out of boards of stock widths and lengths and do the sawing yourself. After deciding what articles you wish to construct, it is a very simple matter to estimate exactly how much material you will require. Of course, enough additional length and width over the finished dimension must be allowed on each piece for the waste produced in sawing and truing up.

In preparing the top for

The Tabouret shown in Fig. 122 (Fig. 126), first plane up the piece to the proper dimensions, then mark off the triangular pieces which are to be removed from the corners and saw them off. If the work has been done carefully, the legs will fit the corners exactly right. Bevel the edges of the legs, as shown, with a chisel. The diagonal leg braces, or *stretchers*, are *halved* at their centers (see *Halved-joint*, page 60). When these have been joined together, lay them across the top piece in the position indicated by dotted lines on the plan, to see that the ends come even with, and at right angles to, the corners. Then procure No. 9, round-head, blued finishing-screws, 1¾ inches long, and screw the pieces together as shown (see *Screws*, page 72).

After making a tabouret or any other piece of furniture,

If you find the Legs rest unevenly upon the floor, it is a simple matter to correct the fault. Locate the short leg and put a chip under it to block it up, then cut a block of wood of just the right thickness to slip under this short leg, and, with it as a gauge, slide it around the four sides of each of the long legs, and *scribe* a knife line across each side on a line with the top of the block. It is then a simple matter to finish off the legs to these lines.

The Tabouret shown in Fig. 123 requires a little more work than that in Fig. 122, as the panel pieces *C* (Fig. 127) are tenoned into the rails *A* and *B*, and the ends of the rails are tenoned into the legs; but mortising is a simple operation once it has been mastered, and the mortise-and-tenon is one of the most commonly used

PLAN OF TOP
ELEVATION
STRETCHER

LIST OF MATERIAL		
PIECES	DIMENSIONS	PARTS
1	13/16" × 11" × 11"	TOP
4	13/16" × 2 1/2" × 16 1/4"	LEGS
2	13/16" × 2" × 13"	STRETCHERS

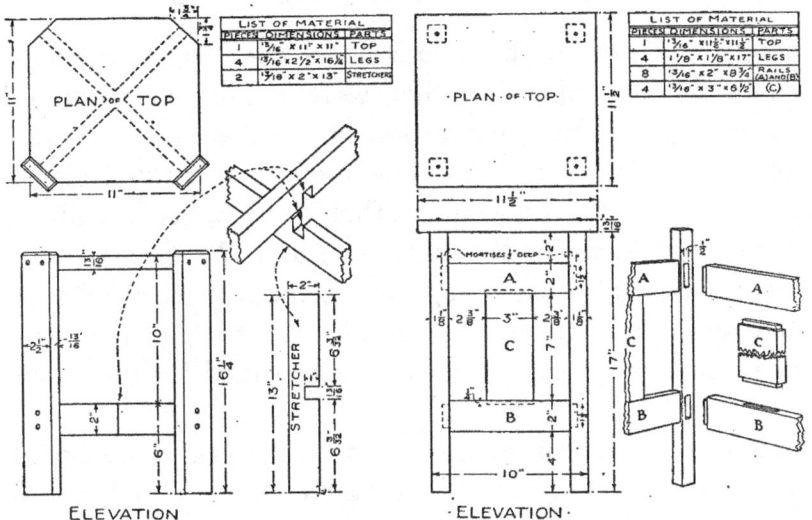

FIG. 126. — Details of Tabouret shown in Fig. 122.

PLAN · OF · TOP
MORTISES 1/2" DEEP
A
B
C
· ELEVATION ·

LIST OF MATERIAL		
PIECES	DIMENSIONS	PARTS
1	13/16" × 11 1/2" × 11 1/2"	TOP
4	1 1/8" × 1 1/8" × 17"	LEGS
8	13/16" × 2" × 8 3/4"	RAILS (A) AND (B)
4	13/16" × 3" × 6 1/2"	(C)

FIG. 127. — Details of Tabouret shown in Fig. 123.

SIDE ELEVATION
STRETCHER
MORTISES FOR PINS
END ELEVATION

LIST OF MATERIAL:		
PIECES	DIMENSIONS	PARTS
1	13/16" × 11 1/2" × 20"	TOP
2	13/16" × 11 1/2" × 15"	ENDS
1	13/16" × 3" × 19"	STRETCHER
1	13/16" ×	PINS.

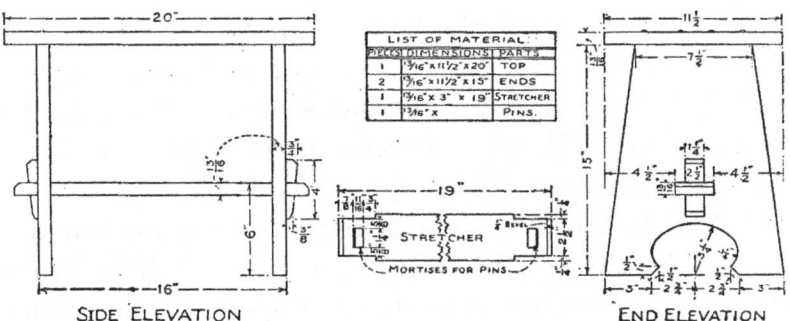

FIG. 128. — Details of Plant Stand shown in Fig. 124.

joints and one of the strongest of the cabinet-maker's methods of joining together work. The operation of *mortising* and the preparation of the *tenons* is fully described on pages 61–65. The mortises for the ends of pieces C need not be more than $\frac{1}{4}$ inch deep, while $\frac{1}{2}$ inch is sufficient for the ends of A and B. See description of *Bench* on page 117 for assembling mortised-and-tenoned work. Secure the top piece to the legs by means of round-head screws such as are specified for the other tabouret.

The Plant Stand illustrated by Fig. 124 is designed more or less along the lines of the much-used mission furniture. For the working-drawings see Fig. 128. The preparation of the mortises and tenons for the connection of the stretcher to the end pieces will be easy, if you have carried out the exercises suggested in Chapter III. The mortises are slightly *undercut* on the outer end to make them correspond with the taper on the pins, and are cut $\frac{1}{16}$ inch inside of the line of the side pieces, as you will see by looking at the dimensions on the stretcher, so that the pins will drive the end pieces tight against the shoulders of the stretcher.

A Footstool, with a shelf below on which the current magazines may be piled, makes a handy piece of furniture for a den or library. An attractive design for one along simple lines is shown in Fig. 125. The working-drawings for this are shown in Fig. 129. After preparing the top, the shelf, and the end pieces, fasten the shelf and

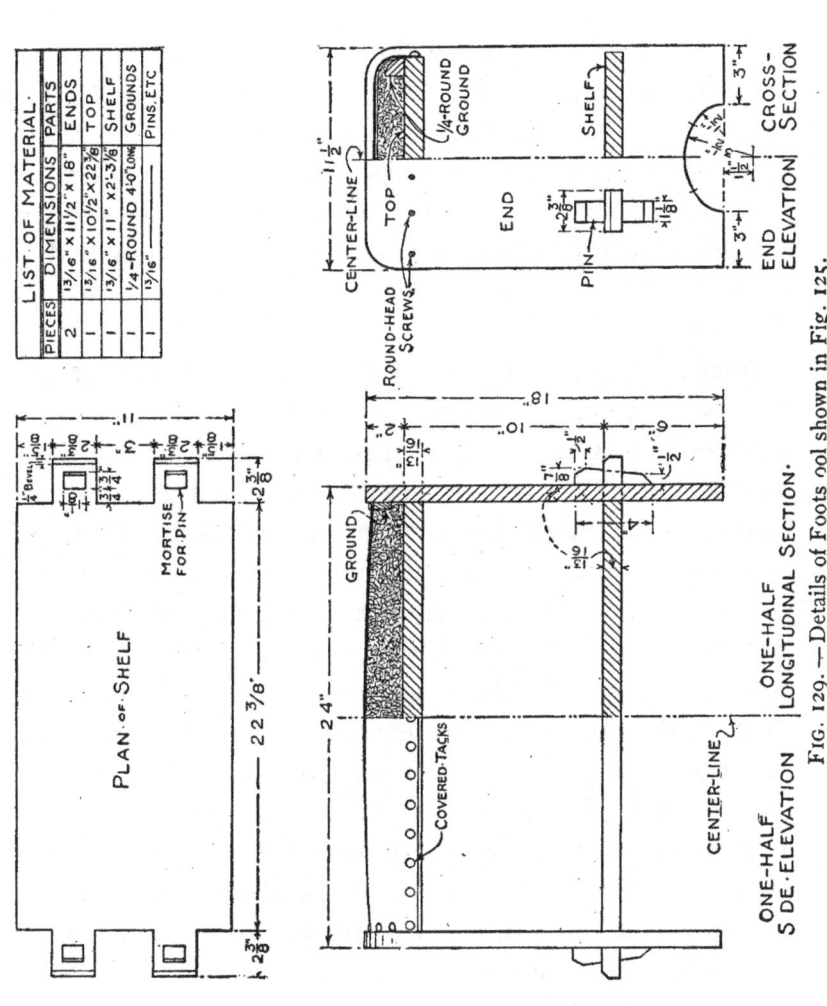

FIG. 129.—Details of Footstool shown in Fig. 125.

ends together by means of the pins, then secure the top between the ends with round-head screws. A strip of *quarter-round* (a small molding) should be nailed to the upper side of the top along each side edge, as shown in the cross-section, for a *ground* to hold out the sides of the upholstering, and a narrow strip should be nailed to each end piece $\frac{1}{2}$ inch below the top for a ground to tack the upholstering cover to.

Upholstering Material can be purchased at almost any dry-goods store. You will require some hair for filling, cheese-cloth or light-weight muslin for covering the hair, 2-ounce cut tacks for fastening the cloth, leather, imitation leather, or heavy denim for the top covering, and large-head tacks covered to match the top material. Perhaps you can get some hair from an old pillow or mattress, and your mother probably can furnish you with the cloth covering. Leather is rather expensive, about $3 a yard, while the imitation leather can be purchased for about $1.25 a yard (1 yard wide), and denim will cost 15 cents a yard. The imitation leather wears better than real leather and is probably the most satisfactory material to use. Tacks with large heads, made of a composition to match leather or imitation leather, can be bought for from 3 to 5 cents a dozen.

To upholster the top of the Footstool, first lay a piece of the cloth over it and tack it to the *ground* along one side and to the *grounds* along the ends, thus forming a pocket in which to stuff the hair. The cloth must be loose enough to allow for sufficient packing, but as it will stretch considerably it may be pulled fairly tight. Pack the hair into the farther side and the two ends, first, and use a small stick with which to push it into the right places. The work is not difficult, but it must be done carefully, and all hollows must be filled out as you go along in order to make a nicely shaped top. When the near side is filled, stretch the cloth tightly over the hair and tack it to the quarter-round *ground*. With the hair held in place by the cloth covering, it is an easy matter to put on the leather or other covering. Draw a line upon the edges of the wood top to indicate the edge of the covering, and $\frac{3}{8}$ inch or $\frac{1}{2}$ inch above this draw another line parallel to it upon which to locate the tack holes; also draw a guide-line along the top of each end *ground* for the end tack holes. Space the holes upon these lines $1\frac{1}{2}$ inches from center to center, or as near to that as will make all the spaces equal, and punch holes for the tacks with a brad-awl which is a trifle smaller than they are. Turn in the edge of the covering material all around, then fasten it in place with the tacks.

The Bench in the photograph opposite page 86, Chapter V, is a neat-appearing piece of furniture suitable for a bedroom or any of the living-rooms. The details for its construction are shown in Fig. 130. First, prepare the legs and end rails, and mortise and tenon them as shown; then, when the pieces have been fitted properly, mark the tenons and the mortises with letters in such a way that

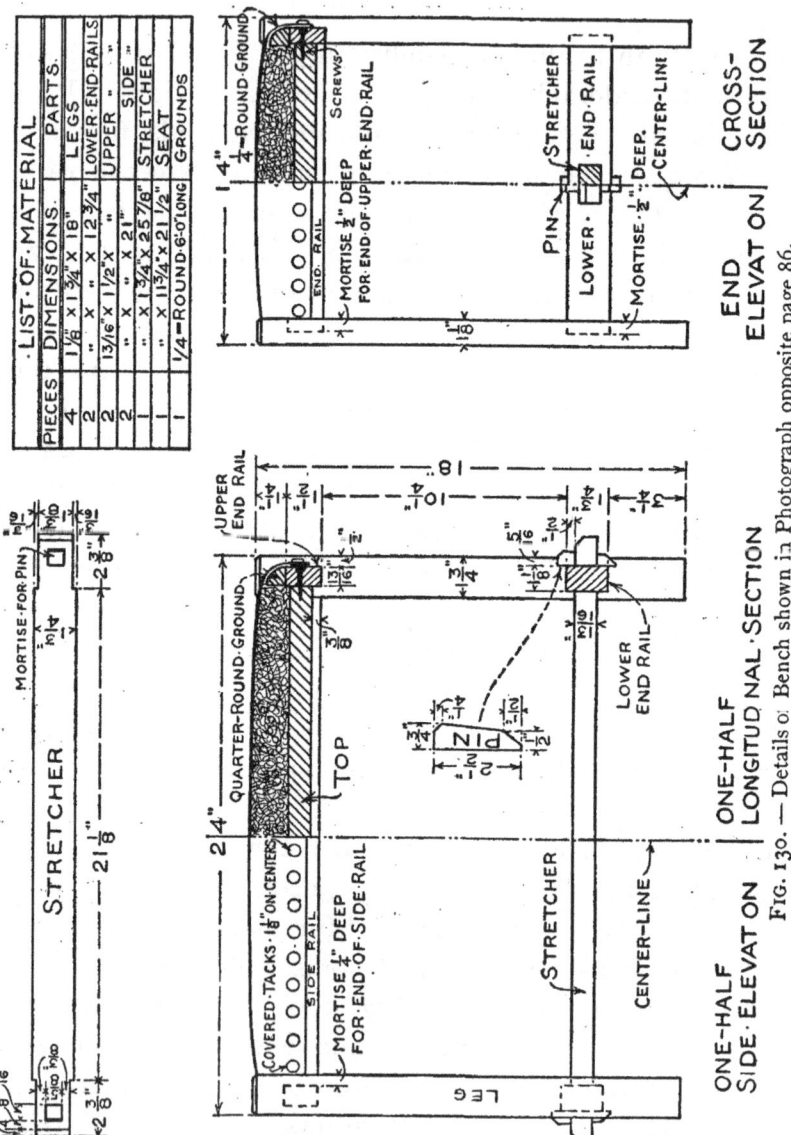

Fig. 130. — Details o: Bench shown in Photograph opposite page 86.

you will know just which fits into which, which edge is up and which face turns out. Next, cut the mortises in the lower rails for the stretcher, then prepare the stretcher as in the detail, trim its ends to fit the mortises in the rails and mortise them for the pins. The side rails should be cut next. Where all the joints consist of a mortise and a tenon, as in the case of this bench, each member should be fitted and tested as cut; then, when all the members have been cut, fit them together and go over the whole piece of work, and if any trimming is required, mark the locations. Then take the members apart, trim where you have found it necessary and sandpaper each piece. The beveling of the tops of the legs and ends of the stretcher may be left until this stage of the construction (do this beveling with a chisel).

Assemble the pieces in the order in which you prepared them, and coat the end of each tenon and the inside of each mortise with glue before fitting them in place. After the glue has had time to set, cut the top piece to fit between the upper rails and fasten it in place with screws. Before boring holes for the screws, locate the places where the large tacks are to go so you can avoid them. Nail a piece of *quarter-round* along the top edge of each of the upper rails to hold in the edges of the upholstering filling.

Finish the wood, then upholster the top in the manner described for the *Footstool.* The covering material must be cut very carefully at the corners and be turned in neatly around the legs. Space the tacks about $1\frac{1}{8}$ inches on centers.

With the general increase in the reading of monthly, semimonthly, and weekly magazines comes the problem of taking care of the back numbers with which the family are not entirely through, for the accumulation is rapid, and a place must be found where they can be piled in some kind of order.

Magazine-racks made upon the plan of open bookcases, but with the shelves spaced closer together, solve the problem of keeping them within convenient reach and at the same time in a tidy manner. The magazine-rack illustrated in Fig. 131 is shown in detail in Fig. 135. As the ends of this spread out at the bottom, the end pieces and the shelves must have their ends cut off on the diagonal. The way to get the proper angle for trimming off these ends is to lay the end pieces upon the floor on their edges, at the given distances apart, and then tack a strip across the edges near the top and bottom to hold them temporarily in that position. Then place the finished top piece against the tops of the end pieces and you will see just how much trimming they require. If you have a bevel (Fig. 34, page 26), set it to this angle and mark off the ends of each end piece accordingly; also mark off the shelf ends. Without the bevel the work may be done with a square, but be very careful to lay out each end of each piece the same, or the pieces will not fit satisfactorily. The

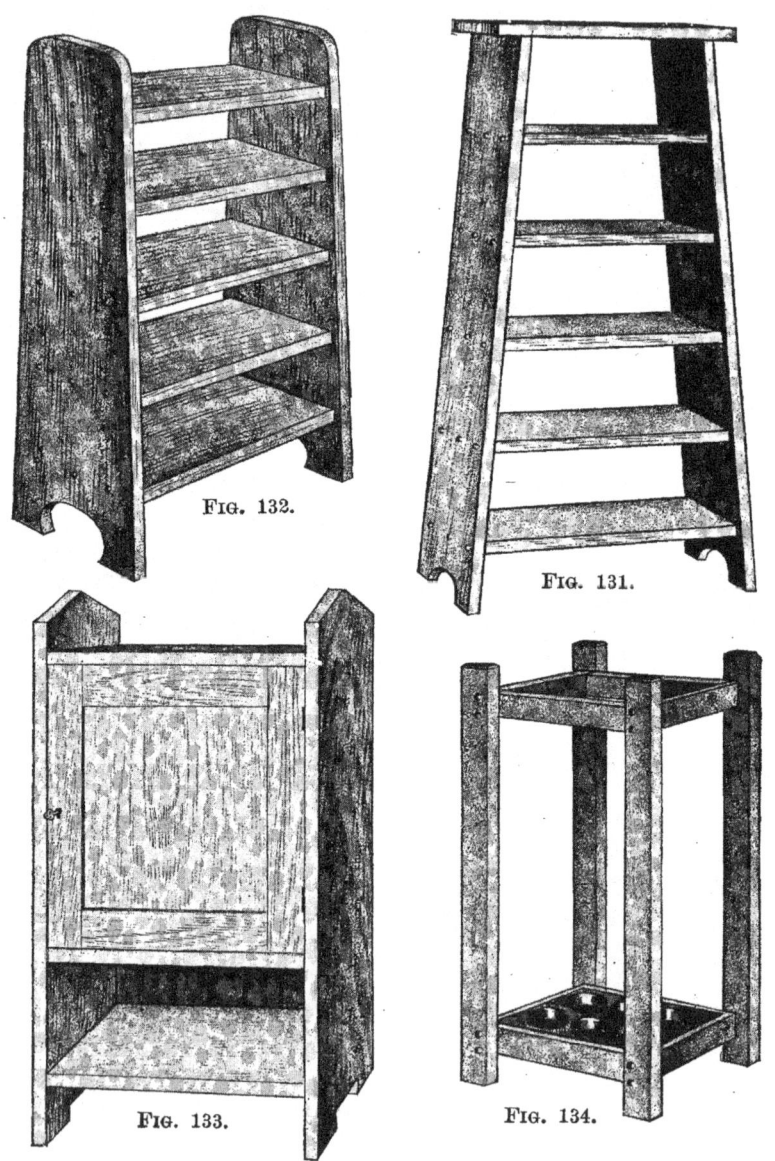

Figs. 131 and 132. — Magazine-Racks.
Fig. 133. — Music-Cabinet.   Fig. 134. — Umbrella-Stand.

·LIST·OF·MATERIAL·		
PIECES	DIMENSIONS	PARTS
1	13/16" × 11½" × 19"	TOP
2	" × 11½" × 3'-3 3/16"	ENDS
1	" × 11" × 14"	SHELF
1	" × 11" × 15"	"
1	" × 11" × 16"	"
1	" × 11" × 17"	"
1	" × 11" × 18"	"

19"
2"
2"
20"
3'-4"
7"
7"
7"
7"
7"
5"
11"
·FRONT· ELEVATION·
·CROSS-SECTION·

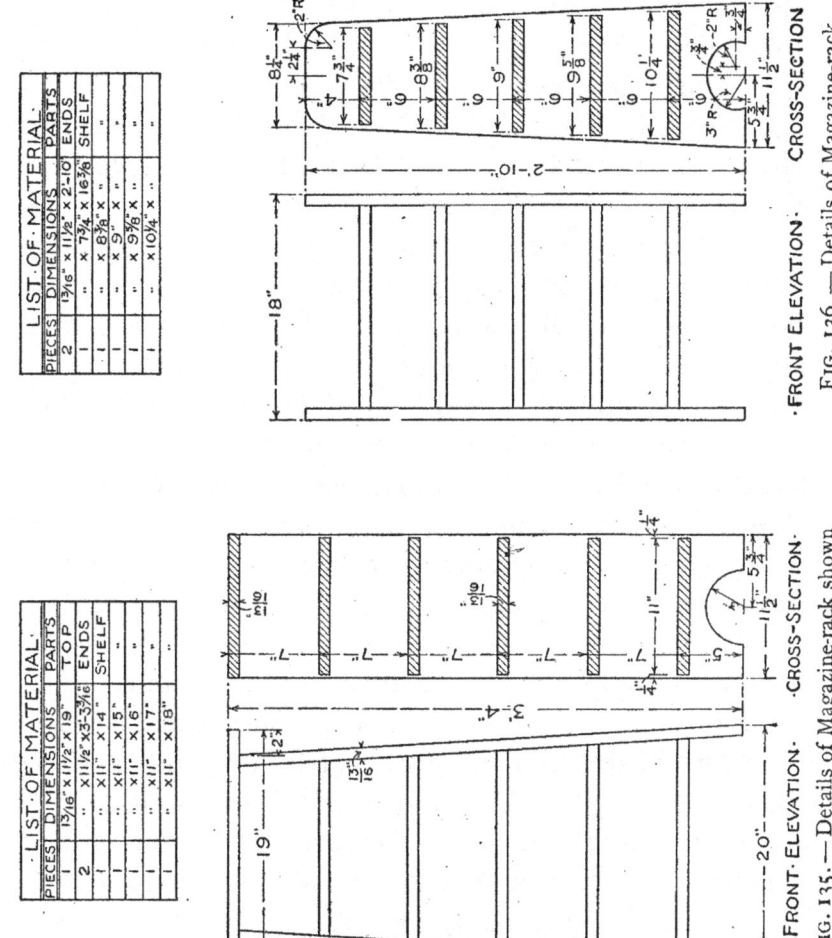

FIG. 135.—Details of Magazine-rack shown

LIST·OF·MATERIAL·		
PIECES	DIMENSIONS	PARTS
2	13/16" × 11½" × 2'-10"	ENDS
1	" × 7¾" × 16⅜"	SHELF
1	" × 8⅜" × "	"
1	" × 9" × "	"
1	" × 9⅝" × "	"
1	" × 10¼" × "	"

18"
2'-10"
2"R
3"R
4"
6"
6"
6"
6"
6"
9"
·FRONT ELEVATION·
CROSS-SECTION

FIG. 136.—Details of Magazine-rack

shelves and top are fastened to the end pieces with round-head screws.

The magazine-rack shown in Fig. 132 has shelves of equal length, but the widths vary, as is shown in the cross-section detail (Fig. 136). Fasten the shelves to the end pieces with round-head screws.

The Music-cabinet shown in Fig. 133 will make an attractive piece of furniture for a music room. First, prepare the end pieces and the shelves (Fig. 137), then after these pieces have been fastened together, put on the back boards and make and hang the paneled door. The best scheme for making a tight-fitting back is to use matched-and-beaded boards (known as M-&-B ceiling). A board always shrinks crosswise of the grain (but not lengthwise), and also expands and contracts to a certain extent with the changes in the atmosphere, and this movement must be provided for in joining pieces together, or there will be trouble. Take the music-cabinet, for example. Here the back will shrink and swell in the width of the cabinet, but the shelves will not, as their grain runs the other way, and under these conditions, if the back boards are wide, and are fitted snugly and nailed to the shelves, they are bound to split in shrinking or *buckle* (bulge out) in swelling, for the shelves will not move with them; but if the boards are narrow, the movement in each piece will of course be very slight, and the small amount that there is may be taken care of in the joints, where, if the boards are matched and beaded,

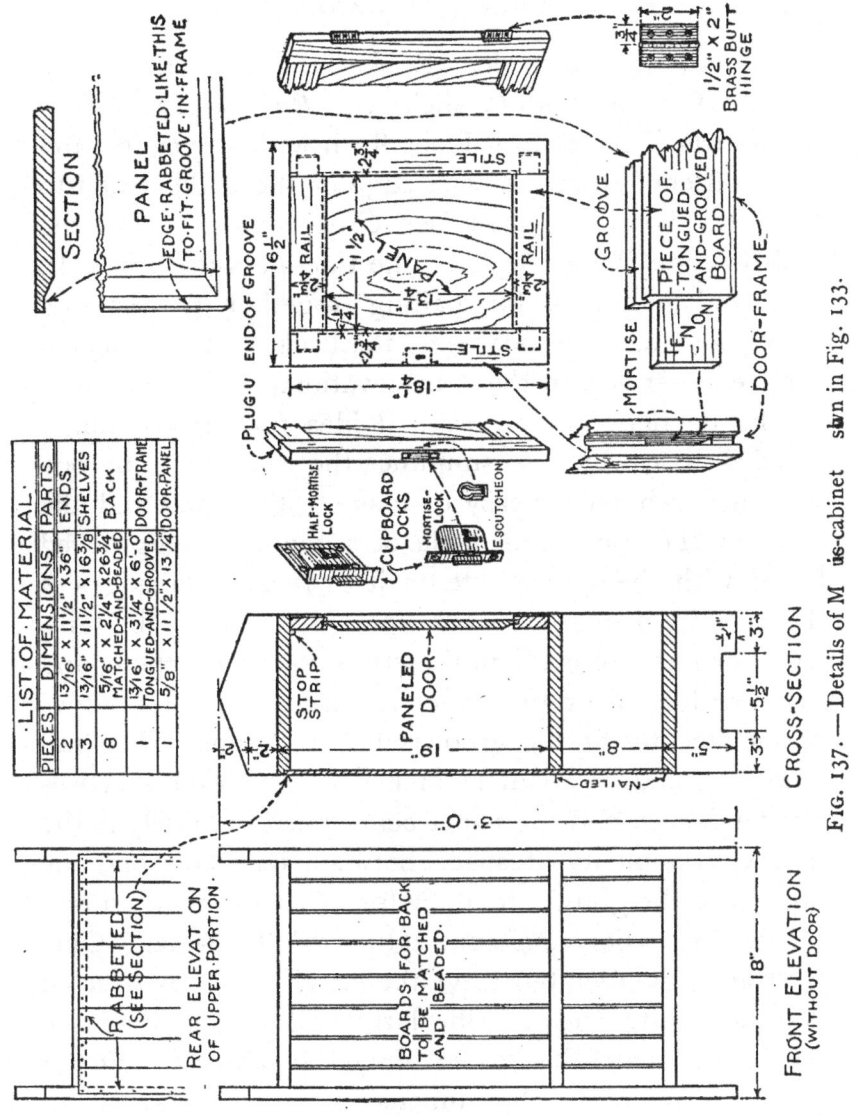

Fig. 137.—Details of Medicine-cabinet shown in Fig. 133.

it will not be noticeable. Rabbet the two side pieces and the top and bottom shelf (see *Rabbet*, page 65) so the boards of the back will set flush with the edges, and plane off enough of the back edge of the middle shelf to allow the boards to pass (see *Cross-section*). Cut the rabbets about $\frac{1}{2}$ inch wide by the thickness of the boards. Use finishing-nails for nailing together the cabinet pieces, and nail the boards of the back to the rabbeted surfaces as shown in the rear elevation.

The details show an original idea for constructing a paneled door, which so simplifies the work that any boy will find such a door easy to make. The *rails* and the *stiles* of the frame are made of a tongued-and-grooved board with the groove left on it to receive the edges of the *panel*. Tenons are cut upon the ends of the rails, and mortises are made in the stiles to receive them, and the board used for the panel is rabbeted on the edges of one face to fit the grooves in the frame. The rail tenons should be about $1\frac{1}{4}$ inches long, and the mortises a trifle deeper, and the panel board must fit loosely in the frame, with plenty of space between its edges and the bottom of the groove, to allow for the movement caused by the expansion and contraction of the wood. Glue the frame together, but leave the panel loose. A paneled door is usually made a trifle larger all around than the opening in which it is to be hinged, to allow for *fitting* it to the opening; the dimensions given provide for this.

Buy a pair of brass butts of the size shown with which to hinge the door in place, and screw these to the edge of the door, notching the edge enough to receive the full thickness of the folded hinge. A cupboard lock, which sets into a mortise cut in the edge of the door stile, as shown in the detail (a *Mortise-lock*), makes the neatest appearing job, but the lock shown just above it (a *Half-mortise lock*) is easier to put on as the cutting is done on the inside face of the stile. With either lock the *selvage-plate* [the front plate through which the *bolt* passes] must be set flush with the edge of the stile. Upon the face of the stile carefully locate the *key-pin*, then cut a hole a trifle larger than the *key* through the stile into the mortise. After the lock has been screwed in place and properly adjusted, tack an *escutcheon plate* over the *keyhole* to finish it off. Locate where the *lock bolt* strikes the side of the cabinet, and cut a small *pocket* at that point for it to turn into. Directly inside of the door tack a narrow strip of wood to the under side of the top shelf and another down each side, as *stop* strips for the door to strike against. These must be adjusted so the door will close properly.

Figure 134 shows a new idea for

An Umbrella-stand, and Fig. 138 the details for its construction. The base holds a tin muffin-pan, each cup of which forms a receptacle for an umbrella end. These pans are made with six, eight, or twelve cups, so you can plan your stand to hold as many umbrellas as you wish. Make the two frames of equal size and just large enough to hold the rim of the muffin-pan (the size of the pan used will determine the dimensions of these frames), using strips 2 inches wide, then cut four uprights of the sizes shown, and fasten them to the four corners so that they will just conceal the joints in the frames (see plan). The muffin-pan should fit loosely enough in the lower frame so it may be removed easily for cleaning. It should be painted with a couple of coats of dull register-enamel to keep it from rusting, as well as to give it a finish.

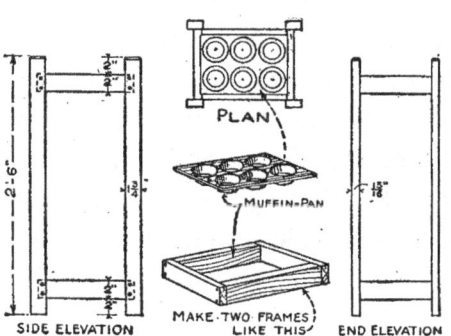

FIG. 138.—Details of Umbrella-stand shown in Fig. 134.

A **Roman Chair** such as is shown in Fig. 139 makes a pretty seat for a hall or reception-room. First prepare the four corner posts and the end rails (Fig. 143), and cut mortises in the posts $\frac{3}{4}$ inch deep to receive the ends of the rails, then prepare the front and rear rails as shown and make mortises in the posts $\frac{1}{2}$ inch deep to receive them. Next cut the stretcher as it is detailed in the plan, mortise the lower end rails for its ends to run through, and prepare pins to fit the stretcher's mortises. Read the instructions given upon page 117 for marking, fitting together, and gluing the mor-

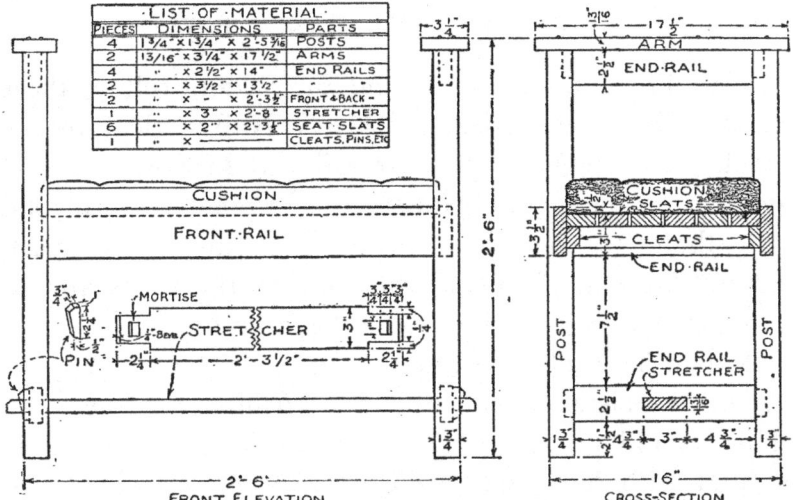

Fig. 143. — Details of Roman Chair shown in Fig. 139.

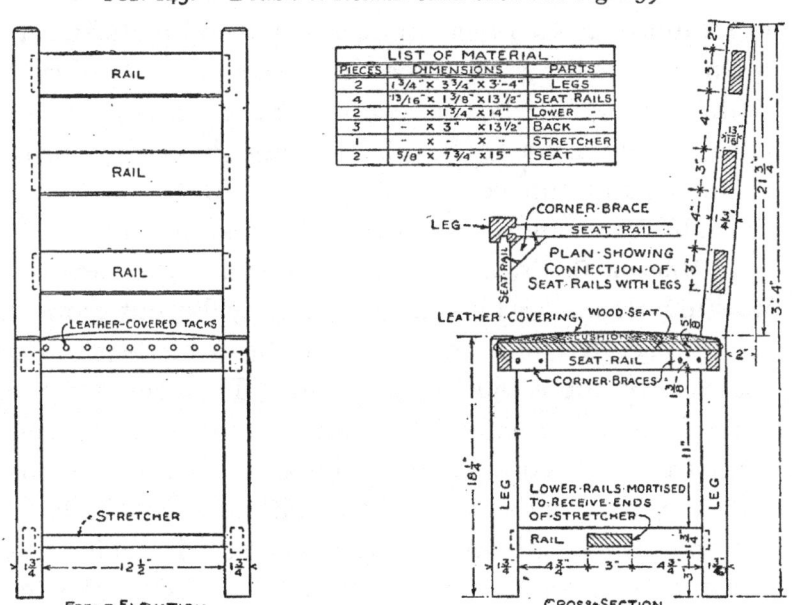

Fig. 144. — Details of Mission Chair shown in Fig. 140.

tised and tenoned pieces of the *Bench*, and follow these in assembling the *Roman Chair*. Nail a cleat to the inside face of the four seat rails to support the seat slats, then cut the slats to the proper length and nail them to the cleats, spacing them $\frac{1}{4}$ inch apart. Screw the arm pieces to the tops of the posts and to the top end rails, using round-head screws.

You will probably require the assistance of your mother or sister in making the cushion for the seat. This should be about $2\frac{1}{2}$ inches thick, and should be stuffed with hair and *tacked* every 4 or 5 inches with strong linen thread to hold the filling in place. By examining a cushion, or even a bed mattress, the method of sewing together the cover so as to give the cushion a square box effect will be understood. The cushion will have to be pliable enough at the corners to fit around the corner posts, as shown.

Figure 140 shows an attractive design for

A Mission Chair, and Fig. 144 includes the necessary working details. The front legs may be cut from the waste piece left after cutting out the back legs; bevel the tops of these pieces as shown. The legs are mortised $\frac{1}{2}$ inch to receive the ends of the rails, the lower rails are mortised $\frac{1}{2}$ inch for the ends of the stretcher, and the seat rails are braced with corner blocks, as shown in the small detail plan. The seat is made out of two pieces of an 8-inch board and is nailed to the tops of the seat rails flush with the outside face of the rails.

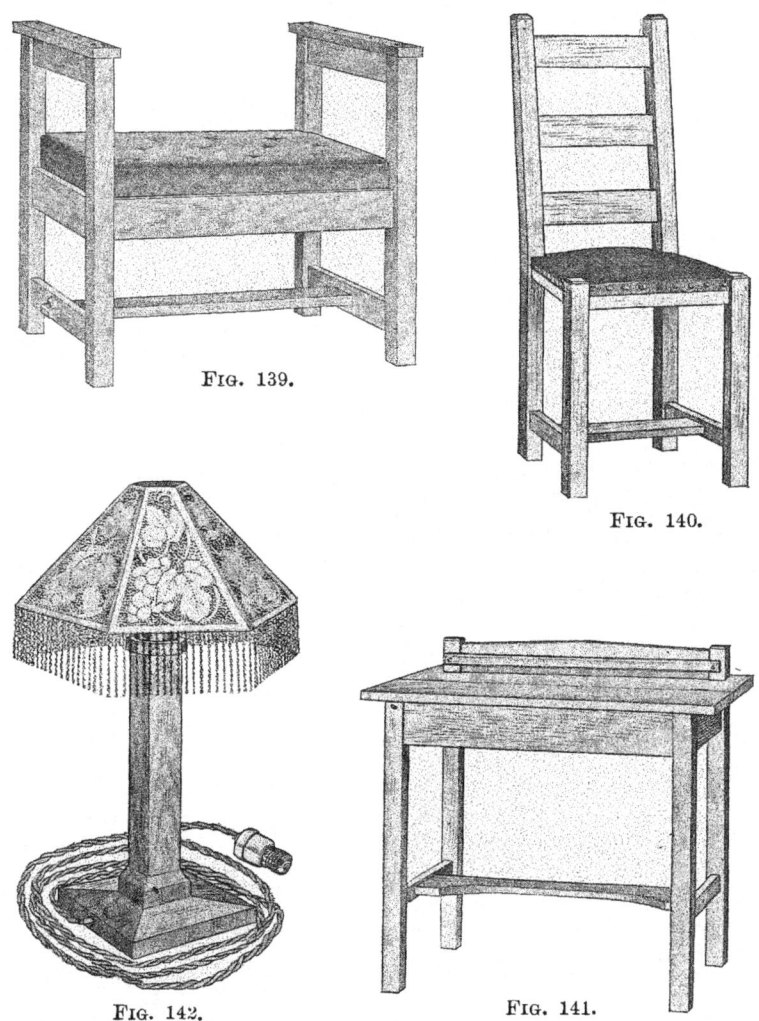

Fig. 139.— A Roman Chair. Fig. 140.— A Mission Chair.
Fig. 142.— An Electric Lamp. Fig. 141.— A Mission Writing-Desk.

Upholster the seat as described on page 116 for the *Footstool*, only do not put on a greater thickness of the hair filling than is shown in the cross-section of the chair.

A Mission Writing-desk such as that illustrated in Fig. 141 is easy to construct. After preparing the legs

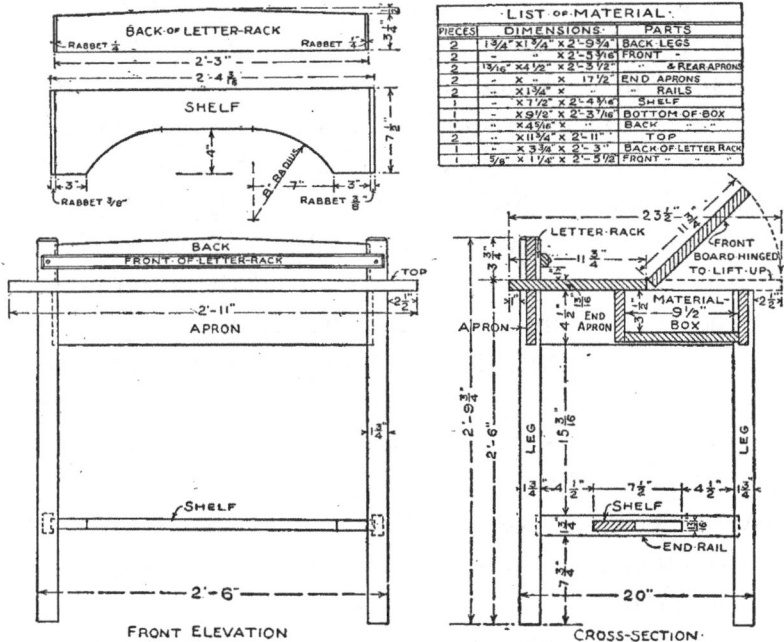

FIG. 145. — Details of Mission Writing-desk shown in Fig. 141.

according to the detail (Fig. 145), cut the end aprons and rails, and mortise the legs to receive their ends. Make the front and rear aprons and cut mortises in the legs to receive them, then prepare the shelf and rabbet the end rails for its ends to set in. The material box is completed by adding two boards, one for the bottom and the other for the back; these may be fastened in place with finishing-nails. As the front portion of the desk top is hinged to the back portion, to give access to the material box, you will be saved the work of gluing up a wide top. The back board of the top must be fitted neatly around the back legs. Hinge the front portion of the top to the back portion with a pair of brass butts $1\frac{1}{2}$ inches by 2 inches in size. The back legs must be mortised as shown, to receive the ends of the back of the letter-rack, and this back piece must be slipped into place at the same time that the shelf ends are slipped into the mortises in the end rails. The front of the letter-rack is screwed to the front face of the back legs.

As mentioned before, in a big piece of work where a number of the parts are mortised-and-tenoned, fit everything together, first, before gluing or nailing any part in place permanently.

With electricity coming into general usage for lighting dwellings, oil and gas lamps are being displaced by electric lamps.

An Electric Lamp with a wooden stand and base is very simple to make. Figure 142 shows an attractive design for a desk or table lamp, fitted with one of the perforated brass lamp-shades described in Chapter XIII. The stand is made in four pieces (A, B, C, and D, Fig. 146). After cutting these to the dimensions given, and

EASILY MADE FURNITURE 131

beveling pieces *B* and *C* as shown, bore a $\frac{3}{8}$-inch hole through the center of each. As the hole through *A* will be too long for your bit, bore it halfway through from each end, being careful to bore perfectly straight so the holes will meet at the center. Also bore a hole of the same diameter through the center of one side of base piece *C*, as shown, to meet the vertical hole. These holes are made for the electric wires to run through.

The Socket for the lamp is a *Snap-switch Wall Receptacle*, and may be purchased together

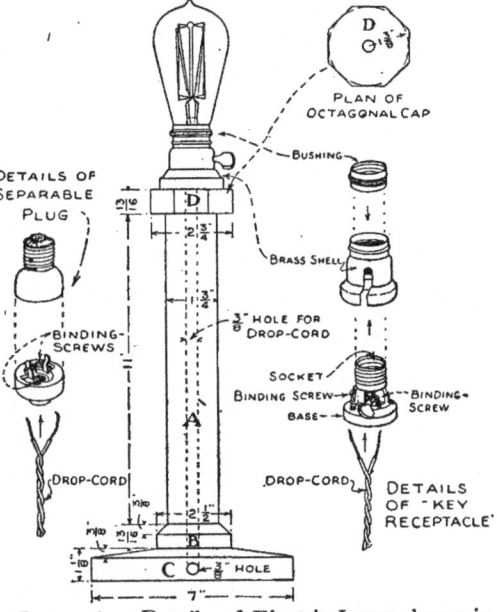

FIG. 146.—Details of Electric Lamp shown in Fig. 142.

with a *Separable Plug* and 10 feet of *drop-cord* for 65 or 70 cents at any store where electrical goods are sold. The detail drawings show the different parts of the receptacle and plug, and *the connections can safely be made by any boy, for the whole thing is wired up, first, without any connection with live wires*, then the upper part of the plug is screwed into a lamp socket in the same way that the plug of any lamp or electrical appliance is attached, and the lower portion is *snapped* into it.

The Wiring Operation is a very simple one. First untwist the ends of the wires as shown, and scrape off the

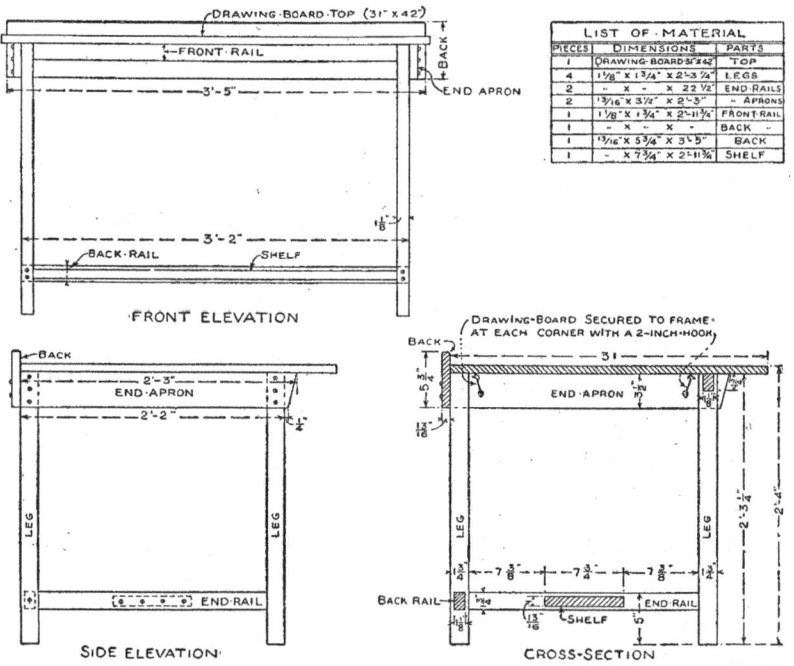

FIG. 147. — Details of Drafting Table shown opposite page 86.

rubber insulation with a knife until the copper wire is bared; also scrape the copper until it is bright and clean. Then separate the *bushing, shell,* and *socket* of the receptacle as shown, slip the wires through the holes in the porcelain *base,* wrap their ends around the *binding-screws,* and tighten the screws to hold them in place. Next run the other end of the wire through the top of the lamp-stand and work it out through the hole in the side of the base piece, then screw the base of the socket to D and put the shell and bushing back in place. The other end of the drop-cord should be connected to the binding-screws of the lower part of the plug.

The *holder* required to support the lamp-shade is shown in Fig. 289, page 215.

Opposite page 86 is shown a view of

A Drafting Table the author has used in his home work-room for a number of years. Probably not many of you boys will do enough drafting to require such a table for the purpose, but it also makes a splendid desk table, and for this reason working details for its construction are given in Fig. 147. The legs, aprons, back, rails, and lower shelf are screwed together, no mortising entering into the table's construction. A drawing-board was used for the top of the table, and this is held securely in place, as shown, by means of hooks and screw-eyes. A large drawing-board can be purchased as cheaply as you can have one made, and it will be built up of well-seasoned material and be properly cleated so that it will not warp out of shape or split. If you want to make

A Desk Table, dowel and glue together the top boards (see *Dowel-joint*, page 68), or, better still, have this work done at a mill if there is one near by. It will not cost much, and you will save a good deal of time by so doing. Of course, the desk table may be used for drafting also, as a drawing-board can be laid upon the table top.

The Electric Fixture shown over the author's table in the photograph opposite page 86 was made out of a piece of brass tubing from an old gas-lamp, fastened to the end of a piece of tubing from an extension curtain-rod. Use your ingenuity and construct a similar fixture for your table, if there is electric light in your house.

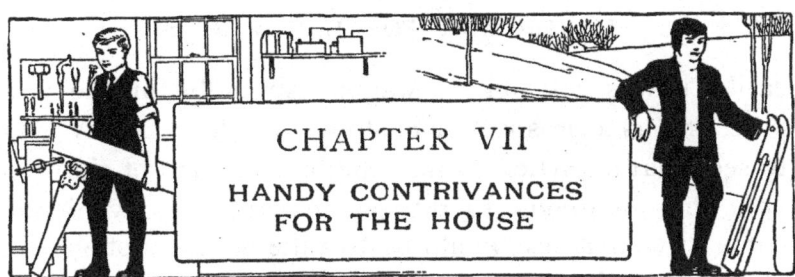

CHAPTER VII
HANDY CONTRIVANCES FOR THE HOUSE

MODERN inventions are doing much to lighten the work of the housekeeper, and the extensive advertising of numerous labor-saving devices now being carried on in the various newspapers and magazines is awakening a general interest in all sorts of household conveniences. The fact that women are adding these articles to their working equipment more and more, as they begin to realize the time and labor which may be saved by their use, should be enough to suggest to you energetic boys who have an eye for business that there is a splendid opportunity to earn money outside of school hours, by taking advantage of the publicity that is being given to these household contrivances and manufacturing a line of articles of your own to sell. Of course, you can hardly expect to have vacuum cleaners and electric flatirons, toasters, percolators, and other such conveniences, but there are many of the simpler things which you can construct, especially those made out of wood, which will be just as good as those sold in the stores.

As a line of samples could not be carried around very

easily, unless you built a wagon especially for the purpose, and as a prospective customer would naturally wish to see what an article is like, the best method of showing your line of goods to those who cannot conveniently come to your house would be to take some photographs of them, or, if you haven't a camera, to make drawings from the objects and prepare blueprints from these as described in Chapter V.

The articles shown upon the following pages will give you a variety of good ideas to start with, and you will probably get suggestions from your mother and her friends for things which they have found very handy; by adding the latter to your list you can make it more complete. You will also find that one idea often suggests another.

The ease with which

A Fireless Cooker may be constructed, together with the fact that the demand for them is growing greater every day, makes this a good article to begin work upon.

This kitchen convenience is claimed to have originated in Norway, where it has been in common use for a great many years, but over there it is generally known as a *hay-stove* from the fact that hay is used around the utensils for packing. Its popularity is due to a number of advantages which it possesses over the cook-stove method of cooking. It is only necessary to place the food over a fire long enough to start it cooking before putting it into the cooker, which not only makes a big saving in the gas-bill, if gas is used for fuel, but also results in a cooler kitchen — which is appreciable in the summer time. The insulation around the receptacles keeps the cooking odors from getting out, and outside dust from getting in, and from the time the food is placed in the

CUSHION MADE IN TWO SECTIONS JOINED ACROSS TOP TO FOLD AS SHOWN.
2'-4"
16"
A
HOLE FOR PAIL 8" IN DIAM.
B
C
HOLE FOR PAIL 10" IN DIAM.
D
WOOD COVER OVER EXCELSIOR INSULATION
CUSHION
14"
PAIL (8" IN DIAM.) WITH POT COVER
WOOD COVER
KETTLE (8" IN DIAM.)
PAIL (10" IN DIAM.) WITH POT COVER
EXCELSIOR INSULATION

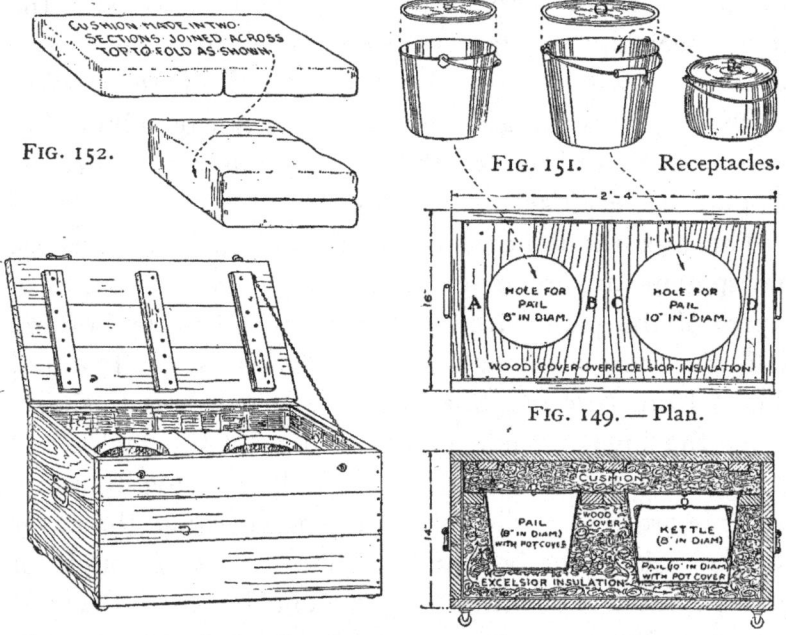

FIG. 152.

FIG. 151. Receptacles.

FIG. 149. — Plan.

FIG. 148. — The Cooker Complete. FIG. 150. — Cross-section.

FIGS. 148–152. — Details of Fireless Cooker.

cooker no further attention is required until it is ready to be taken out and served. These are pointers for you to talk up to prospective customers.

Figure 148 shows a fireless cooker with two receptacles. A well-made packing-box with tight joints can be converted into a cooker, but as the insulation around the receptacles must be as nearly perfect as it is possible to make it, such a box must have its boards driven together with tight joints. If you make the box, and that is the better way, buy matched boards out of which to construct it. Figure 149 shows a plan of the box with the cover opened, and Fig. 150 a cross-section. These two working-drawings have the dimensions of the cooker marked upon them, but the sizes need not be adhered to so long as you allow for the same amount of insulation around the receptacles as is shown.

The box should first be lined, and for this purpose newspapers are good as anything. Tack a couple of layers of the paper around the sides and to the bottom, and over these paste half a dozen thicknesses. The first sheets form a foundation to paste to; the other sheets cover the breaks made in the paper by the tacks and make the insulation continuous. Batten together the cover boards upon the inside as shown, hinge the cover to the back of the box, and provide it with a couple of hooks to hold it down tight, and a check-chain to keep it from opening back too far. Fasten four casters to the bottom of the box so that it can be moved about easily, and a pair of trunk handles to the ends to make it easy to lift.

The receptacles are shown in Figs. 150 and 151. Two tin pails or porcelain-lined pails of the sizes shown make the best kind of receptacles, and a kettle small

HANDY CONTRIVANCES FOR THE HOUSE 139

enough to fit into the larger pail provides a good inner receptacle. Buy two pot covers to fit the large pails (Fig. 151). The kettle will hold cereals and all foods for steaming, and when this is used, the outer pail must be filled with hot water to within about 1 inch of the rim of the kettle. Shallow pans of the proper diameter to fit in the tops of the pails may be provided for smaller receptacles. Large quantities of food may be placed directly in one of the pails, but it is essential to fill as much of the receptacle as possible, because waste space will draw away the heat from the food. This is where the advantage comes in of using the kettle or pans when cooking small quantities of food, for the outer pail may be filled with boiling water. Furnish your customers with these instructions.

Boards A, B, C, and D (Fig. 149) set even with the brims of the pails and conceal the packing. Locate the brims of the pails on these boards, in the positions shown, and saw out the openings with a small saw. Nail cleats along the two sides of the box to nail the ends of the boards to, at the proper height for the larger pail, which must be set 2 inches above the bottom of the box.

Procure excelsior for packing and dampen it with water to make it pack well. Place enough of the excelsior in the bottom of the box to make it of the right height for the larger pail to set upon, and then put in enough more to obtain the proper level for the smaller pail; pack in this excelsior as tight as you can. The openings in the boards will guide you in setting the pails in the right positions. Fill up the balance of the space around the pails to the level of the cover boards with excelsior, and press it down so as to make it as compact as possible. Allow the excelsior to become thoroughly dry before nailing on the cover boards. The pails will draw out of the excelsior easily, as their sides taper.

Make a cushion similar to that shown in Fig. 152 to fill the space between the top of the pails and the box cover. This should be made in two sections, joined together across the top so one will fold over the other as shown, to make it possible to get at one receptacle without uncovering both. Stuff the cushion with excelsior, and make it thick enough so the cover will press it down upon the pail covers.

You boys probably will be interested to know that

The United States Army has tested the fireless cooker as a means of preparing rations while the troops are on the march, and that results have been so satisfactory that, undoubtedly, it will be adopted for such service. The cookers used in the test were made upon a large scale, were packed with the meat, beans, cereal, or other food, at breakfast time, then carted along with the other camp equipment, and when opened at the end of the day's march, supplied a steaming hot meal to the hungry troopers without delay — an improvement, certainly, over the method of awaiting the setting up of stoves, kindling of fires, and cooking of food

HANDY CONTRIVANCES FOR THE HOUSE   141

A Pot-cover Rack such as shown in Fig. 153 provides the most satisfactory way of keeping these covers, as the one desired is always within convenient reach — which is never the case when they are piled up on a shelf or in a drawer.

Figure 154 shows the pattern for the side pieces of the rack. Space the slots as shown, then cut along the side lines of each slot with a saw and remove the wood with a chisel. Notch the back edges as shown, and cut the two connecting cross-pieces 8 inches long to fit in these notches. Nail or screw the cross-pieces in place, and bore a couple of holes through the upper one so the rack may be hung up on nails in the pantry.

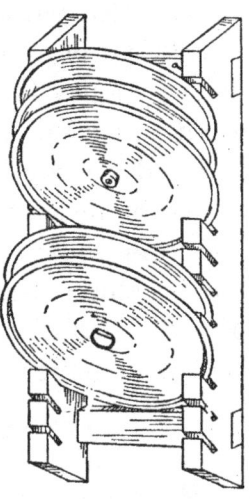
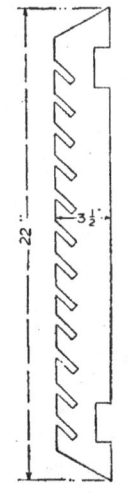

FIG. 153. — Pot-cover Rack.   FIG. 154. — Pattern for Side Pieces.

FIG. 155. — Pantry Shelf Bottle-rack.

The Bottle-rack shown in Fig. 155 is a contrivance which your mother will appreciate, as it will hold all of her bottles of extracts, catsup, Worcestershire sauce, olive oil, etc., and prevent one bottle from knocking over several others when lifted out from behind them.

The rack is made out of a piece of board measuring 9 inches wide and 15 inches long, and the holes for the bottles are laid out and cut as shown in Fig. 156. After cutting the board and planing it up smooth and true, lay off along the edges the measurements given for the centers of the holes and square lines across the board at these points. The centers will be at the intersections of the lines. For the two rows of large holes describe circles $2\frac{1}{4}$ inches in diameter, and for the row of slots describe a circle 1 inch in diameter each side of the vertical center-lines, with a center $\frac{3}{4}$ inch away from the lines, as shown.

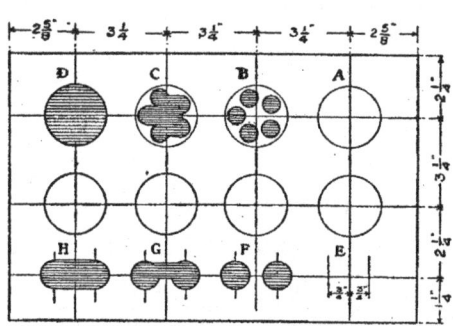

FIG. 156. — Plan of Bottle-rack.
(Showing the four steps in cutting holes larger than your largest auger-bit will bore, and in cutting slots.)

Cutting Large Holes. Unless you have an expansive-bit (Fig. 24, page 21), which can be set to the proper radius, you will have to bore a number of small holes inside of the large circles and then finish the cutting with a chisel. In the first row of holes on the diagram (Fig. 156), A shows the first step — describing the circle; B the second step — boring a ring of holes inside of the circle;

HANDY CONTRIVANCES FOR THE HOUSE 143

C the third step — splitting out the wood between the holes; and *D* the fourth step — trimming up the hole to the circle with a chisel. The diagram also shows the four steps required to cut the slots. *E* shows the centers marked off each side of the center lines, *F* the two 1-inch holes bored at these centers, *G* how the wood between the holes is split out, and *H* how the slot is finally trimmed up. The preparation of this board will give you good practice in handling the bit and brace and the chisel. Place the board in the vise for boring the holes, and bore only until the screw point comes through the opposite side, then turn the board over and bore through the rest of the way from that side. This is to prevent the wood around the hole from chipping off, which it would do if the holes were bored entirely through from one side. Be careful to hold the brace exactly vertical while boring. A $\frac{3}{8}$-inch or $\frac{1}{2}$-inch chisel should be used for trimming the holes, and a half-round wood-file (Fig. 33, page 25) and sandpaper will be a great help in smoothing them.

Nail a cleat to the under face of each end of the board as shown in Fig. 155, and the rack will be completed.

The Flat-iron Rest is another convenience which a housekeeper will be glad to have, as it is much handier than an inverted pie-plate or folded newspaper to set an iron upon, and the sole of the iron may be cleaned by rubbing it on the piece of emery-paper fastened to one half of the board. This is shown in Fig. 157.

Cut the board about 8 by 12 inches in size, tack a piece of tin (a piece from a tomato can will do) over the half which is to hold the iron, and a piece of No. 0 sandpaper over the other half, and then tack some narrow wooden strips around the edge of the tin for a rim to prevent the iron from sliding off. Screw a couple of screw-eyes into one end of the board by which to hang it up.

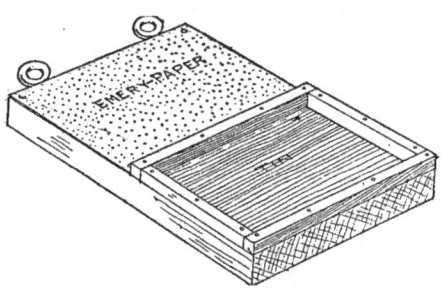

FIG. 157. — Flat-iron Rest.

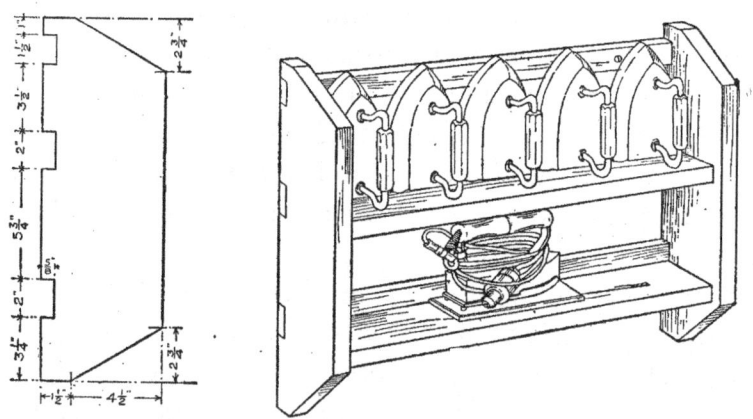

FIG. 159. — Pattern for Side Pieces.   FIG. 158. — Flat-iron Rack.

The Flat-iron Rack (Fig. 158) is easy to make. Lay out the end pieces to the dimensions given on the pattern (Fig. 159), with the top and bottom beveled and the

HANDY CONTRIVANCES FOR THE HOUSE

back edge notched as shown; then, after cutting these, prepare three back strips 22 inches long and to fit the notches, and nail them in place. Cut the two shelves 4½ inches wide by the proper length to fit between the end pieces, and fasten them to the end pieces and to the back strips so the bottoms of the shelves and strips are *flush*. Bore a couple of holes through the upper back strips and furnish your customers with two screw-hooks with which to hang the rack to a wall.

Figure 160 shows a good scheme for

A Sleeve-board, and Fig. 161 patterns for making it. Prepare the two pieces *A* and *B* as shown in Fig. 161, bore the ½-inch holes where

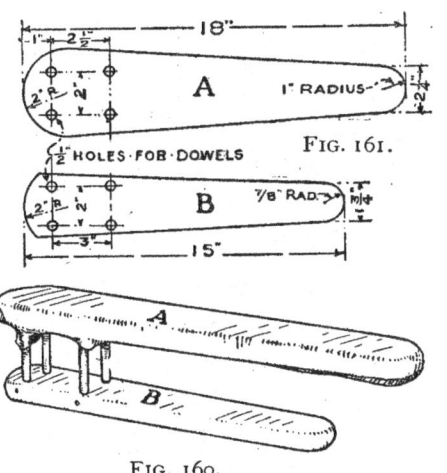

FIG. 160. — Sleeve-board.
FIG. 161. — Patterns for Pieces *A* and *B*.

indicated, and cut four dowels 5 inches long to fit in them. Before connecting *A* and *B*, round off their edges with a plane. Fasten the dowels in the holes by means of finishing-nails driven through the edges of *A* and *B*. The cloth covering on *A* is pinned on in the same way that the covering of any ironing-board is put on, but this is never provided with sleeve-boards, so you need not furnish it with the boards you make to sell.

The Knife-box shown in Fig. 162 has a bottom piece 8 inches wide and 15 inches long, two side pieces 2⅛ inches wide and 15 inches long, two end pieces the shape and size shown in Fig. 163, and a center partition 3 inches high by the inside length of the box. Bevel the top and bottom edges of the side pieces enough to make them square with the bottom and end pieces. Cut the slot shown in the center partition, to form the handle, by boring a ¾-inch hole 2 inches each side of the center of the piece and then cutting out the wood between the holes with a chisel, in the same way as that described on page 142 for cutting the slots in the *Bottle-rack*. Before fastening the partition between the end pieces, tack a piece of felt over the bottom of the inside of the box.

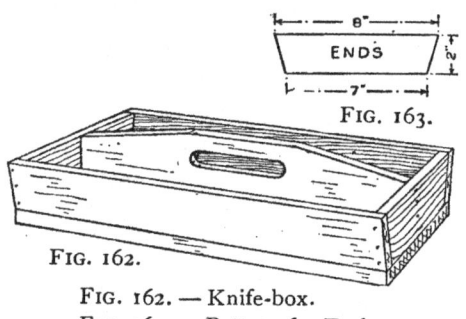

FIG. 162. — Knife-box.
FIG. 163. — Pattern for Ends.

A Scrub-pail Platform will be appreciated by any woman who has experienced the tiresome work of lifting the pail every few minutes while scrubbing, to set it in a different spot, as it is mounted upon casters so that it may easily be pushed along on the floor. Figure 164 shows the completed platform, and Fig. 165 a view of the under side. You will see that this platform can be made very quickly as it consists of only a board a trifle larger each way than the diameter of the bottom of the pail, with strips nailed around its edges to keep the pail from slipping off and a caster screwed to each of the four corners.

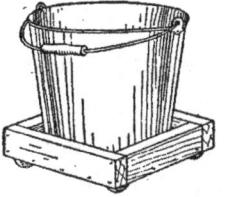

FIG. 164. — Scrub-pail Platform.

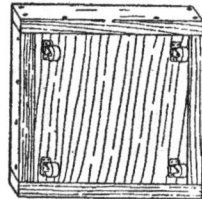

FIG. 165. — Bottom View of Platform.

A Towel-roller is a handy arrangement for holding a kitchen hand-towel, and one similar to that shown in Fig. 166 and finished to match the woodwork of the

FIG. 168. FIG. 167.

CUT SLOTS LIKE THIS IN END PIECES,
OR USE WINDOW-SHADE
SOCKETS LIKE THESE.
SECTION.
BROOM HANDLE

FIG. 166.

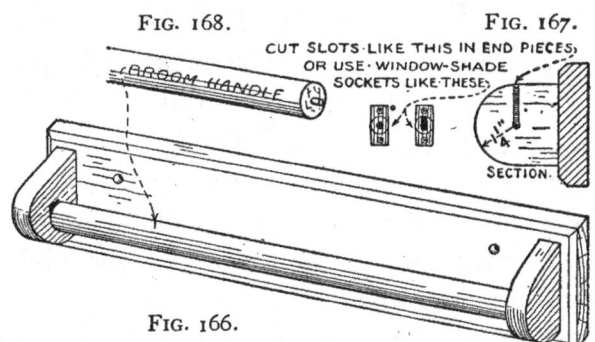

FIG. 166. — Towel-roller.
FIG. 167. — Section showing Slotted End Piece.
FIG. 168. — Broom-handle Roller showing Pivot in End.

kitchen can be screwed to the face of one of the doors. Cut the back board $3\frac{3}{4}$ inches wide and 24 inches long, bevel its edges, and bore a couple of holes in the positions shown through which to screw it to the door. Cut the end pieces 2½ inches square, and round the ends as shown (Fig. 167), then nail them to the back board ¾ inch from the ends. Procure a broom-handle and cut a piece from the lower or straight portion for the roller, and drive a piece of a 20-penny nail into the exact center of each end for pivots (Fig. 168). Cut a slot from the top edge of each end piece down to its center for the roller pivots to turn in (Fig. 167), or buy a pair of window-shade sockets (Fig. 167) and screw them to the end pieces.

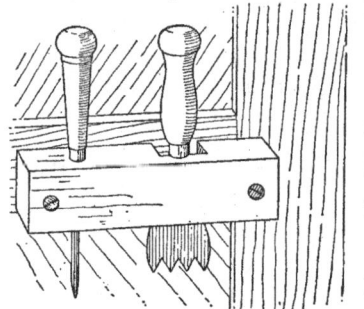

FIG. 169.—Ice-pick and Ice-chisel Rack.

For cutting and chipping ice, an ice-pick and an ice-chisel should be kept within easy reach of the refrigerator, and

An Ice-pick and Ice-chisel Rack screwed to the side of the refrigerator will keep these tools within easy reach (Fig. 169). Make this out of a short block of wood, bore a hole for the pick, and cut a groove in the back edge large enough for the chisel.

Household conveniences such as have been described in this chapter may be made out of pine, cypress, whitewood, basswood, oak, and ash, and they may be painted, stained, shellacked, or varnished, according to the choice of finish your mother, neighbors, or other customers make. For kitchen, pantry, or laundry use, there is no finish better than shellac, or shellac and varnish.

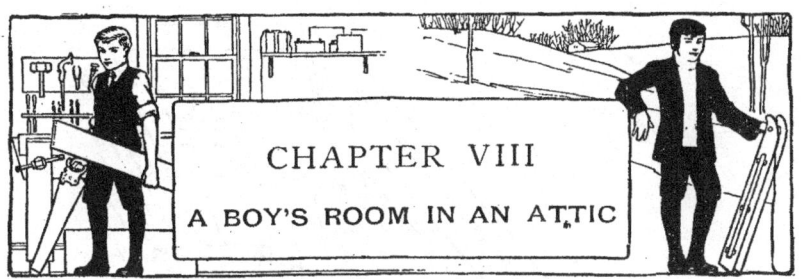

CHAPTER VIII
A BOY'S ROOM IN AN ATTIC

THE attic of the average house presents the best possible conditions for fitting up a boy's room, for generally it is a large unfinished space where a boy will have an excellent opportunity to partition off as large a room as he may require, and furnish it to suit his own taste with home-made furniture and all of his knickknack keepsakes. Usually an attic is the storage place for old trunks, antiquated furniture, and household truck, and this could very easily be packed together in such a way that a large enough space for a room would remain at one end. Figures 170 and 171 show how a room can be made in the attic of a house having a gable roof, but as one attic differs from another just as the house differs from another in plan and design, the suggestions will have to be modified to suit the conditions of your attic. Take a run up to the top of your house, boys, and look things over; then you can tell better just what you can do.

A Dividing Partition to separate the room from the rest of the attic should be built, first, and Fig. 172 shows the proper method of erecting the *studs*. If the attic walls

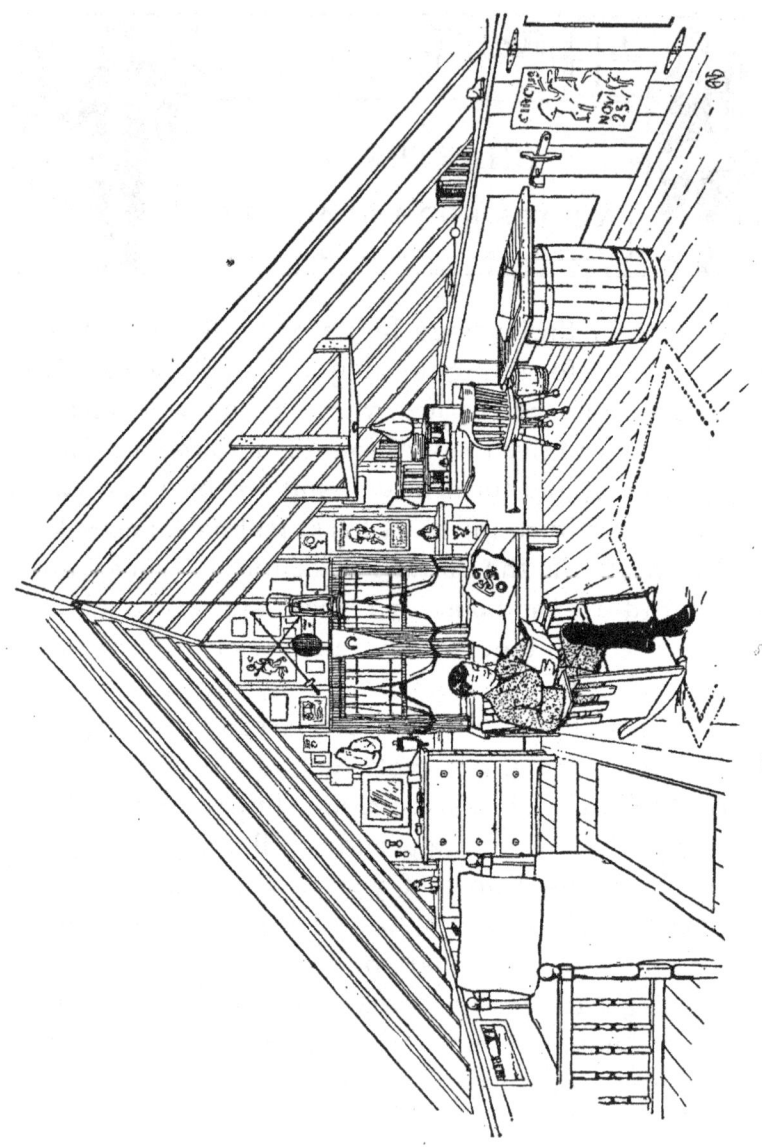

FIG. 17.—A Boy's Room in an Attic.

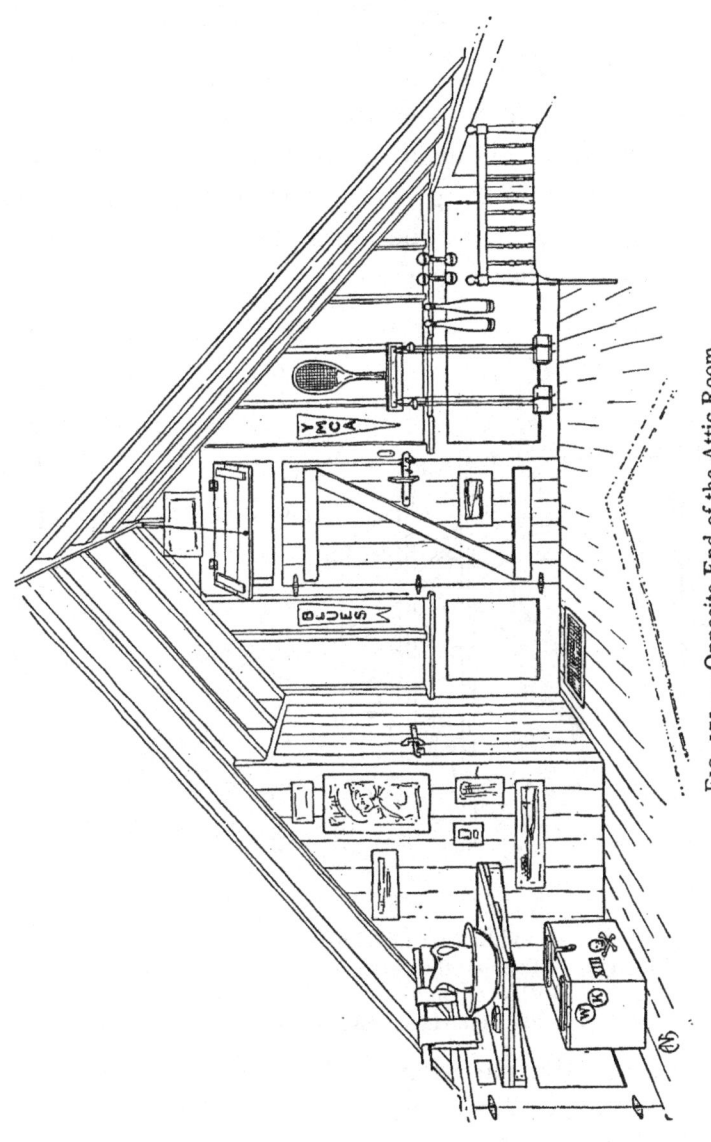

FIG. 171.—Opposite End of the Attic Room.

152   HANDICRAFT FOR HANDY BOYS

are unfinished and of frame construction, as shown in Fig. 170, it will look best to space the partition studs directly opposite the wall studs and nail the boarding on the outside face (Fig. 171); but they may be spaced 3 feet apart, to save lumber, and yet be close enough to support the boards.

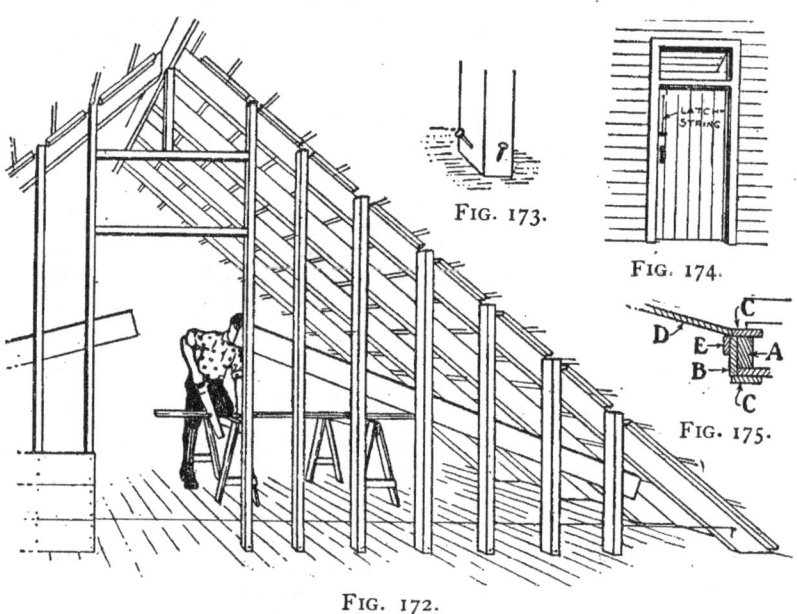

FIG. 172. — Studding for Dividing Partition.
FIG. 173. — Toe-nail the End of the Studs in this Way.
FIG. 174. — View of Outside of Entrance Door.
FIG. 175. — Plan showing Construction of Door Opening.

If you run the partition in the same direction as the roof rafters, locate it so the upper end of the studs may be spiked to the rafters (Fig. 172); if the other way, nail a strip across the bottoms of the rafters to spike your studs to. The illustrations show the partition running in the direction of the rafters, so I shall tell you how to erect it in this way. To get the bottom of the studs in a line, run

A Plumb-line from a nail driven into the face of one of the two rafters, 1 inch or so above the floor, to a nail driven into the face of the opposite rafter, as in Fig. 172. Any strong cord may be used for this line. The studs should also be *plumbed* up and down, as the rafters may not run exactly straight, and for this purpose make

A Plumb-board. This consists of a 4-inch board 5 or 6 feet long whose edges have been planed up straight and true, with a "V" notch cut in the center of one end and a cord with a weight attached tied to a nail driven into the center of the opposite end. By placing this board against the side of a stud, you can tell whether or not it is plumb by the position of the cord, which will hang exactly in the center of the notch when the stud is plumb. (This home-made plumb-board is illustrated on page 13 of "The Boy Craftsman.")

If you locate the door in the center of the partition, first set the two *jamb studs* 3 feet apart (Fig. 172) and *toe-nail* them to the floor and to the rafters (Fig. 173), then spike a cross-piece between these studs, 6 feet 9 inches above the floor, to form the *head* of the door, and fasten another horizontal piece about 20 inches above it for the head of the *transom*. Next, spike the end studs in position, and nail on the temporary *diagonal braces* shown in the illustration to keep the studding plumb until the boarding has been nailed on. Space the intermediate studs at the proper distances apart, and, as soon as each piece is made plumb, tack the brace to it to hold it in position until you spike the ends in place.

It is not necessary to have new lumber for this partition. Boards and studs can usually be bought very cheaply wherever a frame building is being wrecked, and this second-hand stuff and box boards will do very well, for any roughness can be concealed. Studs may be spliced with *fish-plates* when too short (see *Fished-splice*, on page 58).

If the Roof runs down to the Floor along the sides of the room, a partition should be built along each side at a point where the roof is 3 feet above the floor, so the space behind these partitions may be utilized for

Lockers, an addition to a boy's room which cannot very well be dispensed with. These partitions are made as shown in Figs. 176 and 177. Short studs are fitted between the floor and rafters at about every other rafter, a 1-by-2-inch strip is nailed across the studding near the top and another near the bottom, the studs being notched so the strips will set flush with their face, as shown in Fig. 177, and then burlap, denim, or dark-colored muslin is tacked to these strips. The strips and covering should be carried around the other two walls of the room, also, to form a similar

Wainscoting. When the cloth has been tacked on, nail a 6-inch board around the bottom and another board of the same width around the top, and cut a board to fit between the rafters to form a shelf or cap over the wainscoting (Fig. 177).

ROOF BOARDS
RAFTERS
CAP
BOARD
STRIP
CLOTH
STUDS
BLOCK

FIG. 177.

FIG. 176.

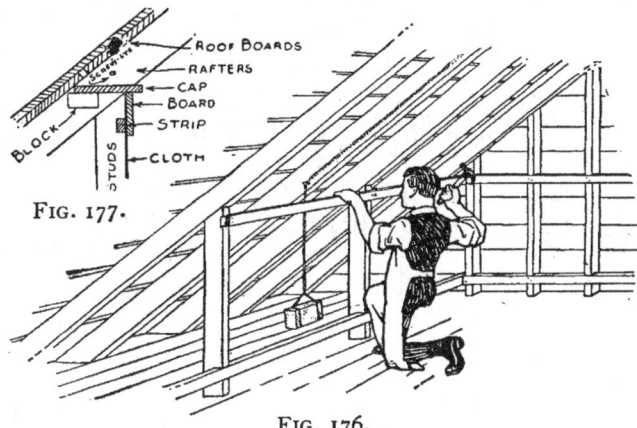

FIG. 176. — How the Wainscoting is put up.
FIG. 177. — Cross-section of Completed Wainscoting.

A Large Clothes Closet should be built in one corner of the room as shown in Figs. 171 and 178, and the inside should be fitted up with shelves, hooks, and coat and trousers hangers. A piece of broom-handle or curtain-pole may be fastened across the rafters upon which to hook coat hangers, hooks may be made out of spools (Fig. 179), and the

Trousers Hangers (Fig. 180) consist of two pieces of wood about 8 inches long, with one face of each beveled (*A* and *B*, Fig. 180), and a wooden button (*C*, Fig. 180).

Screw block *B* to the under side of a shelf, place block *A* parallel to it so the bevels will be about ⅛ inch apart, and screw one end to the shelf; then screw button *C* in the proper position so when the ends of a pair of trousers are placed between the beveled sides of *A* and *B*, it can be turned against strip *A* as a lock to hold the two strips together.

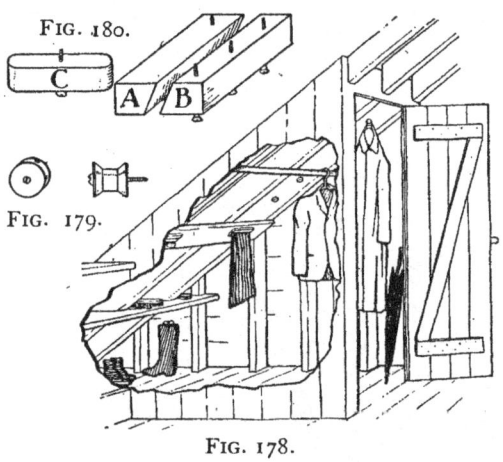

Fig. 178. — Clothes Closet, with Wall broken to show Inside.
Fig. 179. — Spool Hooks.
Fig. 180. — Details of Trousers Hangers.

The Doors should be made of boards battened together as shown in Figs. 171 and 178. To make a nicely finished entrance to the room, conceal the studding around the doorway with *jamb* and *head* boards, and nail a board *trim* around the opening as shown in Figs. 171 and 174. In the plan of the *door jamb* (Fig. 175), the stud on one side of the opening is shown at *A*, the finished *jamb* board at *B*, and the inside and outside *casings* or *trim* at *C*; the door is shown hinged in place at *D*, and the *stop* strip shown at *E* is nailed around the inside of the opening for the door to strike against. Hinge the entrance door and the locker doors on to the casings with strap-hinges (Fig. 171).

A BOY'S ROOM IN AN ATTIC

The Entrance-door Transom is made of boards battened together (Fig. 171) and is hinged at the top to the trim. It is operated by means of a cord which is run from a screw-eye in the bottom of the transom up over a small pulley in the ceiling, and from that down to a nail in the wall.

Figure 181 shows the details for

An Old-fashioned Cabin Latch which will do very well for the doors. By looking at Fig. 171, you will see that the *latch A* (Fig. 181) is screwed at one end to the door, the *guard B* is screwed in place over *A*, and the *catch C* is set into the jamb board. The entrance door should have a *latch-string* with which to open it from the outside (Figs. 174 and 181) and also a wooden *button* (*D*, Fig. 181) with which to lock it on the inside. Make a handle for the outside of the door similar to guard *B* (Figs. 174 and 181).

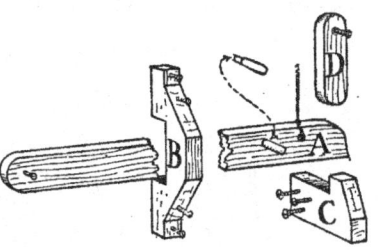

FIG. 181. — Details of Door Latch, Guard, Catch, and Button.

Few unfinished attics are provided with heat, but probably you can obtain

An Oil Heater or Stove for your room. For a coal stove you will have to run a pipe through the partition and over to the chimney, and if there is no opening into the chimney flue, it will be necessary to get a mason to cut one and set a *thimble* into it to receive the end of the pipe; but the latter work will not cost much.

If there isn't any running water in the attic, make

A Wash-stand in a corner, as shown in Fig. 171, to hold a wash-bowl and pitcher. Fasten

A Broom-handle Towel-rack above the wash-stand to the rafters, as shown.

Get a common barn lantern for

Lighting your Room, if neither gas or electricity has been installed in the attic, and construct

A Home-made Hanging Lamp out of it as shown in Fig. 170. Besides the lantern, you will need a *harness snap*,

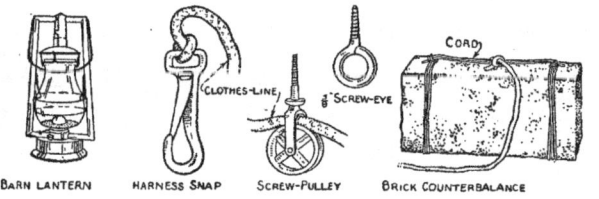

FIG. 182. — These things are required for the Home-made Hanging Lamp.

a *screw-pulley*, a $\frac{5}{8}$-inch *screw-eye*, some *clothes-line* and *cord*, and a *brick* (Fig. 182). Screw the pulley into the ceiling in about the center of the room, then run the clothes-line over the pulley and down the face of a rafter; screw the screw-eye into the rafter just above the wainscot cap (Figs. 176 and 177), slip the clothes-line through this eye and then run it through a hole bored through the wainscot cap, just below, and tie the brick to the end with cord for a counterbalance (Fig. 177); fasten the harness snap to the other end of the clothes-line and adjust it so that the lantern, whose handle is snapped into it, will pull down to within easy reach of the floor. The weight of the brick must be just enough to counterbalance the lantern; if too heavy, break off a piece. Figure 170 shows the lamp pushed up out of the way.

Every one of you will have to suit your own taste in
Furnishing the Room, so the illustrations will serve merely as suggestions for the arrangement of pictures, posters, pennants, fencing foils, tennis rackets, and other things.

Home-made Picture-frames can be made out of laths very easily; *butt* the ends of the laths together instead of *mitering* them and stain the wood *in the rough* instead of planing it off smooth.

The Furniture may be very simple, like the box furniture shown in the following chapter, or some of the designs shown in Chapter VI may be carried out if you wish to spend more time and labor upon it.

You will probably wish to make

A Pirate Chest such as is shown in Fig. 171 and

A Window Seat as shown in Fig. 170. Ask your mother to make a few sofa pillows for the seat.

Some of you Boys will not have an Attic in which to make a room, but those of you who have not will probably find ideas among these suggestions that can be adapted to your present room, whatever part of the house that may be in. If you already have an attic room, you will likely see some ways in which to improve upon its furnishings.

CHAPTER IX

BOX AND BARREL FURNITURE

GROCERY boxes, packing-cases, crates, barrels, kegs, and much of the "truck" to be found in the attic, basement, and wood shed suggest innumerable possibilities for making things, and the fact that these materials can be utilized for many purposes with little or no expense makes them especially well suited to boys' work.

Furniture made from the above materials is naturally somewhat rough, compared with what can be produced with better wood, and some of it will appear clumsy, but no boy will object to this "home-made" appearance on furniture for his own room, if it will serve his purpose — in fact, he will generally prefer something like this in order that his room may be "different" from the other rooms of the house.

The following pages show a number of pieces of furniture which are easy to make, and other ideas will probably suggest themselves while you are working upon these.

The Writing-desk shown in Fig. 183 is fitted around the wall studding, which would be exposed in your room

BOX AND BARREL FURNITURE 161

if it were in the unfinished attic of a frame house; but it also may be fastened upon a plastered wall by supporting it upon brackets nailed to the wall, or by hanging it with chains from hooks screwed into the wall.

Procure a box about 30 inches long, 14 inches wide, and 16 inches deep for the body of the desk. The top

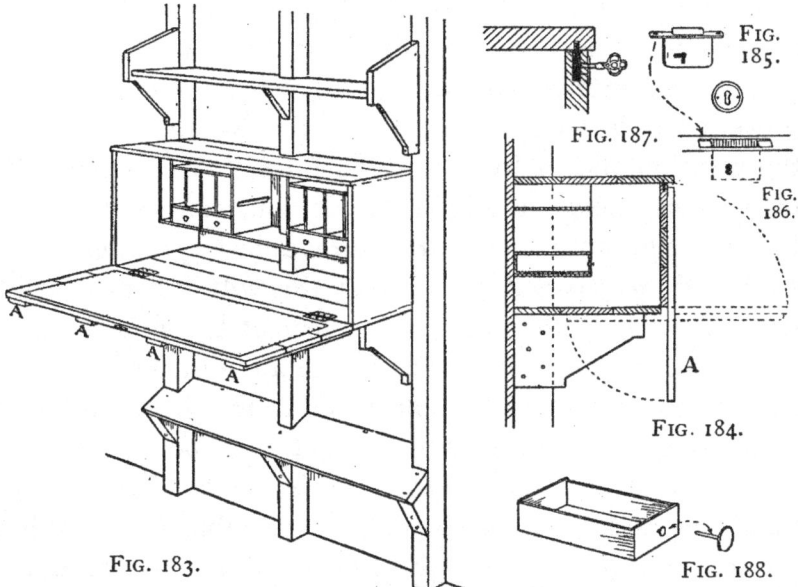

FIG. 183. — The Writing-desk.
FIG. 184. — Section through Writing-desk.
FIG. 185. — A Desk or Cupboard Mortise-lock and Escutcheon for Key-hole.
FIGS. 186–187. — How to set the Lock into the Drop-leaf of the Desk.
FIG. 188. — Cigar Box for Desk Drawers.

of this will form the front of the desk, and then the bottom will be the back, but in case the desk is fitted around the studs, the bottom boards should be removed, as a back will be unnecessary. Figure 184 shows a good shape for bracket supports for the desk; after nailing these in place at the proper height, fasten the box to their tops. Make the *drop-leaf* for the front of the desk out of 1-inch boards and batten them together with four strips (*A*, Fig. 183). Cut the two end battens a little shorter than the width of the leaf, but make the two center ones long enough to project about 10 inches, as in Fig. 184, so they will strike the bottom of the box and prevent the leaf from dropping further when opened to the position shown by the dotted lines. Hinge the leaf in place as shown in Fig. 183. If you want a lock for the desk, go to a hardware store and buy a desk or cupboard *mortise-lock* (Fig. 185); this will cost 15 cents. Cut a mortise in the edge of the leaf of the proper size to receive the lock (Fig. 186), locate and cut the *keyhole*, and then screw the lock in place and fasten the *escutcheon* (Fig. 185) over the keyhole. A slot must be cut in the lower face of the desk top for a *pocket* for the *lock bolt* to turn into, and in order to make it possible to cut this pocket, the front board of the top must be removed and a board about 1 inch wider nailed on in its place; this will make a projection over the drop-leaf as shown in Fig. 187.

Very thin wood should be used with which to partition off the *pigeon-holes*, and pieces of cigar boxes will do nicely. Make the drawer openings of the right size so cigar boxes may be used for drawers (Figs. 183, 184, and

188), and drive brass rug tacks into the ends of the boxes for knobs.

To give the drop-leaf a better writing surface, pad it with a few sheets of newspaper and then cover the paper with a piece of white oil-cloth. Figure 183 shows how a foot-rest may be fastened to the wall, below the desk.

A Shelf for Books may be bracketed to the wall 10 or 12 inches above the desk as shown in Fig. 183.

It is generally an easy matter to find a broken chair, and you ought to be able to get a discarded piano-stool in your storeroom, from some neighbor, or at a second-hand store, as they are being replaced by the more modern piano bench, and having procured these two articles, you can make

An Office Chair such as is shown in Fig. 189. Remove the chair legs, then set the seat and back upon the stool (Fig. 190) and screw it to the top; countersink the screw-heads, fill in over the heads with putty, refinish

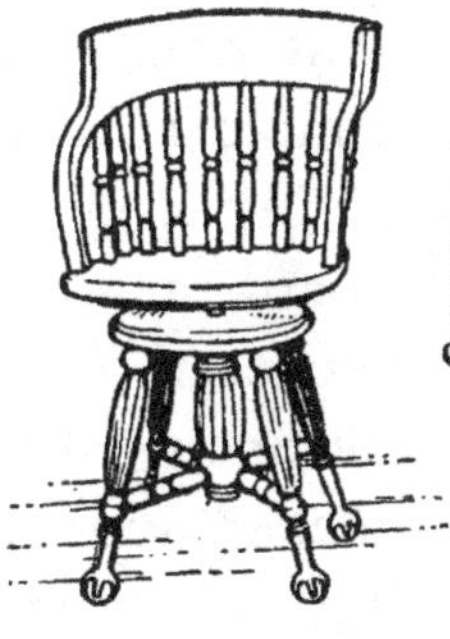

FIG. 189. — The Office Chair.

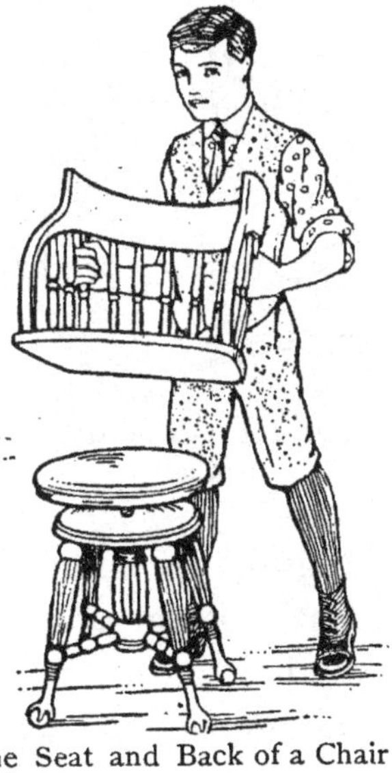

FIG. 190. — How the Seat and Back of a Chair are fastened upon a Piano-stool to form the Office Chair.

the chair to match the stool, and the office chair will be completed.

Procure a fish keg for

A Waste-basket, wash it out thoroughly, and paint it inside and outside. One of these kegs which has been used by the author for this purpose for a number of years is shown in the photograph opposite page 86.

The Arm Rocker shown in Fig. 191 is easy to construct. The seat is made out of a box with the cover boards nailed on, and the back and arm strips are cut out of pieces of boxes or other boards. If you can find a pair of rockers from a broken chair, use them and you will be that much ahead; if not, it is a simple matter to make a pair by laying a chair on its side upon a board, marking out around the rocker, then moving the chair over far enough to mark out the second rocker, and sawing out the pieces and smoothing them up.

FIG. 191. — The Arm Rocker.

Figure 192 shows how the braces *A* should be nailed to the bottom of the box, and Fig. 193 how their ends should be cut to fit over the rockers. By looking at any rocking-chair you will see that the rear ends of the rockers are set several inches closer together than the front ends; provide for this in preparing strips *A*, and be care-

BOX AND BARREL FURNITURE 165

ful to set both rockers the same distance in, so the chair will rock evenly. Screw the rockers to strips *A* as shown.

The lengths of the strips for the back and arms will be determined by the size of the box used for the seat, but in

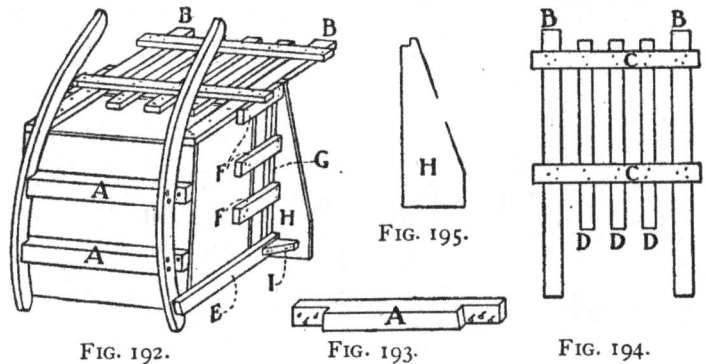

FIG. 192. FIG. 193. FIG. 194.

FIG. 192. — Chair overturned to show how the Rockers are Attached.
FIG. 193. — Brace for the Rockers.
FIG. 194. — How the Back is Constructed.
FIG. 195. — Pattern for the Wide Arm.

order that you may have an idea of the proper proportions, sizes will be given for a box 18 inches by 16 inches by 12 inches. The back should be constructed in one piece as shown in Fig. 194, and nailed to the box as in Fig. 192. Strips *B* are $2\frac{1}{2}$ inches wide by 2 feet 9 inches long, strips *C* $2\frac{1}{2}$ inches wide by 21 inches long, and strips *D* $1\frac{1}{2}$ inches wide by 2 feet long. After the back has been made and fastened to the box, cut the two side strips *E* (Fig. 192) $1\frac{1}{2}$ inches wide by 20 inches long, strips *F* to the same width by 10 inches long, and strips

G to the same width by 16 inches long. Fasten these strips to the box and to each other as shown in Figs. 191 and 192, then cut the right arm *H* (Figs. 192 and 195) 18 inches long by 3 inches wide at the narrow end and 8 inches at the wide end, and cut the left arm of the same length by 3 inches wide. After nailing the arms in place, brace the right arm with the small triangular block *I* (Fig. 192).

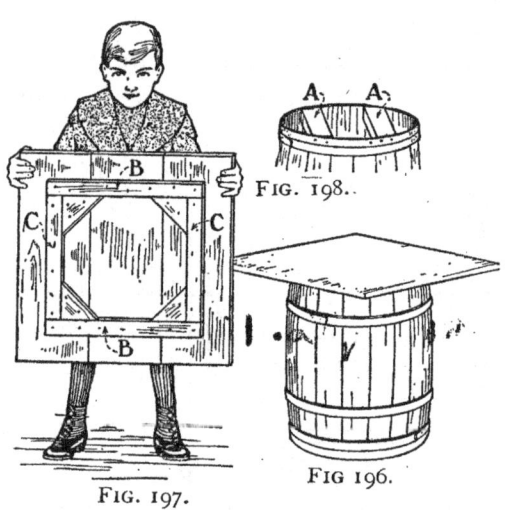

FIG. 197.

FIG. 196. — The Barrel Table.
FIG. 197. — How the Table Top is Made.
FIG. 198. — Cross-pieces in Open End of Barrel to which the Top is Built.

When you have completed your chair, give the measurements of the seat to your mother or sister, and ask her to make a cushion for it.

Procure an apple or potato barrel for the base of

The Barrel Table illustrated in Fig. 196. The table top (Fig. 197) should be about 30 inches square and made of three pieces of boards 10 inches wide. Cut the boards to the proper length and lay them upon the floor side by side. Place the barrel bottom end up upon the exact center of the square formed by the boards, then cut the

BOX AND BARREL FURNITURE 167

cross battens *B* of the right length and nail them to the boards close against the side of the barrel, fit the strips *C* between them close to the sides of the barrel, and cut the triangular corner blocks shown to fit between the strips and the barrel. Turn the barrel right side up again, nail two pieces of 2-by-4 in the open end as shown at *A* in Fig. 198, and nail the top to these cross-pieces.

By covering the top with a piece of heavy wrapping-paper and then tacking a piece of table oilcloth over the top and edges, you will have a smoother table; any unevenness may be padded out with paper before the oilcloth is put on.

Three boxes of exactly the same size, about 3 feet long, 12 inches wide, and 12 inches deep, are required for

The Chiffonier shown in Fig. 199. A dealer in shoes or dry goods will most likely have boxes of uniform size.

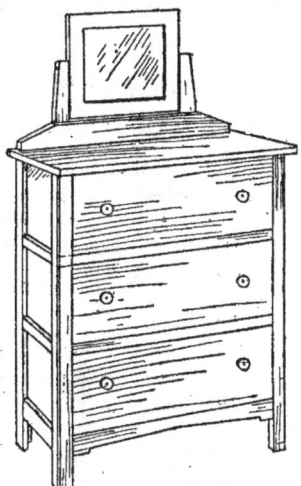

FIG. 199. — The Chiffonier.

Set the boxes on top of one another as in Fig. 200, and then fasten them together at the four corners with strips 6 inches longer than the combined height of the boxes. Nail together the edges of the strips, first, then nail them to the boxes as shown in Fig. 199. The projecting ends of the strips will be the legs, so they must be of exactly the same length or the chiffonier will not rest evenly upon the floor. Fit horizontal strips to the front and ends of the boxes, between the leg strips, to conceal the joints between the boxes (Fig. 199); cut these to the exact width of the front edges. Figure 201 is a view of part of the bottom of the chiffonier and shows the leg strips in place and how the lower portion of the chiffonier is finished off, by nailing a strip shaped similar to that shown in Fig. 202 across the front and a straight strip across the ends (see Fig. 199).

Cut boards of the proper length to make a top with a projection of 1 inch over each end, and nail them to the

FIG. 203.
CUT HERE
NAIL
WASHER
HOLE
FIG. 2C4.
FIG. 205.
BOTTOM
FIG. 201.
FIG. 202.
FIG. 200.

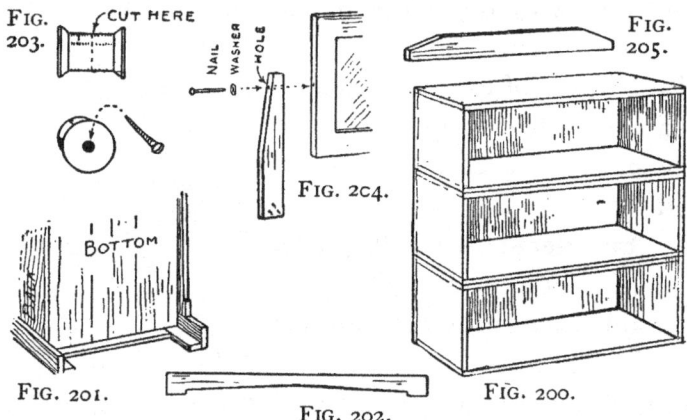

FIG. 200. — Three Boxes of exactly the Same Size are required for the Chiffonier.
FIG. 201. — View of Bottom of Chiffonier.
FIG. 202. — Fit a Strip like this to the Front at the Bottom.
FIG. 203. — Cut Spools in Halves for Knobs.
FIG. 204. — Prepare two Pieces like this for the Mirror-frame Supports.
FIG. 205. — Fasten a Strip like this in Front of the Mirror-frame Supports.

top box so there will be the same projection over the front of the box. The drawers may be made out of boxes cut down to the proper size, or if you do not care to bother with doing this, you may hinge *drop-leaves* to the boxes in the same way that the writing-desk drop-leaf is put on (Fig. 183). Cut spools in halves for knobs (Fig. 203), and screw two of the halves to the face of each drawer or drop-leaf as shown in Fig. 199.

A mirror 10 by 12 inches in size, set in a wooden frame, can be purchased for 50 or 60 cents. To fasten the frame to the chiffonier, cut two uprights 16 inches long, taper one edge of each as shown in Fig 204, bore a $\frac{1}{4}$-inch hole near the upper end as shown, and drive a nail through each hole into the exact center of each side edge of the mirror frame (Fig. 204). Nail or screw the lower ends of the uprights to the back of the top box so the mirror will be exactly in the center of the chiffonier top and about 3 inches above it. Shape a piece similar to that in Fig. 205, and fasten it below the mirror to the mirror-frame supports as shown in Fig. 199, and your chiffonier will be ready for *finishing*.

After making your box furniture either stain it with an oil stain or give it two coats of paint.

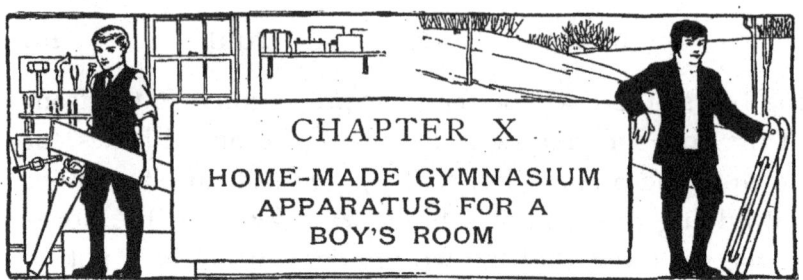

CHAPTER X

HOME-MADE GYMNASIUM APPARATUS FOR A BOY'S ROOM

It is not necessary to go to the basement or attic to fit up a home gymnasium, boys, unless you wish to make large pieces of apparatus, for you can easily equip your own room with *chest-weight*, *chinning-bar*, *hitch-and-kick*, *dumb-bells*, and *Indian clubs*.

A Chest-weight, or "exercising machine," as some boys call it, is shown in Fig. 206, and Figs. 207, 208, and 209 give the details for making it. Select a portion of a wall in your room where it will be most convenient to use the weights, and if the wall is frame,—that is, made of wood and plaster,—locate two of the studs (Fig. 207). Tap upon the plaster with a hammer until you find a portion that sounds solid, make a mark there, then measure 16 inches to the left or right of it, and the chances are you will find the second stud at that point, as studding is generally placed 16 inches from center to center. If the wall is brick, locate two of the vertical strips **to**

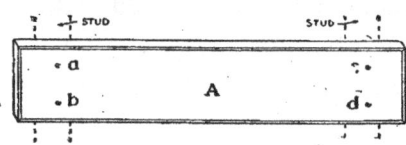

Fig. 207. — Screw the Cross-piece of Chest-weight to Wall Studs like this.

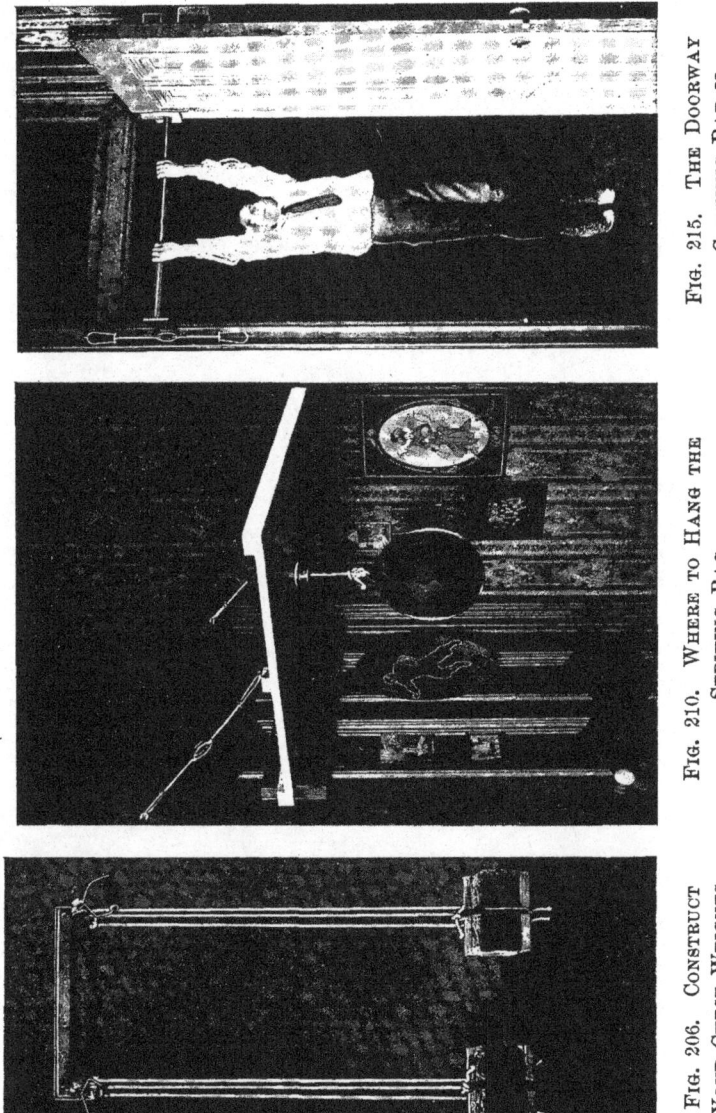

Fig. 206. Construct Your Chest-Weights First.

Fig. 210. Where to Hang the Striking-Bag.

Fig. 215. The Doorway Chinning-Bar is Easily Put Up.

which the laths are nailed. For cross-piece *A* (Figs. 207 and 208) cut a 1-inch piece of oak, pine, or whitewood, 4 inches wide and 20 inches long, plane it up and bevel its

B
A
e
i
f
e
f
PUNCH A HOLE IN TIN END
FIT A WOODEN PLUG IN OPEN END
j
l
k
m
h

FIG. 209.

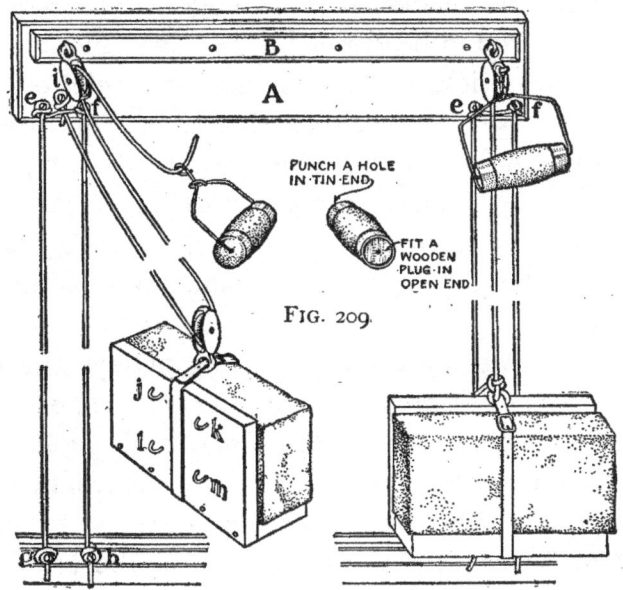

Two-pulley Scheme. FIG. 208. One-pulley Scheme.

FIG. 208. — Two Schemes for Assembling the Weights, Rope, and Pulleys of Chest-weight.

FIG. 209. — Prepare a Pair of Bicycle Handle-bar Grips like this for Handles.

four face edges. Locate holes *a*, *b*, *c*, and *d*, 2 inches from the ends, and bore them $\frac{1}{4}$ inch deep with a $\frac{3}{8}$-inch bit. Spike the board to the wall about on a line with your shoulders, using 20-penny nails and driving them through holes *a*, *b*, *c*, and *d* into the studs. Drive the heads below the surface of the wood with a nail-set, and fill holes *b* and *d* with chips of wood cut to fit over the spike heads (holes *a* and *c* will be concealed by strip *B* as is shown in Fig. 208). Cut cross-piece *B* 19 inches long by $1\frac{1}{4}$ inches wide, bevel its edges, and screw it to board *A* with round-head finishing-screws (Fig. 208).

Procure two bricks of uniform size for weights, make a wooden bracket for each as shown in Fig. 208, and strap them to these brackets with a couple of skate, trunk, or shawl straps. Drive staples into the backs of the brackets at *j*, *k*, *l*, and *m* (Fig. 208), placing *j* and *k* 1 inch to each side of the center and *l* and *m* directly under them.

Purchase two enameled-iron awning pulleys at a hardware store, also get about 25 feet of *sash-cord*, or closely woven clothes-line, for *lifting-lines* and *guide-ropes*. Fasten the pulleys to cross-piece *B* with staples, $1\frac{1}{2}$ inches from the ends. The guide-ropes are fastened to screws *e* and *f* in board *A* and to *g* and *h* in the baseboard. These screws should be placed 2 inches apart, and should center on the pulleys on strip *B*. In attaching the ropes, first fasten them to screws *e* and *f*, then slip their lower ends through staples *j* and *l*, and *k* and *m*, in the weight brackets, and tie them to screws *g* and *h*. You can make either a one-pulley scheme for lifting your weights as shown on the right of Fig. 208, or a two-pulley scheme as shown on the left of the illustration. The latter way has the advantage of a longer rope, but costs a little more on account of the extra rope and pulleys. In the first method the rope is attached to the bracket strap, then run through the pulley and tied to the handle, while in the latter it is tied to screw *i* on board *A*, run through a pulley, slipped over the bracket strap, and then slipped through the upper pulley and tied to the handle.

The handles are made from bicycle *handle-bar grips*, which, if you haven't an old pair, may be purchased for 10 or 15 cents. Glue a wooden plug in the open end of the grip (Fig. 209), then bore a hole through the center of it and punch another hole through the center of the tin cap on the other end of the grip. Run an 18-inch piece of heavy wire through the holes and bend it into the shape shown in the illustrations, with a hook through which to tie the lifting rope. Leave the bricks in their natural color, or stain them with oil paint, and either stain or varnish the woodwork if it is of oak, or paint, stain, or shellac it if it is of pine or whitewood.

A Striking-bag with an elastic cord at each end can easily be fastened in a doorway by screwing a screw-eye in the head and another in the threshold, to which to tie the cords. The upper screw-eye may be left in place and the lower one removed when you detach the bag. But for a bag with a single cord it is necessary to have a platform for it to strike against. You can put up

A Striking-bag Platform in your room by making it detachable, as shown in Fig. 210, so that it may be removed and put out of the way when not in use.

Make the platform 3 feet square, battening together the boards with strips *A*, *B*, and *C* (Fig. 211), and screw hooks *D* and *E* into strip *B*. Cover the under side of this platform with oilcloth to make the surface smooth, first tacking several thicknesses of paper over the boards if there happens to be any uneven places.

To the inside of your room door screw the piece of 2-by-4 *F* (Fig. 212), 2 inches above your head, then

FIG. 214.

J
K

A
B
C
D
E

H
I
G
F

FIG. 212.

FIG. 211.

FIG. 213.

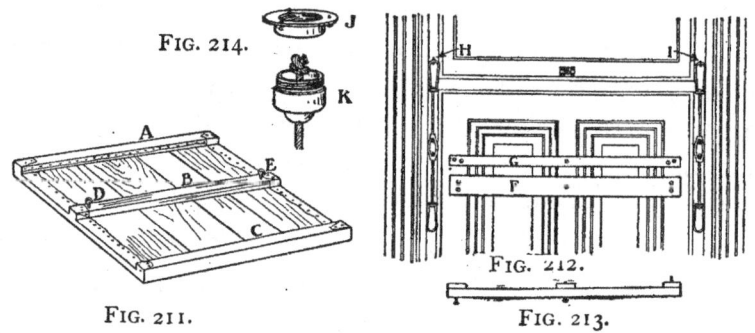

FIG. 211. — How to make the Striking-bag Platform.

FIG. 212. — Attachment of Strips to form Groove for Platform; also Turnbuckles.

FIG. 213. — Block out the Strips thus if the Door has Raised Panels.

FIG. 214. — Details of the Swivel which holds the Bag Cord.

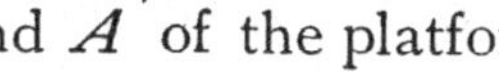

leave a space wide enough for end *A* of the platform to fit in, and screw strip *G* to the door. If the door has raised panels (Fig. 210), block out strips *F* and *G* as shown in Fig. 213. Purchase two buck-saw *turnbuckles* at a hardware store, and fasten one end of each to the door *trim* with staples, at *H* and *I* (Fig. 212); put them just high enough so the lower ends will catch in hooks *D* and *E* (Fig. 211) when the platform is slipped between

HOME-MADE GYMNASIUM APPARATUS

F and *G*. The platform is made solid by turning the turnbuckles. The swivel shown in Fig. 214 costs about 50 cents. The plate *J* is fastened to the under side of the platform with screws, the bag cord is slipped through *K* and knotted, and *K* is screwed on to *J*.

A Chinning-bar is very easily put up in a doorway (Fig. 215). A piece of a curtain-pole will do for the bar, and the socket-blocks for it to set in should be made as shown in Fig. 216. Cut the blocks 4 inches square and make the holes a little larger than the ends of the curtain-pole. Figure 217 shows how to cut the holes by first boring a ring of little holes and then cutting out the center and trimming up with a chisel. Make the hole in block *B* like that in *A*, then saw a piece out of the top. Screw the blocks to the door jambs about 3 inches below the door *head*.

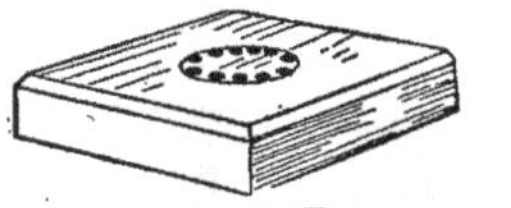

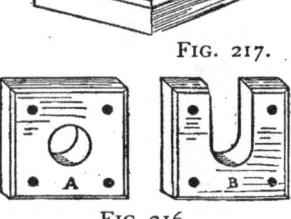

FIG. 216.—Socket-blocks for the Chinning-bar.
FIG. 217.—How to cut a Large Hole.

The Hitch-and-Kick (Fig. 218) is a piece of apparatus that will give you a chance to limber up your leg muscles by practicing the *high kick*. The plate (Fig. 219) may be an old *pot cover* or a *cake-tin*, with three holes punched at *A*, *B*, and *C*. Attach brass chains at these holes, join them at *D*, and at this point connect the end of a piece of chain 12 or 14 feet long. Fasten a small screw-pulley or a screw-eye in the ceiling (Fig. 218), slip the chain

Fig. 218. — The Hitch-and-Kick will give you a Good Chance to Limber up your Leg Muscles.

through it, and bring the end down through a screw-eye and then to a hook which has been screwed into the door or window *trim*. You may have a long stick, graduated into feet and inches, with which to measure the heights of your kicks; or you may tie a short piece of thread through one of the links of the chain, within a foot or so of the loose end, and then lay off some measurements upon the door or window *trim*, in lead-pencil, in such a way that you can easily determine the height of the plate by noting the position of the threaded link.

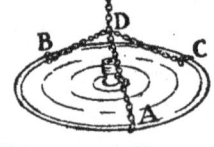

Fig 219 — How to make the Hitch-and-Kick Plate out of an Old Pot Cover.

With the addition of a pair of *dumb-bells*, a pair of *Indian clubs*, and **a wand** made by splicing together two broom-handles, as shown at *A*, *B*, and *C* (Fig. 220), you will have a fairly well-equipped "gym," without sacrificing any floor space of your room for apparatus.

HOME-MADE GYMNASIUM APPARATUS

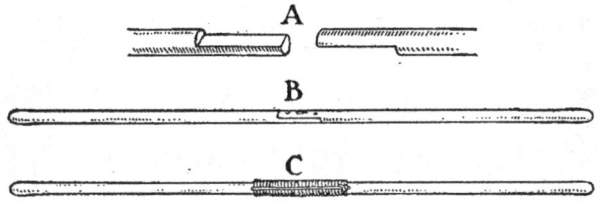

FIG. 220. — A Wand made of Two Broom-handles spliced together End to End.

A Rack for your Dumb-bells, Indian Clubs, and Wand may be made like the one illustrated by Fig. 221. Board *A* is the same size as board *A* of the *Chest-weight* (Fig. 207) and is spiked to the studs in the same way, while board *B* is 2 inches shorter and $2\frac{1}{2}$ inches wide. Make the places for the *bells*, *clubs*, and *wand* to set in as shown in Fig. 222, cutting them as described for the *Chinning-bar* socket *B* (Fig. 216). Screw strip *A* to strip *B*.

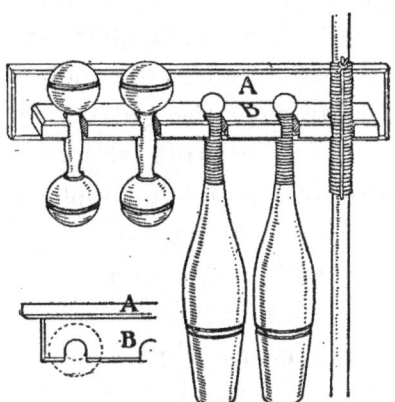

FIG. 222. Plan showing how to cut the Sockets.

FIG. 221. Rack for Dumb-bells, Indian Clubs, and Wand.

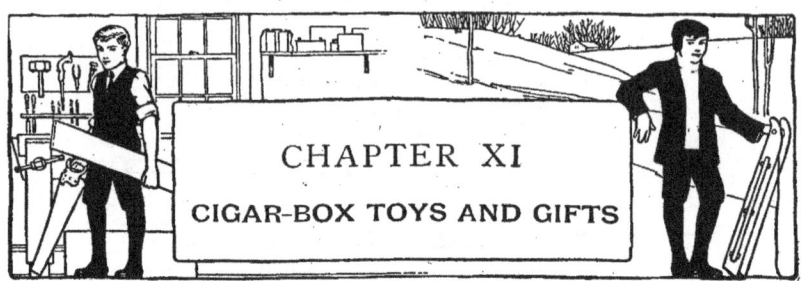

CHAPTER XI
CIGAR-BOX TOYS AND GIFTS

MAKE your Christmas gifts, boys; your own handicraft will be better appreciated by your brothers and sisters, the older folks, and the friends and relatives you wish to remember than anything you can buy, and as the materials may be such as will cost little or nothing, you can save the greater part of the money you usually spend in Christmas shopping. Besides, by showing your work to friends it should be easy to secure orders for duplicate articles.

Probably no material presents as many possibilities for making inexpensive and at the same time attractive articles as the white cedar wood from cigar boxes. You boys very likely know what handy receptacles these boxes are for stamps, coins, marbles, and the hundred and one other things which your pockets will not hold, but here are some ideas for making use of the boxes which you probably never thought of.

The Material will cost you nothing, — except the nails, glue, and finish, — as empty cigar boxes may be procured at any cigar store or drug store. Pick out a good assort-

Fig. 223.

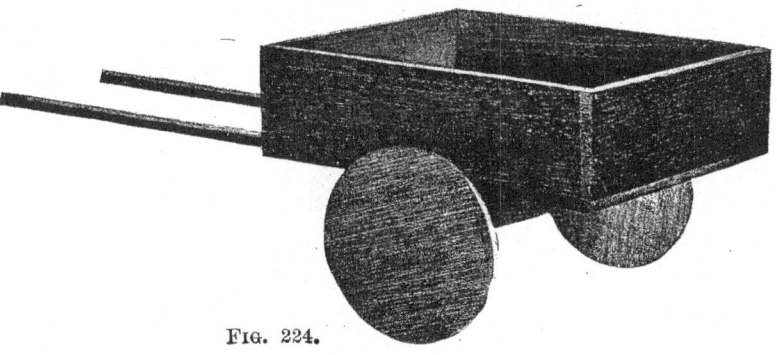

Fig. 224.

Fig. 223. An Express-Wagon.
Fig. 224. A Cart.

ment of shapes and sizes, place the boxes in a tub or wash-boiler of hot water and allow them to soak until the paper labels and bindings loosen, then, when this paper has been removed, bind the covers flat against the bottoms with cord to prevent them from warping, and put them in the sun or near a stove to dry. When the boxes are thoroughly dry, pry them apart, sort out the best pieces and remove the manufacturers' trade-marks with sandpaper (grade No. o).

Brads $\frac{3}{8}$ inch or $\frac{1}{2}$ inch long should be used for nailing, and the heads should be *set* below the surface of the wood and the holes filled with putty colored to match the wood.

Finish the work with two coats of boiled linseed-oil. The oil gives the wood a beautiful rich tone and brings out the markings of the grain.

A scroll-saw, bracket-saw, coping-saw, or a very sharp jack-knife should be used where

Cutting is necessary. Do not attempt to split the wood, as the grain is seldom straight, but lay it down upon a board and *score* it with a knife in the way in which you would score a piece of cardboard; then break it along the scored line, or continue cutting until the piece is cut in two. If you use a saw, cut a little away from the outlines of the work and then trim up with a knife and sandpaper.

The wagons, Jack-in-the-box, and doll furniture shown in this chapter were designed with the idea of saving as much cutting as possible, and you will see by the illustrations that in many cases the boxes are not altered.

The Express-wagon shown in Fig. 223 is made out of a long flat box. Cut down the sides at the front and construct a seat on top of the sides as shown in Fig. 227. Cut the front wheels about $2\frac{1}{4}$ inches in diameter and the rear wheels about $2\frac{3}{4}$ inches in diameter. If you haven't a compass with which to describe the circles, you can mark out the wheels with cups or glass tumblers. Cut the wooden axles as shown in Fig. 227, making the front axle — for the smaller wheels — deeper than the rear one, then fasten them to the wagon and nail the wheels to their ends. Drive a tack into the front of the wagon-box and tie a cord to it, or if you have a small toy horse to hitch to the wagon, fasten a pair of shafts to the under side of the box as is shown upon the two-wheeled cart.

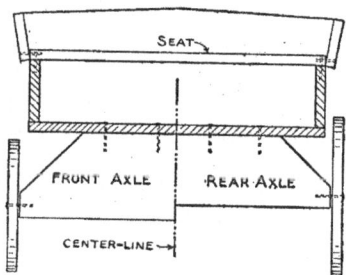

FIG. 227. — Cross-section of the Express-wagon.

The Cart in Fig. 224 is made out of a square flat box with its wheels fastened to the center of the under side. Make the wheels about $2\frac{3}{4}$ inches in diameter.

The Auto Delivery-wagon (Figs. 225 and 226) requires two boxes about $8\frac{1}{2}$ inches long, 5 inches wide, and $2\frac{1}{2}$ inches deep. You will see by looking at the illustrations that one box is inverted upon the other. Before fasten-

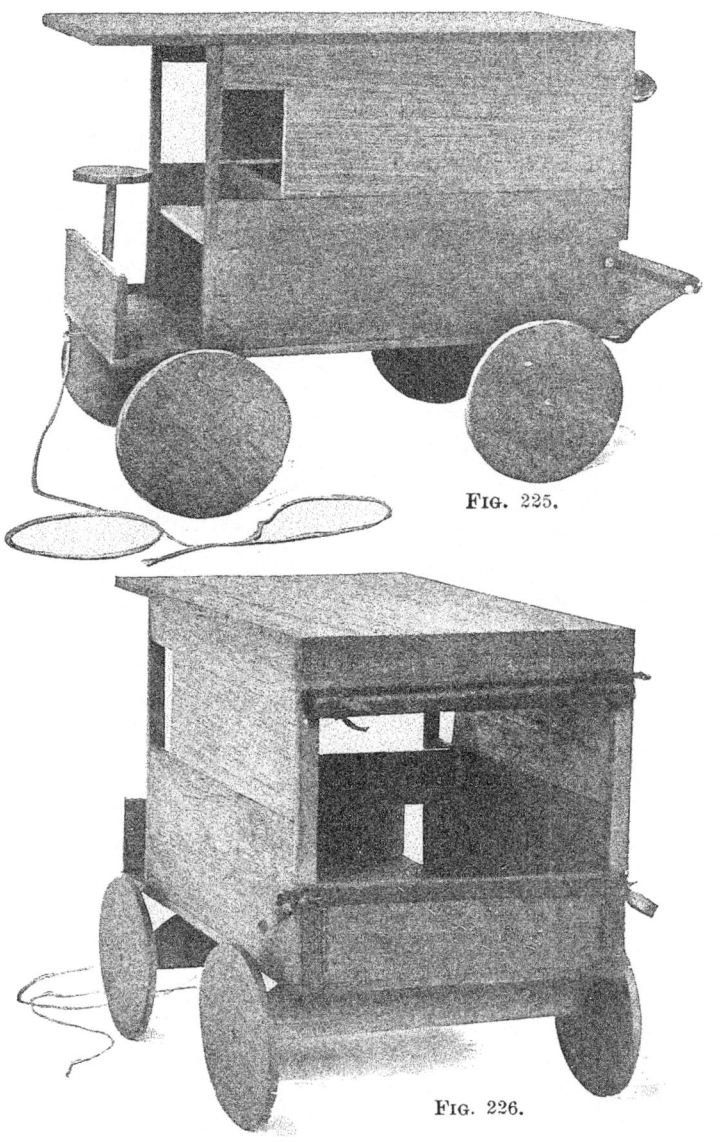

Fig. 225.

Fig. 226.

Figs. 225 and 226. Two Views of an "Auto Delivery-Wagon."

ing them together, remove the two ends of the upper box and the rear end of the lower box (leaving the front end for the *dashboard*), and cut 2 inches off the sides at the front and an additional piece 1 inch by $1\frac{3}{4}$ inches from the sides of the upper box for windows. Fasten the boxes together by nailing strips to the ends of side pieces. Nail a narrow strip across the top of the rear end of the wagon and hinge a drop *end-gate* to the wagon-bed with cloth strips. Support the end-gate with a cloth strap. Tack a curtain of black cloth to the top cross strip and sew two cloth straps to the curtain, so that it may be fastened up in a roll, as shown in the photograph. Make the wheels and axles like those of the express wagon, but cut the front and rear wheels, also the two axles, of equal size. Cut out a small steering-wheel and fasten it on a short wooden rod inside of the dashboard. Make a seat and seat back, nail the back to the seat, and then fasten the seat between the sides of the wagon just below the windows.

A Jack-in-the-box (Fig. 228) is a simpler toy to make than you might imagine. The box should measure about $5\frac{3}{4}$ inches by $5\frac{3}{4}$ inches by 5 inches. Hinge the cover to the top with two pieces of heavy cloth ; glue one piece to the inside of the cover and box, and the other to the outside. Drive a small tack into the front edge of the cover, and below it fasten a small hook onto the box; the hook may be bent from a short piece of wire.

A spiral spring from an old bed-spring will do for Jack's

body, but if you cannot get one of these, it is a simple matter to make a spring. Take a piece of No. 12 gauge wire about 10 feet in length and wind it around a rolling-pin or anything that is cylindrical and about 2½ inches in diameter. Fasten this spring with doubled-pointed tacks upon a piece of wood cut to fit the inside of the box (Fig. 229), then procure a small doll's head, baste a circular piece of cardboard to the top of the spring and to this sew the head. Make a cloth fool's cap to glue on Jack's head, covering his hair entirely, and also a loose jacket to fit over his spiral body; for these use any bright-colored cotton cloth that will fall into folds easily.

Tack the base of the spring to the bottom of the box.

Make the seat for

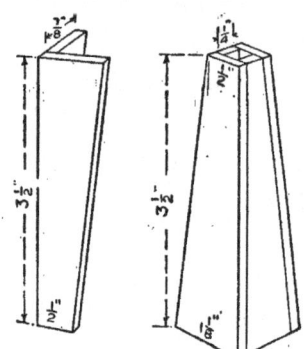

FIG. 236. Leg of Dining-table.   FIG. 235. Pedestal of Center-table.

The Round-seated Chair shown in Fig. 230 2 inches in diameter, the back 5 inches high, 2 inches wide at the top, and 1¼ inches wide at the seat; cut the front leg 2⅛ inches high by 1¼ inches wide.

The Round Center-table (Fig. 231) should have a base built up of four strips as shown in Fig. 235. Cut the circular top 5 inches in diameter. A saucer may be used with which to mark this out.

Select a long flat box for

The Dining-table shown in Fig. 232, and after making

CIGAR-BOX TOYS AND GIFTS

four built-up legs as shown in Fig. 236 fasten them into the four corners of the box.

In making the little

Square-seated Chair (Fig. 233), cut the seat about 2 inches wide by $2\frac{1}{4}$ inches deep, the front legs $2\frac{1}{8}$ inches high by $\frac{3}{8}$ inch wide, and the back legs $4\frac{1}{2}$ inches high by $\frac{3}{8}$ inch wide. Brace the legs and back with crosspieces, and you will have a very firm and artistic diningroom chair.

Select a box about 9 inches by 5 inches by $2\frac{1}{4}$ inches in size for making

The Doll's Cradle shown in Fig. 234. Cut the two rockers by the pattern in Fig. 237 and fasten them to the bottom of the box 1 inch from the ends. Use the rim of a breakfast plate in drawing the arc of the rockers.

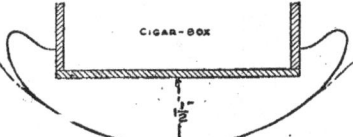

FIG. 237. — Pattern for Cradle Rockers.

The Key-board shown in Fig. 238 is one of the simplest gifts that can be made. Follow the dimensions given upon the pattern (Fig. 243) in laying out the board. Where two sides of a piece correspond, first draw a center-line, then lay out one side, trace it off upon a piece of tissue paper, turn the

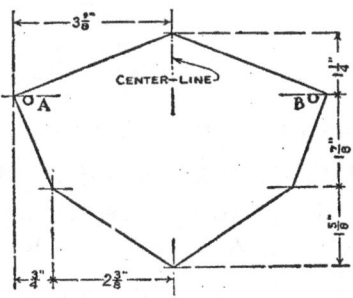

FIG. 243. — Pattern for Key-board.

paper over and reproduce it upon the other side of the center-line. By doing this in laying out all your work you will have no trouble in getting the sides alike. Bore gimlet holes *A* and *B* before cutting out the key board, then there will be little danger of splitting the wood. Space the brass hooks as shown in the photograph.

The Corner Clock-shelf (Fig. 239) is built up of several pieces of wood, the shelf (Fig. 244) consisting of

A
B
FIG. 244.
C
D
E
C&E
D
A
CENTER-LINE
B

FIG. 247. FIG. 245. FIG. 246.

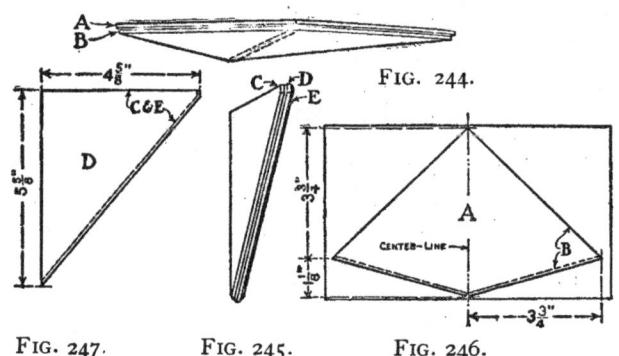

FIG 244. — Shelf of Corner Clock-shelf.
FIG. 245. — Bracket of Corner Clock-shelf.
FIG. 246. — Pattern of Shelf Pieces.
FIG. 247. — Pattern of Bracket Pieces.

pieces *A* and *B*, and the bracket (Fig. 245) of *C*, *D*, and *E*. Figure 246 shows the pattern for *A* and *B*. After cutting these pieces trim $\frac{1}{8}$ inch off of the front edge of *B* (see dotted line, Fig. 246). Cover the lower face of *A* and the upper face of *B* with glue, then place them together with the side edges flush and the front

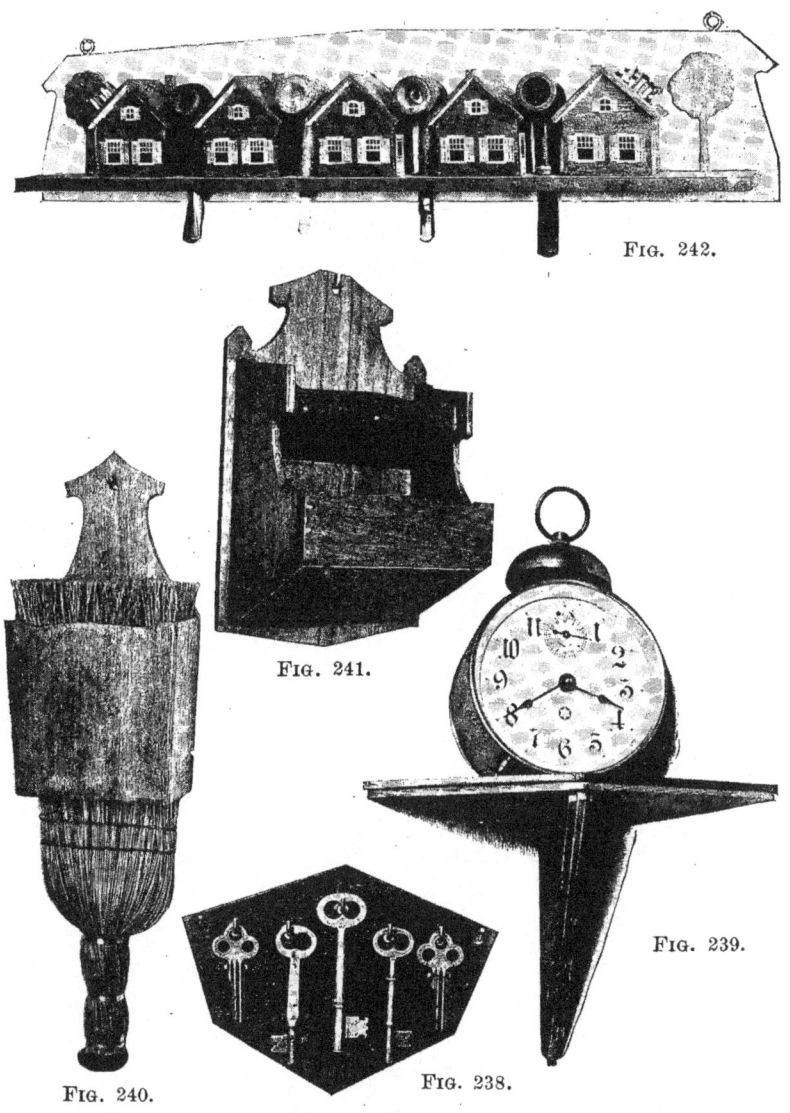

FIG. 238. A KEY-BOARD. FIG. 239. A CORNER CLOCK-SHELF.
FIG. 240. A WHISK-BROOM HOLDER. FIG. 241. A KITCHEN MATCH-BOX.
FIG. 242. A COTTAGE PIPE-RACK AND MATCH-BOX.

edge of *A* projecting over that of *B*. Cut the three bracket pieces as shown in Fig. 247, then cut ⅛ inch off of the long or front edge of *C* and *E* (see dotted line, Fig. 247) so that when they are nailed together the edge of *D* will project beyond *C* and *E* as shown in Fig. 245. The shelf and bracket should be placed under a heavy weight until the glue has set. The photograph shows how to hang the shelf in the corner by means of brads and screw-eyes, the brads being driven into the under side of the shelf and the eyes screwed into the wall for them to stick through.

A Whisk-broom Holder such as is shown in Fig. 240 is a gift which any one will appreciate for his or her room. Make the back and front pieces similar to *A* and *B* (Fig. 248) and cut the side pieces 4 1/16 inches high by 1½ inches wide. Place the side pieces between the front and back in putting the holder together.

A large match-box is a very handy article for the kitchen, where the supply of matches generally disappears so rapidly that an ordinary size of box requires refilling every day or so, and

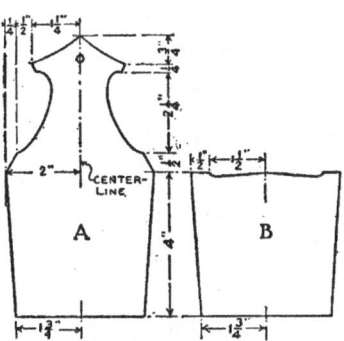

FIG. 248. — Patterns for Whisk-broom Holder.

The Kitchen Match-box shown in Fig. 241 will be appreciated by your mother, because the large receptacle in the lower portion will hold a full box of matches. The upper part of the box is intended for burnt matches.

Figure 249 shows the patterns for the different pieces. A is the back, B the ends, C the front of the upper re-

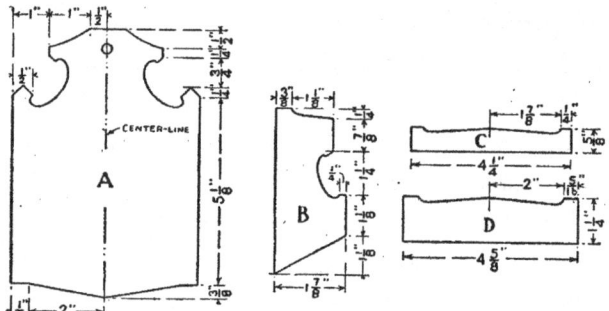

FIG. 249.—Patterns for Kitchen Match-box.

ceptacle, and D the front of the lower receptacle. Besides these pieces you will need a piece $1\frac{1}{2}$ inches wide by the length of C for the bottom of the upper receptacle and a piece $2\frac{1}{4}$ inches wide by the length of D for the bottom of the lower one. The photograph will show you how to put the pieces together. After the box has been completed and given its oil finish, glue a strip of No. 0 sandpaper to the bottom of the lower receptacle.

A gift suitable for the relative or friend who smokes a pipe is

The Cottage Pipe-rack and Match-box shown in Fig. 242. The little cottages are made out of cigar-box wood, but the back and bottom pieces (Fig. 250) are cut out of thicker material; $\frac{1}{2}$-inch pine, whitewood, or basswood will do. Figure 251 shows the dimensions for the cottages and the method of putting them together. As the end cottages are match-boxes, cut an opening in the outer side of their roofs as in Fig. 251. Use glue and $\frac{3}{8}$-inch

OPENING IN ROOF OF END COTTAGES
CLOTH STRIP
2"
3"

FIG. 251.

1"

FIG. 252.

11"
CENTER
BOTTOM PIECE
24"
HOLE
23"

FIG. 250.

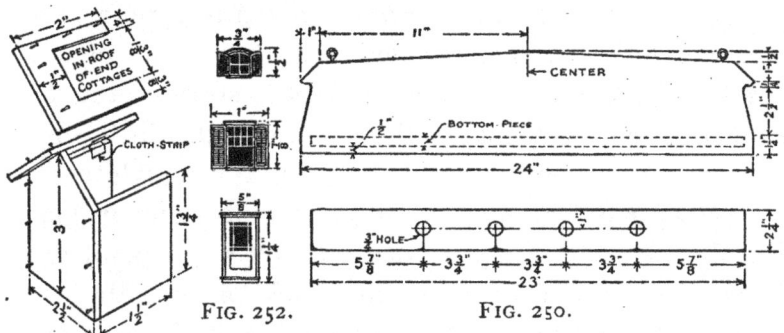

FIG. 250. — Patterns for Back and Bottom Pieces of Cottage Pipe-rack and Match-box.
FIG. 251. — Details of Cottages.
FIG. 252. — Patterns for Paper Doors and Windows.

brads in fastening the pieces, also cloth strips for attaching the roof.

Give the cottages two coats of linseed-oil, then paint the top and edges of the roofs red (*Venetian red*) and the under side white. With a rule and pencil lay out the doors and windows upon a piece of white letter-paper, then draw the lines in ink, paint the shutters green and the glass black (use *water-colors*), and mark off the divisions in the glass with white; then cut these out and glue them on to the cottages as shown in the photograph.

After the back and bottom pieces have been cut and

the holes have been bored in the bottom piece (Fig. 250), rub them down with sandpaper and nail the back to the edge of the bottom piece. Give the back piece two coats of *white lead* and *chrome-yellow* (mixed to form a pretty cream color) and the bottom piece two coats of *olive-green*. Glue the cottages in place, spacing them as shown in the photograph, then cut out the little chimneys to fit the roofs, paint them red with white caps (*Venetian red* and *white lead*), and glue them in place. Cut the trees out of a piece of cigar-box wood, paint them green, and fasten them to the back piece with brads. Screw two screw-eyes into the top edge of the back piece and glue a strip of sandpaper below each end cottage on which to strike matches.

Two, three, and four cottage pipe-racks may be made by changing the proportions of the back and bottom pieces, and

A Cottage Match-box, made by attaching a single cottage to a back piece similar to *A*, Fig. 249, will be a pretty gift. The cottage may be divided through the center for good and burnt matches, in which case an opening must be cut in each side of the roof.

Among the many

Other Gifts which may be made out of cigar boxes are a *letter opener*, a *hall letter-rack*, a cube-shaped *box for string*, a *tooth-brush rack*, a *glove box*, and a *handkerchief box*. Use your ingenuity and work out your own designs for these.

CHAPTER XII
CLOCKWORK TOYS

THE toys shown opposite page 190 are a few of the many mechanical toys which can be operated by clock work, and they are easy to make, too, requiring no more mechanical ability than is possessed by the average boy old enough to handle the simplest of tools.

Generally it is easy to find an old clock somewhere about the house, and a clock which has been discarded simply because it has become worthless as a timekeeper is perfectly good for operating these toys, provided the *mainspring* is in working order. It is not necessary to have a set of works for each toy, for they are so quickly fastened in place that but a minute is required to transfer the works from one toy to another.

Before commencing work upon the toys, get together

The Other Necessary Materials. These will consist of cigar boxes, cardboard, cotton or silk spools, glue, brads, and a few pieces from the woodpile, with one or two additional articles which are mentioned later on. Brads ⅝ inch and 1 inch in length should be purchased for fastening the framework of the toys together, and the cigar boxes should be about 8 inches by 4 inches by 2 inches in size. Remove the paper from the boxes as described in the preceding chapter.

To prepare the Clockwork for use, remove it from its case, detach the hands and face, and pry off the small wheel pivoted directly under the hands; this wheel is shown at *A* in Fig. 257. Remove also the *balance-wheel*

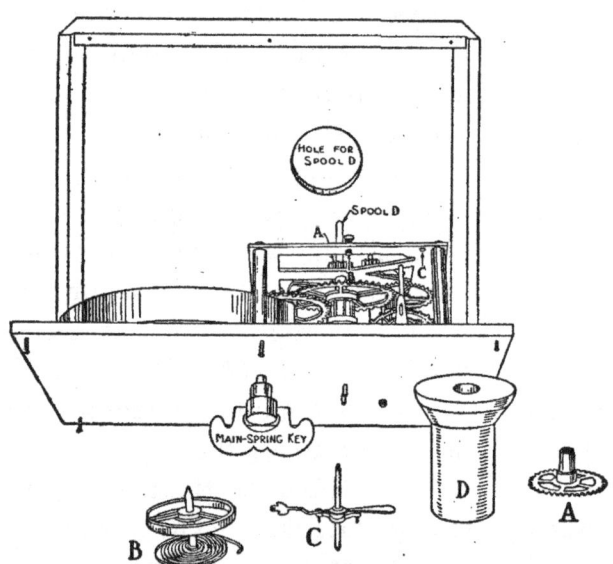

FIG. 257. — How the Clockwork Motor is fastened to the Cigar-box Cover.
(This Box has been cut down to the Proper Length for the Ferris Wheel.)

B (Fig. 257) and the *lever C* pivoted next to it, to increase the speed of the remaining wheels.

Fasten the clockwork motor for

The Merry-go-round shown in Fig. 253 to the cover of

a cigar box, as illustrated in Figs. 254 and 257, boring holes through the cover with a gimlet for the *pivot* ends on the back of the works to set into. Remove the lower flange from a spool (*D*, Fig. 257) and fasten the spool on to the central pivot of the clockwork in the position formerly occupied by wheel *A*. The hole in the spool will be too large for the pivot and must be filled up with sealing-wax. To do this, hold a piece of sealing-wax above the spool and melt it with a lighted match, allowing it to drip into the hole until the latter is about half full, then press the wax down with the end of a match until it is compact, smooth it off on the bottom of the spool, and make a dent in it with a pencil to indicate the exact center of the hole. Heat the end of the pivot with a lighted match, and press it into the dent in the wax, being careful in doing so to get the spool straight upon the pivot. Cut a hole through the bottom of the cigar box belonging to the cover to which you have attached the works, for spool *D* to project through (Fig. 257).

To make the Standard for the merry-go-round, cut four strips of wood 8 inches long, and fasten one to each corner of the cigar box, turning the bottom side of the box up; then cut a piece of $\frac{1}{2}$-inch board 10 inches square, locate its center *F* by drawing diagonal lines from corner to corner as shown in Fig. 258, bore a 1-inch hole through it at this point for spool *D* (Fig. 254), and then nail the box to the center of the board as shown in Fig. 258.

The Tent should be laid out upon heavy white paper as shown in Fig. 259. After describing a circle with a radius of 9 inches, describe another circle within it

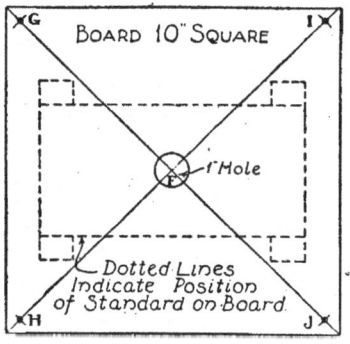

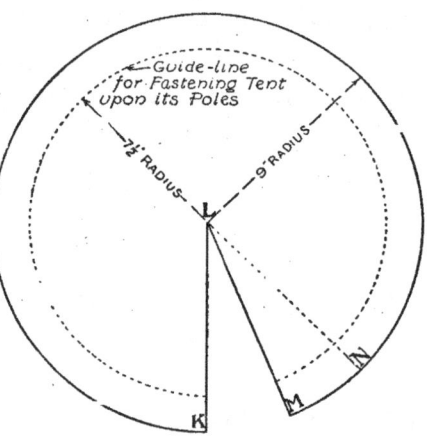

Fig. 258.—Plan of Top of Standard for Merry-go-round.

Fig. 259.—Pattern for Tent of Merry-go-round.

with a radius of $7\frac{1}{2}$ inches, this inner circle (shown by dotted lines in the diagram) being drawn for a guide in fastening the tent upon its tent-poles. Cut out the tent along the outer circle, and from it cut a triangular piece about the size of that included between lines *KL* and *ML* in the diagram. Cover the under edge of *KL* and the upper edge of *ML* with glue, lap *KL* over to about *NL*, and rub down the edges with a cloth to make as neat a joint between the pieces as possible (Fig. 260). Bore a hole through each corner of the standard top (*G*, *H*, *I*, and *J*, Fig. 258), then cut four

Fig. 260.—The Tent ready to be fastened upon a Tent-pole.

FIG. 253. A MERRY-GO-ROUND.

FIG. 255. A FERRIS WHEEL.

FIG. 254. A CLOCKWORK MOTOR.

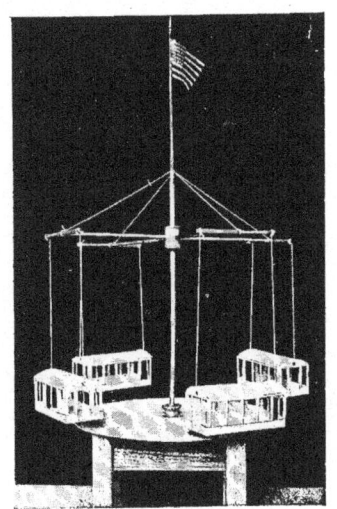

FIG. 256.

CLOCKWORK TOYS

sticks 7 inches long, sandpaper them until smooth, and glue them into these holes for

The Tent-poles. When the tent has dried, tack it to the ends of the poles, being careful to make it set evenly upon them; cut a scalloped border out of red or blue paper and paste it to the edge all around as shown in Fig. 253, and stick a small flag in the peak.

The Horses. A full-size pattern for these is shown in Fig. 261. Take a piece of *tracing-paper* or any thin

FIG. 261.—Full-size Pattern for the Horses of the Merry-go-round.

transparent paper, and place it over the pattern and make an exact copy; then rub a soft lead-pencil over the other side of the paper, turn the paper over with the blackened side down, and transfer the drawing six times upon a piece of light-weight cardboard. Paint the horses with water-colors, using the pattern as a guide for shading and marking them, then cut them out with a sharp knife or a pair of scissors.

Figure 262 shows the pattern for

The Sleighs. Draw this out upon a piece of cardboard, cut it out and fold along the dotted lines, then turn

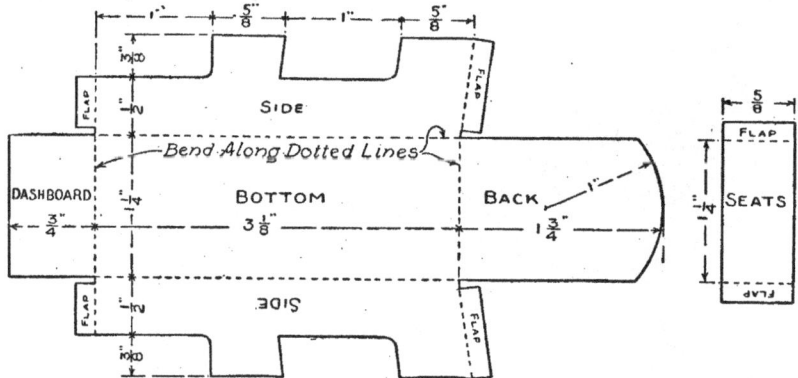

FIG. 262. — Pattern for the Merry-go-round Sleighs.

in the flaps and glue them to the dashboard and to the back. Cut two seats by the pattern given, bend down the flaps and glue them to the sides of the sleigh, and make the back for the front seat like that on the back seat (Fig. 263). Then make another sleigh similar to the one just completed, for two are required for the merry-go-round. Paint the sleighs green or yellow with trimmings of a lighter shade.

CLOCKWORK TOYS

Figure 254 shows

The Shafts upon which the horses and sleighs are mounted. Cut them 5½ inches long, whittle them round, and rub them down with sandpaper. The shafts are fastened in a spool hub which has five holes bored in it (*E*, Fig. 254); bore the holes with a gimlet or small drill, marking them off first with a pencil to be sure of getting them spaced at equal distances. Point the ends of the shafts and glue them

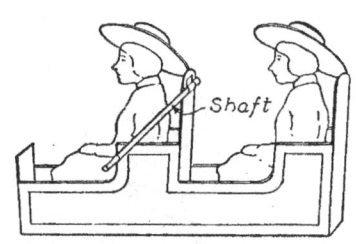

FIG. 263. — A Completed Sleigh showing Attachment to Shaft.

into the holes in the hub, then connect this spool to spool *D* with a piece of a lead-pencil 2 inches long (Fig. 254).

To fasten the horses to the shafts, punch a hole through three of them at *X* (Fig. 261) and slip each one over a shaft, then tack the other three horses to the ends of these shafts at the point *X*. To fasten the sleighs to the remaining shafts, glue one end of a piece of paper to the back of the front seat and the other end around the shaft (Fig. 263).

The Girl Riders for the sleighs are shown full size in Fig. 264, and

The Boy Riders for the horses are shown full size in Fig. 265. Make tracings from the patterns as you made that of the horse and prepare four girls and six boys. Paint their clothes in bright colors. Cut a second leg for each boy rider, so he can be made to sit astride of his horse, and glue the leg to his hip as shown in Fig. 266. Cut a slit in each seat of the sleigh and stick the flaps on the girl riders in them.

For the Platform shown directly under the horses and sleighs in Fig. 253, cut a piece of cardboard 11 inches in

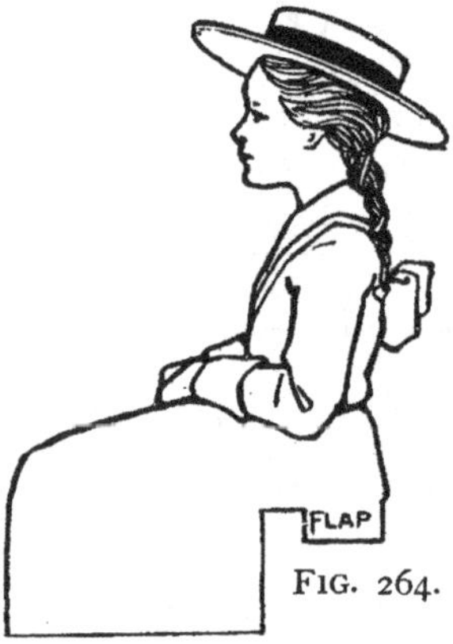
FLAP

FIG. 264.

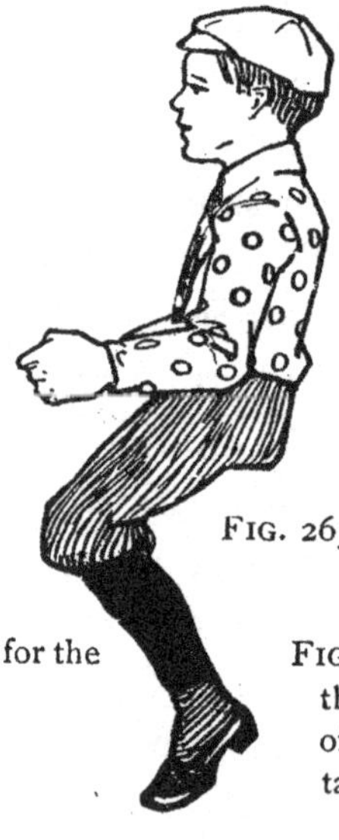

FIG. 265.

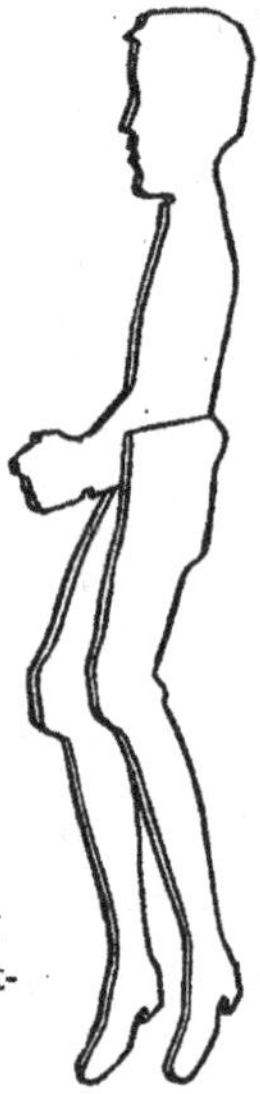

FIG. 266.

FIG. 264.—Full-size Pattern for the Girl Riders.

FIG. 266.—How the Second Leg of the Boy is Attached.

FIG. 265.—Full-size Pattern for the Boy Riders.

diameter; if you choose to make the Ferris wheel before the merry-go-round, you may use the center pieces removed in cutting out the rims, as noted in Fig. 271. Punch a hole through the center of this disk large enough for the peg connecting spools *D* and *E* to slip through. This platform rests upon the top of spool *D* and revolves with it.

To operate the Merry-go-round. The key by which the mainspring is wound up is shown screwed in place on the under side of the cigar-box cover in Fig. 257. While winding the mainspring, it will be necessary to have some means of checking it so it will not unwind at the same time, and the best scheme for a check is to bore a small gimlet hole through the cover of the cigar box and stick a match through this and run it between the spokes of one of the clock wheels so as to prevent it from turning. Then when you have wound up the spring and are ready to start the merry-go-round, all you have to do is to pull out the match.

The model of this toy which the author has before him runs for five minutes with one winding, and any boy can make one which will run as well if he follows the directions given and uses a reasonable amount of carefulness in the work.

Other Animals than horses may be used if you wish to follow the arrangement of some of the latest merry-go-rounds, and pictures of these may be found among the colored cut-outs sold in the stationery stores, or if you can draw well, you may copy them from books and magazines. Great fun may be had by changing the positions of the boy riders, making them ride backward part of the time and sometimes two and three boys on a horse.

Doubtless you have heard of the famous Ferris wheel, and a good many of you have ridden in the smaller wheels patterned after it, at the amusement parks, so you will be interested in making

A Miniature Ferris Wheel like the one shown in Fig. 255.

The Standard for supporting the wheel (Fig. 267) consists of two triangular supports, one with a spool hub fastened to its top for the axle of the wheel to run through and the other with the cigar box inclosing the clockwork fastened to it. Figures 268, 269, and 270 show the construction of these supports. Cut strips P and Q 12 inches long and R 10 inches long, and trim off the upper ends of P and Q, so when they are nailed together, the lower ends will be 8 inches apart; nail strip R to the lower ends of P and Q (Fig. 268). To fasten the spool hub to its support, smear one side of a piece of tape with glue and wind it several times around the spool (Fig. 269), then set the spool on top of the support and press the ends of the tape against the sides of strips P and Q (Fig. 270).

FIG. 267. — Standard for the Ferris Wheel.

The Clockwork Motor for the Ferris wheel is fastened to the cover of a cigar box just as that for the merry-

CLOCKWORK TOYS

go-round was fastened (Fig. 257), but the length of the box is cut down as much as the clockwork will allow to make the box as square and compact as possible.

It is very necessary to have the axle bearings exactly on a line in order to have the wheel run smoothly, so, in fastening the cigar box to its support, be sure that the center of the hole in spool *D* (Fig. 257) is on a level with the spool hub on the opposite support. Nail the supports to a 10-inch by 12-inch board, 8 inches apart, and fasten a cigar box between them for

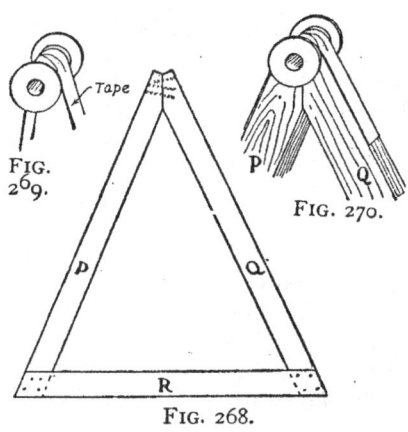

FIG. 268. — Make Two Supports like this for the Ferris Wheel Standard.

FIGS. 269 and 270. — How a Spool is fastened to the Top of the Support for a Hub.

The Station Platform (Fig. 267).

To make the Wheel, first lay out the rims upon a piece of heavy cardboard, using the radii shown in Fig. 271 for describing the circles, then lay the sheet of cardboard upon a board and

Cut out the Rims with a sharp knife, being careful not to run off of the pencil line. The

Hubs of the wheel are spools with six holes bored in them for the spokes to fit in (Fig. 274). Cut six

Spokes $5\frac{3}{4}$ inches long by $\frac{1}{8}$ inch thick for each hub, and cut a slot in one end of each for the cardboard rims to fit in (Figs. 272 and 275). Use a saw rather than a

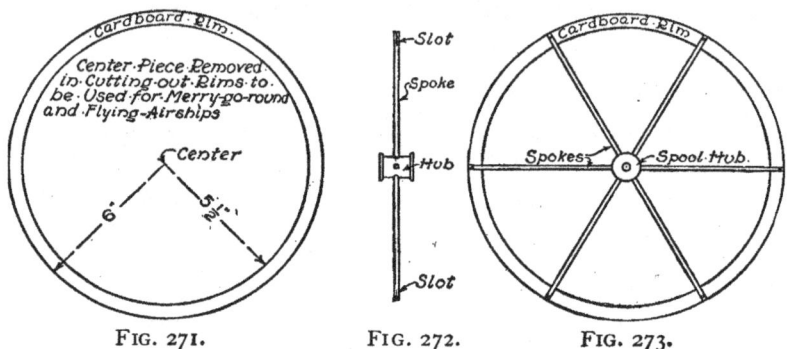

Cardboard Rim
Center Piece Removed in Cutting out Rims to be Used for Merry-go-round and Flying-Airships
Center
6"
5½"

FIG. 271.

Slot
Spoke
Hub
Slot

FIG. 272.

Cardboard Rim
Spokes
Spool Hub

FIG. 273.

FIG. 271. — How to lay out the Cardboard Rims of the Ferris Wheel.
FIG. 272. — The Spokes fitted into the Spool Hub.
FIG. 273. — The Rim slipped into the End of the Spokes.

knife in making the slots, for it will make a kerf of just the right width to receive the cardboard and will not be so apt to split the ends of the slender spokes. Whittle the hub ends of the spokes to fit the holes in the spool hubs (Figs. 272 and 275). In

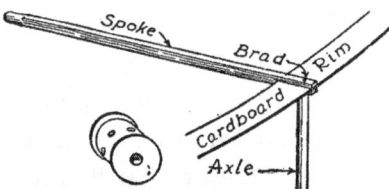

FIG. 274. — A Spool Hub for the Wheel.

Spoke
Brad
Rim
Cardboard
Axle

FIG. 275. — How the Spokes, Rims, and Axles are fastened Together.

Putting together the Spokes, Hubs, and Rims of the wheel, first stick three spokes in a hub and slip a rim into the slots in their ends, then stick the remaining spokes into the hub, one at a time, and spread the rim enough so it can be slipped into their slots (Fig. 273).

When the hubs, rims, and spokes have been assembled,

lay them aside and get some heavy wrapping-paper or thin cardboard out of which

To make the Cars. The pattern for the cars is shown in Fig. 276, and on it you will find all the dimensions

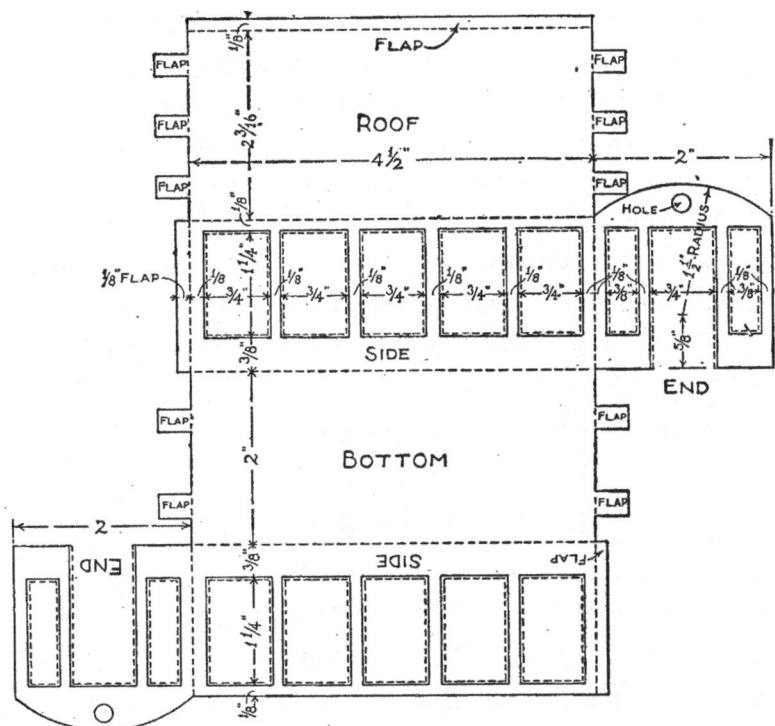

FIG. 276.—Pattern for the Ferris Wheel Cars.

necessary for laying it out to the proper size. It will be understood that the unfigured portions of the drawing are the same as those with dimensions marked upon them. The dotted lines at the door and window openings indicate where the cutting is to be done, while all other dotted lines indicate where the cardboard is to be *scored* and folded. Use a ruler in making the drawing of the car to get the lines straight, and when you have finished it, go over it carefully and compare it with the illustration to be sure it is correct, after which make a careful tracing of it, turn it over and transfer the drawing five times upon cardboard. These and your original drawing will give you the required number of cars. Cut out the openings with a sharp knife and then do the rest of the cutting with a pair of scissors; punch a $\frac{1}{4}$-inch hole in each end of each car with a lead-pencil (Fig. 276), being careful to get the holes exactly opposite.

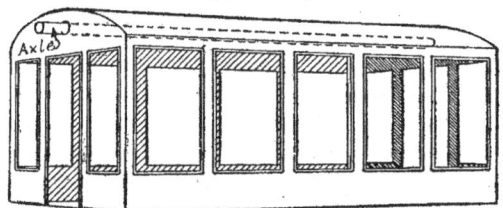

FIG. 277.— A Completed Car for the Ferris Wheel.

In folding and gluing the cars, slip the flaps inside and bend the roofs so they will follow the curve of the ends (Fig. 277).

When the cars have been completed, cut six sticks 5 inches long, whittle them down until they are about $\frac{1}{8}$ inch in diameter, and sandpaper them until they are perfectly round and smooth. These sticks connect the rims of the wheel and form

The Axles from which the cars are hung (Fig. 277). Great care must be used in fastening them between the rims, for they are easily split, and the best way to do is

CLOCKWORK TOYS

to start a hole first in the ends of each axle with an awl, or by driving a brad part way in and then withdrawing it; then drive a brad through each spoke of one rim into an axle (Fig. 275); slip the other ends of the axles through the holes in the ends of the cars (Fig. 277), and nail the spokes of the other rim to them.

To mount the Wheel upon its standard, whittle an axle $8\frac{1}{2}$ inches long to fit the hubs, then hold the wheel between the two uprights, with the hubs on a line with the spool bearings and run the axle through the holes (Fig. 255).

Build Steps at each end of the platform out of heavy writing-paper or light cardboard. Fold the paper or cardboard back and forth, making pleats about $\frac{1}{4}$ inch wide, for the steps, and after gluing it in place, cut out the *balustrades* and glue them to the edges of the steps. Make the top step low enough so there will be about $\frac{1}{4}$-inch clearance between it and the bottom of the cars (Fig. 255).

After you have made a final inspection to see that everything has been put together properly, your toy will be ready for operation, and I am sure that when you set the clockwork machinery in motion, and the little wheel begins to revolve slowly with each little car balancing upon its axle, you will agree that you have constructed a very interesting toy.

The "Flying Airships" is a riding device consisting of a number of cars suspended by steel cables from large arms pivoted to the top of a tower. When the machinery is started, the arms begin to revolve slowly, and the motion produced causes the cars to swing out away from the center. As the speed of the arms increases, the cars swing out farther and farther, until when the highest speed has been reached the cables by which the cars are suspended have taken an oblique position and raised the cars some distance above the ground; then the speed of the engine is gradually diminished, and the cars finally regain their former position. This piece of apparatus is also known as an *aërostat*.

You will find the miniature flying airships (Fig. 256) easy to construct after making a merry-go-round or Ferris wheel, as many of its details are identical with those of the other toys.

The Standard for the toy is made similar to the one for the merry-go-round (Fig. 253), except that the top board is omitted and a circular piece of cardboard of the size of the disks removed in cutting out the rims of the Ferris wheel is substituted in its place. Cut a hole through the exact center of the piece large enough so it will fit over spool D (Fig. 254).

Cut a Mast about 14 inches long and of the diameter of the hole in the spool and stick it into spool D; then 3 inches below the top of the mast fasten a spool with four horizontal arms 6 inches long glued into holes bored in it. Fasten a cross-piece $4\frac{1}{2}$ inches long to the end of each arm with brads, and from these suspend

Cars made similar to those of the Ferris wheel with cords. Set a small flag in a hole bored in the top of the mast and then run cords from the top of the mast out to the ends of the arm pieces.

With this toy the cars cannot be swung out obliquely as on the large flying airships except by

Increasing the Speed of the Clockwork. This can be accomplished by removing one or two of the wheels of the clockwork, but it is not advisable to take out more than one wheel in addition to those removed for the merry-go-round (Fig. 257) because the mainspring would require rewinding too often to make the toy enjoyable.

CHAPTER XIII
BRASS CRAFT

OF the modern handicrafts requiring materials other than wood, those in which metal is used are probably the most interesting to boys, for metal is one of their principal materials for all work of an electrical or mechanical nature; and as metal handicrafts require tools such as most boys are accustomed to handle, the work is probably better suited to boys than to girls.

Brass-piercing is an interesting metal craft, the material is inexpensive, and the work is simple. Following are

The Tools and Materials Required: —

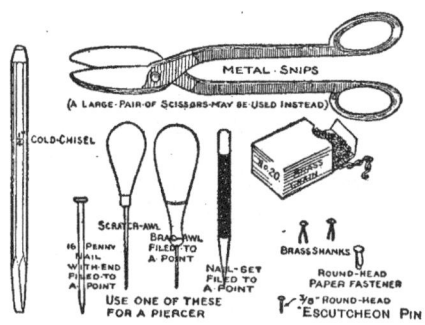

Fig. 278. — Some of the Tools and Materials Required.

Hammer
Piercing Tool (see Fig. 278)
$\frac{1}{4}''$ Cold-chisel (see Fig. 278)
Flat or Half-round Metal-file (see Fig. 33, page 25)
Board (Whitewood or Basswood) $\frac{1}{2}'' \times 12'' \times 20''$
Pencil, Eraser, and Compass
Drawing-paper and Carbon Paper
No. 30 Gauge Sheet Brass for small work

BRASS CRAFT 207

No. 28 Gauge Sheet Brass for large work
6-oz. Tacks
$\frac{3}{8}''$ Round-head Escutcheon Pins (Fig. 278)
Brass Shanks or Paper Fasteners (Fig. 278)
$\frac{1}{4}''$ Brass Screw-eyes
Box of No. 20 Brass Chain (or Bead Fringe) (Fig. 278)
Metal Polish and Lacquer

To make easy the work of laying out designs for the articles illustrated in this chapter, suitable designs are shown at a small scale. Those which are more or less elaborate may be drawn full size by the process of

Enlarging by Squares, which is easy to carry out. Each of the small squares drawn across these designs represents a space on the full-size pattern $\frac{1}{2}$ inch square (Fig. 281). The first thing to do is to lay out, full size, the outlines and marginal lines of the piece of brass required for the article upon a piece of drawing-paper, using the dimensions given upon the diagram. Take one side of the 12-by-20-inch board for a drawing-board and use the other side to do the piercing on; tack the paper to the board. Then when you have carefully checked up the measurements with those upon the diagram, lay off the squares upon it, making each of those shown $\frac{1}{2}$ inch each way; then number one end of the horizontal lines and letter one end of the vertical lines as shown, and it will be a simple matter to locate each portion of the design upon your pattern just where it is shown in the book, for, by the lettering and numbering, corresponding squares can be located quickly. When the design has been drawn out full size, it is a simple matter to trace off the entire pattern — outline and design — upon a piece of brass, by placing a piece of carbon paper between the drawing-paper and the brass and then carefully tracing over the lines with a sharp pencil. Carbon paper such as stenographers use upon their typewriters for making duplicate copies of typewritten matter may be used. Where two sides of a design are similar (Fig. 285), enlarge one half, make a tracing of it, reverse the tracing, and trace it off upon the opposite side of the *center-line;* if the design is repeated several times, lay it out upon one section and then trace it off upon the other sections. By doing this it is easier to get all portions alike. Leave a margin of about $\frac{1}{4}$ inch around the edges of the outline to allow for *turning in.* Be sure not to cut out the piece from the sheet until after you have pierced the design, except in cases where the brass is to be mounted upon wood, for the square piece will be easier to hold to the board during this operation.

When ready

To pierce a Design, first follow the outlines of the entire design and pierce a continuous row of small holes along them, placing the holes as close together as possible and making them of equal size; then fill in a series of coarser holes in the spaces between these rows of holes to form a background to the design. As the piercing tool is tapered to a point, the size of the hole is, of course, determined by the depth to which it is driven through the brass. Drive the tool with a hammer. The background holes should not be spaced off in even rows nor in the form of a pattern, for the effect would be such as to detract from the design, but they should be scattered over the field in such a way that the spaces between will be about equal; this will give the background an even tone.

Wire brushes are sold for

Polishing the Brass, but you will find that any sort of metal polish or scouring powder will answer the purpose very well. Of course the brass will tarnish and must be polished from time to time to keep it bright, unless some finish is put upon it. Brass lacquers — transparent or in color — may be purchased at the art stores, but you will find

A Home-made Antique Green Lacquer of the following formula very pretty and a simple solution to make up: —

    1 part ammonia muriate
    1 part ammonia carbonate
    12 parts cold water

The metal should be cleaned thoroughly and the solution should be applied with a brush. Several applications of the lacquer will improve the depth of the finish.

With these general instructions in mind, you can begin work upon some of the simpler articles illustrated in this chapter.

A Tea-pot Stand such as is shown in Fig. 279 consists

of a circular wood disk upon which a piece of perforated brass is mounted. Use a piece of $\frac{1}{2}$-inch whitewood or basswood for the disk. Make it $5\frac{13}{16}$ inches in diameter, cut it out with a compass-saw or other fine saw, and smooth the edges with a wood-file or chisel; then sandpaper it. Cut a strip of brass of the proper width and length to form a metal band for the edge of the base, and tack it to the edge with *escutcheon pins* (Fig. 278), spacing them about $\frac{3}{4}$ inch apart.

SECTION
DRIVE 3 RUG-TACKS INTO BOTTOM FOR FEET

FIG. 280.

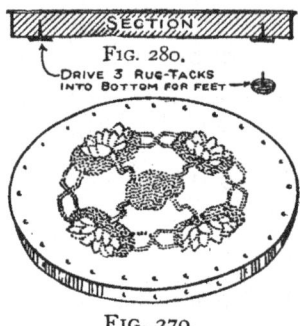

FIG. 279.

FIG. 279. — A Tea-pot Stand.
FIG. 280. — Section through Stand.

The pattern for the top brass covering is shown in Fig. 281. After the design has been laid out full size upon brass, the piece should be cut out before the perforating is done and fastened to the base with escutcheon pins. Describe a circle about $\frac{3}{16}$ inch inside of the edge of the brass, locate positions for the pins around this, $\frac{3}{4}$ inch apart, and punch the holes at these points with the piercer before driving the

A B C D E F G H I J K L M
1 2 3 4 5 6 7 8 9 10 11 12 13
3" RADIUS

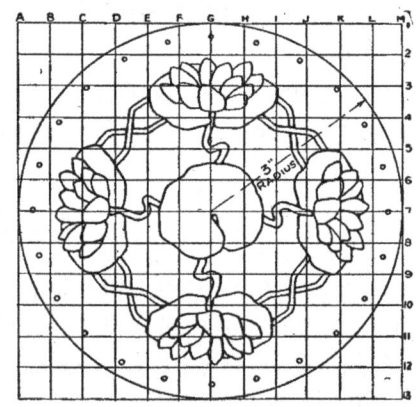

FIG. 281. — Pattern for Top of Tea-pot Stand and Calendar Board.

(On the full-size pattern make each of the small squares shown above $\frac{1}{2}$ inch square, to guide you in enlarging the design.)

BRASS CRAFT

pins into the base. The edge of the brass top will project about $\frac{1}{16}$ inch over the brass band (Fig. 280). Drive three rug tacks into the base, as shown, for feet.

A Calendar Board like the one shown in Fig. 282 will make a pretty Christmas or New Year's gift. Its construction is similar to that of the tea-pot stand, with the omission of the feet and the addition of a brass screw-eye screwed into the top by which to hang it up. A small calendar can usually be bought at a stationery store, and this should be attached to the exact center of the board by means of two escutcheon pins driven through the corners of the top margin.

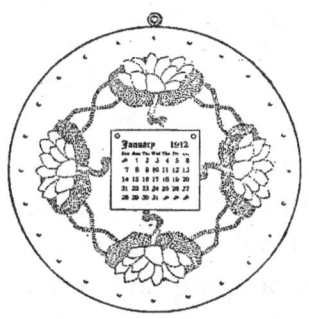

FIG. 282. — A Calendar Board.

The Pen Tray illustrated in Fig. 283 requires a bottom block of the size shown in Fig. 284. After preparing

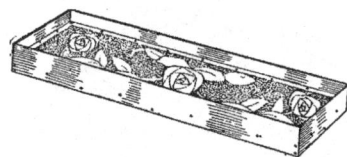

FIG. 283. — A Pen Tray.

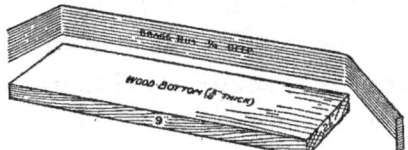

FIG. 284. — Wood Bottom and Brass Rim for the Pen Tray.

this, cut a piece of brass of the exact width and length of the block and fasten it to the top with escutcheon pins, spacing the pins about as shown in Fig. 283. Then enlarge the design shown in Fig. 285, trace it off upon the brass, and perforate it. After this has been done, cut a strip of brass ¾ inch wide, bend it to fit around the edge of the bottom block, as shown in Fig. 284, and tack it to the edge to form a rim to the tray.

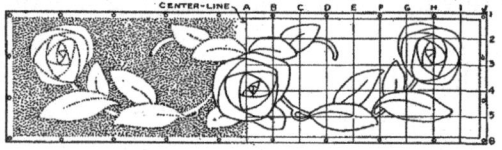

FIG. 285.— Design for Bottom of Pen Tray.
(Enlarge the right half and reverse it for the left half.)

The ends of the strip should be made to lap at one corner as in Fig. 283. File off the top edge of the rim smooth and glue a piece of felt to the bottom of the tray to prevent it from scratching any surface upon which it is placed.

Lamp and candle shades are among the most popular pierced brass articles. Fig. 286 shows

A Lamp-shade of six sides, and Fig. 287 how the sides appear when laid out on a sheet of brass. The design is shown upon two of the panels, in the pattern: on one as it will appear when the background is perforated, and on the other with the squares marked off upon it to help you in enlarging it. After laying

FIG. 286.— A Lamp-shade of Six Sides.
(See Fig. 142, Chapter VI.)

out the design full size, trace it off upon each of the panels. The piece should be cut out, after the perforating has been completed, and folded along the dotted lines. Bend the brass over the sharp edge of your board. The flaps along the top and bottom edges should be turned in and

TURN IN
TURN IN
BEND IN
TURN IN

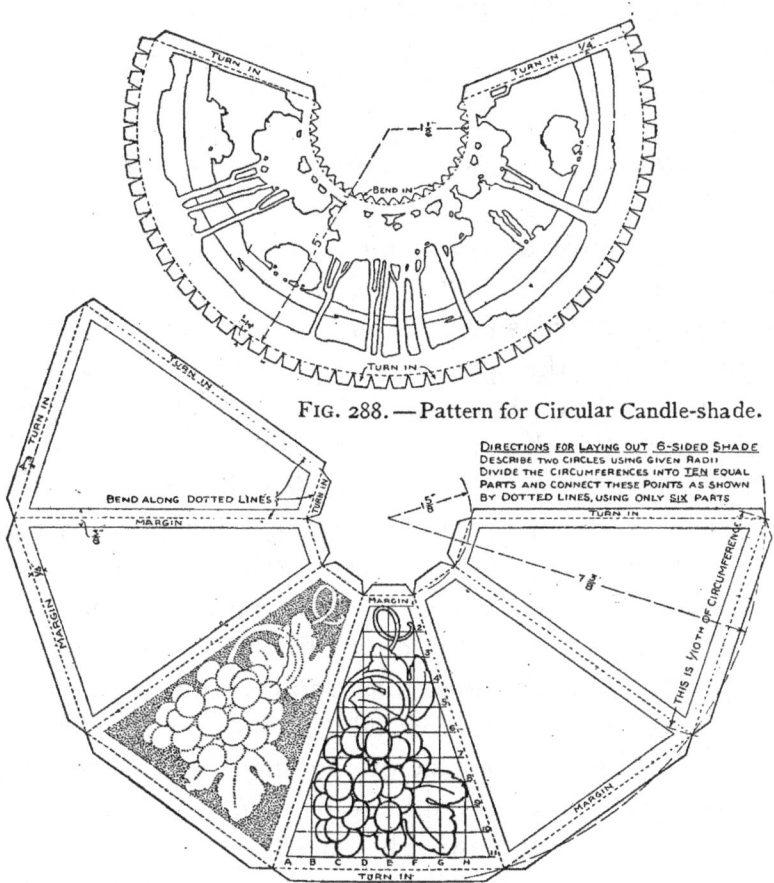

FIG. 288.—Pattern for Circular Candle-shade.

DIRECTIONS FOR LAYING OUT 6-SIDED SHADE
DESCRIBE TWO CIRCLES USING GIVEN RADII
DIVIDE THE CIRCUMFERENCES INTO TEN EQUAL
PARTS AND CONNECT THESE POINTS AS SHOWN
BY DOTTED LINES, USING ONLY SIX PARTS
TURN IN
BEND ALONG DOTTED LINES
MARGIN
THIS IS 1/10TH OF CIRCUMFERENCE
A B C D E F G H

FIG. 287.—Pattern for Lamp-shade of Six Sides.

hammered flat against the sides of the shade, and the end edges should also be turned in and one lapped over the other. Fasten the end edges with brass shanks, paper fasteners, or escutcheon pins (Fig. 278), bending the ends over upon the inside. If you use the pins, cut them off short and clinch them upon the inside by placing them on the head of a hatchet and hammering the heads with a hammer.

Chain Fringe is cheaper and more interesting to put on than the bead fringe frequently used upon brass shades. Figure 278 shows the size which should be bought. Cut this up into 3-inch lengths and fasten the pieces to the lower edge of the shade about $\frac{3}{16}$ inch from center to center, hooking the opened link on the end of each piece of chain through a hole punched through the brass, and then pinching it closed.

The Candle-shade on the candle-stick in Fig. 291 should be laid out by the pattern in Fig. 288. As the landscape design is very simple, it will not be necessary to enlarge it by squares. After piercing and cutting out the piece of brass, snip the top and bottom edges, cutting out small triangular pieces as shown, and then bend over the little flaps thus formed and hammer them down flat against the inside face of the shade. The edge of one end of the piece should also be turned in (see dotted line on pattern), and this should either be lapped over the other edge and the two fastened as described for the other shade, or the other edge should be folded out and one edge hooked into the other as the edges of a tin can are joined, and the two hammered down so as to make a neat edge. Attach chain fringe to the rim as described for the other shade.

Figures 289 and 290 show two forms of **Shade Holders**, the former for an electric lamp and the latter for a candle. These can be bought where light-fixtures are sold and cost about 10 cents apiece.

The Candle-stick shown in Fig. 291 is easy to make, and when the wood is carefully covered with the brass, makes a very neat-appearing article.

FIG. 289.

FIG. 290.

FIG. 289.—Electric Lamp-shade Holder.

FIG. 290. — Candle-shade Holder.

Figure 292 shows the sizes of the pieces of brass, together with the designs which are to be perforated upon them. First prepare the wood blocks for the base, upright, and top pieces, making them $\frac{1}{16}$ inch less than the dimensions given upon the patterns, to allow for the thickness of the brass. Before fastening the blocks together, prepare the brass pieces, nail them in place, lay out the designs, and perforate them. The sides should be made in one

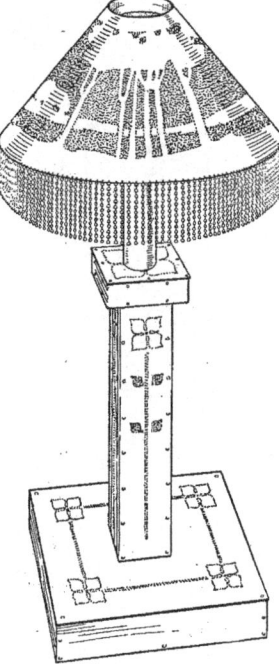

FIG. 291.— A Brass Candle-stick with Circular Shade.

piece and be bent around the corners. The upper covering of the top and base pieces should project about $\frac{1}{16}$ inch

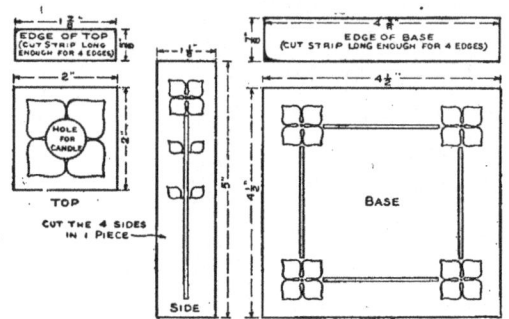

FIG. 292. — Patterns for Brass Pieces of the Candle-stick.

(Cut the *wood blocks* $\frac{1}{16}$ inch less than the above dimensions to allow for the thickness of the brass.)

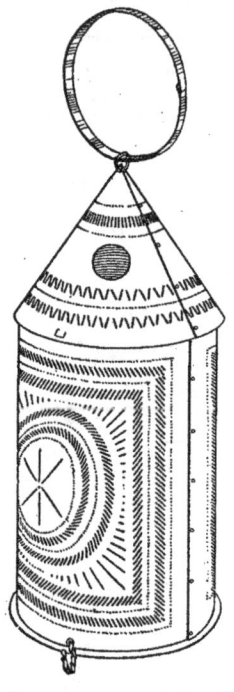

as shown in Fig. 291. After nailing the blocks together, glue a strip of felt to the bottom of the base piece.

The "Paul Revere" Lantern shown in Fig. 293 differs from the lanterns used in the colonial times only in this respect — it is lighted by removing the bottom instead of through a door-

FIG. 293. — A "Paul Revere" Lantern.

way in the side. The door has been omitted to make the construction simpler; however, if you wish to make an exact copy, you may make a door and hinge it in place with pieces of wire. For this lantern the proper size for an opening would be $3\frac{1}{2}$ by $6\frac{1}{2}$ inches.

The right-hand portion of the patterns for the side

BRASS CRAFT 217

and top pieces (Figs. 296 and 297) shows the main measurements for the design, and at the left the design is shown perforated. After laying out lines to the measurements given, divide up the spaces between into the number of spaces shown. The small holes of the design are made with a piercer, and the slits are cut with a cold-chisel (Fig. 278). Space the perforations as shown, and be careful to keep the ends of the slits within the guide-lines

 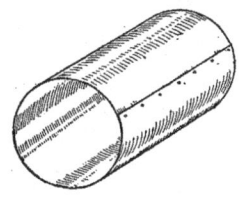

FIG. 295. — The Lantern Bottom.   FIG. 294. — The Lantern Sides.

The tips on the upper edge of the side piece slip through the slots cut in the top piece (Figs. 296 and 297), and hold the top to the sides when bent over, while the two holes near the bottom edge are made to receive the pins which hold the bottom in place (Figs. 293, 294, and 295).

Fasten the ends of the side piece together with brass shanks (Fig. 294), then cut a circular block of wood to fit in the bottom end of this cylinder (Fig. 295), and fasten to it a circular piece of brass of a large enough diameter to make a $\frac{1}{4}$-inch projection beyond the sides of the lantern. Make a candle-holder out of a strip of brass, as shown in Fig. 295, and tack this to the base block. The pins for holding the bottom in the lantern are made out of two brass screw-eyes, by filing off the threads, and these are held to the bottom with short pieces of brass chain to keep them from being lost when the bottom is removed for lighting the candle. Before fastening the top to the sides

FIG. 297.

FIG. 298.

LAP
VENT
VENT
VENT
BRASS STRIP FOR LANTERN RING
LAP

FIG. 296.

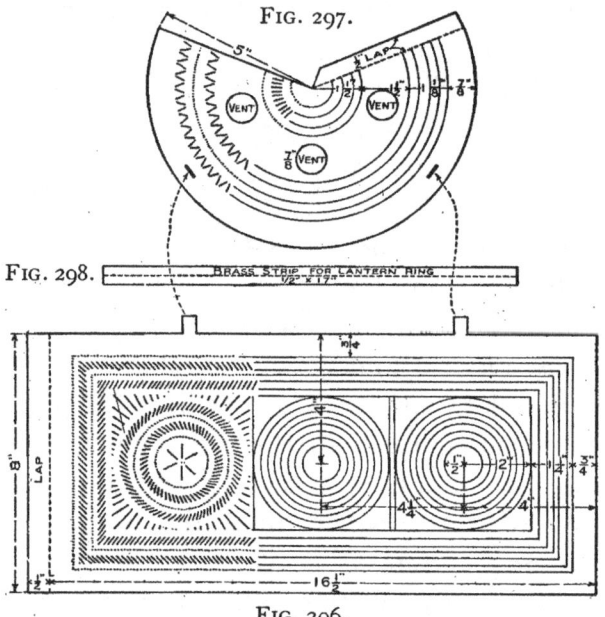

FIG. 296. — Pattern of Lantern Sides.
FIG. 297. — Pattern of Lantern Top.
FIG. 298. — Brass Strip for Lantern Ring.

prepare the lantern ring. Cut a strip of brass of the size shown in Fig. 298, bend it over along the center to make it stiff, and then bend it into a ring and clinch the ends together like the sides of a tin can are clinched. Wire the ring to the peak as shown in Fig. 293.

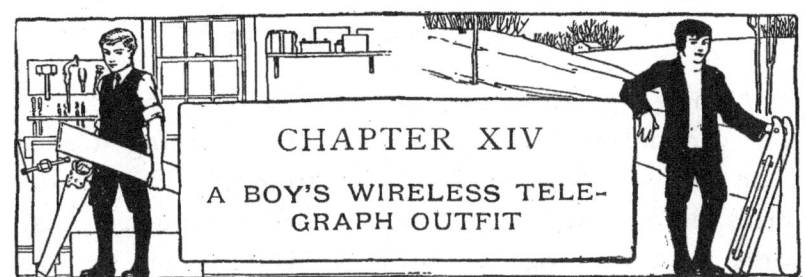

CHAPTER XIV

A BOY'S WIRELESS TELEGRAPH OUTFIT

MARCONI's experiments from 1895 to 1899 to devise instruments for the transmitting and recording of messages without the use of wires, resulted in a number of successes which astonished the scientific world, but when he so perfected the apparatus that he was enabled on December 12, 1901, to transmit across the Atlantic Ocean from Newfoundland to England, this crowning success was accepted by one and all as one of the greatest achievements of modern times.

Though wireless telegraphy was looked upon by many as depending upon a mysterious phenomena, far too deep for the amateur to understand, it was not long after articles treating at length upon the subject began to appear in the newspapers and technical journals that boys started to study into it. Soon after the establishment of a wireless station at the Charlestown Navy Yard, the operators became aware one day that somebody was tampering with their messages, for they began to pick up remarks, which were of a decidedly unofficial character. The interference became very annoying, and it was a number of days before the source could be located; then a crudely arranged mast upon a shed roof, a few squares from the Navy Yard, furnished a clew and, as might naturally be expected, wires from the top of the mast were found to lead down into the shed where it was discovered that two boys had fitted up a home electrical shop and installed a complete sending and receiving apparatus. The investigators were of course greatly surprised to find that they had been baffled by *mere boys*, but you can well imagine their chagrin when, upon examining the equipment, they found that it was mostly home-made and that though part of it was constructed out of nothing more or less than junk, it was serving the purpose of the government's complicated and costly apparatus.

This just goes to show, boys, that if you can't make something out of nothing, you can often come pretty close to it, and that with the things you can ordinarily find about the house, the shed, and in the junk dealers' stores you can construct all sorts of things, many of which your father and men manufacturing those very things would not believe could be made except with the materials customarily used. I do not mean to convey the impression by this that you can construct a wireless outfit out of such stuff alone; but it can be used to advantage to help out.

Other boys naturally followed in the footsteps of

the pioneer boy experimenters in making wireless outfits, and it has been estimated that, at the present time, there are in the neighborhood of five thousand amateur stations in the country, to say nothing of countless thousands of boy enthusiasts who would own outfits if they but knew what is required, what parts they can make, how to do the work, and how to go about installing the outfit. Everywhere you go, now, you are likely to see the earmarks of the amateur station in the masts set up on the housetops, used to support the *aerials*. In Chicago there are nearly three hundred of these stations, and in some parts of the city where the enthusiasm runs high you can count a score or more of poles within the range of the eye.

To show you

What Some Boys have accomplished let me quote from two of their letters. Richard Cobb, who lives in Cambridge, Massachusetts, writes the following in a letter published in the *Boston Herald*: —

"I have erected at my house a simple wireless telegraph station. I receive all the government stations in the district. At 10 o'clock each night I hear the wireless telegraph station Wellfleet, and amateur stations between times. Once in a while I hear the two revenue cutters, the *Gresham* and *Acushnet*, and once in a while I hear Brant Rock, which is very high-pitched and sends D. When sending a message it repeats each word.

"I suppose each boy that has a receiving set receives the time at 12 o'clock each day. I receive the time each day except Sundays. It comes in very loud. I set my watch by it each day. My call is I L in the Continental and I X in the Morse code. My set comprises a silicon detector, fixed condenser, double-slide tuning-coil, one pair of 500-ohm receivers, 101 feet antennæ and a gas pipe for a ground. I have very good results."

The making of the same forms of instruments as Richard mentions, with the exception of the receivers, is described in this chapter. In the same paper, Fulton Rindge, also of Cambridge, says: —

"I began to study wireless telegraphy about two years ago, just before the *Republic* sent out that famous C Q D. My first set was only for receiving and a very simple one. It consisted of a poorly made tuning-coil, a silicon detector and a telephone receiver. My second set was a good deal better, and I had a pair of receivers. I have had quite a number of sets, but the one I have now I think is pretty good.

"All my instruments are home-made. I can send about 10 miles."

Most of the boys are highly successful with their home stations, and with simple apparatus are able to receive everything within a radius of 100 miles and to transmit a distance of several miles. Any boy is free to receive government and commercial station messages, for this does not cause any disturbance, but *he must not interfere with such messages*, for such interference has made much trouble and resulted in the enactment of a law forbidding it under a severe penalty.

The Chicago amateurs have a society known as **The Chicago Wireless Club**, and under the guidance of their president, Mr. Royal C. Dickson, a pioneer amateur wireless experimenter and now an expert for one of the large commercial companies, they are making remarkable progress. At the regular meetings lectures upon the subject are given, and all details about which any of the members have had difficulty in understanding are clearly explained. Each member is furnished with a large *code card*, upon which the Morse and Continental codes are printed in large type, and a sheet containing a *call list* of all the members; and so that he may be strictly up-to-date he is supplied with *aërogram blanks* (Fig. 299) and envelopes.

FIG. 299. — Form of Aërogram Blank used by the Boys of "The Chicago Wireless Club."

Some of the boys in one of the suburbs have opened up

Amateur Commercial Stations and transmit aërograms at the rate of ten words for 5 cents, which might be a good way of earning money if it were not for the almost universal installation of the telephone. Still, the novelty of sending an aërogram might make it possible to obtain enough business to make such a venture pay.

Mr. Dickson, who, by the way, was a schoolmate of the author, probably knows better than any one else about the difficulties which an amateur experiences in installing a wireless outfit, and, realizing that he could give you boys the most practical suggestions, the author succeeded in getting him to consent to work up and describe for you the material presented in this chapter. The illustrations have been made directly from the models furnished by him, and some of these models, boys, have been tested out on one of the large lake boats. Many of the published articles on wireless outfits describe parts of the equipment which are very difficult for a boy to make, — such as the construction of an induction-coil, — and a boy undertaking the work is often discouraged before it is more than half completed, or finds after he has finished it that it will not operate. Mr. Dickson's suggestions will be found easy to carry out, and the apparatus will work splendidly.

The illustrations show, besides the pieces which you can make, the best forms of the parts which must be purchased.

Before undertaking the construction and installation of the wireless instruments, you should know something about

The Fundamental Principles of Wireless Telegraphy. Throughout all space a substance is supposed to exist, though nothing definite is known about it, and this substance, which is colorless, odorless, and without weight, and called *ether*, is supposed to have remarkable qualities for transmitting vibrations through space. You boys have noticed how when a moving boat disturbs the sur-

FIG. 300. — A Good Way to arrange the Wireless Instruments upon a Table in your Room. (See Wiring Diagram, Fig. 325.)

face of a body of water, the disturbance is communicated in the form of waves to the surrounding water, and that all other craft within range of these waves start to bob up and down as soon as they are reached. Now, just for example, let us imagine that a body of water is the ether I have been telling you about, that there are a number of yachts, motor boats, and other craft at anchor, and that each of these is the aërial of a wireless telegraph station. Then let us suppose that one of the boats in the midst of the others weighs anchor and gets under way, and that the resulting action upon the water represents the transmitting of a message through the ether, and each wave which rolls out from the wake of the passing boat represents a *dot* or *dash* of a message, and you will get a pretty good idea of how a wireless message travels; but the waves in the ether (they are known as *electromagnetic* or *Hertzian* waves) travel very rapidly, so rapidly, in fact, that they are recorded practically the instant that the electric discharges are made, no matter what length of space they have to travel through

Electricity is used by which to produce the waves in sending a wireless message, and in our small outfit this is obtained from batteries, the current from which is passed through an induction-coil to increase the *voltage* and then jumped across the space between the ends of two metal rods of a piece of apparatus known as a *spark-gap*, producing a spark whose duration determines the *dot* and *dash* (these are used in " wireless " just the same as in the codes of the ordinary telegraph). The current is then carried by the wires to the aërial wires and there discharged in all directions, in the form of long and short discharges. The earth has a great capacity for electricity, and electricity will run through anything connected to it that is of a proper conducting material. Therefore, when the waves produced by the discharges from an aërial spread out, all the aerials within their range which are *grounded* receive them just the same as the lightning-rod receives the lightning discharges, and the current runs down into the ground in the same way that a bolt of lightning runs down a lightning-rod into the ground. The long and short discharges are recorded by means of telephone receivers after they have been regulated by a number of pieces of apparatus, which will be taken up later.

The first thing to consider is

The Aërial or *antennæ*. The success of the whole undertaking rests so much upon this that it ought to be the best that can possibly be made. With a good aërial results can be secured even with inferior instruments, but the most excellent instruments will not respond when connected to a poor aerial. Two things should be figured upon, the height and the length. Each is important, and the longer and higher the aërial is, the better the results will be. It should be at least 30 feet high at one end and at least 50 feet long. It may be vertical, horizontal, or slanting, but usually the best results are obtained when it is supported horizontally or slanting between two supports (Fig. 301). A very satisfactory aërial is one which is 70 or 80 feet long and 50

FIG. 301. — The Length of the Aèrial Mast can be reduced by erecting it upon a Roof. Use Two Masts if One End cannot be supported as Above.

feet or more high. With such an aërial and the instruments described upon the following pages receiving can be accomplished within a radius of several hundred miles. Of course the dimensions of the aërial will necessarily depend upon the character of the place, and if the masts are erected upon the housetop or the roof of a shed, the height can be obtained with shorter material (Fig. 301).

The aërial should have not less than six strands of wire, and eight or ten are better, and these should be spaced 1 foot apart (Fig. 302). A six-strand aërial will require a *spreader* at each end 5 feet 6 inches long and an eight-strand aërial will require one 7 feet 6 inches

Screw-eye
Bamboo Fish-pole Spreader
Porcelain Cleats
Wire
These wires should be at least 50 feet long
And should be spaced 1 foot apart
Spreader
To Mast or Other Support
To Switch

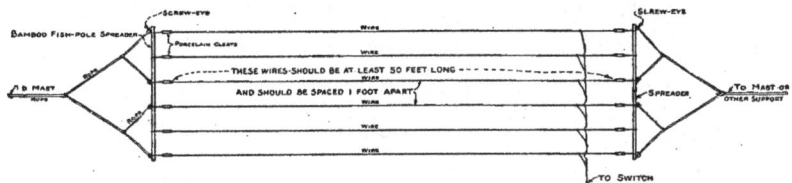

FIG. 302. — How to construct a Six-wire Aërial or *Antennæ*.

long. These can be made of any light, strong pieces of wood. The heavy end of a bamboo fish pole furnishes excellent material as it is very light as well as tough and strong. The wires should not be fastened directly to the spreader, but first to an insulator as shown in Fig. 302. Ordinary *porcelain cleats* (Fig. 303) make excellent insulators and cost less than 1 cent a piece, but if you cannot get these, necks of bottles may be used instead. After the wires have been fastened to the spreaders as shown in the diagram of Fig. 302, and ropes have been attached to screw-eyes screwed into the spreaders near the ends, rope stays must be run from these ropes back to the spreaders as shown in Fig. 302; otherwise, the spreaders will bow in at the center and cause the center wires to slacken.

FIG. 303. — Porcelain Cleat.

FIG. 304. — Battery Porcelain Insulator.

Any sort of wire, except iron or steel, may be used, and this may be bare or insulated. Bare wire is cheaper, of course, but sometimes the builder may have insulated wire on hand that can be used to advantage. The wire should not be smaller than No. 16 B. & S. gauge, and larger wire is better, No. 14 being standard for small outfits.

The wire leading in from the aërial must be insulated very carefully at the point where it enters the house, by passing it through a porcelain insulator. A battery insulator (Fig. 304) will serve the purpose. Figure 300 shows how a hole may be bored through the top rail of the upper window sash large enough to receive the insulator. This wire must be supported on insulators wherever support is necessary, all the way from the aërial to the instruments.

The Masts which support the aërial should be equipped with pulleys, like rigging a flagpole, so that the aerial may be hoisted or lowered at any time for repairs. Clothes-line pulleys such as are shown in Fig. 208 (page 171) and a stout hemp clothes-line may be used for the rigging. The poles must, of course, be braced very strongly with wire stays (Fig. 301), and it is a good idea to set in *turnbuckles* (see *H* and *I*, Fig. 212, page 174) so that the stays may be kept taut. If one end of the aërial can be run down to the house and fastened to the window-frame, as in Fig. 301, of course only one mast will be necessary.

Grounding the Aërial. When not in use, the aërial should be disconnected from the instruments, and be connected to the *ground wire*, as a precaution against lightning. The ground wire is fastened to a water-pipe or to a metal rod driven 6 feet or more into the ground, or in one of the other ways described below. A good ground connection is one of the essentials of a wireless outfit. In cities a water-pipe makes an excellent ground, but where none of these are installed, other means must be adopted. A pump with a pipe extending down to a deep well will be satisfactory, or a metal plate placed in any stream or lake and connected to the instruments will work very well. If none of these are available, connection must be established by digging down to moist earth, embedding a sheet of metal of 10 square feet or more of surface, and then pouring several bucketfuls of brine upon it before replacing the earth dug from the hole. The buried plate may be of any metal except iron or steel.

A wire should extend from the switch of the instruments to the *ground* wire (Fig. 325).

Instead of removing the aërial wire from the instruments after use, and connecting it to the *ground* wire, a handier scheme is to get a *double-throw, single-pole knife switch* and connect it between the aërial and the *double-throw, double-pole knife switch* shown in Figs. 325 and 331. This switch has three connections instead of the six on the *double-throw, double-pole switch*, and the aërial is connected at the center, the ground at one end, and the wire from the aërial connection on the switch shown in Fig. 325 to the other end.

As many boys are satisfied with a receiving set only, this will be described first.

A Good Receiving Outfit consists of one or a pair of *telephone receivers*, *detector*, *tuning-coil*, and *condenser*, to which a *potentiometer* and a *dry battery* and a second *condenser* must be added when a detector of the microphone type is used. Of these

The Telephone Receivers must be purchased; the remaining instruments can be made by any boy. The cheapest good telephone receivers, consisting of two receivers mounted on a head-band with a double connecting cord (Fig. 305) cost about $4, while a single receiver without a head-band (Fig. 306) can be bought for about $2. When buying a single receiver, take care to get one that is a part of a double set, so that you may add the other parts as you can afford them, and thus make up a complete set without having any unused parts left over. The ordinary receiver such as is used on telephones is not at all sensitive enough. The receiver should be one especially made for "wireless" and should have *1000 ohms resistance* (see *Ohm*, on page 252). An ordinary receiver may be used until a "wireless" one can be

TO TUNING-COIL-SLIDER
TO DETECTOR OR TO BATTERY AND POTENTIOMETER

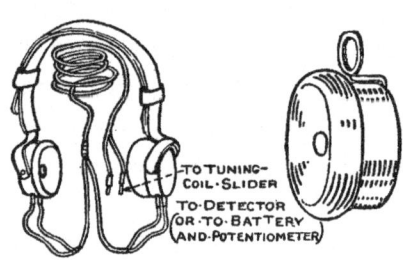

FIG. 305. — A Good Pair of Telephone Receivers with Head-band and Cord.

FIG. 306. — A Single Receiver.

A BOY'S WIRELESS TELEGRAPH OUTFIT 233

obtained, and interesting results can be secured with it, but as so much depends on a good receiver, most experimenters have a pair and pride themselves on possessing a very sensitive set.

There are a great many types of

Detectors, some of which require a battery in connection, while others work better without. The detector is necessary to change the "wireless" waves into such form that will enable the telephone receivers to render them audible, so that each wave will sound like a buzz and be distinguished easily.

The very best detector is the *silicon* type, but as silicon can be obtained only at certain supply houses, and as the experimenter is usually anxious to proceed without delay, descriptions of some good detectors made of easily obtainable materials will be given first.

For making one form of

Microphone Detector, you will require two flat carbons from dry batteries, a wood base about $\frac{3}{8}$ inch by 3 inches by 4 inches, four binding-posts (these may be taken from carbons of old dry batteries), some strips of brass, copper, or tin, a needle, and a paper fastener, or other small piece of metal, for a weight.

Figure 307 shows the completed detector and Fig. 308 how the pieces of carbon should be cut from the battery carbons, how their ends should be tapered to a sharp edge with a file, and how the brass, copper, or tin strips should be cut and bent. Cut the carbon pieces $1\frac{1}{4}$ inches high and the brass pieces $2\frac{1}{4}$ inches long by the width of the carbons. Cut the projecting tips shown on the top edge of the brass pieces, as a means of preventing the needle which spans the space between the carbons from being knocked off,

FILE END TO A SHARP EDGE THUS
BREAK OR SAW OFF ABOUT HERE
PAPER-FASTENER
NEEDLE
TO POTENTIOMETER-SLIDER ALSO TO CONDENSER NO 2
CARBON FROM OLD DRY BATTERY
FIG. 308
NEEDLE
CARBON
WASHER
NUT
BRASS PIECE
SCREW
BINDING POST
FIG. 307.
TO TUNING-COIL SLIDER ALSO TO TELEPHONE-RECEIVERS
WOOD BASE
SECTION

FIG. 309.

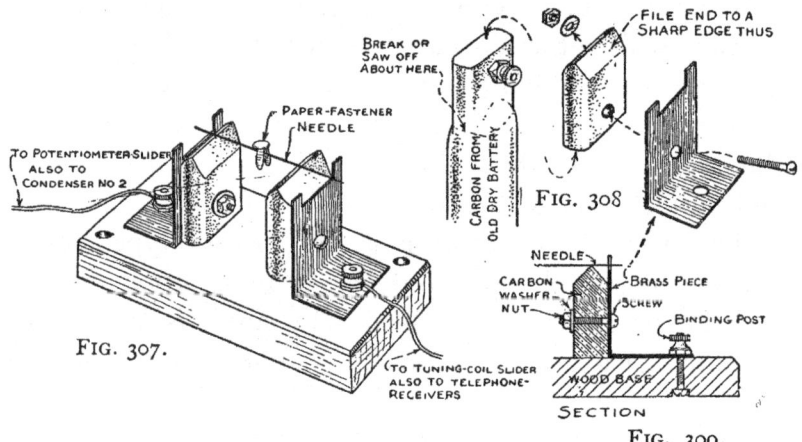

FIG. 307. — A Home-made Microphone Detector. (See Fig. 326.)
FIG. 308. — How to prepare the Carbon and Brass Pieces.
FIG. 309. — Section showing how to fasten the Pieces Together.

and make the edge between the tips lower than the carbon tops (see Fig. 309), as the needle must rest on the carbons only, and not touch the metal anywhere. Punch holes through the brass pieces in the proper places for connecting them to the carbon pieces, and make others for connecting them to the base block. The carbons should be placed parallel and about 1 inch apart. The needle should be considerably longer

than the distance between its bearing points, and the paper fastener, or other metal weight, should be placed at the center to make it bear upon the carbons with the right amount of pressure. By varying the weight the most satisfactory adjustment can be found. In no case should the weight be heavy, for if it is, the detector will not operate at all. If you bend the needle slightly, it will be easier to keep it in position. The proper method of connecting the detector to the other instruments is shown in Figs. 307 and 326.

A Razor Blade Microphone Detector requires a base of the size specified for the other detector, two old blades from a safety razor, four binding-posts, two strips of

TO TUNING-COIL SLIDER,
ALSO TO TELEPHONE-
RECEIVERS
TO POTENTIOMETER SLIDER;
ALSO TO CONDENSER NO.2.
GRAPHITE FROM A NO.3 PENCIL

FIG. 310.

SAFETY-RAZOR BLADE

FIG. 311.

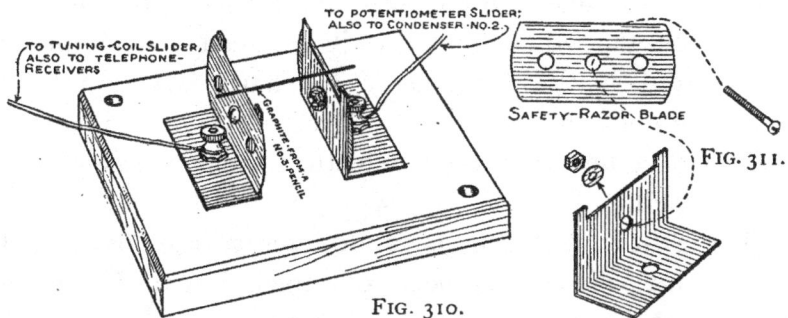

FIG. 310. — A Safety-razor Blade Microphone Detector. (See Fig. 326.)
FIG. 311. — How to prepare the Brass Pieces.

brass, copper, or tin, and a No. 3 lead-pencil. This detector is shown in Fig. 310.

The metal strips should be cut and bent as shown in Fig. 311, and holes should be punched through the upper part opposite the center hole in the razor blade and in the center of the lower part, as shown, for connecting the blades to the strips and the strips to the block by means of the binding-posts. When completed, this detector will resemble, somewhat, the one previously described, the razor blades being placed parallel and about 1 inch apart. The No. 3 pencil should be split open, the graphite removed, and a piece of it placed across the blades just as the needle was placed across the carbons in the other detector. The projecting tips should be cut on the brass pieces, as shown, to prevent the graphite from rolling off. If the pencil is soft, the detector will not *restore*, that is, after a "wireless" wave has actuated it, it must be jarred or tapped before it will be ready for another wave; and if the graphite is too hard, it will not be sensitive enough. The best degree of hardness is found in a No. 3 pencil. This detector is easily made and works well.

The Silicon Detector is undoubtedly the best, and when the silicon has been obtained, it can be made very quickly. Silicon is not expensive, a generous-sized lump usually being sold for 25 cents. Figure 312 shows a simple form of this detector.

The silicon should be held to a base block by a strip of brass having holes punched through it large enough for the bolt of a binding-post to stick through (Fig. 313), and a small piece of springy wire should be bent as shown in Fig. 314 and be secured at one end to the base block by a binding-post in such a way that the other end will press very lightly on the silicon, as shown in Fig. 312. In using this detector the end of the wire which rests on the silicon should be moved around until the most sensitive spot is found. The wire must never bear heavily on the silicon.

WIRE
FIG. 314.
TO TELEPHONE-RECEIVERS
SILICON
BRASS
FIG. 313.
BINDING-POSTS
TO TUNING-COIL SLIDER; ALSO TO SWITCH
FIG. 312.

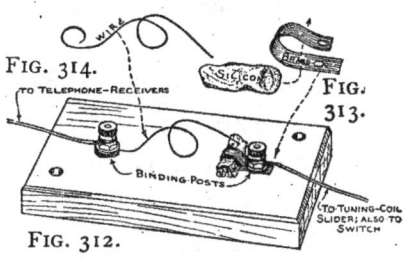

FIG. 312. — A Home-made Silicon Detector. (See Fig. 325.)
FIG. 313. — Strip of Brass with which Silicon is held to Binding-post.
FIG. 314. — Bend a Piece of Wire like this and connect as shown in Fig. 312.

Since no two wireless stations, probably, have exactly the same size aërials, or exactly the same adjustment of the sending instruments, it would be very difficult for different stations to communicate unless some arrangements were made to compensate for the differences in construction and adjustment. The simplest device for this *tuning*, as it is called, is

The Tuning-coil or *Tuner*. It is a very essential part of the outfit and should be constructed as soon as a detector has been completed.

The tuner consists of a single layer of wire wound upon a cylinder not less than 2½ inches in diameter. A rolling-pin is of just the right size, and the handles of the pin may be left on it to turn it by while winding on the wire, and sawed off afterwards. For a cylinder of this thickness, a length of 11 inches is necessary to secure a sufficient amount of wire. The tuner should be wound with copper wire not larger than No. 20 B. & S. gauge and not smaller than No. 24. Do not use cotton-covered wire or any other kind of insulated wire, if you can obtain that which is enameled. The latter is the very best, but as it can be obtained only from the larger supply houses, you may not be able to get it, in which case you will have to use bare wire.

Before winding, give the core two coats of shellac; this will form a yielding surface for the wire to cut into and will keep the wire in place even though the wood core shrinks after the coil has been completed. If you use enameled wire, simply fasten one end to the rolling-pin with a tack, near its end, and have an assistant turn the pin while you guide the wire on to it closely and neatly, until you reach the other end; then secure the wire with another tack and cut it off, leaving about 12 inches for connections. The bare wire will be a little more difficult to wind than the enameled wire, as it will be necessary to keep each turn from touching the adjacent turn by winding a thick thread, or thin cord, in between the wire as is shown in Fig. 316, winding this thread on at the same time that you wind the wire. Even though this requires some patience, it is much better than winding the tuner with the ordinary cloth insulated wire and then attempting to scrape bare the strip along which the sliders run. After the tuner has been wound, give it two more coats of shellac (this not only adds to its appearance, but helps to keep the winding in

FIG. 317.
ROLLING-PIN
FIG. 318.
BRASS
$\frac{1}{4}$" x $\frac{1}{4}$" x 12"
BRASS ROD
WIRE
THREAD
FIG. 319.
BINDING-POST
FIG. 316.
SLIDER
TO SWITCH (GROUND)
TO SWITCH (AERIAL)
TO RECEIVERS
FIG. 315.

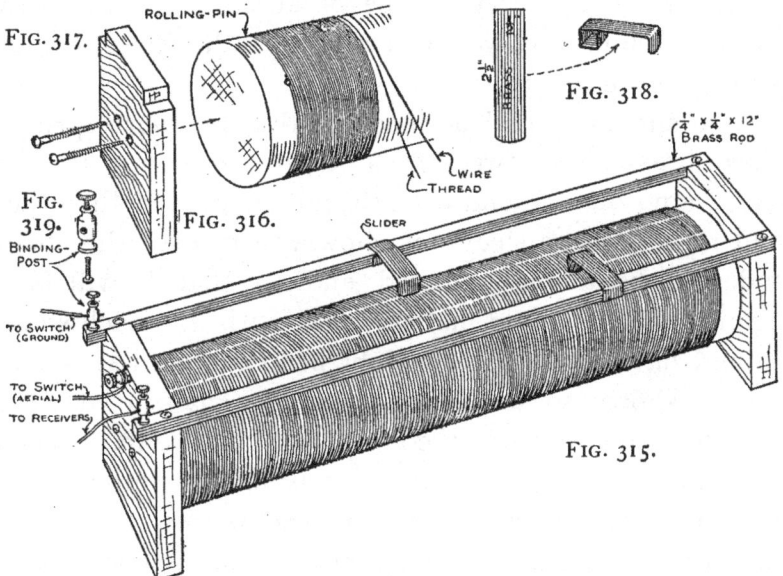

FIG. 315. — A Home-made Tuning-coil or Tuner.
FIG. 316. — How to wind Thread between the Turns of Wire if Bare Wire is used.
FIG. 317. — Prepare Two End Pieces like This.
FIG. 318. — How the Sliders should be cut and bent.
FIG. 319. — Use this Form of Binding-post.

place), then cut off the handle ends of the rolling-pin. Two end pieces $2\frac{3}{4}$ inches square and $\frac{3}{8}$-inch thick, with $\frac{1}{4}$-inch notches cut out of two corners (Fig. 317), should now be prepared and screwed to the ends of the cylinder, to support it and the slider rods. The rods should be of brass of the size marked in Fig. 315, and two $\frac{1}{8}$-inch holes should be drilled through each near one end, and one $\frac{1}{8}$-inch hole through each near the other end. The rod can be procured at almost any machine shop, and you can also get the holes drilled there for a few cents.

The sliders should be made of thin but very springy sheet brass. Cut two pieces of the size shown in Fig. 318, round off one end of each, and then bend the other end into a square sleeve, as shown, to fit over the slider rod, and bend the rounded end so that it will bear against the tuner and make contact with it. Each slider should have another very slight bend made in its upper face as shown, so as to form a spring that will keep the rounded end in perfect contact with the wire. When the sliders have been bent properly, slip them on to the rods and screw the rods to the end pieces with small round-head screws. If the tuner has been wound with enameled wire, the enamel must be scraped off carefully along the path of the slider, and if bare wire has been used, the shellac must be removed from the path of the sliders with sandpaper. The sliders must make good contact both with the square rod and the wire winding, or the wireless outfit will not operate.

Fasten a one-hole binding-post such as is shown in Fig. 319 in the two remaining holes in the rods, and fasten an ordinary binding-post to one end piece as shown. Fasten the end of the wire winding to the last-

A BOY'S WIRELESS TELEGRAPH OUTFIT 241

mentioned post, and the apparatus will be ready for installation. The proper connections are marked in Fig. 315.

The Fixed Condenser. Unless one has a fair knowledge of electricity, it would be hard to explain to him the part played by the condenser; however, it makes such a big difference in the strength of the signals received that it is necessary to use one. When a micro-

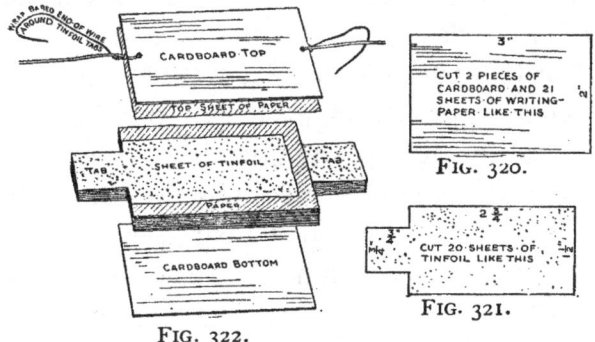

FIGS. 320–322. — Details of a Home-made Fixed Condenser.

phone detector is used, a second condenser must be wired up in connection with it as shown in the wiring diagram (Fig. 326).

The materials required are a few sheets of tin-foil, which can be procured from any florist, some sheets of good writing-paper, cardboard, and some ordinary tire tape. Cut as many sheets of cardboard and paper as is specified in Fig. 320, of the size shown, and the number of pieces of tin-foil indicated in Fig. 321 of the shape and size shown.

Begin building up the condenser by placing one of the pieces of cardboard upon a flat surface; upon this lay a sheet of the paper, then on this place a sheet of the tin-foil with the tab projecting at the left end; over this lay another sheet of the paper, and then place another sheet of the tin-foil on top of this with the tab projecting at the right end. Continue to build up the condenser in this way, reversing the tab on the alternate layers of tin-foil (Fig. 322) until all of the sheets have been used. Over the top sheet of paper lay the second piece of cardboard. Cut two pieces of insulated wire 12 inches or so in length, bare one end of each, run them through the ends of the cardboard top, and give them a couple of twists (Fig. 322); then carefully press together the projecting tabs on the tin-foil, and wind the bared ends of the wires around them as shown on the right end in Fig. 323. By running the wires through the cardboard as directed, whatever strain is brought to bear upon the terminal wires will come upon the cardboard and not the delicate tin-foil. With the terminal wires in place wrap the entire condenser with tire tape, beginning at one end as shown in Fig. 323, and lapping each turn partly over the previous turn. One of these condensers should be connected directly across the telephone receivers as shown in Figs. 325 and 326, and when a

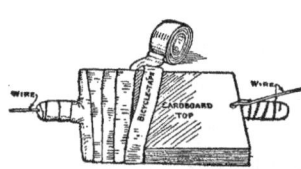

FIG. 323. — The Fixed Condenser is completed by covering it as above with Bicycle Tape. (See Figs. 325 and 326.)

microphone detector is used, a second condenser should be set in between the detector and the switch (Fig. 326).

If you have constructed the silicon detector first and do not care to use any of the other forms described, it will not be necessary to make

A Potentiometer, but with a microphone detector you will require one. Its purpose is to regulate with great precision the battery current in the *receiving circuit.* It is made like the tuner, except that it has only one slider instead of two and is much smaller (Fig. 324), and must

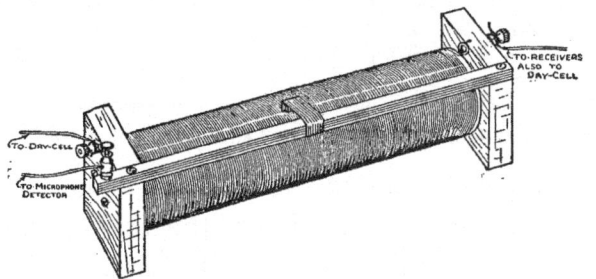

FIG. 324. — A Home-made Potentiometer.
(See Fig. 326.)

be wound with German-silver wire instead of copper. This wire will not be expensive to buy, as about two ounces will be enough, and this amount costs about 25 cents. A piece of a 1½-inch curtain- or rug-pole 8 inches long is of ample size for the cylinder.

Wind the cylinder with a layer of No. 24 bare German-silver wire, separating the turns with thread wound in between as directed for the bare-wire tuner (Fig. 316). In the tuner only one end of the winding was connected to a binding-post, but in making the potentiometer each end of the wire must be attached to a binding-post. Give

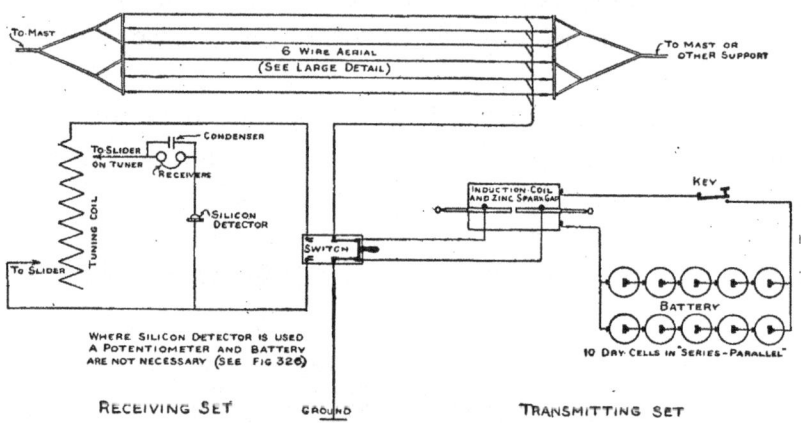

Fig. 325. — Complete Wiring Plan — when a Silicon Detector is used.

the coil a couple of coats of shellac, then make a rod and slider similar to the ones made for the tuner; screw the rod in place to the end pieces and fasten a binding-post to its end. The slider must make good contact with both the wire and the slider rod.

This completes the receiving instruments. They should be arranged upon a board or table in some such manner as shown in Fig. 300 and wired up as shown in Fig. 325 or Fig. 326, according to which form of detector is used. With either receiving set you should be able to hear commercial companies for a distance of a hundred miles, with the proper aërial, and all amateur stations in your vicinity. The arrangement of the instruments is discussed upon page 248.

The Transmitting Outfit is more expensive than the receiving set, for nearly all of the instruments have to be

TO MAST
AERIAL
TO MAST OR OTHER SUPPORT
CONDENSER NO. 1.
TO SLIDER ON TUNING-COIL
RECEIVERS
TUNING-COIL
MICROPHONE DETECTOR
POTENTIOMETER
1 DRY-CELL
TO SLIDER-ON POTENTIOMETER
TO SLIDER
CONDENSER NO. 2
SWITCH
INDUCTION-COIL AND ZINC SPARK-GAP
KEY
BATTERY
10 DRY CELLS IN SERIES-PARALLEL
RECEIVING SET
GROUND
TRANSMITTING SET

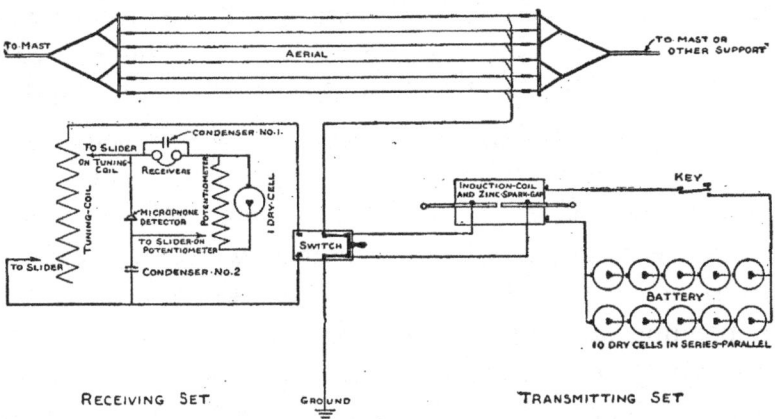

FIG. 326. — Complete Wiring Plan — when a Microphone Detector is used.

purchased, as they are too complex to make. The outfit consists of an *induction-coil* (*spark-coil*), *spark-gap*, *battery*, *key*, and *switch*.

The Induction-coil (Fig. 327) consists of a few layers, usually three or four, of a large size of insulated copper

SECONDARY
PRIMARY

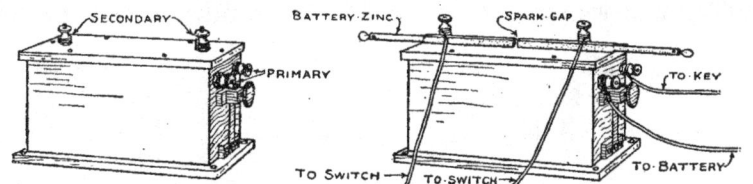

FIG. 327. — An Induction-coil or *Spark-coil*.

BATTERY ZINC
SPARK GAP
TO KEY
TO SWITCH
TO SWITCH
TO BATTERY

FIG. 328. — How to make a Spark-gap on Coil Box with Battery Zincs.

wire wound upon a core of soft, bare-iron wires; this first winding is called the *primary*. Over this is wound a great many turns, in many layers, of a very fine wire; this is called the *secondary*. As explained in the first part of the chapter, it is necessary to have a spark with which to send out " wireless " waves. The dry cells alone are not capable of producing the right kind of spark as their *voltage* is too low. But by sending a current of a few volts' pressure through the primary of the coil another current of quite high voltage will be induced in the secondary; in fact, the voltage will be sufficient to cause the electricity to jump across a considerable gap, depending on the size of the coil. Coils are usually rated according to the length of spark they are capable of giving. The coil will not operate on a continuous current, so an *interrupter* is used in connection with the primary.

A 1-inch coil costs about $5, and with a good aërial, will send several miles. A ½-inch coil is only a little cheaper than the 1-inch, while its sending radius is less than one half as much.

The Spark-gap can be made by binding two battery

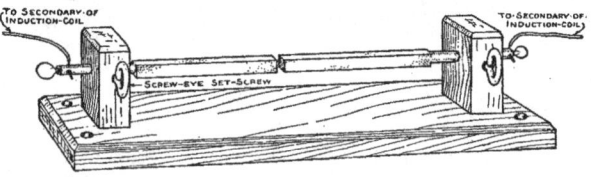

Fig. 329. — A Home-made Spark-gap.

zincs on the secondary terminals of the spark-coil, as shown in Fig. 328, or a simple frame may be made to hold the zincs, as shown in Fig. 329. If you make a frame, set in a couple of screw-eyes as shown for set-screws.

The induction-coil may be operated by dry cells or a storage battery.

A Storage Battery is expensive in first cost, but more satisfactory and cheaper in the end. Sometimes a good second-hand one can be bought cheap at a near-by garage.

Dry Batteries, or *dry cells*, can also be obtained from a garage, where they are discarded when too weak to spark an automobile; these are still plenty good enough for the "wireless" coil. The 1-inch coil will require five dry cells, but if another five can be obtained, they should also be used. Instead of connecting all ten in *series*, that is, connecting the carbon of each to the zinc of the one next to it (Fig. 333), connect each five in series and then connect the end cells in *parallel*, or *multiple*, that is, connect the carbons of one pair of end cells and the zincs of the other pair of end cells (Figs. 325 and 333). This form of connection is known as *series-parallel*. When all the zincs are joined together, also all the carbons, the connection is called *parallel*, or *multiple* (Fig. 333). If five cells are used in a series and you wish to add more cells, you must add another complete set of five, as *there must be the same number of cells in each series.*

The *dots* and *dashes* of the telegraph code are made on

The Wireless Key (Fig. 330), which makes the spark jump for a longer or shorter period of time according to how pressed. A good cheap key costs about 50 cents, a full brass key about $1

As the aërial is used alternately for sending and receiving, some means must be employed for connecting

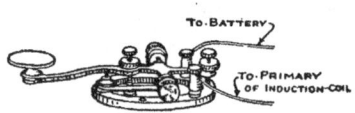

FIG. 330. — A Good Form of Wireless Key.

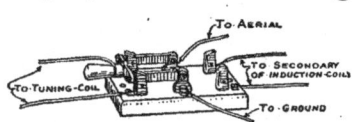

FIG. 331. — A Double-throw, Double-pole Knife Switch.

the sending instruments and then in turn the receiving instruments. This is accomplished by

The Knife Switch shown in Fig. 331, known as a *double-throw, double-pole knife switch*. This will cost between 30 and 50 cents, according to where purchased. The connections are marked upon the illustration of the switch and are also shown upon the wiring diagrams (Figs. 325 and 326).

By studying the diagrams you will find the manner of connecting up all the instruments clearly indicated. This should not be done until after they have been arranged upon a board or table. Figure 300 shows

A Good Arrangement for the Instruments if you wish to have them in your bedroom, and that is where most boys generally keep them so that they are always within easy reach. If you haven't a desk or table in your room, you can construct one similar to one of those illustrated in

Chapters VI and IX. The idea is to place the instruments where they can be operated handiest. Screw the base of each instrument to the table to keep it in position.

Operation of Instruments. When the key of the transmitting set is pressed, the vibrator on the end of the spark-coil box will buzz, and a shower of sparks will jump across the gap between the zincs of the spark-gap. When the aërial and ground are not connected to the spark-coil, it will give a long spark (about 1 inch if it is rated as a 1-inch coil), provided the battery is strong enough; but when the aërial and ground are attached,— one to each secondary binding-post of the coil,— it will be impossible to get a spark longer than $\frac{1}{4}$ inch, as the aërial and ground will be acting as a "capacity"; that is, the coil will be carrying a "load." If the coil gives a good spark with the ground connection, but no spark at all when connected to the aërial, it shows that the insulation of the wire leading in from the aërial is defective somewhere. This wire must be supported on insulators *at every point* from the aërial down to the switch.

To Receive a Call. If two complete stations are erected within a few miles of each other, one station should begin calling the other at certain times previously agreed upon, while the operator at the station called should listen carefully through his receivers, slowly moving backward and forward the sliders on his tuner and occasionally adjusting his detector until he hears the station calling him. When the station ceases calling, the receiving operator should throw over his switch and answer. Each station should be designated by a *call*, usually the initials of the owner. The amateur should not do things in a haphazard way, but should become familiar with the regular practice used in commercial wireless stations. To receive government and commercial stations you must of course know their calls in order to be able to know who is calling. The electrical journals advertise pamphlets containing all the principal stations, which can be purchased for 10 or 15 cents.

To make a Call. Suppose station *CGS* wishes to call station *CMW*. He proceeds to call the letters *CMW* several times and at intervals signs his own call, like this: *CMW CMW CMW*, followed by a slight pause, and then *CGS*; then he repeats the operation, finally ending by making *3*, which is the finish signal. When the operator at *CMW* picks up the call, he does not answer until he hears the *3* signal; then hearing nothing else, he knows definitely that the operator at *CGS* has stopped calling, has placed his switch in position for receiving, and is waiting for him (*CMW*) to answer.

Two Codes are used in " Wireless," the Morse code and the Continental code (Fig. 332). While there is not very much difference between the two, the Morse code is used almost entirely in this country and is the one you should learn. The *dots* and *dashes* of the code will be heard through the receivers as short and long buzzes. Adjust the sliders on the tuning-coil until the signals

A BOY'S WIRELESS TELEGRAPH OUTFIT 251

are heard the loudest, and adjust the slider on the potentiometer in the same way if you use one in your receiving set. Do not regulate the latter so that the current from the battery cell is too strong, for it is better to have it a little too weak than so strong that the detector will not operate.

A Good Way to learn the Code is to connect your telegraph key with an ordinary electric buzzer and one dry cell. After the code has been memorized, a friend can *send* on the buzzer while you copy the message he sends; then you may take your turn sending while he *receives*. A good buzzer costs about 25 cents.

In learning the code, the numerals, comma, period, and question mark, as well as the letters, should be memorized, as it is a very great mistake to get a smattering of the alphabet and neglect the punctuation and numerals.

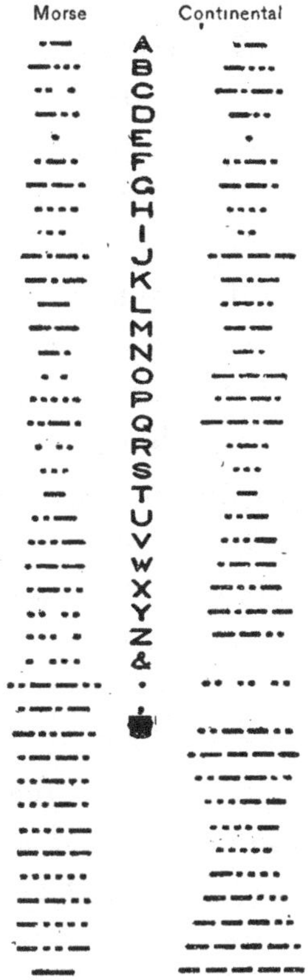

Although any boy interested in "wireless" can successfully install and operate an outfit from the directions given, it will be a very great aid to visit, if possible, some amateur station, for the use and purpose of the different instruments will

FIG. 332. — The Two Codes used in Wireless Telegraphy. The Morse code is generally used in this country.

be better understood and many valuable ideas gained from seeing them in operation.

While many units are used in

Electrical Measurements, only three need be considered by the amateur operator. These are the *volt*, the *ohm*, and the *ampere*.

The Volt is the unit of electrical pressure,

The Ampere is the unit of current strength, and

The Ohm is the unit of resistance. The latter is probably most readily understood by those not familiar with electrical work. Any conductor of electricity, such as wire, sheet-metal, carbon-rod, etc., offers resistance just as the sides of a ditch offer resistance to water flowing through that ditch. If the ditch were made of smooth cement, the water would flow through it more readily than if the sides were of rough projecting logs. In the same way some substances have low resistance to electrical currents, while others have high resistance. Silver has the least resistance, copper comes next, iron has considerable, and an alloy, known as German silver, has so much that it is used for making resistance coils and for other purposes where resistance is required (see *Potentiometer*).

Water will not flow in a ditch unless forced to do so. If the ditch ran down the hillside, of course the water would flow downhill in the ditch, and the steeper the hill, the greater the pressure would be. In the same way, electricity will not flow unless there is a pressure behind it, and the higher the pressure (*voltage*), the more readily it will flow.

The ampere represents the broadness of the "ditch," that is, the depth and breadth of the "stream of water," as this is decidedly a different quantity than the pressure behind it.

A better understanding of the volt and the ampere will be gained through practical work. The ohm is readily grasped when it is learned that about 150 feet of No. 18 copper wire has a resistance of 1 ohm.

Connection of Dry Batteries. Batteries, or, more properly speaking, *dry cells*, may be connected in *series*, *parallel* (also known as *multiple*), or a combination of both ways, called *series-parallel*. These connections are described

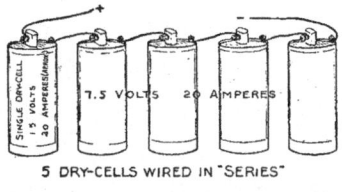
5 DRY-CELLS WIRED IN "SERIES"

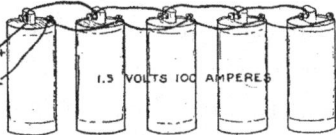
5 DRY-CELLS WIRED IN "PARALLEL" OR "MULTIPLE"

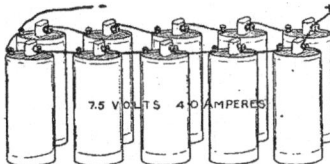
10 DRY-CELLS WIRED IN SERIES-PARALLEL

FIG. 333. — The Three Methods of Wiring Battery Cells.

(Showing 5 cells and the voltage and approximate amperage obtained by each method.)

under *Dry Batteries* on page 247, and shown in Fig. 333. Now for an application of the two units, volts and amperes. If the cells are connected in series, the whole set will have the combined voltage of all the cells, but the current in amperes will be only that of one cell (if the cells are alike and uniform); while, if the cells are all connected in parallel, the voltage will be that of only one cell, but the current strength, or amperage, will be equal to the combined amperage of all the cells. For example, if each dry cell is capable of giving 1.5 volts and 20 amperes, five cells connected in series (see Fig. 333) would give 5 times 1.5 volts, or 7.5 volts, and 20 amperes. If they were connected in parallel, there would be no change like this in the voltage, which would remain 1.5 volts or the voltage of a single cell, but the current strength would be 5 times 20 amperes, or 100 amperes (Fig. 333).

It is not difficult to determine the result of connecting cells in series-parallel. In Figs. 325 and 333 there are ten cells connected in series-parallel, five cells in each of two series. Each set will give 7.5 volts and 20 amperes, but when the two sets are connected parallel, the combined output will be 7.5 volts and 40 amperes, which you will understand from the examples given. It must be borne in mind, however, that while a dry cell will give as high as 20 amperes by test, this is an excessive amount of current to draw from it and would exhaust it in a very short time. Four or 5 amperes is as much as should be used, and if more than this is required, the cells must be placed in series-parallel. As mentioned before, each series of a series-parallel combination must contain the same number of cells. For instance, a set of three cannot be put in parallel with a set of four, for the voltage of the four set is greater than that of the three set, and a current would flow from the four set through the three set and in time exhaust the four set.

The ordinary spark-coil requires considerable current, and it pays to lessen the heavy burden on the battery by using two series in parallel. Four cells may be used for each series, but five are better.

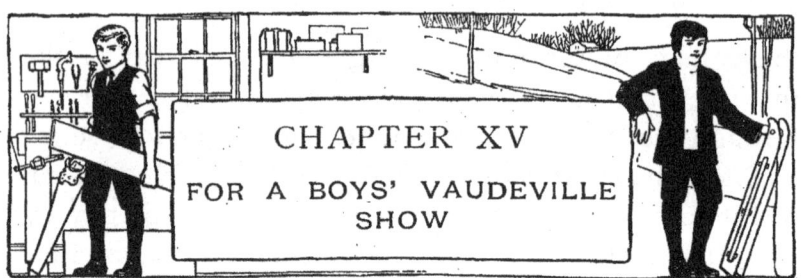

CHAPTER XV
FOR A BOYS' VAUDEVILLE SHOW

ABOUT the best kind of show for a neighborhood of boys, a boys' club, or a school organization to give is one in which each boy can do a special act or "stunt." It may be an exhibition of magic-lantern views, a sleight-of-hand performance, panorama or puppet show, boxing-match, or one of an endless variety of entertaining acts. The *strong man, magical mortar, boy with a wonderful voice, crack-shot*, and *ventriloquist* acts described in this chapter are easy to prepare.

Sam Dow, the strong man (Fig. 334), should wear a long-sleeved shirt with the shoulders and sleeves padded out to form large muscles, and should also pad the calves of his legs; if this padding throws the muscles out of their natural positions, so much the better.

For the great act of

Holding out a Chair upon which a Boy is seated, you will need an old seatless chair or a box with the ends knocked out and two uprights and crosspieces nailed to it for a back (Fig. 335). Drape the chair or box with a sheet or a piece of cloth of any kind large enough to

FIG. 334. — Sam Dow, "The Strong Man," holding a Seated Boy at Arm's Length.

hang down to the floor all around when the chair is held out at arm's length (Figs. 334 and 336), leaving the seat opening uncovered. Next get a pair of short trousers, stuff the legs, fasten a pair of stuffed stockings to the knees, fit the feet into a pair of shoes, and then fasten the legs to the chair, as shown in Fig. 336. The boy who is to appear to be seated upon the chair stands in the opening in the seat with the waist of the false trousers fastened and concealed under his coat (Fig. 334). While the chair stands on the floor, the boy rests on his knees, but when the strong man

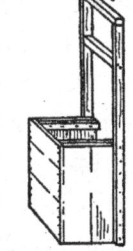

FIG. 335. Framework of Chair.

grasps the back of the chair with his hand and commences to lift, the boy slowly arises to his feet, taking the position shown by the dotted lines in Fig. 334.

Two attendants should carry the chair on to the stage, and the "seated" boy should hold on to the sides and lift his feet so as to give the boys an actual load to carry in. After Sam Dow has held the chair by each hand, and then by one finger, the audience will be convulsed with laughter if the chair is allowed to remain in the air a few seconds after he has released his hold upon it. A great deal of additional fun can always be furnished to the audience by "giving away" the trick in some such manner after a performance of this kind.

FIG. 336. — The Draped Chair with False Legs Attached.

The famous

Dumb-bell Lifting Feat must not be overlooked. Make the 2000-lb. dumb-bell like that shown in Fig. 337, preparing each end out of two barrel-hoops crossed at right angles with the cross-piece *A* fastened in the center (Fig. 338). Make the handle out of a piece of curtain-pole or iron pipe; if the latter is used, it can be struck by the strong man to show the audience that it really is made of iron. Fasten the ends of the handle in holes bored through cross-pieces *A*. Cover the hoops with cloth, then on top of this place enough padding to

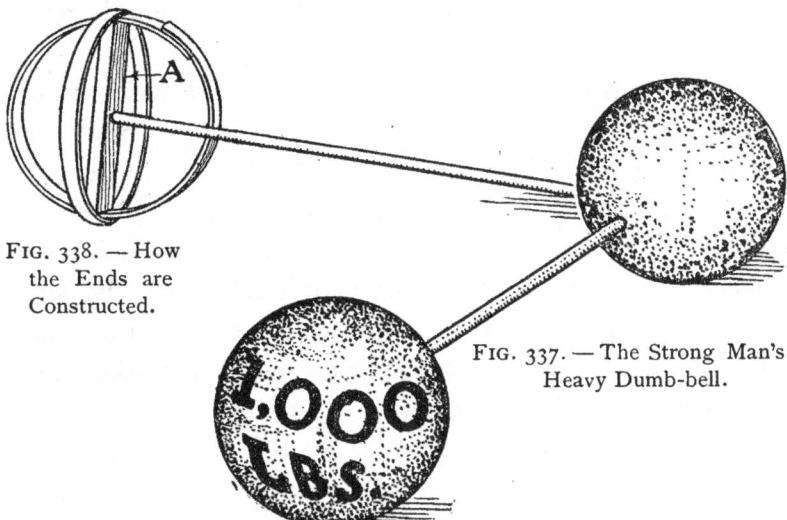

FIG. 338. — How the Ends are Constructed.

FIG. 337. — The Strong Man's Heavy Dumb-bell.

fill out the flattened portions and make them perfectly round, and cover the padding with black cloth. Paint the handle black and letter the weights upon the ends with white paint.

A couple of boys should drag the dumb-bell on to the stage, then Sam Dow should demonstrate his strength by lifting it with each hand, holding it upon his chin, balancing it on end upon his head, lying down upon his back and lifting it with his feet, and lifting it with his teeth by means of a piece of rope tied around the handle.

The strong man may demonstrate his ability as a juggler by

Juggling with Heavy Balls — croquet or bowling balls covered with silver or black paper, and he should introduce as a special attraction

Bonehead, the man with a head of solid ivory, upon which 500-lb. cannon-balls can be dropped without any apparent effect. Two balls of exactly the same size must be used in this stunt — an association foot-ball or a basket-ball for one, and a large bowling ball for the other are just the things if you can get them, otherwise use a croquet ball and a rubber ball of the same size. Cover the balls with black paper or tin-foil to make them look as nearly alike as possible.

Sam Dow should first pick up the heavy ball and allow it to crash upon the stage floor to let the audience see that it is solid; then he must pick up the rubber ball as though it were of the same weight and with an apparent effort toss it into the air so that it will land upon the head of Bonehead. Sam Dow should catch the ball as soon as it bounces off of Bonehead and toss it to one side of the stage out of view of the audience. A cracking sound should be made the instant the ball strikes Bonehead, and a louder crashing noise when Sam Dow throws it to one side. The strong man's stunts always make a big hit.

The Magical Mortar (Fig. 339). Get a sugar barrel from your grocer and a packing-case about 30 by 30 by

FOR A BOYS' VAUDEVILLE SHOW

40 inches in size at a dry-goods store, out of which to construct the mortar. If the barrel has wire hoops, fasten them to the staves with small staples; if wooden hoops, fasten them to the staves with small nails. Knock out the bottom of the barrel and saw away part of one side, as shown in Fig. 340, and cut away a little of one end of the box for end A of the barrel to fit in (Fig. 339); set end B inside of the box (Fig. 339) and fasten its hoops (D, Fig. 340) to the box sides. Make the bearing blocks as shown at C (Fig. 339) and tack

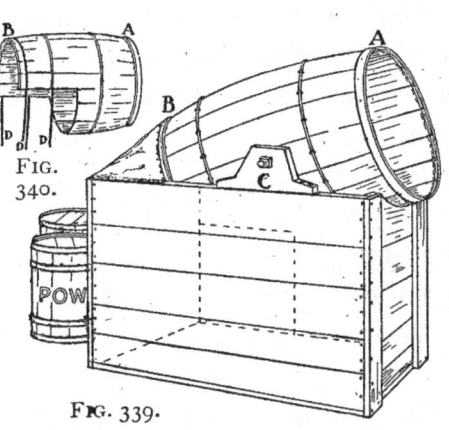

Fig. 339. — The Magical Mortar.
Fig. 340. — How the Barrel is Cut.

a piece of cloth over end B and to the edges of the box. Cut a 20-inch opening in one side of the box for a door (see dotted lines, Fig. 339).

The Professor exhibiting the mortar must have two assistants, No. 1 to operate the mortar from within the box, and No. 2 to wait upon him. For

The Wonderful Hat Trick, the professor should take an old derby, fedora, or straw hat, a duplicate of which has been placed inside of the mortar, and in full view of the audience tear it into bits, then put the pieces into a paper bag, throw the bag into the mortar, and shoot the hat from the mortar in a whole condition. Of course as the mortar is discharged assistant No. 1 throws out the duplicate hat, having first placed it in the bag after removing the pieces of the torn hat.

The mortar is charged from the nail keg "powder cans" standing behind it, and the report is produced by having some one strike a piece of sheet-iron with a hammer.

Other Mortar Stunts. The professor may place a dog in the mortar and fire out his "remains" in the form of a string of sausage, and transform all sorts of things in a similar manner.

Assistant No. 2 should wear a false-face in order to be prepared for

The Professor's Final Exhibition. Having run out of "gun powder," the professor sends assistant No. 2 for more, and after he has gone, moves the mortar to one side of the stage in such a position that assistant No. 1 can crawl out through the opening in the side. The professor no sooner turns around to the audience than there is the sound of a terrific explosion (strike a piece of sheet-iron with a hammer), and what appears to be the assistant's body is thrown upon the stage, with its head, arms, and legs dismembered.

The professor mourns the loss of his assistant and "powder," then thinks of the magical mortar and announces that he will put the man together again.

He gathers up the members of the body, places them in the mortar, goes out and rolls a barrel of " powder " on to the stage, and after moving the mortar back to the center of the stage, loads and discharges it. Instantly the assistant jumps forth whole and very much alive. Of course he crawls into the box, through the hole in the side, while it is over at one side of the stage.

Make the Dummy Assistant, thrown in at the time of the explosion, out of old clothes, ripping off the sleeves and legs of a coat and pair of trousers and stuffing each part with newspapers. Make a stuffed head, and fasten upon it a false-face similar to the one worn by the assistant so the heads will look exactly alike.

Falsetto, the boy with a wonderful voice, proved a great success in an amateur vaudeville. He stands in front of a curtain stretched across the stage, and back of this curtain are four assistants, — two boys, one with a bass, the other with a tenor voice, and two girls, one with an alto, the other with a soprano voice. Your sisters will probably be willing to help you out in this unseen part of the performance.

At the left of the stage the young vocalist sings the first verse of a song in *pantomime*, while the assistant with the tenor voice stands directly behind him on the other side of the curtain and does the actual singing. Responding to the applause, — which he is certain to receive, Falsetto bows, walks over nearer the center of the stage, and goes through with the second verse, in a soprano voice; for the third verse he moves a little farther over to the right, and here his voice changes to bass; and in an alto voice he sings the fourth verse at the extreme right of the stage.

With a little practice a boy will be able to get the proper expression to the mouth; and when well done you will find that this act will make one of the biggest hits of the show.

The Ventriloquist who throws his voice into the mouth of a doll in such a way that it sounds to the audience as though the doll were actually speaking is always a good entertainer.

It is a simple matter to make

A Ventriloquist's Doll (Fig. 341), and if you haven't the power of throwing your voice and talking without moving your lips, you can obtain just about as good results by having an assistant behind a curtain back

FIG. 341.—The Ventriloquist operating the Speaking Doll.

of the doll do the talking while you operate the doll's head and mouth.

Make the head framework (Fig. 342) out of 1-inch strips, and buy a false-face for the face. Cut strip *A* 4 inches long, *B* and *C* 9½ inches long, *E* 5 inches long, and *F* 16 inches long. Fasten the end of *A* between *B* and *C*, and center *E* upon *B* and *C* (Fig. 342). Cut the false-face as shown in Fig. 343, tack the upper portion to strips *A* and *E* at 1, 2, and 3 (Figs. 342 and 343), and the chin to strip *D* at 4; pivot the end of *D* between strips *B* and *C* with a nail. With a little care in pivoting the jaw in place, the mouth will open and close to a nicety. Fasten a rubber band between *A* and *D* and a piece of string with a small ring tied to its end to the under side of *D* (Fig. 342). Set strip *F* between the lower end of *B* and *C*, and after fastening it in place whittle the lower part round as shown.

1
A
B
C
2
E
3
4
D
F
FIG. 342.

1
2
3
CUT HERE
CUT HERE
4
FIG. 343.

G
H
I
L
J
K
FIG. 344.

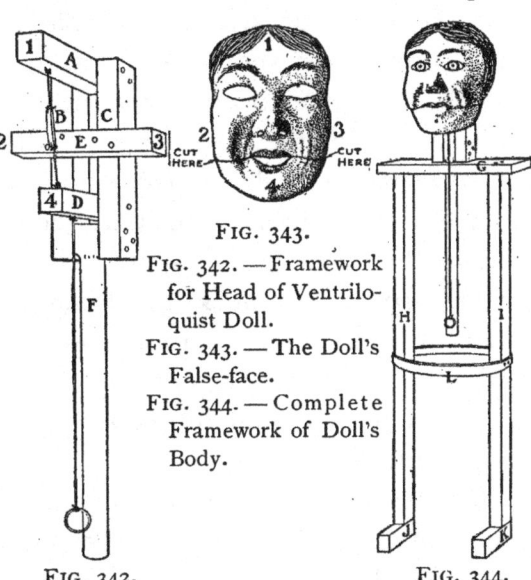

FIG. 342.—Framework for Head of Ventriloquist Doll.
FIG. 343.—The Doll's False-face.
FIG. 344.—Complete Framework of Doll's Body.

Cut the body strips H and I (Fig. 344) 30 inches in length, the foot blocks J and K 6 inches long, and the shoulder cross-piece G 15 inches long. Nail the pieces together as shown, and fasten a barrel-hoop to strips H and I at L; bore a hole in the center of G large enough for the neck strip F to turn in.

With the framework prepared it is a simple matter to put a suit of clothes upon it and stuff it out with rags and newspapers. Paste paper across the eye-openings and paint the pupils with water-colors; build out the back of the head with paper and cover it with cloth. Fasten a collar and necktie around the doll's neck and a pair of stuffed gloves in the ends of the sleeves for hands. Pin up the tails of the coat, so you can reach the end of stick F, and slip your finger through the cord jaw-manipulator.

Prepare a conversation to carry on with the doll, select several songs for him to sing, and request your audience to talk with him. The success of this act depends entirely upon how well the ventriloquist manipulates the head and jaws of the doll and keeps the movements in time with the talking assistant. If there is enough space behind the curtain for the assistant to walk from side to side of the stage, the ventriloquist may carry the doll about.

Willie Shute, the crack shot of the world, shoots portraits upon targets, an act which will interest any audience.

The Targets are easy to prepare. For these get some fresh pieces of heavy manila wrapping-paper at the grocery store. Sketch a simple outline of a head (Fig. 345) upon one sheet, then get a piece of small brass tubing (an old gas-burner will do) and file one end to a

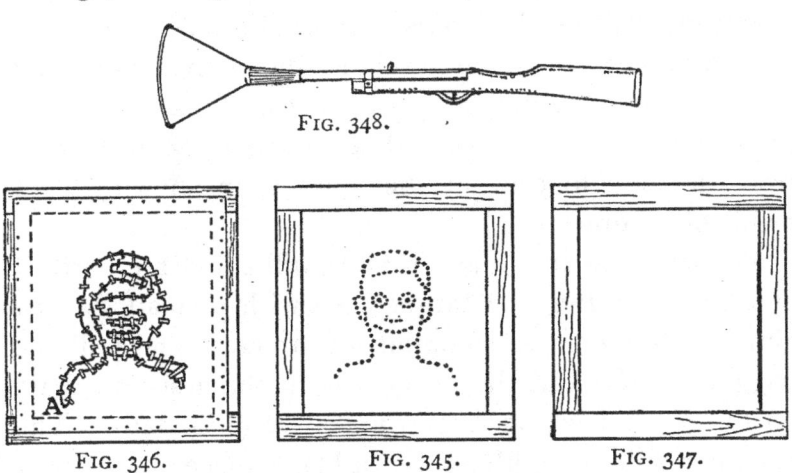

FIG. 348.

FIG. 346.   FIG. 345.   FIG. 347.

FIG. 345. — The Outline of the "Portrait" shot out by "Willie Shute."
FIG. 346. — The Reverse of the "Portrait" showing the Paper Strips over the Holes.
FIG. 347. — The Blank Paper which the Audience first sees.
FIG. 348. — Blunderbuss made for "Willie Shute."

sharp cutting edge. Lay the sheet upon a piece of linoleum, and, with the tubing as a punch and a hammer to strike it, punch out holes along the sketched outline (Fig. 345). Lay this punched sheet upon another sheet of the same kind of paper and mark the location of each hole, then cut away all except enough to cover the holes. Tack the punched sheet upon a wooden frame, stretching the paper as tight as possible, then fasten the cut-out portion of the second sheet over the back of the holes with small paper strips (Fig. 346). Make several portraits, also write out the names of a few of the audience whom you expect, and for a final stunt have a target on which to shoot the words " Good Night!"

The frames should be set in a row upon a table and be surrounded by draperies to conceal the assistant behind them. The light should be thrown upon the targets from in front, to prevent the holes from showing as a result of shadows.

Willie Shute announces that he will shoot the portrait of a boy upon the first target, then with a small gun he aims at the target and commences to cock and pull the trigger. As fast as the trigger snaps the assistant tears off the paper backing, beginning at *A* (Fig. 346). The audience will see nothing but a blank piece of paper at first (Fig. 347), but as each hole is uncovered it will show up black (Fig. 345). With

A Blunderbuss made by fastening a tin funnel upon the end of a toy gun (Fig. 348) an entire portrait can be made in one shot. If you haven't a toy gun, you can whittle one out of a stick and attach some kind of trigger that will make a clicking sound.

A Program Board upon which to announce each act of your performance is shown in Fig. 349. Make the board 12 inches by 18 in size, and cut strips *A* and *B* 16 inches long and *C* and *D* 8 inches long. Paint the board white and letter the word "Program" across the top with black paint. Cut the *"number" slips* 4 inches by 19, out of cardboard, and letter the names of the acts upon them.

Hang this board at one side of the stage where an attendant can reach it easily to change the number slips.

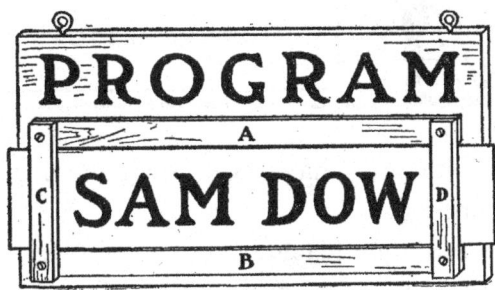

FIG. 349. — A Program Board.

Have the boy who owns a printing-press

Print the Admission Tickets, with the type set up in the form used for theater tickets.

CHAPTER XVI
MOVING PICTURES

You may have your own moving pictures at home by making

A Simple Machine such as shown in Fig. 350. This toy consists of a cardboard cylinder with slots cut in its sides, which is mounted upon a wooden base fastened to the end of a stick, while the pictures are made on strips of cardboard and represent a man, horse, dog, or some other subject, in action, drawn in just the positions in which it would appear in a series of photographs taken in rapid succession. The strips of pictures are placed, one at a time, inside of the cylinder close to the sides and facing in, then the cylinder is whirled around by means of the stick upon which it is pivoted, and by looking through the slots, in the sides you see a number of men, horses, dogs, or whatever the figures may be, moving just as they would appear upon the screen at a regular moving-picture show.

FIG. 350. — A Moving-picture Machine.

MOVING PICTURES 271

The Wooden Base for the cardboard cylinder is the first thing to make (Fig. 351). Upon a piece of board about $\frac{1}{2}$ inch thick describe a circle $5\frac{1}{8}$ inches in diameter with a compass, or if you haven't a compass, hunt up a jug or china saucer of this diameter and mark out around its rim. With a scroll-saw or a coping-saw it will be easy to follow the circle in sawing out the base, but with a large saw it will be necessary to cut off first the four corners of the board close to the circle, then the eight corners thus produced, then the sixteen corners, and so on until it is as round as you can get it, and then finish off the edge with a chisel and sandpaper.

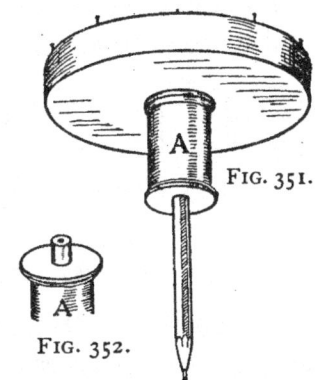

FIG. 351.—The Base for the Cardboard Cylinder.
FIG. 352.—The Spool and Pencil which are glued to the Base.

Bore a $\frac{1}{4}$-inch hole through the center of the base, then get a lead-pencil 6 inches long (or whittle a stick to the same size) and three spools, two of which will fit tight upon the pencil and the third loose. The holes in spools of different shapes vary a trifle in size, so probably you will find that mother or sister has just what you want. Push the upper end of the pencil through spool A so that about $\frac{1}{2}$ inch projects (Fig. 352), cover it and the top of the spool with glue, and stick it through the hole bored in the base (Fig. 351); then press spool

A against the base until it is glued fast. Slip spool *B* on to the pencil and glue spool *C* on to the end (Fig. 354).

For the Cylinder get some light-weight cardboard that will be easy to cut, mark out a piece $3\frac{1}{2}$ inches wide and

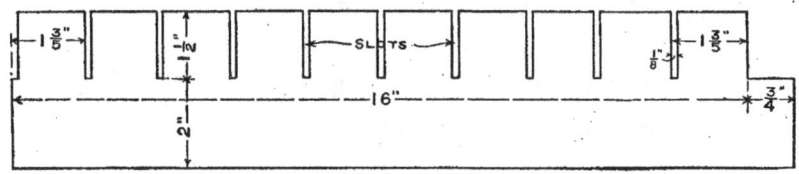

FIG. 353. — Pattern for Cardboard Cylinders.

$16\frac{3}{4}$ inches long (Fig. 353), and mark off the ten slots at equal distances apart. Cut out the cylinder with a pair of shears or a sharp knife, then tack its lower edge to the edge of the wooden base, as shown in Fig. 354, and glue the ends of the cardboard together.

The Clown and Ball Pictures (Fig. 355) are shown four pieces, as are

The Circus Horse and Hound Pictures (Fig. 356). Each set when joined together end to end will make a strip just long enough to reach around the inside of the cylinder. They are drawn full size, so all you will have to do will be to trace them off upon a piece of transparent paper and then transfer them upon a piece of heavy paper or light-weight cardboard, plac-

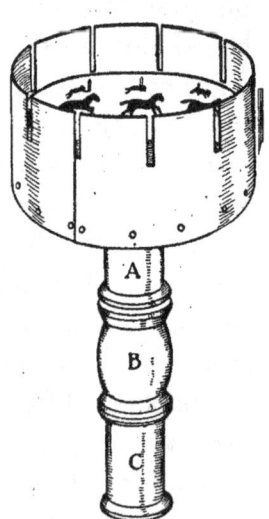

FIG. 354. — The Completed Moving-picture Machine.

MOVING PICTURES 273

ing the ends *A*, *B*, and *C* together so as to form a continuous strip. To hold the strips in place against the sides of the cylinder, drive a number of small brads into the top of the base just far enough away from the edge so the strips will slip between them and the cylinder (Fig. 351).

To operate the Toy, hold it by the middle spool with one hand and make the cylinder revolve by turning the bottom spool with the other hand (Fig. 350).

The Automobile. Figure 357 shows a modern adaptation of an old form of optical illusion. Give the book

FIG. 357. — Give the Book a Circular Motion and see the Automobile Run.

a circular motion, at the same time looking steadily at the center of the picture, and the wheels will immediately appear to revolve and the machine to run.

By cutting out a side view of an automobile from a magazine or newspaper advertisement and mounting it

FIG. 355. — Moving Picture Set No. 1.

FIG. 356. — Moving Picture Set No. 2.

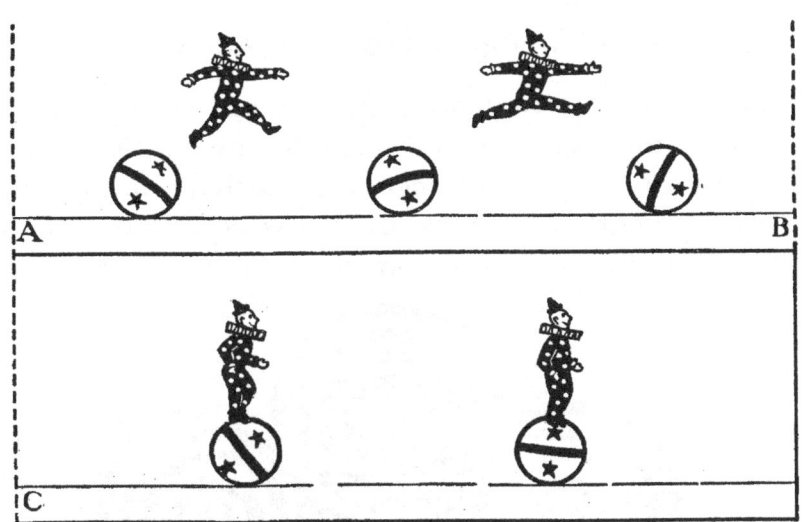

"The Clown and Ball."

Adapted from Muybridge's "Animals in Motion."

"The Circus Horse and Hound."

276 HANDICRAFT FOR HANDY BOYS

upon a piece of cardboard, then preparing two circular disks of the same size as the wheels with a series of concentric circles inscribed upon them as shown in Fig. 357, and pasting these over the printed wheels, you will have this optical illusion in a more convenient form to handle

FIG. 358. — The Revolving Wheels. The inner wheel runs in the opposite direction from the outer wheels.

and in such shape that you can carry it about in your pocket to show to all your friends.

Another interesting optical illusion is

The Revolving Wheels shown in Fig. 358. By giving the book a circular motion and gazing at the center of

MOVING PICTURES 277

the illustration the outer wheels will begin to revolve rapidly, just as those of the automobile did, and the inner wheel will turn very slowly in the direction opposite to that in which the outer wheels run.

If you own a pair of compasses, you will find this illustration very easy to lay out upon a piece of paper or cardboard. The inner circle should be described first, then a larger circle upon which to locate the centers of the outer wheels should be drawn with the same center

FIG. 359. — A Boxing-match. Gaze steadily at the center of the picture, draw the book up to your face, and the boys will appear to come together; lower and raise the book in succession, and you will see a lively boxing-match.

and the radius of this larger circle will be the proper spacing for the centers of the wheels.

An illusion of an entirely different kind but no less interesting is

The Boxing-match shown in Fig. 359. The directions for looking at this are printed below the illustration.

You may make cards with pictures of automobiles, motor cycles, and aëroplanes in similar positions, as it is easy to find side views of these machines in the advertisements in magazines; then when you have mounted these at the proper distance apart, you will have a set of moving pictures showing automobile and motor cycle smash-ups — which are now common occurrences — and airship collisions — which we will probably witness within a short time.

CHAPTER XVII
A SNOW BATTLESHIP

HERE, boys, is a new idea for a snow fight. A snow battleship is, in construction, really a snow fort, with the addition of turrets, conning-tower, funnels, mast, and fighting-tops (Fig. 360). This extra equipment is easy to make and adds greatly to the sport of a snow fight. A little carpenter work is necessary, but this is simple to do, and all sawing and a good portion of the nailing may be done indoors. The pieces may then be carried to the spot on which you are going to build the ship and set in place.

The central portion of the ship, directly below the conning-tower and known as

The Central Station, requires a framework such as is shown in Fig. 361. Out of any boards you can get make two frames similar to that shown in Fig. 362, driving three or four nails through each corner and clinching their ends. The corners may be braced with diagonal strips, but this is not necessary, for the frames will be held rigid enough when embedded in snow. Cut two boards 3 feet 6 inches long for the cross-pieces E

and *F*, and enough boards of the same length with which to roof the top of the framework.

FIG. 361.—Framework of the Central Station.

On the site selected for the battleship set up the two frames as shown in Fig. 361; fasten the cross-pieces *E* and *F* between them 2 feet above the ground, and nail roof board *G* in place; leave a space of 22 inches for the conning-tower, then roof the rest of the top with the boards you have cut for the purpose (Fig. 361).

If there is plenty of snow,

Build the Hull of your battleship alike on both sides, but if there is not enough

FIG. 362.—Make Two Frames like This.

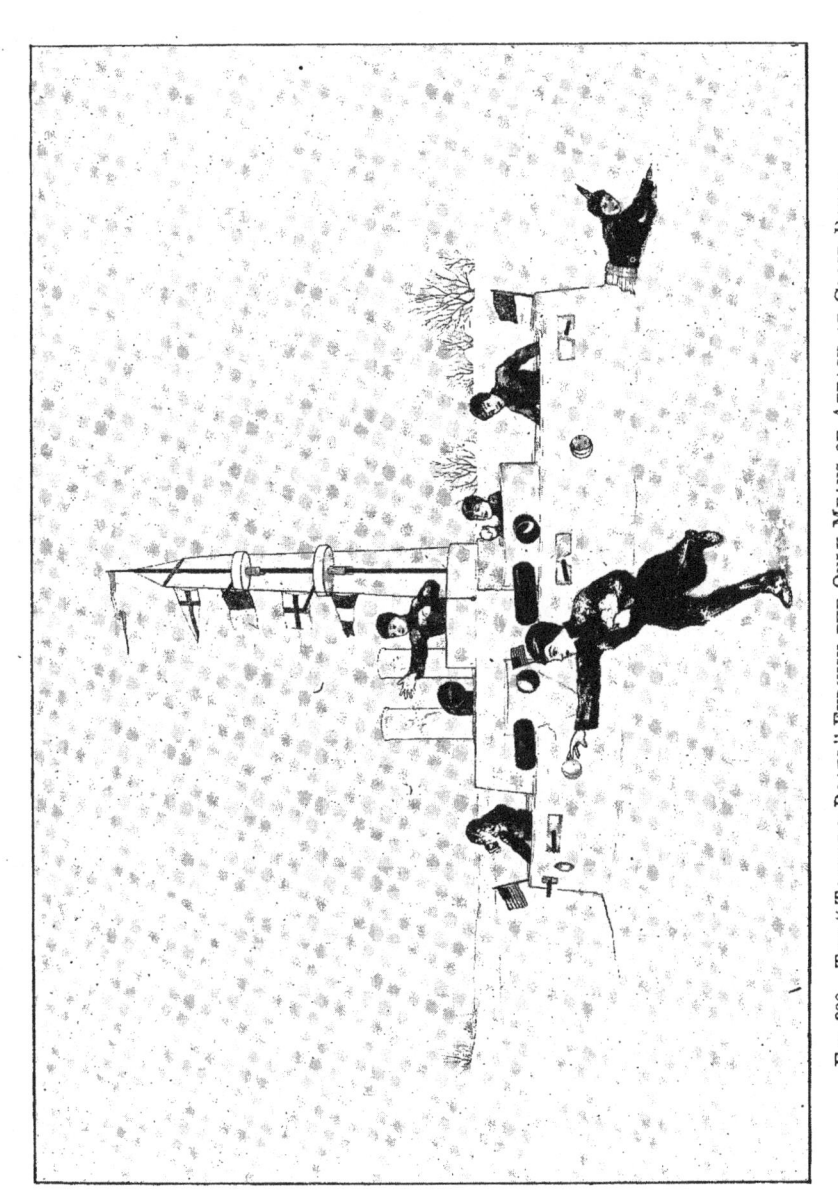

FIG. 360. THE "TORPEDO-BOATS" FURNISH THE ONLY MEANS OF ATTACK AT CLOSE RANGE.

to do this, stand the framework against the fence or wall and build only one side.

Figure 361 shows how the hull should be marked out in the snow with the sides converging toward the bow and stern. The inside of the bow should be about 7 feet from the central station framework, the inside of the stern about 4 feet from the framework. The illustration shows the stern end of the hull partly built up, and by this you will see how the sides should taper from a thick base to a thinner wall at the top. The inside of the walls should be straight, so as not to make the inside space too small, but you will find it much easier to build the wall roughly and then finish it off with a shovel afterward.

Set a barrel in the bow for

A Torpedo Tube (Fig. 363), and when the sides have reached a height of 30 inches, set the ends of a 4-foot board in them 2 feet forward of the central station (see *H*, Fig. 363) upon which to build the forward turret; at the same height set two or three boards into the walls inside of the framework, at *I* (Fig. 363), for the conning-tower platform. Build up the sides of the hull to a height of 3 feet 6 inches, and inclose the framework of the central station with a 5-inch wall of snow, leaving a passage fore and aft below cross-pieces *E* and *F* (Fig. 363) wide enough to crawl through. Offset the wall above the hull a trifle.

Cover the top of the central station —

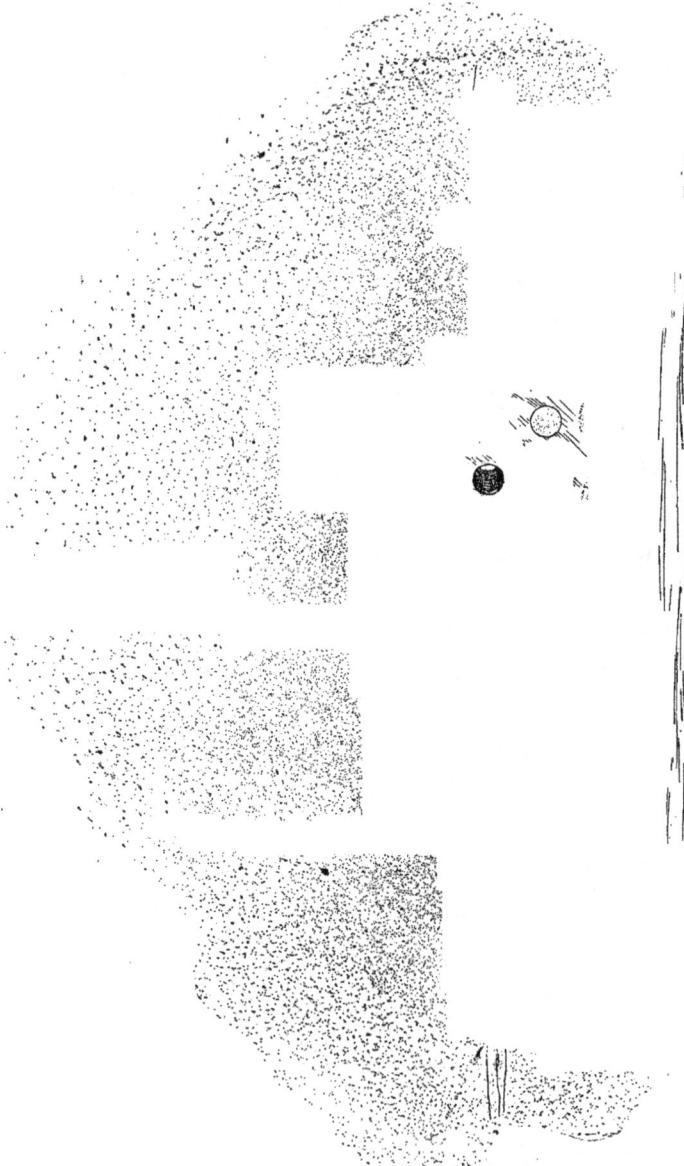

Fig. 363. Two Battleships in Action, showing a Longitudinal Section of One Battleship.

A SNOW BATTLESHIP

The Superstructure Deck — with enough snow to hide the boards. Build the wall of

The Conning-tower 12 inches above the superstructure deck (Fig. 363), and that of

The Forward Turret 12 inches above the sides of the hull; build

The Midship Turret on to the side of the ship. The shaping of the conning-tower and turrets can be done with a shovel or a shingle. To lessen the apparent height of the hull, bank snow around the base (Fig. 363).

The Mast should be about 11 feet long and can be made by splicing together a couple of curtain- or clothes-poles.

For the Fighting-tops (Fig. 366) take two barrel-hoops, fasten a piece of 2-by-4 in each (Fig. 364), and bore a hole in the center large enough for the mast to slip through. Tack a 4-inch rim of cardboard around the hoops and cover the bottoms with the same material (Figs. 365 and 366). Wire pieces of broom-handle to the cross-pieces for

Rapid-fire Guns (Fig. 365). The fighting-tops should be supported upon *trestletrees* — two blocks of wood tied or nailed to the mast (Fig. 366).

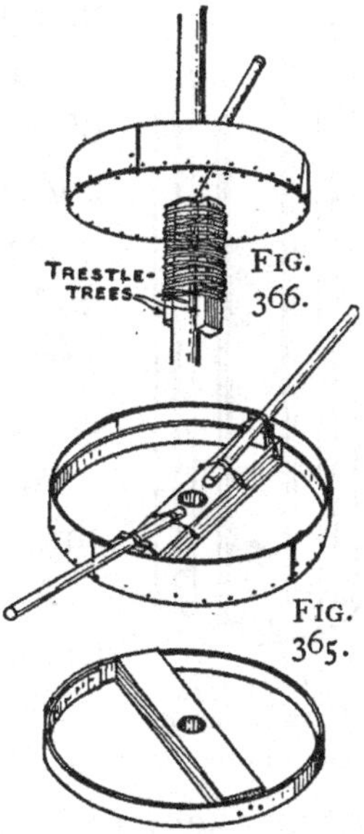

FIG. 366.

FIG. 365.

FIG. 364.

FIGS. 364, 365, and 366. Construction of the Fighting-tops.

Fasten the upper top 3 feet below the masthead, and the lower one 2 feet 6 inches below that.

The Crosstree should be 2 feet long; tie it securely at its center to the mast at *J* (Fig. 363).

Make a Coach-whip Pennant out of wrapping-paper or cloth to fly from the masthead, and to one of the *maststays*, which should be fastened to the masthead and to the ends of the crosstree, fasten three or four

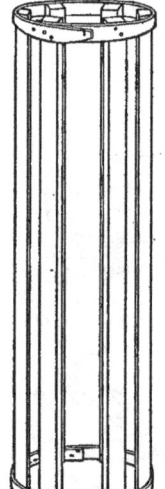

FIG. 367. Framework of the Funnels.

Paper Signal Flags (Fig. 363). Pictures of these flags, in color, may be found in an encyclopedia.

After rigging up the mast, run it 18 inches into the wall of the conning-tower and tie the ends of the maststays to stakes driven into the snow.

Make a Union Jack for the bow of the ship and

A National Ensign for the stern, and tack them upon sticks for staffs.

The Construction of the Funnels is shown in Fig. 367. Unfasten four barrel-hoops and make them 12 inches in diameter, and cut twelve sticks 3 feet 6 inches long. Nail the sticks to the inside face of the hoops (Fig. 367), then cover the framework with heavy wrapping-paper. Place these funnels upon the deck as shown in Fig. 363, and pack enough snow around their bases to hold them in position. For

FIG. 234. A DOLL'S CRADLE.

FIG. 230. A ROUND-SEATED CHAIR.

FIG. 228. A JACK-IN-THE-BOX.

FIG. 231. A ROUND CENTER-TABLE.

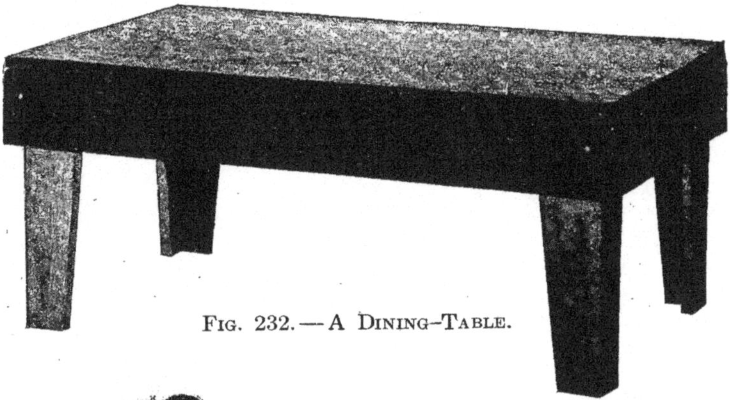

FIG. 232.—A DINING-TABLE.

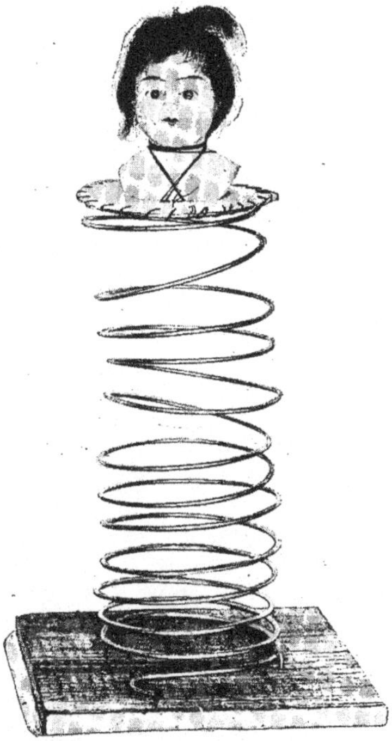

FIG. 229.—THE SKELETON OF THE JACK-IN-THE-BOX.

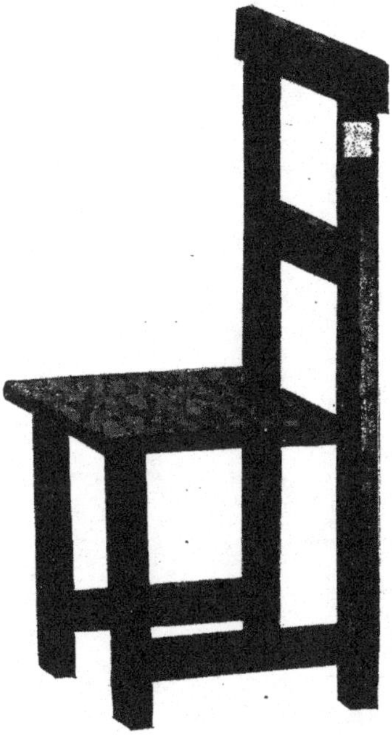

FIG. 233.—A SQUARE-SEATED CHAIR.

A SNOW BATTLESHIP

Ventilators procure a couple of stovepipe elbows.

Stovepipe or pieces of fence-posts may be used for your

Main-battery Guns, two of which should be placed in each turret. Cut three 8-inch *portholes* in the sides of the hull for peepholes, and make four depressions or recesses, as shown, for the

Secondary-battery Guns, which may be pieces of broomhandle.

Figure 363 shows the interior of your ship while in action. This illustration will suggest

The Arrangement of Amunition Stores, the idea being to keep the main supply of snowballs in baskets and boxes in the central station — the *magazine* — and from these to fill the pockets and baskets in the turrets and on the deck.

The Captain of the Ship, whom you must choose beforehand, will command from the conning-tower (Fig. 363), and must appoint the other men to their respective places on the forward deck, in the forward turret, the central station, and aft. He also selects the boy *torpedo boats*.

For a Naval Battle there should be at least two ships built with broadsides opposite (Fig. 363). Of course you can have a land and naval battle if the enemy prefer to build a fort, but there will be more fun with battleships. Certain

Rules must be observed in a snow fight, just as in any other boys' game, and the rules for a naval battle will differ somewhat from those of a snow-fort battle.

The main object of this game is to inflict as much damage as possible upon the enemy's ship (nothing but snowballs being allowed), and to capture and sink the "torpedo boats." A battleship is sunk if its mast is knocked to the ground. If neither ship is badly disabled when it is necessary to discontinue action for any reason,

A White Flag of Truce should be displayed by each side, and during this period of truce you can all set to work and repair the ships.

The "Torpedo Boats" furnish the only means of attack at close range. Each side should have two of these — two boys who must each wear a small flag stuck in his cap, as shown in Fig. 360. The "torpedo boats" must not fire upon one another, but if the flag is knocked from the hat of one boy and a "torpedo boat" of the enemy reaches him before he can replace his flag, he is considered captured, sunk, and out of the game until his side captures an enemy's "torpedo boat," when an exchange may be effected.

Repairs. The paper-covered funnels, the fighting-tops, and the signal flags will be damaged the most and will have a fine battered appearance. These may easily be removed, carried indoors, and repaired in a few minutes.

In this kind of snow fight

Good Marksmanship counts for more than strength, and the small boy with an accurate aim is as valuable a man as his big brother.

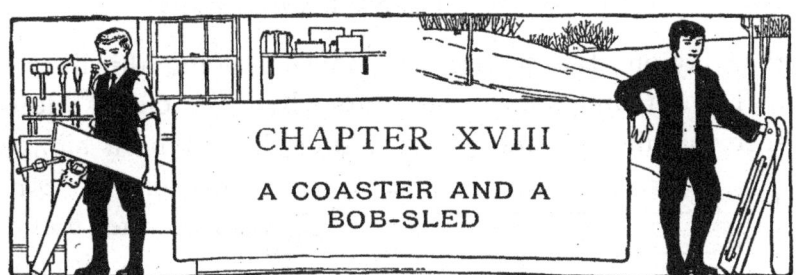

CHAPTER XVIII
A COASTER AND A BOB-SLED

A HOME-MADE sled that is properly put together generally outlasts the store sled, not because it is more substantially built, perhaps, but because the boy who has spent the necessary time to construct it realizes its worth and takes a pride in keeping it in good condition.

The Coaster shown in Fig. 368 is simple to make, but in cutting out the various pieces and putting them together

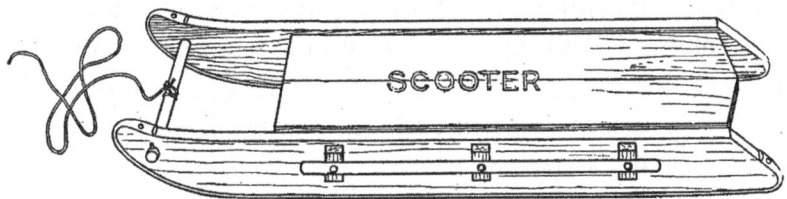

FIG. 368. — A Home-made Coaster.

you must do the work carefully in order to get the best results.

Lay out the Runners by the pattern shown in Fig. 369. This has been marked off into squares, at the ends, to aid you in laying out the curves. Measure off the total length of the runner upon a 1-inch or $1\frac{1}{4}$-inch board, then lay out the squares as shown, spacing the lines 1 inch apart, and locate the points where the curves intersect the lines on the pattern; then it will be a simple matter to connect the points by a continuous curved line After one runner has been laid out and cut from the board it can be used for a pattern for marking out the other runner.

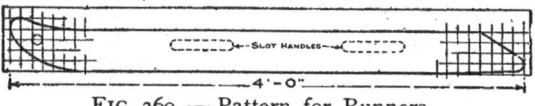

FIG. 369. — Pattern for Runners.

(Lay out the squares as shown 1" × 1" as a guide for drawing the curved ends.)

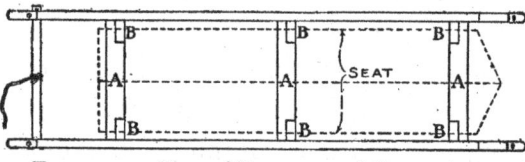

FIG. 370. — Plan of Runners and Cross-pieces.

If you can get only pine or other soft wood out of which to cut the runners, you can reënforce them after cutting them out by driving 16-penny nails, or short pieces of iron rod, into holes bored vertically 8 or 10 inches apart.

Oiled wooden runners will slide over an icy surface, but **Shoes** either of *hoop-iron* or *half-oval iron* are to be preferred if you can get them. A blacksmith is the man to go to for these. Take the runners to him and have him bend the irons to fit and make the screw holes so you can screw them in place. The holes along the bottom should be countersunk so the screw-heads will set flush with the iron (Fig. 376). Five screws for each runner will be plenty.

A COASTER AND A BOB-SLED

Cut the three

Connecting Cross-pieces (*A*, Figs. 370 and 371) 12 inches long, 2 inches wide, and 1½ inches thick and prepare the ends of each as shown at *A* (Fig. 372); then cut the six braces *B* (Figs. 370 and 371) as shown in Fig. 372, to fit the mortises in the ends of *A*. Screw the braces to the cross-pieces and to the runners (Fig. 371), then screw the cross-pieces between the runners. They should be ⅞ inch below the top — one 11 inches from the front end, another 7 inches from the rear end, and the third halfway between the two.

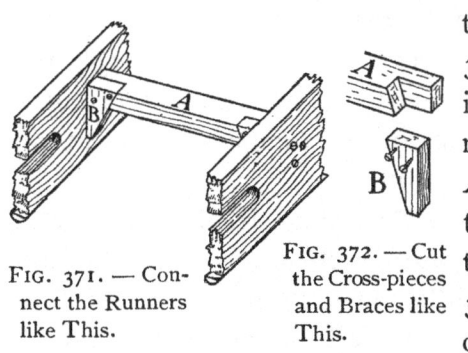

FIG. 371. — Connect the Runners like This.

FIG. 372. — Cut the Cross-pieces and Braces like This.

Make the Seat in two pieces (a wide board would be likely to split) and screw the boards to the cross-pieces.

There are a number of forms of

Sled Handles, any one of which you may use. One of the simplest kind of handles consists of slots cut through the runners as shown in Figs. 369 and 371. The slots should be cut as described on page 142 (see Fig. 156). To make the handle shown in Fig. 368, cut two pieces of broom-handle 28 inches long and four wooden blocks 2 inches square; nail two of the blocks to each runner, then bore ⅝-inch holes through the broom-handle pieces and through the blocks and runners, and bolt the handles in place with ⅝-inch carriage-bolts 4 inches long. Drawer-pulls, such as are used upon the fronts of kitchen pantry drawers, are another form of handles which may be used.

Bore a 1-inch hole through the bow ends of the runners and cut a piece of broom-handle to fit in them for

The Foot-bar. If you drive a nail through each end of the broom-handle, close to the runners, it will prevent the bow end of the runners from spreading.

Paint your coaster with at least two coats of paint. You may suit yourself about the colors, but a good combination would be to paint the runners yellow or green and the seat and handles red; then if you want to letter a name upon the seat, put it on with black paint.

Every one of you boys can own

A Bob-sled, for there is nothing difficult about constructing one, and the material required is inexpensive.

FIG. 373.—"Every boy can own a bob-sled."

A bob consists of two sleds built

A COASTER AND A BOB-SLED

along the lines of a coaster, placed tandem, and connected with a plank long enough to hold three or more boys (Figs. 373 and 374).

The sleds must be built first, and as they are identical in construction

The Four Runners may be cut out by the same pattern (Fig. 375). The pattern shows the curved ends marked

FIG. 374. — A Home-made Bob-sled.

off into squares, just as the pattern for the runners of the coaster was shown, and one runner should be laid out first, just as described for the other sled, and the others marked out from this. Make them out of oak or other strong wood, if possible, as the bob-sled's runners are subjected to a great deal of strain. If you must use soft wood, do not fail to reënforce them as suggested for the runners of the coaster.

For connecting the Runners and bracing them, cut six cleats $1\frac{1}{4}$ inches thick, 2 inches wide, and 10 inches long (*A*, Figs. 376 and 378), and buy twelve 2-by-2-inch iron angle-braces, such as are shown in Fig. 377, at a hardware store. Nail the runners to the ends of the cleats, using three cleats for each sled and spacing them as shown in Fig. 378, and then screw the angle-braces to the runners and to the cleats (Figs. 376 and 378). Cut

The Sled Seats 22 inches long out of 10-inch boards and screw them to the cleats.

The Seat of the Bob-sled shown in the illustration is a 2-by-10-inch plank 7 feet 6 inches long and is bolted to the bow sled and hinged to the stern sled. Cut the two

C
B
E
F
WASHER
D
A
FIG. 378.
NUT
5/8" BOLT
FIG. 381.
FIG. 379.
FIG. 380.
FIG. 377.
SEAT
CLEATS
DRAW THE LINES WHICH FORM THE SQUARES 1-INCH APART
2'-6"

FIG. 375. FIG. 376.

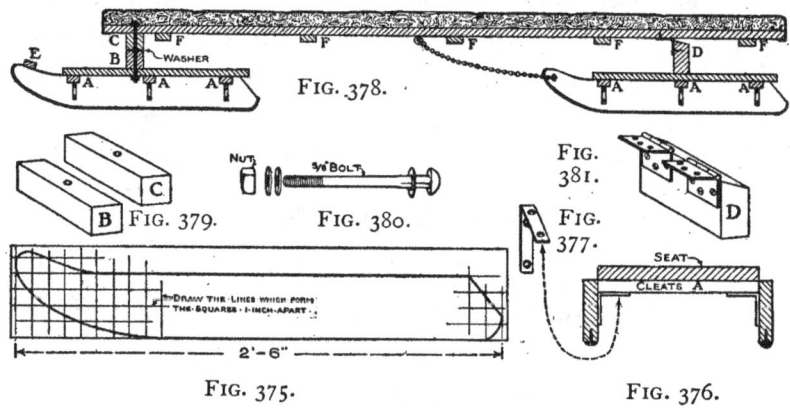

FIG. 375.—Pattern for Runners.
FIG. 376.—Cross-section of Sled showing how Runners are Braced.
FIG. 377.—Iron Braces for bracing the Runners.
FIG. 378.—Longitudinal Section of Completed Bob-sled.
FIG. 379.—Blocks for connecting Seat to Front Sled.
FIG. 380.—Use a $\frac{5}{8}''$ × 7″ Carriage-bolt for a King-bolt.
FIG. 381.—Block for connecting Seat to Rear Sled.

blocks *B* and *C* (Fig. 379) $1\frac{3}{4}$ inches wide, $1\frac{3}{4}$ inches thick, and 10 inches long, and bore a $\frac{5}{8}$-inch hole through the center of one side of each, then nail block *B* to the board seat of the sled and block *C* to the under side of the plank, and bore the $\frac{5}{8}$-inch holes through both the board seat and the plank. Buy a $\frac{5}{8}$-inch carriage-bolt 7 inches long (Fig. 380) and drop it into the holes in the plank, block, and sled seat, putting a washer between the bolt-head and seat, another between blocks *B* and *C* and a washer and nut upon the lower end.

The Seat is hinged at the Stern End so the stern sled will rise and fall as it runs over uneven ground, independent of the bow sled. Cut block *D* (Figs. 378 and 381) out of hard wood 2 inches thick, 4 inches wide, and 10 inches long, and plane off the top edge as shown. Get a pair of 4-by-4-inch wrought-steel butts at a hardware store for the hinges, and screw them to this block and to the plank seat with screws $1\frac{3}{4}$ inches long; then spike the stern sled to the block. Connect the bow ends of the runners of the stern sled with the bottom of the plank seat with

Check-chains, or ropes, fastened to screw-eyes (Fig. 378).

Cut the Steering Foot-bar *E* (Fig. 378) 20 inches long, nail it to the runners of the bow sled, and attach

The Steering Lines to its ends (Fig. 374).

For Handle-bars cut the cross-bars *F* (Fig. 378) 20 inches long and screw them to the under side of the plank seat, and bolt pieces of broom-handle to their ends, as shown in Fig. 374.

The Seat should have a Cushion, and an old carriage, wagon, or boat cushion may be remodeled for it, or the top of the plank may be padded with excelsior or straw and then covered with a piece of oilcloth or carpet (Fig. 378). The padding should be spread out evenly and be secured to the plank by stretching a piece of cloth over it and tacking it to the edges of the plank with cord before putting on the top covering (see directions for upholstering on page 116); then the covering should be pulled tight over the padding and tacked to the under side of the plank. *Tufting* the cushion every 4 or 5 inches, by driving nails through the covering and padding into the plank, will prevent the padding from shifting and becoming lumpy (Fig. 374).

Two Coats of Paint applied to all the woodwork will give the sled its finishing touches, then, with a snow-covered hill or slippery toboggan-slide to coast upon, you will be ready to give all of your friends a ride upon your new home-made bob.

PART II
Spring and Summer Handicraft

AERO CLUB OF THE CHICAGO CALUMET HIGH SCHOOL.

A MODEL AEROPLANE MEET OF THE CALUMET AERO CLUB.

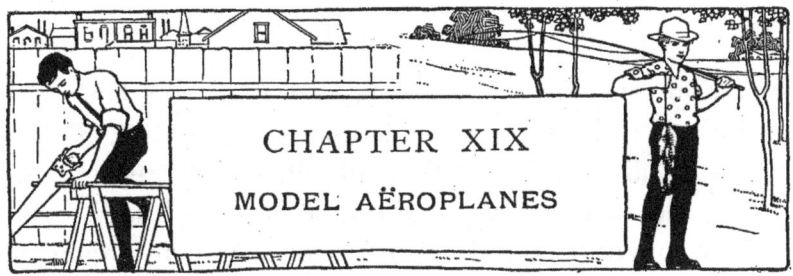

CHAPTER XIX
MODEL AËROPLANES

Boys cannot study well while some one or something from without is attracting their attention, and it is this very condition of things which makes indoor work difficult after the first signs of spring have arrived. As soon as the Weather Man throws over the switch marked "balmy weather," Mother Nature takes heed and sends forth her messengers in their little "airyplanes" to arouse a greater activity in every living creature, and to awaken each growing thing from its winter sleep. We all receive the call in the "airygrams," which reach us through the gentle breezes, and through the fragrance from the fields and forests which fill our nostrils; and each little squealing or chattering animal, and each chirping or scolding bird, seems either to invite us to come out into the open and work, or to mock us for not doing so. Then there are the brooks and the streams, whose jumping fish remind us that the "fishin'" is fine, and the old "swimmin'" hole, the sight of which tempts us to take an afternoon off and go "swimmin'." So it is no wonder that, with all these invitations thrust upon us at one time, we become restless, and that you boys find it difficult to keep your minds upon your studies, for it is to these calls of Nature that all within us is responding.

But the days are getting longer now, and soon there will be lots of time before and after school to devote to outdoor work and play, and, with all day Saturday in addition and the spring vacation in sight, you fellows will have very little reason to complain.

Since the making and flying of model aëroplanes has developed into one of the greatest of pastimes for boys, it has been added to the list of boys' sports, and, although a model aëroplane requires calm weather rather than the breeze necessary for kite flying, aëroplane flying seems to belong to the spring of the year, for it furnishes the first opportunity to try out the models which have been devised and constructed during the winter months; so the first spell of warm weather of each year is probably destined to be known hereafter as aëroplane time, as well as kite, marble, and top time.

A model aëroplane contest is as much more fascinating than a kite contest as an automobile race is than a horse race, and what makes it more interesting than kite flying is probably the fact that it requires more skill to build a light and evenly balanced model, and that a successful flight depends upon the model itself, rather than the guiding hand of its flyer, as in kite flying.

The Lengths of Flights have been limited on account of the lack of a long-running light-weight motor, but the dis-

MODEL AËROPLANES

tances covered have gradually been increased from some 60 odd feet, one of the first records made several years

Courtesy of " The Chicago Daily News."
Junior Aëronautics.
Ideas which are more Ingenious than Praiseworthy.
(See details in Chapter XX for a *safe* and *practical* " boy-carrying " machine.)

ago, to a distance of over 350 feet, recently obtained. This shows how boys have succeeded in developing better and better models, through the discovery of more satisfactory working material, better forms for the planes and propellers, and improved methods for installing the motive power and for joining together the various parts of the models.

Junior Aëro Clubs have been organized in schools and in branches of the Young Men's Christian Association, in many parts of the country, and it is very probable, if the model aëroplane increases in popularity at the rate at which it has during the past few years, that fully two thirds of the boys of America, as well as a large proportion of their English cousins, and the boys in all other countries in which aëronautics are holding the public's attention, will soon become enthusiastic builders of model aeroplanes.

The Chicago Calumet High School boys organized an aëro club in the winter of 1910, and, under the tutorage of Mr. Arthur Booth, their instructor in mechanical drawing, have designed and built many successful models. The photographs opposite page 297 show some of the club members with their home-made models, also the start of one of their aëroplane races, while two of the photographs opposite page 302 show other views of several of their models.

Model Aëroplane Meets. Each aëro club has its own rules for its contests, but they do not differ very materially. There are usually three judges — a starter, a recorder, and a head official — to govern the race, and it is generally stipulated in the rules that all models shall be the product of the boys entering them. In some races it is required that the models start from the ground; in others they must be released from the hand without giving them any forward motion; in a third form of race they must be launched from a table top, chair, or bench; and for a fourth way they are launched from the hand and may be given as much of a push as the contestants wish. Sometimes a dozen models are started off at one time, but usually the number is limited to five or six, to avoid collisions.

The lengths of the flights are figured from the starting line to the points at which they first touch the ground. The winner of a race is usually awarded 10 points, the holder of second place 5 points, and the holder of third place 3 points. In the races in which the machines start from the ground, the model which rises within the least number of feet from the starting line scores 10 points, and the one which rises next best scores 5 points, which results in heavy handicaps for models capable of covering long distances, but slow in taking to the air.

Three cups, each having a valuation of $100, were awarded last year by business men of New York City for the winners of the contests held under the auspices of the Young Men's Christian Association. The first of these was deeded with the condition that it be won three times in succession by a contestant before becoming his property, the second was for the longest flight of the year, and the third for the best-designed model among the winners of all the contests. These prizes have stimulated a desire in New York boys to put forth their very best efforts, and have resulted in some surprising records and an astonishing array of styles of models, from careful reproductions of the large successful flyers to a variety of forms which only boys' ingenuity could produce.

The Three Types of Machines used in designing models are the *glider*, or motorless model; the *monoplane*, which is constructed more or less along the lines of a bird; and the *biplane*, or double-decked aëroplane. Gliders may be of either the monoplane or biplane type.

The glider is the best form for a boy to make first, as it is the simplest and will enable him to learn the main points to be observed in building a successful flyer; then, after he has succeeded in producing a good glider, he can go a little farther and add a motor, and then he will be prepared to undertake the construction of some of the more elaborate monoplanes. A number of successful biplane models have been made, but so far none has been produced which can equal the records of the monoplane model. They are usually not as stable a machine, the greatest difficulty being that a very slight disturbance in the air will upset them and cause them to crash to the earth, usually resulting disastrously, if not in total destruction.

The Support of an Aëroplane. There are several fundamental principles which must be taken into consideration in designing an aëroplane, in order to make it so it will ride the air successfully. It is necessary to so plan the wings, or *planes*, that the center of the upward pressure exerted upon them by the supporting air beneath will come at the *center of balance*. The instant the center of this pressure shifts to one side, the planes tilt, with the result that the machine loses its equilibrium and upsets. To illustrate this action, take a piece of paper or cardboard and drop it from your hand. You will find that as long as it remains flat it floats, but the instant the center of the air pressure beneath shifts to one side, the opposite edge drops, and the piece overbalances and falls. Cardboard is stiffer and will keep its balance longer than the piece of paper, as the air pressure is held under its center of balance for a longer time. If you let a piece of cardboard glide out of your hand, you will discover another factor which must be counted on; you will find that the forward end is forced upward, and, as a result, the card instantly slips backward, then upsets and drops to the ground. This is caused by a change in the center of the air pressure, immediately the card starts to move forward, from the center of balance to a point between that and the forward end. This tendency to upset is neutralized by counterbalancing, or by adding *stability planes* in such positions as will help to retain the original center of balance.

A Cardboard Bird Glider may be fashioned on the lines of the body of a bird, as shown in Fig. 382. Mark out a circular piece of cardboard, using a compass or the rim of a small plate for the purpose; cut a couple of wedge-shaped pieces of equal size out of the edge, leaving the piece between for a tail; and turn over about $\frac{1}{4}$ inch of the edge directly opposite the tail, as shown, and stick a piece cut in the shape of a head and neck in a slit made through the folded front edge. The head should have some sealing-wax dropped upon it to give it weight; this can then be used as a counterbalance, and be extended or pushed back into the body as much as is necessary to equalize the upward pressure upon the forward end. The bird should glide to the ground in a long, graceful curve; if it dives head first, you may know that the weight is too heavy, and that the head must be pushed closer to the body; while if it rises and then collapses, the head must be extended a little farther front.

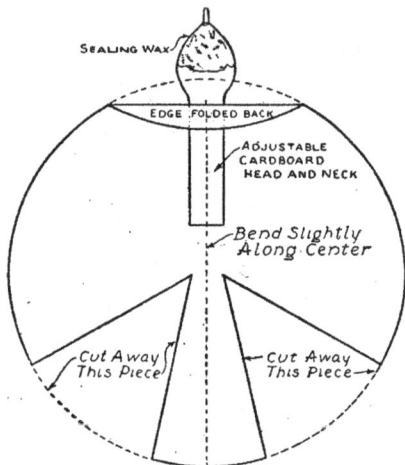

FIG. 382. — A Cardboard Bird Glider.

A Simple Monoplane Model is shown in Fig. 383. This makes a splendid form of glider as well. Figure 384 shows the model without the planes, and Fig. 385 shows the details for the propeller.

Use a $\frac{1}{4}$-inch or $\frac{3}{8}$-inch pine flagstaff for

The Center-pole, and get one which is split down the center, if possible, so the slot in which to slip the card-

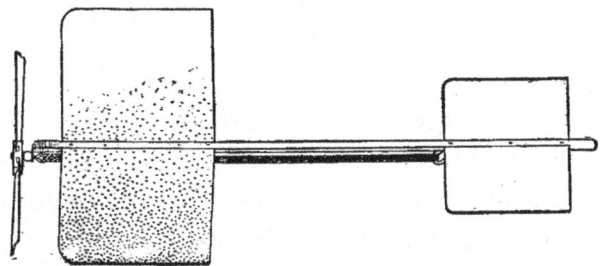

FIG. 383. — A Simple Monoplane Model.

board wings will already be prepared. If you cannot find an old staff nailed up somewhere, from which the flag has been washed by the rain, you may use a cabinet-

SECTION
TIN PROPELLER BLADE
(CUT TWO OF THESE OUT OF A TOMATO CAN)
WIRE SHAFT
HUB
GLASS BEAD
BRASS BEARING
FIG. 385.
FLAGSTAFF
SCREW HOOK
4 STRANDS OF RUBBER BANDS
BEAD
SHAFT
FIG. 384.

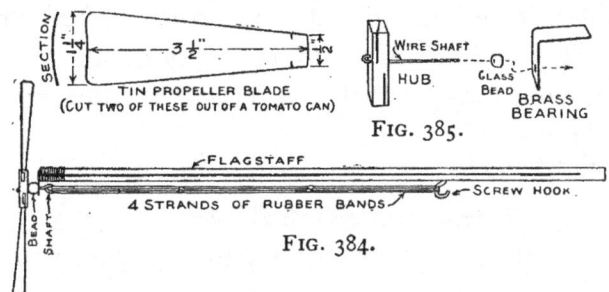

FIG. 384. — Center-pole of Monoplane with Motor in Place.
FIG. 385. — Details of Propeller, Shaft and Bearing.

maker's dowel stick and rip one end for a distance of 5 inches and the other for a distance of 6 inches. Cut this center-pole about 18 inches long.

Before attaching thé propeller,

Cut the Two Planes out of cardboard of a light weight, yet stiff enough to support itself. The sizes of these planes must be determined by experimenting, as they will depend upon the weight of the material, but will be approximately 5 inches by 12 inches and 4 inches by 6 inches. The large plane should be fastened about 1 inch from one end of the pole, and the rear plane should be placed about the same distance from the opposite end. You have now completed a glider, and this should be tried out before the motor is attached. Adjust the rear plane fore and aft until the model will glide in long, graceful sweeps; but do not fasten it permanently in place if you intend to install a motor, for after this has been put in place it will be necessary to readjust this plane.

A Glider Race may be started from a shed or barn roof, or, if you live in an upper story of an apartment building, you may use the rear porch from which to start the models.

The details for

An Easily Made Propeller are shown in Fig 385. The blades are cut out of tin from a tomato can, which you will find of just the right curve. Remove the ragged edge of the cut end of a can, by holding the can over a flame until the solder melts and the end drops off; then mark out one blade to the dimensions given, cut it out, and mark out the second blade with it as a pattern.

Cut a block $\frac{3}{8}$ inch by $\frac{3}{8}$ inch by $1\frac{1}{4}$ inches in size out of hard wood for a hub; drill a small hole through the center for a shaft, and slot each end diagonally for a distance of $\frac{1}{2}$ inch with a saw, as shown in the detail. Notch each edge of the blades near the narrow end, as shown in the pattern; then slip the blades into the slots in the hubs, bend the ends over against the hub, and drive a tack through the wood and the tin to help hold them in position.

Cut a short piece of wire for

The Shaft, and after slipping it through the hub bend the end over and stick it into another small hole made in the hub.

The Shaft Bearing should be made out of a piece of brass $\frac{3}{8}$ inch by $1\frac{1}{2}$ inches in size. Drill a hole of a little larger diameter than the shaft, near one end, and, $\frac{1}{2}$ inch away from this end, bend it as shown; then set it into the split end of the center-pole, and bind it in place by winding the end with strong linen thread. Coat the thread with glue, or with shellac, to hold it in place.

Strands of rubber are used for

The Motive Power of model aëroplanes almost exclusively, as this is the most efficient light-weight material which has as yet been found for the purpose. For the simpler models, No. 32 rubber bands are often looped together chain fashion, and several strands of these used; but for the larger machines strands of rubber about $\frac{1}{16}$ inch thick are generally used. Rubber strands $\frac{1}{16}$ inch thick can be purchased wherever model aëroplanes are sold, and will cost about $1 for a piece 100 feet long; you will find the addresses of dealers, who make a specialty of furnishing model aëroplane parts, in the magazines. Some of the boys of the Chicago Calumet High School have tried the rubber from old golf balls, and have found this very satisfactory.

The number of strands necessary for a motor will depend, of course, upon the age of the rubber, and its diameter. If you use No. 32 rubber bands, which are $\frac{1}{8}$ inch wide and 3 inches long, from four to six strands will usually be sufficient, while if you use $\frac{1}{16}$ inch rubber, there should be from ten to eighteen strands.

Slip a glass bead on to the propeller shaft for a thrust-bearing, then slip the shaft through the hole in the hub, bend the end into a hook, and slip the rubber over it. The other ends of the strands should be looped over a screw-hook, and the hook should be screwed into the center-pole about 12 inches away from the propeller shaft. The strands should be just loose enough to remain taut when unwound.

The propeller of model aëroplanes is usually placed at the forward end, rather than in the rear as on the large machines, and the model is really drawn through the air instead of propelled. It has been found that the model flies steadier by this arrangement.

When winding up the Motor for a Flight, the propeller should be given from 100 to 175 turns, according to the strength of the rubber and number of strands used.

Figure 386 shows a monoplane patterned after **A French Model.** This, like the model just described,

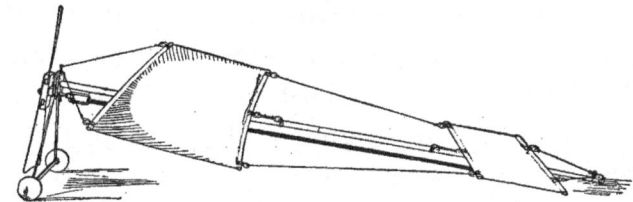

FIG. 386. — A French Monoplane Model.

may be equipped with a motor or may be used without as a glider.

The Center-pole is made out of a piece of bamboo, for which the end of a bamboo fishing-rod may be used (Fig. 387). Prepare blocks *A* and *B* as shown in Figs. 387 and 388, making *A* $\frac{1}{4}$ inch thick, $\frac{1}{2}$ inch wide.

BAMBOO CENTER-POLE 29" LONG
A
B
C
D
E
6 STRANDS OF 3-INCH RUBBER BANDS OR 18 STRANDS OF 1/16-INCH SQUARE RUBBER CORD
4"
SECTION
TIN PROPELLER BLADE

FIG. 387.

MACHINE SCREW
WOODEN WASHER
A
RING FROM TOP OF AN ALARM CLOCK FLATTENED ON SIDES
B
SCREW HOOK

FIG. 388.

WIRE
BAMBOO
BUTTON MOULD

FIG. 389.

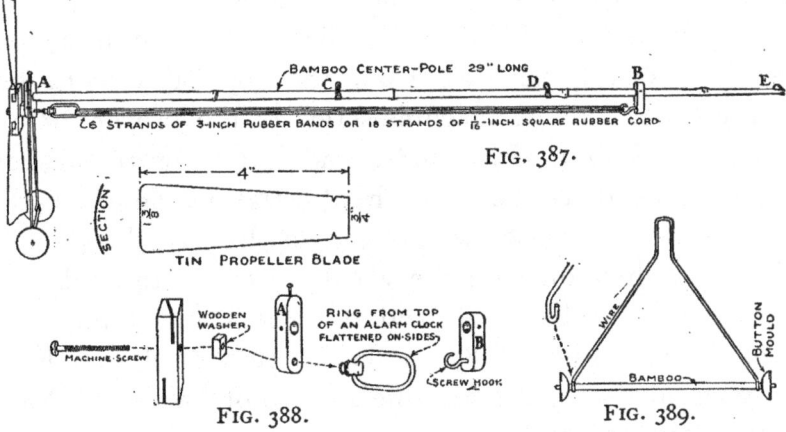

FIG. 387. — Center-pole and Motor of Monoplane Model shown in Fig. 386.
FIG. 388. — Details of Propeller and Motor Connections.
FIG. 389. — Details of Running-gear.

and $1\frac{1}{2}$ inches long, and B of the same width and thickness by $1\frac{1}{4}$ inches long. The necessary holes should be bored through these blocks before they are trimmed up to the proper size, to avoid splitting them. Locate the holes of the proper diameters for the center-pole, propeller shaft, and a screw-hook. Fasten the blocks to the center-pole with glue and brads, placing A at one end and B 23 inches away from it. Bind three fancy-work rings to the center-pole at C, D, and E (Fig. 387). Bind ring C $11\frac{1}{2}$ inches from block A, D 8 inches from C, and E at the end of the pole.

The Propeller is made similar to the one described for the other monoplane, but is of different proportions. The pattern for the blades is shown in Fig. 388, and the hub, also shown in the detail, should be $\frac{3}{8}$ inch by $\frac{3}{8}$ inch by $1\frac{3}{4}$ inches in size. For the propeller shaft, procure the ring from the top of a worn-out alarm-clock; also a machine-screw of the proper thread to screw into it (Fig. 388); and cut a small washer of hard wood, as shown. The illustrations show clearly how the machine-screw should run through the propeller hub, then through the wooden washer, through the lower hole in block A, and then be screwed into the clock ring. Figure 387 shows the number of strands of rubber necessary for an efficient motor; also how they are connected to the clock ring and to the screw-hook in block B.

A Running-gear is not necessary for a simple monoplane like this, but it is easily made and attached, and is a big protection to the propeller blades, which are likely to be bent out of shape if of metal, or broken if of wood, by coming in contact with the ground.

Figure 389 shows a simple way to construct the frame out of wire and bamboo, and how the ends of the bamboo axle run through the wheels. Button molds can be purchased at any dry-goods store for about 5 cents a dozen, and these make excellent wheels; they turn upon the axle and are held in place by driving short pins through the bamboo ends. Fasten the wire frame to block *A* with small tacks or thread, or with both (Fig. 387).

Some boys provide their models with bamboo

Skids constructed similar to the runners which were originally used upon the large machines, but wheels look neater upon the model machines, and produce less friction.

The Planes for this model do not require a framework. Only two sticks are necessary for each, and these slip through the hems sewed on the edges of the covering (Fig. 390). Silk should be used for the covering of the planes, and, if your mother hasn't any scraps large enough in her scrap-bag, you can buy enough for the two planes for 25 cents. If your mother or sister will do the necessary sewing on the sewing-machine, the rest of the work can be finished up very quickly; however, any boy who is at all handy can manage a needle and thread well enough when he has to, and does not find it hard, either. Make a hem along each of the long edges to run the sticks into, and a narrow one along each narrow edge to keep the silk from raveling. The pattern (Fig. 390) shows the proper dimensions for the planes. The sticks may be whittled out of pine, but bamboo is lighter and stronger.

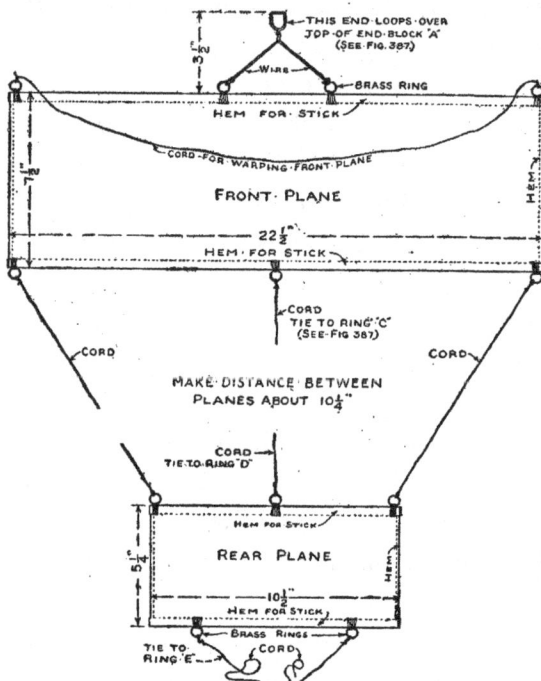

FIG. 390. — Pattern for Planes and Connections for Monoplane Model shown in Fig. 386.

After the silk has been prepared and the sticks have been slipped into the hems made for them, sew a dozen small brass rings to the edges, in the positions indicated upon the pattern, being careful to place each pair of rings the same distance away from the center. To the two center rings on the front edge of the front plane fasten the ends of a piece of wire bent as shown in Fig. 390, with a loop in the end to fit over the top of block *A* of the center-pole. Attach a cord to the rings at the ends of the front plane, for *warping* the plane; connect the two planes about $10\frac{1}{4}$ inches apart with cords tied to the end rings as shown; and tie a short piece of cord to each of the remaining rings by which to fasten the planes to rings *C*, *D*, and *E* on the center-pole. In attaching the planes to the center-pole, first slip the wire loop over the top of block *A* (Fig. 387), then pull the cords on the rear edge of the rear plane until the sticks in the front plane are bowed, and tie them to ring *E*; tie the cords on the center rings to rings *C* and *D* to keep the planes centered upon the center-pole.

After you have completed this model, go over it and examine each part; see that the silk covering of the planes is stretched taut; sight along the model, lengthwise, to see that the planes are in line with each other; test the warping of the front plane to make certain that it is the same on each end; and, if necessary, readjust the bracing cords to correct any of these faults.

If the model dives when you try it, loosen the bracing cords and move the rear plane a little forward; if it rises and then slips backwards to the ground, move the plane back until a perfect balance is obtained. When the planes have been properly adjusted, tie the cords securely so they will not slip. Some boys coat the knots with glue to make them doubly secure, but two half-hitches will make a perfect fastening.

The upper center photograph in the group opposite page 302 shows this model monoplane held aloft with the

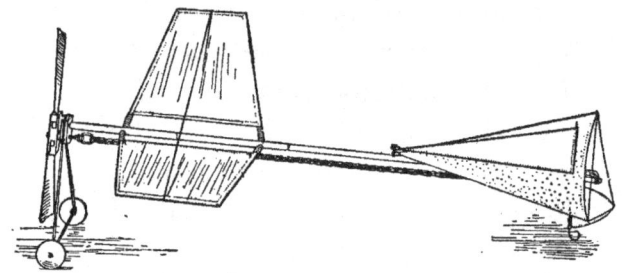

FIG. 391.—Antoinette Monoplane Model.

motor wound up, ready to be released for a flight. When carefully made, this model will fly distances of 100 to 200 feet.

The Antoinette Model shown in Fig. 391 is a neat monoplane and one that is easily made.

The Center-pole is shown in Fig. 392, and consists of a piece of a bamboo fishing-rod or bamboo umbrella handle, 24 inches long and $\frac{3}{8}$ or $\frac{1}{2}$ inch in diameter. Prepare the blocks *A* and *B* similar to blocks *A* and *B* in Fig. 388, and fasten *B* in place $21\frac{1}{2}$ inches away from block *A*. Run a piece of stiff wire through the center-pole at *C*, which should be $2\frac{1}{2}$ inches from *A*, and another at *D*, which should be 6 inches away from *C*; also run a piece of wire, cut $5\frac{1}{2}$ inches long and having its lower end bent into the form of a hook, through a vertical hole bored through the center-pole $\frac{1}{2}$ inch back of block *B*. Drive a screw into the top of the pole at *F*, which should be 7 inches away from block *B*, and fasten a brass ring to the rear end of the pole, as shown at *G*.

Use the details given in Fig. 388 in preparing

The Propeller for this model, and connect up the rubber motor as described for the other model.

Figures 393 to 396 show the patterns for the wings, tail, fin, and rudder.

A
C
D
F
B
E
G

FIG. 392.

RING
8"
HEM FOR WIRE
2"
FIN

FIG. 395.

11 1/2"
1"
HEM FOR WIRE OR STICKS
CORD FOR WARPING WINGS
WING
4
6"

FIG. 393.

WIRE IN EDGE
2"
2 1/2"
RUDDER

FIG. 396.

CORD IN EDGE
TAIL
RING
9 1/2"
RING
HEM FOR STICK
CORD IN EDGE
8

FIG. 394.

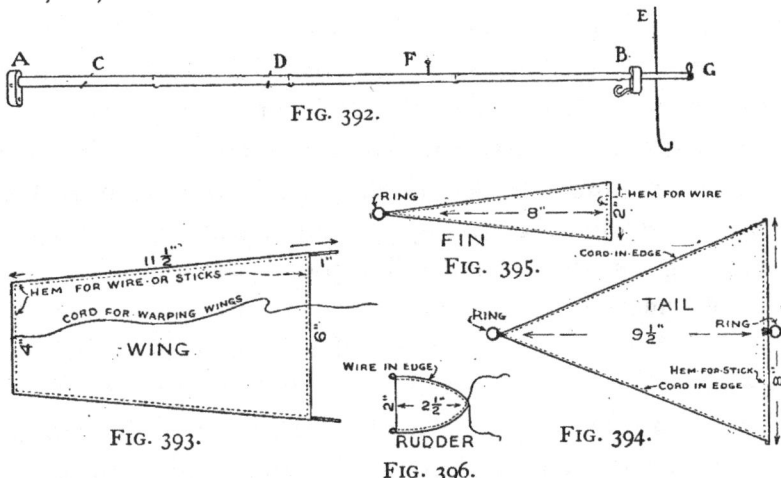

FIG. 392. — Center-pole of Antoinette Monoplane Model.
FIG. 393. — Pattern for Wings.
FIG. 394. — Pattern for Tail.
FIG. 395. — Pattern for Fin.
FIG. 396. — Pattern for Rudder.

The Wings require frames made of wire, or of four bamboo sticks bound together at the corners with linen thread, as indicated by the dotted lines in Fig. 393, and they are covered with silk. The projecting ends on the side pieces are provided for connection to the ends of wires C and D on the center-pole (Figs. 392 and 391); bind them in place with linen thread (Fig. 391). Connect the ends of the wings with a thread or cord, and make this short enough to warp the wings $2\frac{1}{2}$ inches (measurement at center, and from string to center-pole).

The Tail has one stick, which slips into a hem in the short edge of the cloth, and cords run through hems on the other two edges. Fasten one end of each cord to the stick and the other end to a small brass ring. This plane should be warped $\frac{3}{4}$ inch, by attaching a warping cord to the ends of the stick, as shown in Fig. 391.

The Fin is prepared similar to the tail plane, but, instead of having a stick run through it, the seam on the short edge slips over the upper end of wire E (Fig. 392). The rings on the fin and tail slip over the nail at F.

The Rudder has a piece of wire run through its edge to give it stiffness, and the ends of this wire are bent into hooks and fastened to the lower part of wire E (Figs. 391 and 392). Attach a thread to the rear of the rudder and fasten the ends of this to the ends of the tail plane, setting the rudder in line with the center-pole, or at an angle, according to whether you wish to have the model fly straight or in a curve.

The Running-gear is to be constructed the same as for the other model.

A More Elaborate Monoplane Model is shown in Fig. 397. This is one of the forms of monoplane models used by the boys of the Chicago Calumet High School

MODEL AËROPLANES 317

in their study of aëronautics. It is more difficult to make than those which have been described, but any handy boy who has built some of the simpler models successfully should be prepared to undertake its construction; for he will have learned that exact workmanship is necessary in model making, that the weight and

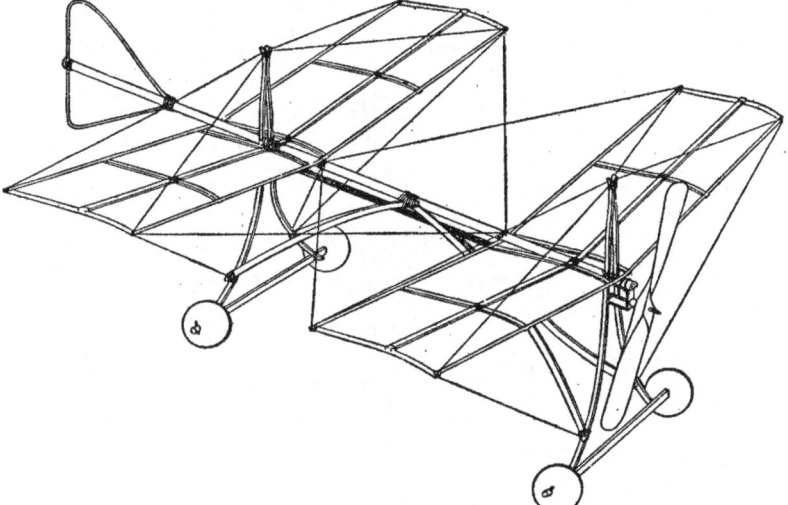

FIG. 397. — A More Elaborate Monoplane Model.

strength of materials used must be carefully considered, that each part must be carefully tested as prepared, that the planes must be warped or bowed to the same degree at both ends, and that an efficient propeller is one half of the secret of producing a record-breaking model.

As so many measurements are necessary for this model, in order that each part may be properly propor-

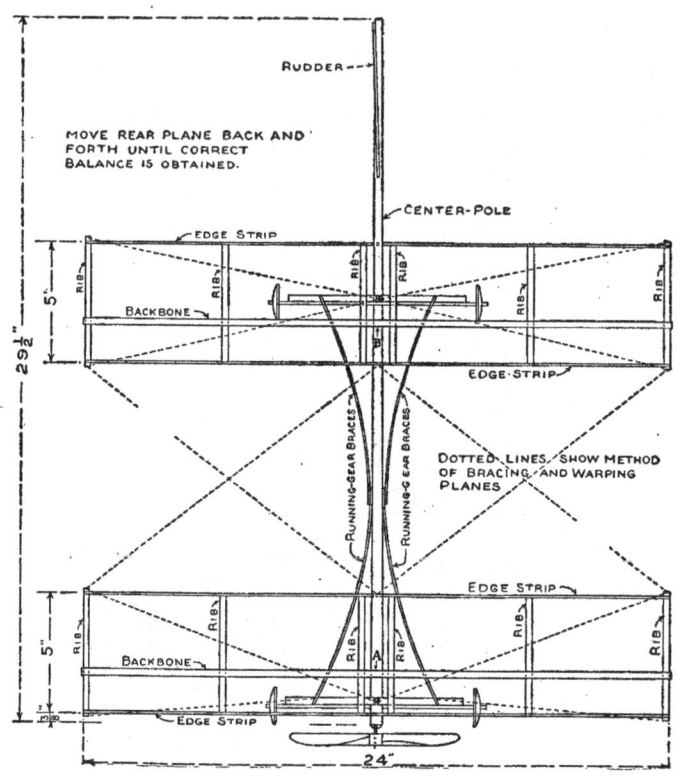

FIG. 398.—Plan or Top View.
(Scale $\frac{1}{8}'' = 1''$.)

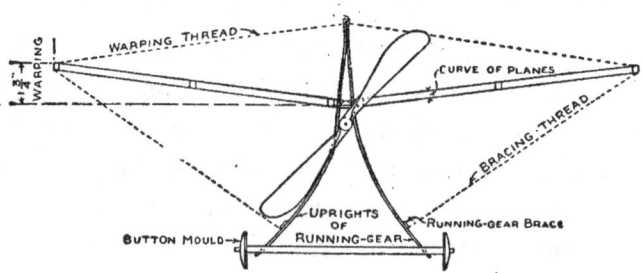

FIG. 399.—Front Elevation of Monoplane Model shown in Fig. 397.
(Scale $\frac{1}{8}'' = 1''$.)

MODEL AËROPLANES 319

tioned and properly placed, working-drawings are shown to a scale of ⅛ inch to the inch; that is, the plan or top view (Fig. 398), the front elevation (Fig. 399), and the side elevation (Fig. 400) are reproduced upon the pages at such a size that ⅛ inch of the drawing on the page represents 1 inch on the model, which you will understand if you have studied the instructions in Chapter IV for making working-drawings. By placing an ordinary ruler upon the pages you will be able to tell exactly what any measurement is.

Unless you have had some experience in reading mechanical drawings, there is one thing which may puzzle you, and which I shall explain. If you look at the propeller in Figs. 398 and 399, you will see that it is shown shorter in the plan than in the front elevation; the plan does not, in this case, show the correct length, but represents the top view when the propeller is turned to the angle shown in the front elevation. It is *foreshortened* in the plan. The propeller is foreshortened in the same

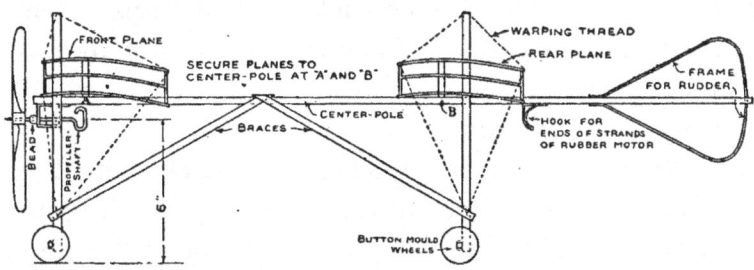

FIG. 400. — Side Elevation of Monoplane Model shown in Fig. 397.
(Scale ⅛″ = 1″.)

way in the side elevation (Fig. 400), which shows it as it would be seen in a side view when it is turned as shown in the front elevation. As all other portions set at an angle are foreshortened in a similar manner, in all views in which you do not look squarely at them, be careful to use the drawing which shows the true length, in taking off the measurements.

The Center-pole of this model is made out of a piece of bamboo, for which a fishing-rod or Japanese parasol handle may be used, and should be about $\frac{1}{2}$ inch thick; and the framework of the running-gear, the braces, and the backbone and ribs of each plane are made of strips of split bamboo $\frac{1}{16}$ inch thick by $\frac{3}{16}$ inch wide, and the edge strips of the planes and rudder are made of pine about $\frac{1}{16}$ inch in diameter. The ribs from a Japanese parasol may be used for the bamboo strips, and the sticks from a *sink splasher*, — a contrivance made to keep the walls around a sink from being splashed, which can be purchased for 5 or 10 cents at a department store — are just the thing for the $\frac{1}{16}$-inch sticks; small strips of bamboo may be used instead of the round sticks, if they are easier to obtain.

Strong linen thread is

The Best Material for Binding the sticks together. Wire is sometimes used, but thread is very much lighter and easier to handle, and if you brush the connections with a thin coat of glue after wrapping the thread around them, they cannot possibly separate. The binding was

MODEL AËROPLANES 321

not shown on the connections on the plan and elevations, in order not to make the drawings complicated, but you will readily see where it is necessary by looking at Fig. 397.

The Running-gear consists of two triangular frames, on each of which a pair of button molds are mounted for wheels. Measure off the lengths of the strips, from the drawings, and fasten the strips together as in Fig. 401. Whittle down the ends of the axles to fit the holes in the button molds, and drive pins through them to hold the molds in place. After completing the frames, bind them to the center-pole and brace each upright with a diagonal brace, as shown in Figs. 398 and 400.

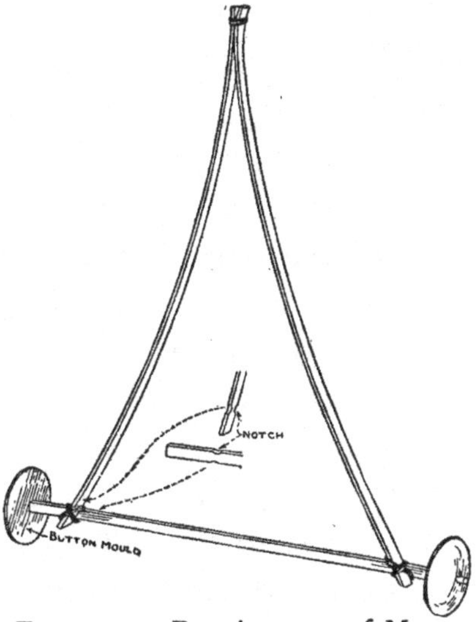

The Propeller shown in the drawings is a true form of screw-propeller. The making of one of these is

FIG. 401. — Running-gear of Monoplane shown in Fig. 397.

difficult, and it requires a great deal of accuracy in both laying out and cutting to produce one that is efficient. Many boys succeed in preparing very satisfactory propellers out of pine, spruce, or walnut, and sometimes *laminations* (layers) of walnut and white holly wood, while other boys buy them already made. A very effective 10-inch propeller can be purchased for about $1. If you make your propeller, follow the dimensions shown upon the drawings.

The Shaft Bearing is shown in detail in Fig. 402. Make this of brass or copper, of any gauge heavy enough to keep its shape, and not over $\frac{1}{16}$ inch thick. Flatten the under side of the center-pole for it to rest against, and wire it in place about $\frac{1}{8}$ inch away from the end.

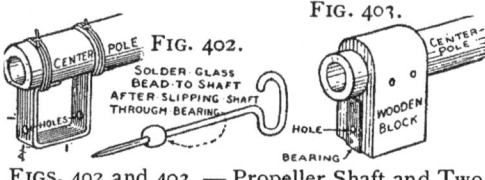

FIGS. 402 and 403. — Propeller Shaft and Two Forms of Shaft Bearing

If you have only very thin brass, copper, or tin out of which to make the bearing, you may prepare a block to fit on the pole and tack the bearing to the under side and ends of this, as shown in Fig. 403.

The Shaft is made out of a piece of stiff wire (Figs. 400 and 402). File a square taper upon the propeller end of this, so that the propeller will not turn upon it, and, after slipping it through the bearing, solder a glass bead on to it 1 inch from the end, as shown, to relieve the propeller of all motor strain. Drive the propeller on to the end of the shaft, carefully, so as to avoid the danger of splitting it. It is not necessary to clinch the end of this shaft, if you drive the propeller on to it properly; and there is an advantage in not clinching it, in the fact that the propeller can easily be removed then, in case

MODEL AËROPLANES

of accident, or if you have a number of forms of propellers, you can quickly interchange them. In drilling the hole through the shaft bearing, be sure to place it low enough so the hook will clear the center-pole, in revolving

The hook for the rear end of the rubber motor should be bent out of a piece of brass, and be wired to the under side of the center-pole to a flattened surface, as shown in Fig. 400.

The Rubber Motor described for the other models will be satisfactory for this machine (see page 307).

The Construction of the Planes is clearly shown upon the working-drawings. Bend the ribs to the exact curve shown in Fig. 404, and be careful to get them all alike.

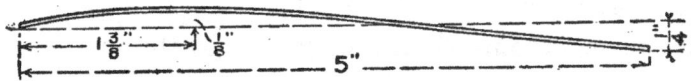

FIG. 404. — Curve the Ribs of the Planes like This.

Bind together the ends of the backbone, ribs, and edge sticks carefully, then test each framework to see that it balances at the center; this it must do, and it will if you have cut the sticks of equal size and have connected them at equal distances each side of the center. Cover the planes with silk or with Japanese rice-paper, stretching the covering as tight as possible, and cross-stitching the silk or gluing the paper. If you dampen the paper first, before putting it on, it will dry out as tight as a drumhead.

Bind the planes to the center-pole at *A* and *B* (Figs. 398 and 400), being careful in doing so to place them exactly at right angles to the pole. The rear plane will have to be readjusted, after the model has been completed, to a point which will produce a perfect balance of the machine, but the position shown is an approximate location and a good one for a first trial.

The Bracings, shown by the dotted lines in the illustrations, are fastened to the ends of the sticks. Use strong linen thread and fasten each end with two half-hitches. You may notch the ends of the sticks on the edges, in the same way that you notched the frame pieces of the running-gear, to avoid the possibility of the thread slipping off, but with well-tied half-hitches this precaution is not necessary.

The Rudder Frame should be lashed to the center-pole, as shown in Figs. 397 and 400. Cover the frame with thin paper or silk.

Finish. To make the framework more shipshape, it should be finished in some way. First rub it down carefully with sandpaper, then give it a couple of coats of shellac or aluminum paint. The aluminum paint such as is sold for stoves and radiators is inexpensive, and by using this the model's framework will appear to be made of aluminum.

Flights this Monoplane is capable of Making. Some of the boys of the Chicago Calumet High School's aëro club have made models of this type which have covered distances of from 200 to 325 feet. If you are a good mechanic, you may be able to turn out a machine which will exceed this longest flight, and if you are a genius, you may be able to discover improvements which will develop it into a record breaker. The photographs opposite pages 297 and 302 show this model in various sizes, and some of the models, you will notice, are provided with additional fins, placed below and above the center-pole, while others have a horizontal tail plane. After you have made the model for which the working-drawings are given, work out some of these extra parts, using your ingenuity, as well as the photographs, to determine the proper proportions for them.

Model aëroplane making, like the building of man-carrying machines, is in its infancy as yet, and for this reason probably offers a better opportunity for the boy inventor to show his skill and originality than does any other experimental work occupying the attention of men and boys at the present time. The making and flying of the small machines is keeping pace with that of the large ones. Each boy owner of a machine usually sets out with a determination to make a name for himself, and the frequency with which records are made and smashed in the junior aëro contests would make it difficult for any one but an enthusiast to keep track of the latest records.

Some of my readers will doubtless be holders of model aëroplane records, and when the honor comes to you, I want you to let me know.

The boy who devises a motor which will be more efficient than the rubber strand motor used at the present time, will do more to advance this new pastime than can come from any other form of development, so here is a good field for your experiments.

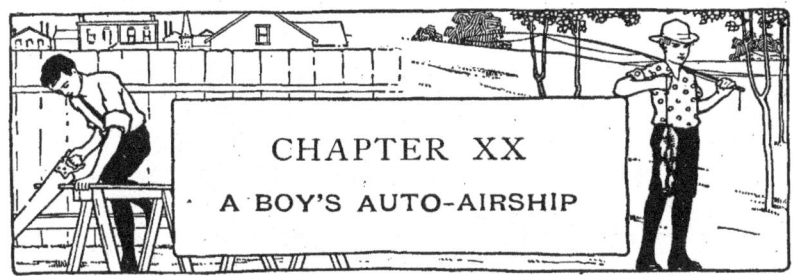

CHAPTER XX
A BOY'S AUTO-AIRSHIP

PROBABLY after making a number of different forms of model aëroplanes, you boys will become ambitious to construct something in which you yourselves can ride. Although the airship and aëroplane have been developed to the point where successful flying is an accomplished feat, they are a long ways from the stage of perfection whereby one can fly without endangering life or limb. However, to help satisfy you restless fellows who desire to fly, I am going to show you a scheme which will enable you to sail through the air. This will not contain the elements of danger or foolhardiness attendant upon leaping from a tree-top or shed roof with an umbrella for a parachute, or any of the ingenious ideas shown in Mr. Bradley's cartoon on page 299, which any lad who has suffered the consequences by breaking a limb or smashing the dining table and other furniture in such reckless endeavors, will tell you are not a success; instead, the auto-airship described and illustrated upon the following pages will provide a greater safety to the pilot than is afforded the coaster upon a toboggan-slide, or coaster railway, to-

FIG. 405.—The Auto-airship in Flight.

gether with many of the thrills of flying. As you will see by looking at Figs. 405 and 406, the rope cable along which the airship flies is hung low enough to keep the

FIG. 406. — Making a Landing.

course of the young aviator always close to the surface of good old Mother Earth.

For the Framework of the Balloon (Fig. 407), procure eight barrel hoops and three 1-by-2-inch strips 12 or 14 feet long, and purchase at a hardware store two wooden *single blocks* (the size for ¾-inch rope, with *hooks* and *beckets*, Fig. 411), 3 pounds of No. 12 steel wire, and ½ pound of small copper staples (Fig. 408).

From the 1-by-2-inch strips cut A, B, C, and D 5 feet 8 inches long, and crosspieces E, F, G, H, I, and J of the lengths shown in the top view of the framework (Fig.

409). Remove the beckets from the single blocks, unscrewing the bolts which hold them in the iron straps (Fig. 411), and bore a hole, the size of those in the straps, through strips *C* and *D*, $1\frac{1}{2}$ inches from each end. Then

NAILED
STAPLE
NAIL
BOW
RIB-BAND
STERN
RIBS
STAYS
FIG. 407.
BECKET
¼"x4" BOLT
FIG.
408.
LOOSE HOOK

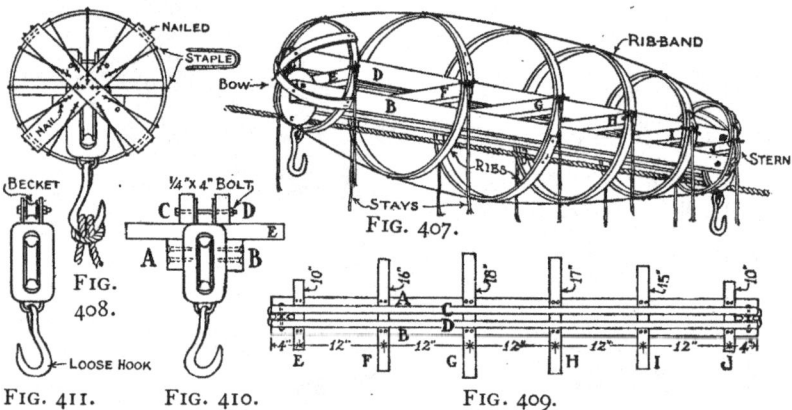

FIG. 411. FIG. 410. FIG. 409.

FIGS. 407 and 408. — Side and End Views of Framework of Balloon.
FIGS. 409 and 410. — Top and End Views showing Framework before Ribs and Rib-bands are attached.
FIG. 411. — Wooden Single Block.

bolt *C* and *D* to the becket straps (Figs. 409 and 410), using 4-inch bolts. Nail the crosspieces to *C* and *D*, spacing them as shown in Fig. 409; then nail strips *A* and *B* to the crosspieces, and screw their ends to the wooden shells of the blocks (Fig. 410). Two nails should be used at each point of nailing, to insure a strong framework.

The Barrel Hoop Ribs are fastened to the ends of the crosspieces (Fig. 407). Remove the nails which hold the hoops together, and turn in the ends until the inside diameters equal the length of the crosspieces, then drive several nails through the ends and clinch them on the inner side of the hoops. To build out the bow and stern of the framework (Fig. 407), cut the two remaining hoops in halves, cross a pair of these halves at right angles for each end, and fasten their centers together; then nail the ends to the end ribs and drive in a nail at the points where the hoops cross strips *A*, *B*, *C*, and *D* (Fig. 408). Clinch all nails wherever it is possible to do so.

Cut Twelve Rib-bands from the No. 12 wire, fasten one across the bottoms of the ribs, another across the tops (Fig. 407), and space the remaining ten between them at equal distances. The intermediate rib-bands are shown in Fig. 408, but have been omitted in Fig. 407 to make that illustration clearer. Fasten the rib-bands to the ribs with staples (Fig. 408).

Before inclosing the framework, cut twelve 6-foot lengths of heavy cord for

Stays, and tie one to each rib just above the crosspiece (Fig. 407); also run a cord through the blocks, so that when you are ready to slip the balloon on to its rope cable, you can tie the end of the cord to the rope and, by means of it, pull the rope through the wheels of the blocks.

You will require $4\frac{1}{2}$ yards of cloth for

The Balloon Envelope. A black, brown, or gray cambric or muslin will make the most durable covering, but any cloth you can get, such as old sheets, can be used.

Put the cloth on lengthwise of the framework in two strips, stretch it as smooth as possible, and fasten it to the ribs with tacks and to the rib-bands with thread. On top of the envelope sew a band of white cloth around the center of the balloon (Fig. 405).

The Construction of the Car requires but little explanation, as Figs. 412 to 418 show the details clearly. Pro-

SUSPENSION-STAYS
SEAT-BACK
SHAFT
BRACKET
BATTEN
SEAT
SEAT
SEAT RISER
FOOT-BOARD
K
L
1/4" HOLE
SHINGLE PROPELLER-BLADE
6"
3"
14½"
WASHERS
10 PENNY NAIL
FIG. 414.
FIG. 415
FIG. 417.
FIG. 418.
FIG. 413.
FIG. 412.
FIG. 416.

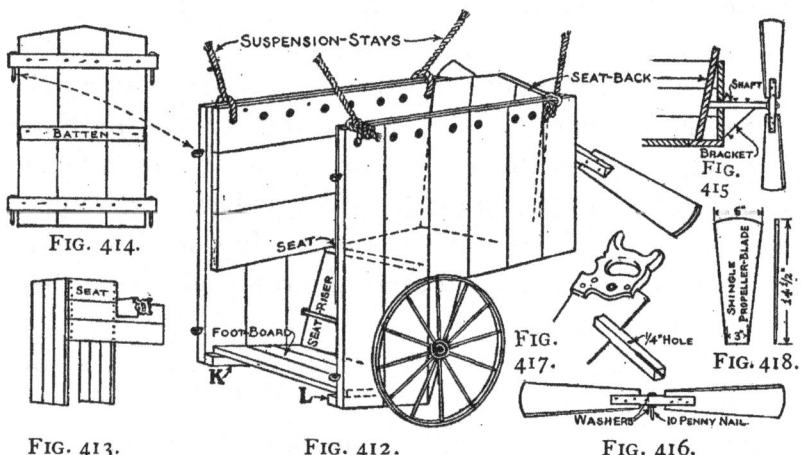

FIG. 412. — The Car.
FIG. 413. — First Step in making over a Box for a Car.
FIG. 414. — Gate for Front of Car.
FIGS. 415 to 418. — Details of Propeller.

cure a box about 16 inches deep, 20 inches wide, and 3 feet long; remove the bottom and one end, nail the bottom boards crosswise to form the car seat (Fig. 413), and saw off the projecting ends. Reënforce the sides of the box with vertical boards (Fig. 412). Cut the first two boards long enough to support the pitched foot-board, which should be fastened 14 inches below the seat, and make the first board on each side project 1 inch beyond the box (Fig. 412) to form a rabbet for the gate to set in. Nail cleats K and L to the side boards, where shown, and fasten the foot-board upon them. Fit the seat-riser between the seat and foot-board, make a seat back as shown in Figs. 412 and 415, and attach a pair of wagon wheels to the sides.

Fasten the gate boards together with three battens, making the top and bottom battens long enough to project $1\frac{1}{2}$ inches on each side; drive a 20-penny (4-inch) nail through each end of the projecting battens, and screw four screw-eyes into the front of the car for sockets, in which to set them (Figs. 412 and 414).

Bore eight $\frac{5}{8}$-inch holes through each side of the car, $1\frac{1}{2}$ inches below the top, through which to tie the stays (Fig. 412); then cut two 6-foot lengths of $\frac{1}{2}$-inch rope for the suspension stays, and tie the ends of one through the two front holes, and the ends of the other through the two rear holes (Fig. 412).

The Propeller (Figs. 415 to 418) requires a hub strip 1-by-1-by-10 inches in size, with a $3\frac{1}{2}$-inch slot in each end (Fig. 417), and two blades similar to Fig. 418. Notice that the slots are cut diagonally across the ends of the hub strip, and that one is at right angles to the other. Bore a $\frac{1}{4}$-inch hole through the center of one side of the hub strip (Fig. 417), then fasten the blades in the slots. Cut a stick 11 inches long for the propeller shaft (Fig. 415), fasten the propeller to one end, and insert the other end in a hole bored through the back of the car; nail it securely in position, and brace it with a wooden bracket.

If you stretch the cable for your airship upon a hillside, you will require

A Starting Platform just high enough to lift the car off the ground, but if the ground is level, or nearly so (Fig. 405), it will be necessary to construct a platform 8 feet or so above the surface to give the rope cable sufficient pitch.

This platform is built between two trees, 3 or 4 feet apart, and is supported by four brackets. Each bracket consists of three pieces of 2-by-4, as you will see by looking at Fig. 405. Cut the piece marked M 4 feet long, and N and O 2 feet 6 inches long; miter the lower ends of N and O, and let their upper ends into M. Nail the pieces together and spike two brackets to each tree; then spike crosspieces P and Q across the trees, directly under top piece M of the brackets, as additional supports. Cut the railing uprights R, S, and T 5 feet long, mortise the upper ends for the gate (U) to slide through, and spike them to the brackets. Brace the lower ends with the diagonal pieces V and W, and their upper ends with boards X and Y. Cut the gate (U) long enough to reach from R to T, insert a short stick in a hole bored near one end, for a handle, and nail a strip across the other end to prevent it from pulling through the mortise in upright R. Nail the platform boards in place, and fasten

A Push-off Platform (Z) between the trees, 18 inches above the main platform, for the car.

Build a ladder from the ground to the main platform.

The Rope Cable. Purchase $\frac{3}{4}$-inch Manila rope for the cable, and get whatever length you will require in one piece. Fasten one end of this rope to a tree a few feet in back of the upper station platform (Fig. 405), then run it through the single blocks in the balloon framework, and while you pull on the rope to take up as much of the slack as possible, have some one tie the lower end to the center of a rope stretched between two trees at the lower end of the airship's course (Fig. 406). If there doesn't happen to be a tree directly in back of the upper station, you can attach that end of the rope between two trees, in the same way that you fastened the lower end. Tie the lower end of the rope low enough so the car will run upon the ground for a few feet, and slow up, before reaching the end. Throw some loose earth over the point of landing, and from there as far as the end of the rope, to retard the speed of the wheels.

To attach the Car, hitch the loops of the suspension stays over the block hooks (Fig. 405), and tie the ends of the intermediate stays through the holes in the sides of the car.

To pull back the Airship to the Starting Platform,

attach a strong cord to the hook in the stern block, run it through a small pulley attached to the upper end of the cable (Fig. 405), and bring it down below the platform to a windlass constructed as shown in the illustration.

If several of you boys club together in building an auto-airship, you will have to "toss up" to see who shall have the first ride; then, after all of the "directors" and workmen have ridden, you will want your friends to enjoy a trip. By charging a small fare you can make the airship pay back, in a short time, what you have expended for material.

Fig. 122.

Fig. 124.

Fig. 123.

Fig. 125.

Figs. 122 and 123. Tabourets.
Fig. 124. Plant Stand.
Fig. 125. Footstool.

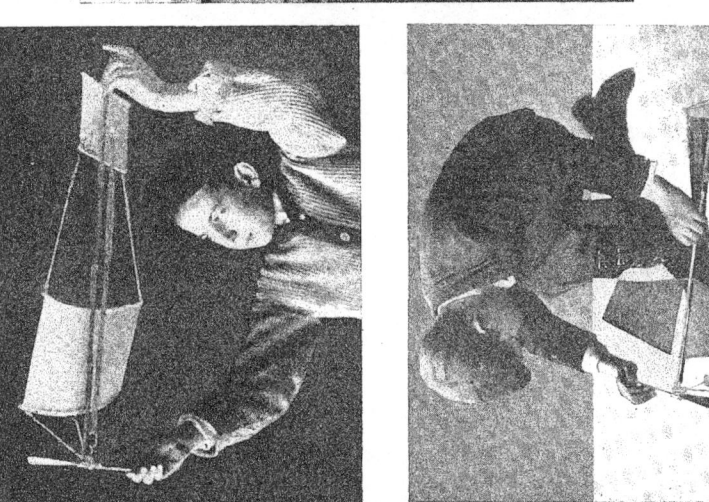
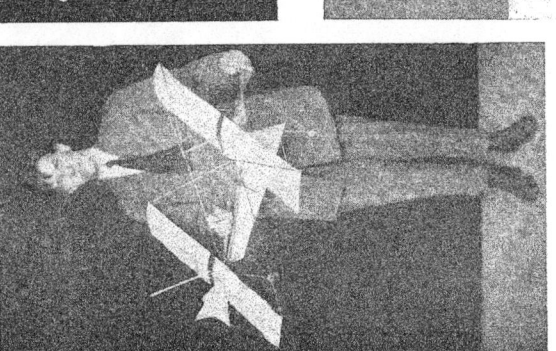

Some Good Forms of Model Aeroplanes.

CHAPTER XXI

CAMPING EQUIPMENT

WHEN the last day of school arrives, isn't it with a sense of relief that you pack up your books, carry them home, and throw them on to a high shelf, or into your bedroom closet — somewhere out of sight? And isn't it hard to realize that you need not think of lessons again for more than two months, and that you are free to do whatever you choose for the balance of the summer days? It used to be that way when the author was a boy, and conditions probably haven't changed much in this regard.

Some of you boys will experience the joys of camping out for the first time this summer, — the trip which always remains freshest in one's memory, as it generally is so full of amusing incidents, — and those of you who have camped out before will probably not miss an opportunity to do so again this year; but, if it is not possible for you to go away from town, there is no reason why you cannot camp out near home, in some vacant lot, or in your back yard, or on the porch or roof.

A Tent is one of the first parts of the camping equipment to look after. The prices of tents vary in different locations, but you can get an 8 foot by 10 foot " A " tent (Fig. 419) of 10-ounce duck, complete with poles and stakes, in New York, Chicago, Denver, or San Francisco, for about $7, and a wall tent of the same size (see photo-

FIG. 419. — An "A" Tent.

graph opposite page 340) for about $9, while a *fly* will cost about one half as much as the tent.

If you wish to make a tent yourself, you will not find the work difficult, and you will save considerable on the cost. The sewing together of the strips of canvas is the hardest part of the work for a boy; probably your mother will be willing to do this for you on her sewing-machine. Eight-ounce duck, 29 inches wide, retails at about 15 cents a yard, and the 10-ounce weight, which is better for the purpose, at about 18 cents a yard.

For making an " A " Tent of the size shown upon the diagram (Fig. 420), you will require 30 yards of material. The diagram shows the completed tent as it would appear when spread out flat upon the ground, and also the dimensions for cutting the different lengths of canvas. You will see that strips *A*, *B*, *C*, and *D* are of equal length, and that strips *E*, *G*, *J*, and *K* are of one shape and size, as are also the triangular pieces *F*, *H*, *I*, and *L* and strips *M* and *N*. Lap each strip a full 1 inch over the edge of the adjoining pieces, as indicated by the dotted lines on the diagram, and sew each seam near the edges with a double row of stitching. After all of the pieces have been cut and sewed together, turn back the outside edges 1 inch, as indicated by dotted lines, to finish them off and at the same time, reënforce them. Buy one dozen 1-inch iron harness rings for the ridge and guy-rope eyelets, set two in the canvas at the ends of the ridge, and one at the end of each of the side seams, and buttonhole stitch them in place. The canvas should be reënforced with a square patch in the places where the eyelets are to be set in in the ridge. Sew canvas loops and straps to the flaps, in the locations indicated, and tie the guy-ropes through the eyelets provided for them.

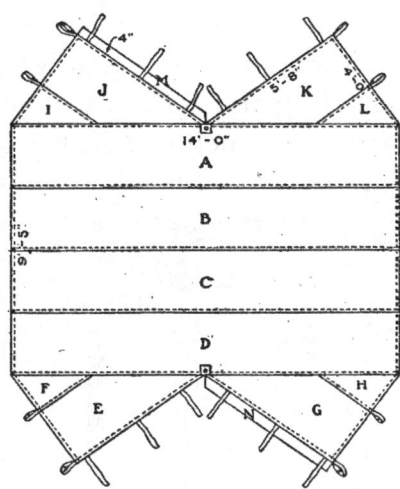

FIG. 420. — Diagram for Making an "A" Tent, 7 feet by 9 feet and 5 inches.

Figures 421 to 423 show the details for

The Ridge-pole and Uprights. These should be cut out of pieces 1¾ inches square, which may be ripped out of a piece of 2-by-4. Cut the uprights about 5 feet 10 inches long, which will allow for setting the ends 3 inches into the ground, and the ridge-pole 9 feet 5 inches long. Round off the top of the ridge-pole as in Fig. 423. Drive a piece of ⅜-inch or ½-inch iron rod into one end of each upright (Fig. 422), and bore two holes, ⅛ inch larger than the rods, through the ridge-pole in the proper positions for the rods to fit in (Fig. 421). A piece of tin bent around the ends of the pole, as in Fig. 423, will prevent the rods from splitting them.

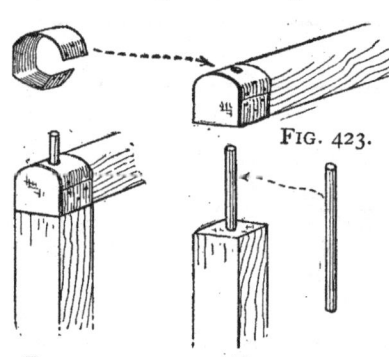

FIG. 423.

FIG. 421. FIG. 422.

FIG. 421.—Connection of Ridge-pole with Upright.
FIG. 422.—End of Upright.
FIG. 423.—End of Ridge-pole.

Fourteen Tent Stakes will be required, and these should be prepared at home, to save delay in pitching the tent after you reach your camping ground.

Pitch your Tent upon a level spot, close to your water supply if possible, and dig a little trench around it to catch the surface rain-water, which would otherwise run into the tent; make a couple of outlets from the trench, on the low side, so the water will drain away. Do this

A-Wall Tent, Eight Feet by Ten Feet, with Fly.

Flapjacks for Two.

trenching as soon as you have pitched your tent; otherwise, you may be caught unprepared for a storm, and it is unpleasant to be compelled to do the work during a drenching rain.

A Tent Ground-cloth, which should be of waterproof material, should be laid upon the ground and lapped up around the sides of the tent; this will prevent the dampness of the ground from penetrating your bedding.

If there are spruce or pine trees in the vicinity of your camp, be sure

To make a Mattress upon which to spread your blankets. Cut a number of boughs, and lop off enough of the tips of the branches to form a good-sized pile of twigs. Then carry these to your tent and, beginning at the proper point for the head of your bed, place a row of the twigs upon the ground-cloth with the tips toward the back of the tent. Next, place another layer of the twigs over these, and lap the tips over the butt ends of the first row, and continue to lay row after row in this manner, which is just the way in which the shingles on a roof are lapped, until you have reached the foot of the bed. The degree of softness of this mattress will depend entirely upon the care with which the twigs are placed and how well the butt ends are concealed by the tips. To avoid hard lumps, use only the slender portions of the branches. Spread your blanket upon the mattress, and your bed will be complete.

If the nights are cold in the region in which you intend to camp, take along

A Sleeping-bag. By folding over your blanket along the center, lengthwise, and then sewing it along the side and across the bottom, a very satisfactory bag may be made. The author has found such a bag very comfortable, and, when camping in the mountains where the temperature at night drops below "freezing," has used two of these bags, slipping one inside of the other, to give double warmth. With the top of the bag pulled snugly around your neck, there is no possibility for the cold air to reach you. The bag can be turned inside out every morning and aired. With covers in common, you are likely to awaken some night, feeling cold, to find that one of the other boys has been over-generous to himself with the clothes, unless you know how to "cling" to your portion; but with a sleeping-bag you are safe from disturbance.

Other Equipment. No two boys will carry the same equipment with them when going camping, and every boy will find after he has reached camp that he has taken along lots of needless things and left behind many articles which would add greatly to his comforts; but this is something which most campers experience, and it is doubtful if ever a man carries exactly the same outfit on two trips, for the reason that he is continually finding some way wherein he can make it more compact and complete. The greatest trouble lies generally in taking along too much. The location of your camp will determine to a great extent what special articles should be included in the outfit, and an experienced camper, familiar with that part of the country, will be a good one to consult about your requirements.

A frying-pan, kettle, saucepan, baking pan, coffee-pot, wash-basin, two water pails, tin plates and cups, spoons, knives and forks, and a can-opener will be required for the kitchen outfit; and towels, rags, soap, rope and twine, matches, a lantern and a can of kerosene oil, candles, an ax, a sharpening stone, hammer, saw and nails, will just about complete the general equipment. It is a good plan to take several sizes of nails, — 8-penny, 10-penny, 16-penny, and 20-penny, — for there will probably be things which you will wish to make while in camp.

An Electric Flash Lamp is a very handy article to have for locating things in and about the tent, when you do not care to bother with lighting your lantern.

Packing. Wrap your matches in paraffine paper, and then place them in a tin can to protect them from dampness; and put all the other small articles of your equipment in small bags provided with draw strings; salt and flour sacks may be fixed for the purpose. Pack the sacks, and all other things belonging to the general equipment which are not too bulky, in grocery boxes. When you get to camp, you will find the boxes handy for keeping things in, and those not required for this purpose will make good stools and will be good for setting things on.

A Safety Match-box, a strong jack-knife, and fishing-tackle should be made a part of the personal equipment of each boy of the camping party, and if each has

A Duffle Box (Fig. 424) in which to carry his outfit, he will save a general mix-up of things, possible loss of small articles, and resulting unpleasantness with the other fellow whom he may think is to blame

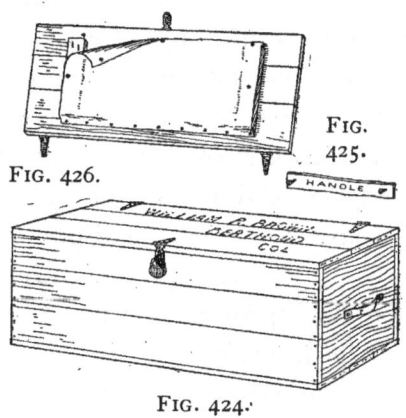

FIG. 424.— Camp Duffle Box.
FIG. 425.— Strap Handle.
FIG. 426.— Pocket on Inside of Cover.

A grocery box will serve the purpose, but this should be gone over carefully, and all boards whose nails show signs of loosening should have additional nails driven into them. Batten together the cover boards on the inside, hinge them to the box with strap-hinges, and fasten a hasp to the front so the box may be padlocked for transporting, and whenever you are away from camp. Handles may be made out of pieces of a strap, or several thicknesses of cloth tape, and be secured to the box with screws (Fig. 425). By fastening a piece of canvas or heavy cloth to the inside of the cover, over the battens (Fig. 426), tacking it along the bottom edge, and making buttonholes in the side and upper edges to button over large-head tacks, the space between the battens will serve as a pocket for writing materials.

If any boy in your party has had experience in camp cooking, leave to him the matter of purchasing

Food Supplies. But if you are all "green" at it, you had better get your mothers to help you make out your grocery list. Each mother will have a pretty fair idea of the size of her son's appetite, and it ought to be an easy matter for her to estimate on the proper quantities and varieties of supplies to do him. But she should be warned, beforehand, to allow for an increased appetite; also to select such things as can easily be prepared. Then compare all the lists and compile one complete list from them.

Fish and game may possibly be secured while in camp, but it is best not to count upon this as a certainty, and to take along plenty of everything, unless you know that your camp will be within easy reach of supplies.

If you are to be Cook, find out how to make flapjacks, graham muffins, biscuits, and johnny-cake, and watch your mother to see how she prepares breakfast cereals, coffee, and tea; also try your hand at cooking these things while at home, instead of waiting until you get into camp and starving your companions, as well as yourself, during the experimental period. It will save lots of unpleasantness all around.

The trouble met with in

Making an Open Fire for cooking generally arises from

getting it too large, so that it is all blaze and smoke. What is necessary is a small fire of hot coals. If you have watched an experienced camper prepare his fire, you have noticed that he confines it to a small place.

The Backwoodsman's Scheme of building his fire between two logs placed alongside of each other, about 6 inches apart at one end and 12 inches apart at the other end (Fig.

FIG. 427. — The Backwoodsman's Camp Fireplace.

427), is very satisfactory for a fireplace, as the fire is confined between the logs, and, by keeping the wide opening turned toward the wind, a splendid draft is obtained.

The logs should be green, and, to prevent the fire from getting under them, it is well to plaster mud against their inner faces. Two forked branches are driven into the ground, one at each end of the fireplace, and a horizontal pole, known as a *lug pole*, rests in the forks and supports the pothooks.

CAMPING EQUIPMENT

The Pothooks may be made from forked sticks cut to the proper length, with nails driven into them near the lower ends (Fig. 428), or out of pieces of heavy wire bent into hooks at one end and loops at the other end (Fig. 429), the loops being made large enough so they will slide back and forth on the lug pole. Both the stick and wire pothooks may be made short enough to accommodate the largest pot you have, and then lengthened to suit the small utensils by means of S-shaped extension hooks bent out of wire (Fig. 430). A piece of tin from an empty tin can may be tacked across the logs for the coffee-pot and for handleless utensils which are too small for the logs to support.

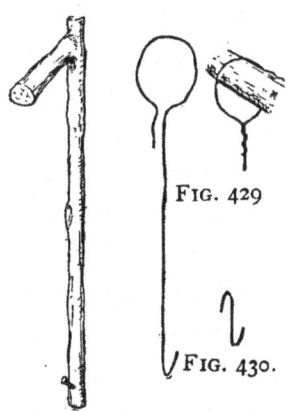

Fig. 428.
Fig. 428.—Stick Pothook.
Fig. 429.—Wire Pothook.
Fig. 430.—Extension Hook.

Such a fireplace as the above can be built anywhere, even in a back yard, with perfect safety, and any boy can use his ingenuity to rig up his pothooks and supports out of plain sticks if he cannot find suitable branches for the purpose.

A Sheet-iron Camp Stove, such as is shown in the photograph opposite page 340, is very commonly used by campers, and is handier and easier to cook on than the open fire. A stove of the size shown in the illustration can usually be bought complete with stovepipe for $1.50.

A Dutch Oven is a good substitute for the camp stove, and answers almost every purpose. It consists of a shallow iron pan or kettle, supported upon iron legs and furnished with a tight-fitting cover. It is set in a bed of red-hot coals, then after the biscuits, muffins, beans, meat, fish, or other food which is to be baked, stewed, or roasted is placed in the pan, the cover is fitted on and hot coals are heaped up at the sides and over the top. A medium-sized oven will cost $1.00.

A Camp Fireless Cooker is another handy contrivance, inasmuch as food can be prepared in it while you are away from camp, so that it will be ready to eat immediately upon your return at night tired and hungry. A cooker may be constructed out of a grocery box; and hay or dried leaves may be used for packing. See directions on page 136 for making a fireless cooker. By setting the cooker box into a hole in the ground, and throwing earth over the cover after placing the food within, the insulation will be more nearly perfect.

To build a Fire properly, whittle a few shavings and cut a number of small sticks, — some to about the size of a lead-pencil and others a little larger, — spread the shavings along the bottom of the fireplace, and upon these pile up the sticks, loosely and crisscrossed, so as to allow plenty of openings for draft. Set fire to the shavings, and as soon as the sticks have kindled, add a few larger pieces of wood to the pile; but be careful not to put on too many pieces before the fire has made a good

CAMPING EQUIPMENT

start, or you will choke out the flame. A good fire is obtained only by careful building, and requires continual attention to be satisfactory for camp cooking.

Always keep a good supply of wood at hand, some place under cover where it will be protected from rain and dew, so you will never be without dry wood with which to kindle your fire.

Camp Furniture. A table and a few seats add to the comforts of camp life, and the making of these furnishes interesting occupation for days when you wish to stay around camp. The three tools mentioned among the camp equipment are all that are necessary for making camp furniture, because fine work is neither required nor desirable in the woods.

Figure 431 shows

A Camp Chair that is easily made. You will notice that the edges of all the pieces are left square, instead of being beveled to fit the adjoining surfaces, that the seat board *B* is nailed to the diagonal brace *C*, and the two fastened to the chair back *A*, with cleats *D* and *E* nailed on to support them, and that the diagonal leg *F* is slanted as much as you wish to have the chair back slant, and is braced by the two side braces *G*.

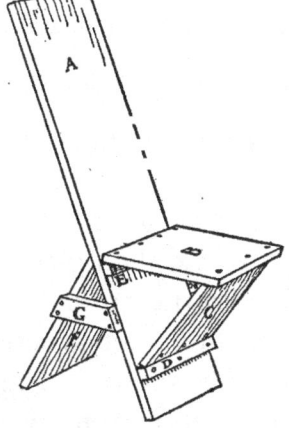

FIG. 431. — A Camp Chair.

A Camp Table (Fig. 432). By fastening together several

boards with battens, a good table top can be made, and this may be supported at one end on a cleat nailed across a tree trunk (Fig. 433), and at the other end on a couple of stakes driven into the ground (Fig. 432).

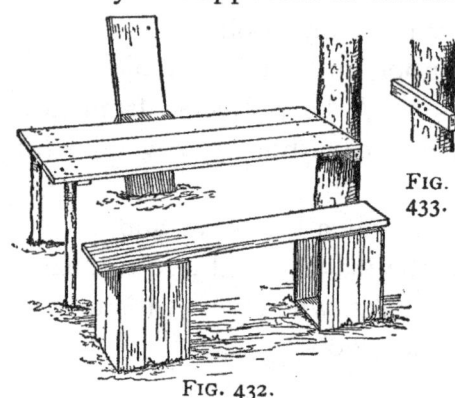

FIG. 432.
FIG. 432. — A Camp Table and Bench.
FIG. 433. — Cleat Support on Tree.

Boxes can usually be picked up in the vicinity of an old camp, and these, added to those in which you brought your outfit, can be utilized for many things.

A Good Table Bench is obtained by laying a plank across the tops of two boxes (Fig. 432), and

A Comfortable Box Bench is made by removing one side of a box, then placing the box on the ground, bottom up, and constructing a back as shown in Fig. 434. To keep it from overturning, nail the box to stakes driven into the ground. Use your ingenuity in constructing

Box Cupboards to hang in the tent and upon the trees.

FIG. 434. — A Comfortable Box Bench.

CHAPTER XXII
A HOME-MADE PUNT

GOOD workmanship is necessary in boat building, not so much for the sake of appearance as for safety and durability, but neat appearance will not be found lacking in a properly planned and carefully built boat. The nearer a boat approaches the square lines of a box, the easier it is to build, and it is well for a boy to try one of the simplest forms, such as the punt shown in Fig. 435, for a first attempt. The principles of boat building are easily learned, and after you have constructed a punt you will have had enough experience to enable you to tackle other forms of craft of more complicated construction.

Dimensions. The punt shown in the illustration is 12 feet long, 3 feet 6 inches wide, and 18 inches deep, but these dimensions can easily be increased or reduced if you wish a boat of other proportions.

Material. Get pine or cypress for your building material, and be sure to see that it is well seasoned, dry, and free from knots and other defects. Stock 18 inches wide is generally hard to find, nowadays, in most localities, so probably you will have to use an 8-inch and a 10-inch board, or a 6-inch and a 12-inch board, for each side. The bottom boards should be either 4 or 6 inches wide and

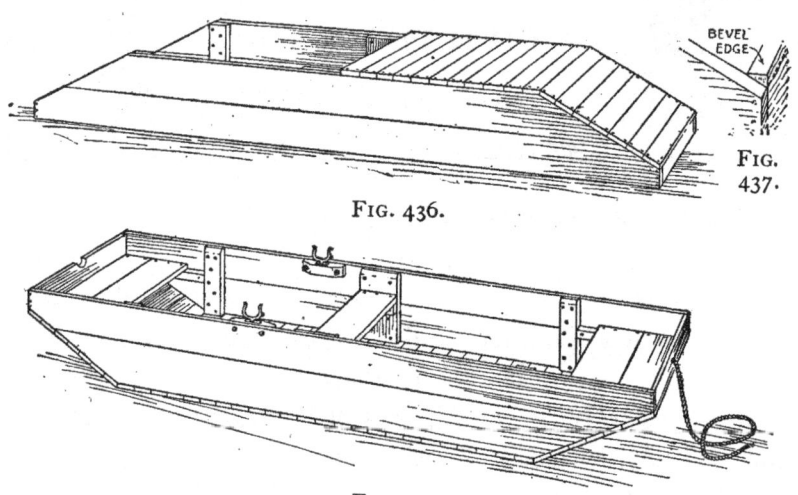

Fig. 436.

Fig. 437.

Fig. 435.

Fig. 435. — A Home-made Punt.
Fig. 436. — How the Bottom Boards are Put On.
Fig. 437. — Bevel off the Bottom Edge of the Stem and Stern Pieces.

have plain edges, not tongued and grooved, and the seats may be made of any scraps you have on hand.

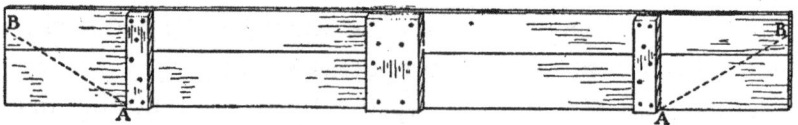

Fig. 438. — Batten Together the Side Boards like this.

Figure 438 shows how

The Side Boards should be battened together. Make the center batten 10 inches wide and the other two battens about 4 inches wide; fasten the latter in place about

24 inches from the ends. Short nails will not hold such pieces as battens very well, and the clinching of long nails, where they are exposed to view, is not very desirable, so it is a good plan to use screws of the proper length for the purpose.

When the boards of the side pieces have been battened together, locate the points *B* 4 inches below the top edge, then connect them with points *A* by the diagonal lines *AB*, as shown, and saw off the ends on these lines.

Cut the Stem and Stern Pieces 4 inches wide and 3 feet 4 inches long, then turn the side pieces over on their top edge as shown in Fig. 436, and fit these pieces between their ends.

Cut the Bottom Boards 3 feet 6 inches long, out of the 4-inch or 6-inch boards mentioned before. Coat the edges of the side pieces and the edges of each bottom board with white lead, and drive each board as close as possible to the preceding piece. Use copper or galvanized nails for fastening the boards; these will stand the exposure to water, but wire or wrought-iron nails without galvanizing will not, and will soon rust through and break off.

The bottom edge of the stem and stern pieces will have to be beveled off with a plane as shown in Fig. 437, as will also one edge of the first and last bottom boards, and one edge of the bottom boards at the ridges, in order to make the boards fit together perfectly at those points.

Fasten an Inner Keel Board to the bottom of your boat along the center, from bow to stern, as a protection to the bottom boards, and nail a cleat to it in the proper place to brace your feet against while rowing.

Figure 435 shows the arrangement of the three

Seats. Fasten these to cleats placed about 3 inches below the top of the sides. Make the center seat out of a 10-inch board, and the end seats out of a 10-inch and an 8-inch board (which will make them about 18 inches wide), and nail a short batten across the under side of the end seats as shown in Fig. 439, to prevent them from springing apart and catching one's clothes between them.

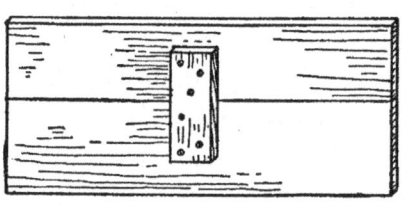

FIG. 439. — The End Seat.

Rowlocks. A pair of galvanized wrought-iron rowlocks, of the form shown in Fig. 440, can be purchased for 25 or 30 cents, and it is an easy matter to make the socket blocks for them to set in (Fig. 441). Cut two blocks about 8 inches long, $1\frac{1}{4}$ inches wide, and 2 inches thick; bevel the ends, and bore a $\frac{1}{4}$-inch hole near each

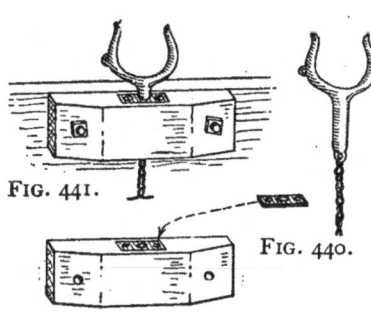

FIG. 441.
FIG. 440.

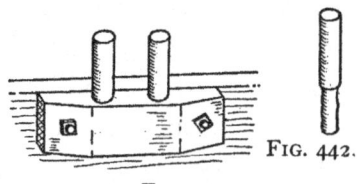

FIG. 443.
FIG. 442.

FIGS. 440 and 441. — Rowlocks.
FIGS. 442 and 443. — Thole-pins.

end for bolting, and a ½-inch hole from the center of the top down through each for the rowlock to drop into. The socket plate (Fig. 440), which comes with the rowlock, should be set into the block flush with the top. Bolt the blocks to the sides of the punt (Fig. 441) so the centers will be 14 inches from the center of the center seat.

In case you cannot conveniently get rowlocks,

Thole-pins may be made and used as a substitute. Figure 442 shows a pin cut from a piece of broom-handle, and Fig. 443 shows how a pair of them should be set into holes bored in a block similar to those shown for the rowlocks. The holes for the pins should be placed about 3 inches apart.

The Painter may be knotted on the end and slipped through a hole bored in the stem piece, and a circular notch may be cut in the top edge of the stern piece to admit an oar or paddle for steering.

Finishing. Set all nail-heads, putty up the holes thus made, and all other holes and defects, and then give the boat two or three coats of lead paint, inside and out, in color to suit your taste.

CHAPTER XXIII
A HOME-MADE SHARPIE

ALTHOUGH there is more work to the construction of a sharpie than the punt described in the last chapter, it is much easier to row on account of its wedge-shaped bow; at the same time, the material required will cost no more than that for the other boat. The flat-bottom boat is generally considered one of the best forms of cheap rowboats, and you will find it in common use

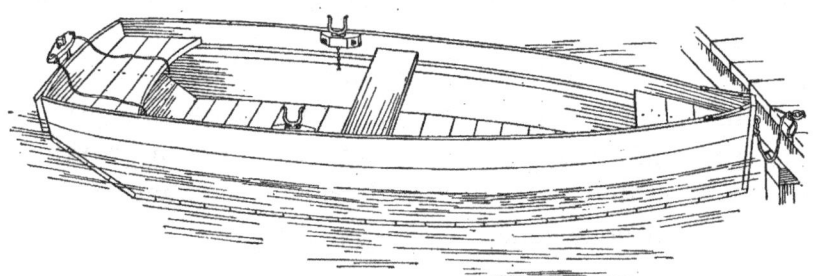

FIG. 444. — A Home-made Sharpie.

upon the rivers and small lakes, at summer resorts and at private piers. It is not difficult to build one.

Dimensions. Figure 444 shows a sharpie 13 feet long, 3 feet 6 inches wide amidships, and 18 inches deep.

You may alter these proportions if you wish, but, in case you do, draw out your revised plan and figure out the sizes for all the pieces before beginning work, so that every part will fit properly.

As it is difficult to get boards wider than 14 inches,

13'-4"
SIDE · PIECES
11'-0"
FIG. 445.
3'-0"
STERN PIECE
2'-8"
FIG. 447.
3'-4"
BATTENS
STRETCHER
18"
2'-10"
3"
FIG. 448.
FIG. 446.
A
B
USE EITHER FORM OF STEM PIECE
TEMPORARY BRACE

FIG. 449.

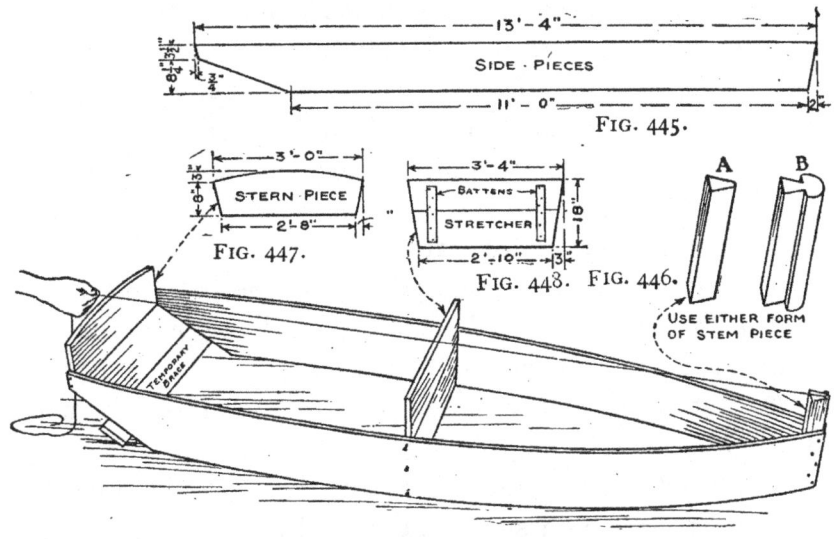

FIG. 445. — Pattern for the Side Pieces.
FIG. 446. — Two Forms of Stem-piece.
FIG. 447. — Pattern for the Stern-piece.
FIG. 448. — Pattern for the Stretcher.
FIG. 449. — How the Above Pieces are put Together.

and 12 inches is usually the widest stock material, you will have to use either a 12-inch and a 6-inch board, or a 10-inch and an 8-inch board, for

The Side Pieces. The boards should be of 1-inch stock,

and should be dressed on both sides. Figure 445 shows the pattern for the lower boards, with the dimensions for cutting the slants on the bow and stern ends.

Cut the Stem-piece like one of the forms shown in Fig. 446. *A* is the simpler form to cut, but *B* makes the neater appearing bow, as it finishes off the ends of the side pieces; the side boards fit into the rabbets cut in the sides of piece *B*. If form *A* is used, the ends of the side pieces must be finished off by nailing a strip 3 inches wide to the edges of the side pieces and the stem-piece (*C*, Fig. 452).

Figure 447 shows the pattern for

The Stern-piece, and Fig. 448 shows the pattern for

The Stretcher, both of which should be prepared as soon as the stem-piece has been cut.

To put together the sides, stem-and stern-pieces, and the stretcher (Fig. 449), first nail the ends of the side pieces to the stem-piece, then nail them to the ends of the stretcher, which should be placed in the exact center of the length of the sides. Draw the stern ends toward each other until they are of the required distance apart for the stern-piece to fit between, and tack a temporary piece across the edges to hold them in position (Fig. 449). It is necessary to bend each side piece the same amount, in order to turn out a boat which will not have a tendency to swerve to one side with each stroke of the oars, and the best way to get the sides symmetrical is by attaching a cord to a nail driven into the center of the

A HOME-MADE SHARPIE

end of the stem-piece, stretching it along the entire length of the boat and holding it at the center of the stern-piece (Fig. 449); if this crosses the center of the stretcher, you may know that the work is right, and you can fasten the stern ends permanently in place; if it does not cross the stretcher at the center, it will be a simple matter to bend one side piece a little more and the other a little less, until the string crosses the center of the bow, stern, and stretcher in a straight line.

The stretcher may be fastened permanently in place, or the nails may be driven part way in (Fig. 450) so

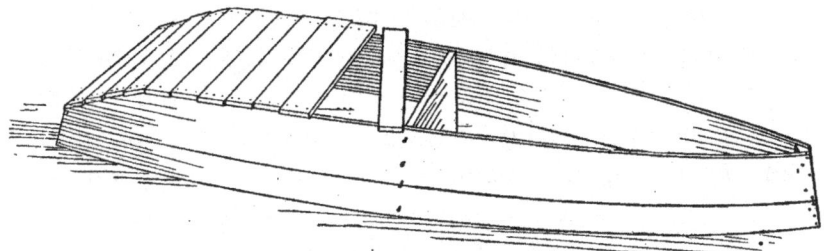

FIG. 450. — How the Bottom Boards are put On.

they may be removed and the stretcher taken out after the center seat has been put in place and the bracing is no longer required. The top boards of the sides should be nailed on as soon as the framework has been trued up, and the ends of these should be cut off even with the stem- and stern-pieces.

The Bottom Boards should be either 4-inch or 6-inch boards of 1-inch stock, dressed on two sides and two edges. Get the dryest material you can, for the pieces must not shrink to any marked degree after being put in place or the seams will open and cause the boat to leak; dry stuff will swell when exposed to the water, and the seams will close up very tight. The boards must not have tongued-and-grooved edges. Before putting on the boards, it will be necessary to plane off the bottom edges of the side pieces, because, as a result of the change in the twist of the boards between the bow and stern, these edges will be slightly curved. Do this work carefully so as to provide a straight and true surface to nail the bottom to. Cut the boards a little longer than is necessary, and then, starting at the stern end, nail the pieces in place, driving each board as tight as possible against the preceding piece. The edges of the boards and the side pieces should be given a thick coat of white lead to caulk up the seams. See instructions given for putting on the bottom of the *Punt* (page 353).

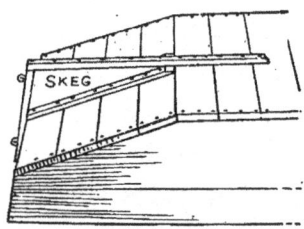

FIG. 451.—Attachment of Skeg.

It will not be necessary to attach a keel along the entire length of the bottom of the boat, but

A Skeg should be prepared for the sloping stern as shown in Fig. 451. This triangular piece may be cut out of 1-inch stuff and should be of the proper size so, when nailed in place, the lower edge will line up with the straight part of the bottom of the boat, and the end will

A HOME-MADE SHARPIE

line up with the face of the stern-piece. The illustration shows how the piece should be attached and braced with small wooden strips. The skeg must be in an exact line with the center of the bow and stern; its position can be determined by stretching a cord through the centers. The strip at the end of the skeg not only holds this piece to the stern, but forms a strip in which to screw the screw-eyes for the rudder hooks.

Fasten an Inner Keel Board in the bottom as described on page 353 for the *Punt*.

Seats should be fastened in the bow and stern ends and in the center as shown in Fig. 444. These should be supported upon cleats, and the neatest way to put on the cleats is to make them continuous as shown in the illustration, and fasten them low enough so they will cover the seams between the side boards. Batten together the pieces of the bow and stern seats as shown in Fig. 439, page 354.

The Bow of the Boat should be completed next. If you have made a wedge-shaped stem-piece (*A*, Fig. 446), cut strip *C* (Fig. 452) 3 inches wide, and long enough to extend from 1½ inches above the stem-piece down to the under side of the bottom boards; then

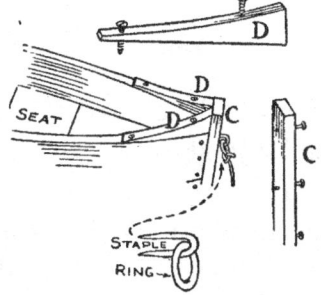

FIG. 452.— Finishing of Bow.

prepare two triangular pieces similar to *D* to fit against strip *C*, and screw them in place as shown. If stem-piece

B was used (Fig. 446), fit two pieces similar to *D* (Fig. 452) against it in the same way.

For the Painter secure a small staple, and a yacht or harness iron ring, and attach these to the bow as shown in Fig. 452.

An Easily Made Rudder is shown in Figs. 453 to 457. Figure 453 shows it completed; Fig. 454 shows how screw-eyes are screwed into the strip fastened to the stern-piece,

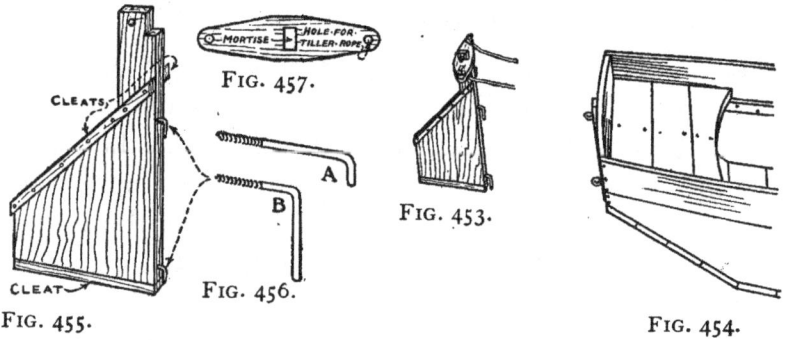

FIGS. 453–457. — Details of an Easily Made Rudder.

into which to hook the rudder hooks; and Figs. 455, 456, and 457 show the details for constructing the rudder.

The cross-bar of the rudder (Fig. 457) should be mortised to receive the end of the rudder, as shown, and a hole should be bored through the rudder through which to drive a pin to hold the cross-bar in place (Fig. 455). Get two 7-inch iron hooks (*A*, Fig. 456), bend the ends out straight, and then bend a new 4-inch hook on each (*B*, Fig. 456). Screw these hooks in the proper positions so they will hook into the screw-eyes in the stern.

The Rowlock Blocks should be prepared and attached as shown in Fig. 441 or Fig. 443, page 354, and either

Rowlocks or Thole-pins should be fitted into them (Figs. 440 and 442, page 354).

Finish the Boat as directed for the *Punt* (see page 355).

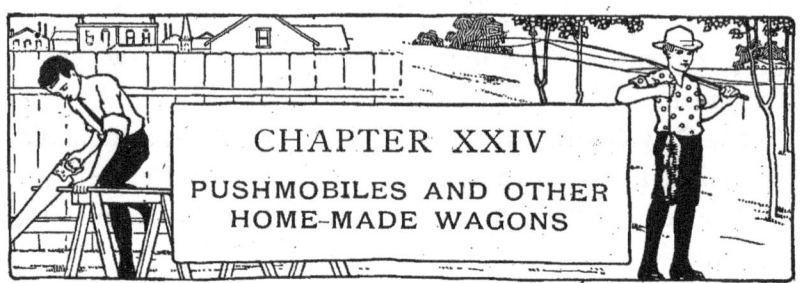

CHAPTER XXIV
PUSHMOBILES AND OTHER HOME-MADE WAGONS

WITH the necessary wheels in hand, it is possible to make all sorts of wagons, from a simple two-wheeled dog-cart to a model automobile. There are a number of sources from which a boy can procure wheels if he doesn't own any. Oftentimes a pair can be picked up at a second-hand store or at a junk shop, for 50 or 75 cents a pair; sometimes a neighbor who has a grown son can find a few for you by a little rummaging through the shed or barn loft; and often you will run across a boy with whom you can strike a good bargain. Wagon, bicycle, tricycle, velocipede, and baby-carriage wheels may be used.

A Pushmobile is a unique form of home-made wagon that has been developed from the simple wagons which the boys used to make for coasting, and for pushing from behind, when the automobile was unknown. It is patterned as nearly as possible after an automobile, and it is pushed by the mechanician, who runs behind, while the driver rides and attends to the steering. Working details for making one of these unique wagons are shown in Figs. 458 to 471.

 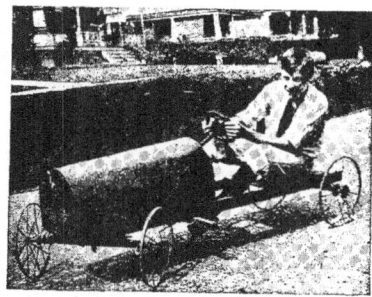

SOME OF THE COMPETING CARS IN THE FLUSHING PUSHMOBILE CLUB RACES.

PUSHMOBILES AND OTHER HOME-MADE WAGONS

Paul Towne of Flushing, Long Island, was probably the first boy to build a pushmobile, and as a result of the rivalry which sprang up among the boys who made

FIG. 458.—A Pushmobile.

similar "machines," each of whom claimed superior advantages for his car,

The Flushing Pushmobile Club was organized in the autumn of 1906 for the purpose of promoting pushmobile races. The *Brooklyn Daily Times* of Dec. 15, 1906, contained an interesting account of the work of the club, from which the following details of several of its races are taken:—

"The Flushing Club has held three great races during its active career. The first was an intersuburban affair and was to determine whether championship honors should go to Flushing, College Point, or Bayside, membership in the club being from all these 'foreign' countries. The honors in this race went to Flushing, for President Paul

Towne and his brother Herbert were the winners. The second race was for the Vanderbilt cup, so called. Many of the Murray Hill and Flushing merchants contributed toward it, but the largest individual subscription came from Mr. Vanderbilt. The trophy was valued at over $50. According to the deed of gift the trophy must be won three times to become the property of the winner. The first race for this cup ended in a fluke, for the car winning the race was protested. It was then decided that the race should be run over. The second event was won by Brown and Lawrence, who won the first race. This was a very popular victory under the circumstances. The third big event was a race for the Reiger cup, a beautiful trophy presented by Charles Reiger of Flushing. This event brought out the full strength of the club, for there were twenty cars in the race. The trophy was won by Donahue and Johnson."

The photographs opposite page 364 show several of the competing machines, while those opposite this page show the start of one of the club's races and one of the winning teams. The winning team in

The Vanderbilt Cup Race covered the course, which was ten times around a city block, in 27 minutes and 12 seconds. This was one of the most interesting races.

You will notice by the photographs that the boys have shown considerable ingenuity in working out the plans for their pushmobiles. Various kinds and sizes of wheels have been used; some of the bodies are built low and others high; some of the models have been copied after foreign racing machines, and others have been patterned after roadsters and runabouts. The hoods have been made of grocery boxes, sheet metal, barrel hoops covered with canvas, or built up with box boards; and one boy, who wanted to get the pointed nose effect of the

WINNING CAR IN THE VANDERBILT CUP RACE.

AT THE START OFF. A FLUSHING PUSHMOBILE CLUB RACE.

French racer, used the sawed-off bow of a row boat for his. To furnish the " chug," " chug," and " smell " of the automobile, one lad equipped a dummy car with a gasoline engine, and this was run over the course for the benefit of the spectators.

The *Brooklyn Daily Times* published the following interesting

Description of a Pushmobile Race :—

"Is a pushmobile race exciting? Ask any of the hundreds of spectators who crowd the course. They will tell you that it is almost as interesting as a real auto race. There will be men and women with score-cards, pencils, and stop-watches. The cars are timed for each lap. Seconds count as much, if not more, than in the big races. The cars come singly, three, four, and half a dozen at a time. It takes an expert to keep all the records accurately. This car is now ahead, and then that one leads. One car is gaining a lap on all the rest and looks like a winner. There are spurts in which the boys on the cars use every bit of strength and endurance they possess. As the contest comes to a close, it is seen that some two or three are leading. Now if no accident happens, if only there is not a breakdown! That is the hope expressed by each man and woman with the score-card. Then the rush for the finish. The first car to complete the ten laps, and then the figuring for elapsed time, and finally the declaration of the winner and the shouts for the successful car."

Now, boys, if you have not become fired with enthusiasm after reading the above accounts of the work of the Flushing Pushmobile Club, the author has missed his guess; if you *have*, get to work and construct a machine like the one shown in Fig. 458 and described upon the following pages, then show it to your boy friends, and the chances are there will be enough machines in your town within a few days to make it possible to

Organize a Pushmobile Club, or to make pushmobile racing a feature of your present neighborhood or school club.

To construct a Pushmobile. When procuring wheels for a pushmobile, get the iron axle rods and nuts and washers that belong to the wheels, if possible; it will be easy enough to refit nuts and washers to the axles if they are lost, but if you cannot get the axles or find another pair that will do, you will have

To make New Axles. A couple of round iron rods of the proper diameter to fit the hubs of your wheels can be procured at almost any hardware store, wagon shop, or blacksmith shop, and you can have them cut to the proper length, threaded for nuts, and drilled in two places near each end, by a machinist, plumber, or gas-fitter. You will have to decide upon the width of your wagon before you can determine the length for the rods, and of course the length of the wheel hubs will have to be considered also. The first hole in the rod is provided for an iron pin, the purpose of which is to keep the wheel from running too far back on the axle, and the second hole is made for a stove-bolt or screw for fastening the iron axle to the wooden axle and wagon-bed (Figs. 477 and 478).

The Wooden Axles should be constructed first (Figs. 459 and 460). The sizes of these will depend upon the length of the iron axles, the height of the wheels, and whether you want a high or low body. The drawings show a machine with a body that is higher than most of

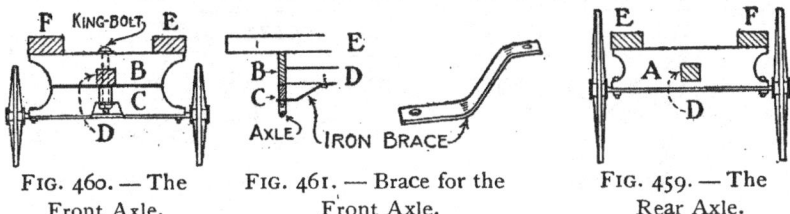

FIG. 460. — The Front Axle. FIG. 461. — Brace for the Front Axle. FIG. 459. — The Rear Axle.

those shown in the photographs, but this makes a car that is easier for the mechanician to push, for he does not have to stoop over as much. After cutting out piece *A*, you must make *B* and *C* of the proper widths so the top of *B* will be level with the top of *A* when the wheels are in place. *C* is fastened to *B* by means of a king-bolt (Fig. 460).

Connect the wooden axles by means of a piece of 2-by-2 (*D*, Figs. 459 to 462), and brace the king-bolt of the front axle to this strip with an iron strap, to prevent it from bending (Fig. 461); the brace should be about $\frac{1}{8}$ inch thick and 1 inch wide, and should be bent and drilled as shown in Fig. 461.

The Wagon-bed pieces *E* and *F* are 2-by-4's and connect the tops of axle pieces *A* and *B*, to which they are nailed. These will be of whatever length you have determined to make your car.

For the Steering-wheel get an old sewing-machine driving-wheel, if possible, and use a broom-handle for a

G
H
I
E
F
B
C
D
J
A

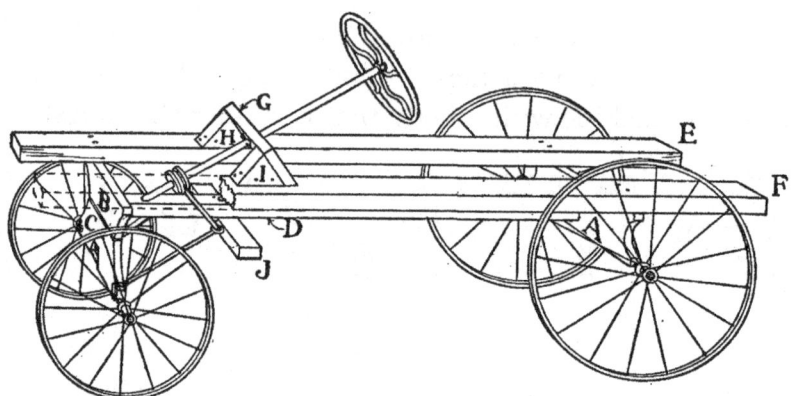

FIG. 462. — Framework of the Pushmobile.
(The front end of the strip *F* is broken off so that you can see the steering-gear.)

shaft (Fig. 463). Screw the wheel to the end of the broom-handle (Fig. 465). If you cannot get a sewing-machine wheel, a wooden or iron wagon-wheel may be wired to the end of the broom-handle (Fig. 466). The shaft must be provided with a *drum* upon which to fasten the steering ropes (Figs. 462 and 463), and this drum should be made out of three circular blocks as shown in Fig. 464. Lay out the center block 3 inches in diameter, and the outer, or flange, blocks 4 inches in diameter, and before cutting them out

PIN
SCREW
ROPE
SCREW
WIRE

FIG. 465. FIG. 466. FIG. 463. FIG. 464.

FIG. 463. — Steering-wheel and Shaft for the Pushmobile.

FIG. 464. — Three Disks like these for Drum of Steering-wheel Shaft.

FIG. 465. — How to attach a Sewing-machine Wheel to a Broom-handle.

FIG. 466. — How to wire a Wagon Wheel to a Broom-handle.

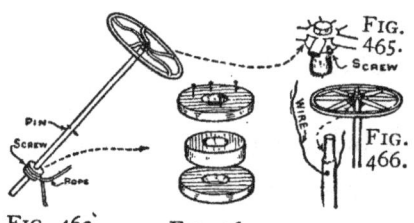

bore a 1-inch hole through the center of each. Nail the blocks together, and slip the completed drum over the end of the broom-handle; but do not fasten the drum in place until after you have mounted the shaft on the framework.

Fasten a board to the wagon-bed, as shown at *G* (Fig. 462), on blocks similar to *H* and *I*; the blocks must be cut to the proper slant so the position of the board will be at right angles to the steering-wheel shaft. Then fasten the cross-piece *J* to the under side of strip *D* with a bolt and nails. Board *G* should have a 1-inch hole bored through its center for the steering shaft to turn in, and a hole should be bored part way through strip *D*, directly in line with the hole in *G*, for a socket for the end of the shaft. To connect the drum on the shaft to the wheels, take some strong rope, pass it around the drum, cross the ends on the under side (Fig. 463), run them through screw-eyes screwed into the cross-piece *J* on each side of strip *D*, and attach them to the ends of the wooden axle. It is important to cross the rope after passing it around the drum, for otherwise the pushmobile would turn to the left when you turn the wheel to the right, and *vice versa*.

When the steering-gear has been carefully adjusted, fasten the drum to the shaft with a screw, and screw or nail the steering line to the drum; also drive a pin into the broom-handle about $\frac{1}{4}$ inch in front of board *G* to prevent the shaft from pulling out of place (Figs. 462 and 463).

HANDICRAFT FOR HANDY BOYS

When the frame of the pushmobile has been completed, it is a simple matter to finish the body.

The Hood is made out of a box with the cover and bottom removed, and a three-sided top constructed upon it. If you cannot find a box of the right size, you can cut down a large box or build the hood out of boards. Figures 458

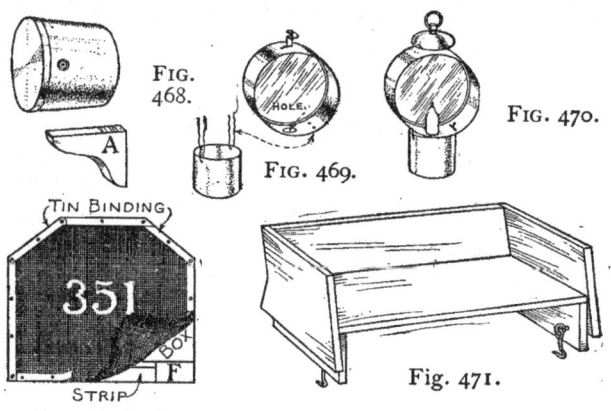

FIG. 467. — Radiator-front.
FIG. 468. — Lard-can Headlight and Bracket.
FIG. 469. — Clock-case and Can for Side Lamps.
FIG. 470. — The Completed Clock-case Side Lamp.
FIG. 471. — Seat for Auto Wagon.

and 467 show the shape of the top. Fasten a small pill box to the top of the hood, as shown, for the cap to the "radiator" (Fig. 458).

After fastening the hood to the frame of the pushmobile, tack a piece of screen wire over the front for

The Radiator-front, and then attach a strip of tin around the edge, as shown in Fig. 467, to finish it off.

The Seat, back, and arms of the body are made out of a box cut down, and the rear end is built up of boards.

Headlights. Two lard cans with their covers fitted on make splendid imitation headlights (Fig. 468). Cut two wooden brackets similar to *A* (Fig. 468), nail or screw them to the sides of the radiator-front, and then nail or screw the cans to the brackets and to the radiator-front.

Side Lamps. Bicycle lamps may be used for these, or you can make lamps out of the cases of two old alarm-clocks (Figs. 469 and 470).

To make a Clock-case Side Lamp, remove the works from the case and put back the screws necessary to hold the glass in place; then cut a $\frac{3}{4}$-inch hole through the center of the bottom for the candle, and wire the case to the top of a small tin can of about the size of a 1-pound paint can, punching holes through the clock-case and the can through which to run the wire. The candle sets down in the can and is lighted by removing the tin back of the clock-case. Nail or screw the case to the side of the hood.

Paint your Machine with two coats of paint, using any color you choose. Of course you will want to make the body of one color and the trimmings of another.

Paint your License Number upon the radiator-front with white or red paint.

A Racing Pushmobile may have a much simpler body than the machine just described, or you may make portions removable so the machine may be dismantled for a race.

An Auto Wagon. The wagon shown in Fig. 472 has a body built similar to that of the pushmobile, except that

FIG. 472. — An Auto Wagon.

the bed is made solid out of boards 1 inch thick. Make the sides out of 8-inch boards with a 2-inch strip nailed along the top edge, and make the dashboard out of two pieces of board battened together.

The Steering-wheel should be made out of a sewing-machine wheel and piece of gas-pipe as shown in Fig. 473. Get a gas-fitter to prepare a piece of gas-pipe with a T connection at one end, and a short piece of pipe run through the T crosswise, as shown in the illustration, and have him drill a hole through the vertical piece of pipe near the upper end, and two holes through the cross-piece — one near each end. Screw two screw-eyes into the inside face of the dashboard, then slip the steering shaft through a hole bored through the bottom of the wagon-bed, and through the screw-eyes. Fasten the wheel to the end of the pipe by means of a metal pin driven through the hole in the pipe and wheel hub, wrap some wire around the pipe on a line with the top of the dashboard, and solder it in place, to keep the pipe from slipping down (Fig. 473), and run rope or chain from the ends of the lower cross-piece to the axle ends.

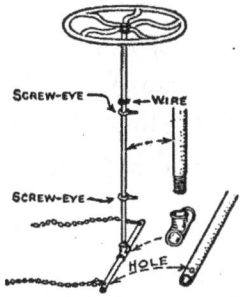

FIG. 473. — Details of a Sewing-machine Wheel and Gas-pipe Steering wheel.

Another Steering-gear. The steering shaft and cross-piece may be made of wood, but of course the iron pipe scheme is much stronger and is much better in the case of the auto wagon, where the weight of the driver comes directly over the wheels, bringing a greater strain upon each part. If you want to, you may rig up a dummy steering-wheel and shaft, and provide for steering by running ropes from the axle ends around the sides of the wagon to the back, where the mechanician can attend to it. It might be a good plan to provide for this method of steering, anyway, so in case you give a child a ride at any time you can place him in the front seat and do the steering yourself from the rear.

Build the Seat as shown in Fig. 471, and screw a hook into each end of the seat, and a screw-eye into each side of the wagon in the proper position for it to hook into, to hold it securely to the wagon sides.

Procure a Trip Gong for the front of the dashboard, or fasten an electric bell upon it and place a dry battery inside of the wagon.

Figure 474 shows

A Simple Push Wagon. A 2-inch plank, 6 or 8 inches in width, should be procured for

FIG. 474. — A Simple Push Wagon.

The Wagon-bed; a board 1 inch thick may be used, but of course it will not have the stiffness that the thicker piece would have. Also get a strong box, knock out one end, nail a cleat to the ends of the side and bottom boards to hold them together, and fasten the box to one end of the wagon-bed as shown in Figs. 474 and 475.

The Rear Wheels should be 16 or 18 inches in diameter and should set under the center of the box (Fig. 475). Nail two blocks of the same thickness as the wagon-bed to the bottom of the box, and fasten the axle across them

WAGON BED
STAPLES
FIG. 476.
FIG. 477
PIN
STAPLE
STOVE-BOLT, OR SCREW
KING-BOLT
WASHER
WOODEN AXLE
IRON AXLE
FIG. 478.
NUT
WASHER
WAGON BED
STAPLES
FIG. 479.
BATTEN
BLOCK
IRON AXLE
BATTEN
BOTTOM VIEW OF WAGON-BED
IRON AXLE
KING-BOLT
BLOCK
WOODEN AXLE
FIG. 475.
BATTEN

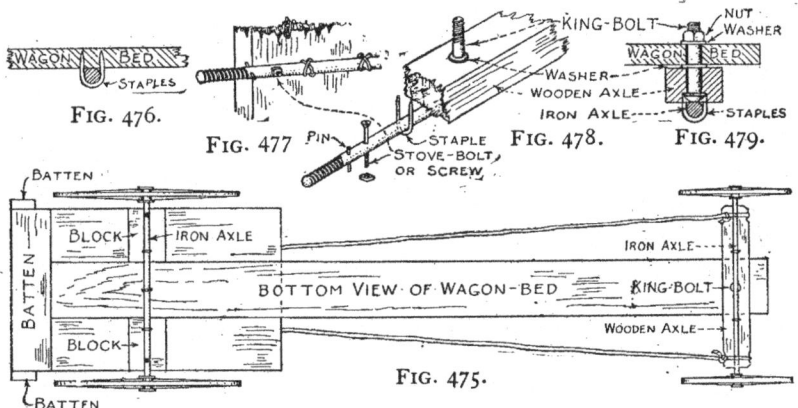

FIG. 475. — Bottom View of Wagon-bed.
FIGS. 476 and 477. — The Way to attach the Rear Axle.
FIGS. 478 and 479. — The Way to attach the Front Axle.

as shown, running a stove-bolt or screw through the holes (Figs. 477 and 478), and using either staples or nails bent over as additional fastenings (Figs. 476 to 478). Drive a metal pin through the outer hole in the axles to keep the hubs of the wheels from rubbing against the wood (Figs. 477 and 478).

The Axle for the Front Wheels is fastened to a wooden

axle (Fig. 478), which in turn is pivoted to the wagon-bed by means of a king-bolt as shown in Figs. 478 and 479. Bore a hole through the wagon-bed for the bolt, and put washers where shown before screwing the nut in place.

CHAPTER XXV

BIRD-HOUSES

BIRDS seem to show a practical rather than an artistic sense in choosing their homes, and, unlike us, do not care whether their houses are plain or highly ornamented. A common box properly arranged is just as much of an attraction as one on which a great deal of time has been spent in working out fancy roofs, porches, and doorways, provided it is placed where there will be ample protection from cats and other enemies of birds, and where there will be a plentiful supply of seeds and insects for food near by, and water for drink and bath. But carefully designed houses, of course, appear neater and more pleasing to us, so it is best to take pains in planning and constructing our garden bird homes.

Tomato cans, apple and sugar barrels, fish kegs, nail kegs and white lead kegs, cheese boxes, butter firkins, wooden pails, and small boxes such as soap and starch come in can be procured by any boy, and from these materials there are many kinds of houses that can be made. You will find a variety of new ideas for easily made houses in this chapter, and the materials mentioned are sufficient for the greater part of the construction of these.

A Box Bird-house such as is shown in Fig. 480 can be made out of an empty starch box, or you may cut out the pieces and put together the box yourself. In case you make the box, the top edge of the end pieces can be cut slanted to allow for the slanted roof, but if you use a

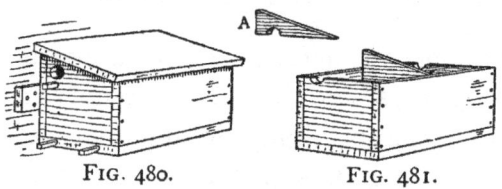

FIG. 480.   FIG. 481.
Details of a Box Lean-to Bird-house.

ready-made box, a triangular piece will have to be added to the edges (*A*, Fig. 481). If you make the box, cut the center partition, which divides the box into two bird compartments, the same size as the end pieces; but for a box already made, cut this piece first and then use it for a pattern for laying out the triangular pieces to be added to the ends. The doorway in each end can be cut with a jackknife; this will be very easy to do if the ends are in two pieces, for one half of the hole can be cut out of the edge of each piece (Fig. 481).

For wrens and other small birds the holes need not be more than $1\frac{1}{2}$ inches in diameter; and 3 inches will admit any of the larger birds that may be attracted to your boxes.

After the ends of the box have been pieced out, nail a strip to the back to make it of the same height, then cut the roof board large enough so it will project about 1 inch

BIRD-HOUSES

over the front and ends of the box, and nail it in place. Fit the perch sticks into holes bored in the ends of the box as shown in Fig. 480.

This house may be mounted upon a clothes-post, but it will look better if bracketed to a wall on account of the style of its roof. A wooden bracket may be cut out and nailed to the wall, or a strip 6 or 8 inches longer than the box may be nailed to the back and the ends of this nailed to the wall (Fig. 480).

Another Box Bird-house is shown in Fig. 482. This is similar to a house which the boys of some of the Chicago public schools have constructed and placed in the trees of the parks, with the addition of the pan bath. The illustration shows clearly how the back, sides, and roof are cut and fitted together, and how the water pan is bracketed out from the lower end of the back board, and I am going to let you work out the sizes for the various pieces according to what you think they ought to be.

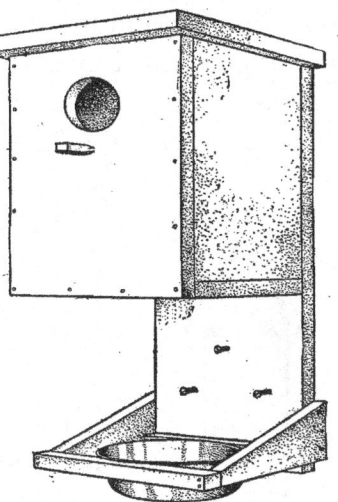

FIG. 482. — Another Box Bird-house with a Pan for Drinking Water.

The lower portion of the back board may be screwed or nailed to a wall or post, or if you omit the pan and place the box in a tree, it can be tied securely by running a piece of clothes-line several times around it and the tree trunk.

A cheese-box cover and one of the small kegs in which mackerel and herring come to the market furnishes the materials for making

A Bird Tower such as is shown in Fig. 483. The keg must be thoroughly washed out with hot water and either washing soda or lye, and should be painted inside, to remove the fish odor. Bore four openings in the side of the keg, and fasten a perch stick in a small hole below each opening.

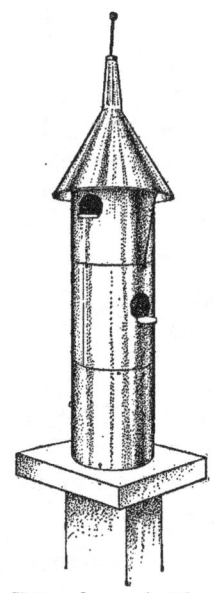

FIG. 487.— A Tin-can Bird Tower.

The illustration shows the keg mounted upon the end of a rug-pole, but if you cannot get one of these, the top of a clothes-post, or a piece of 2-by-4 set into the ground, will serve the purpose. Nail the keg to the support, then set the cheese-box cover on top and nail it in place.

The lower perches should run through the support as shown in the illustration, and may be of pieces of broken flagstaffs or cabinet-maker's dowel sticks.

Figure 487 shows

A Tin-can Bird Tower. This is made out of empty tomato cans. Cut a hole $1\frac{1}{2}$ inches in diameter in the side of three cans about $1\frac{1}{2}$ inches from the top; do not remove the piece of tin,

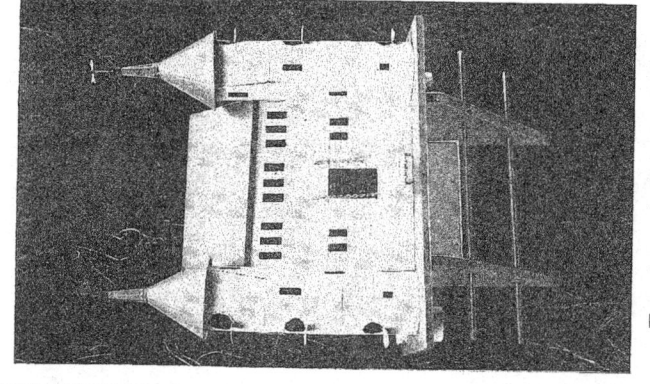

Fig. 484. A Bird Castle.

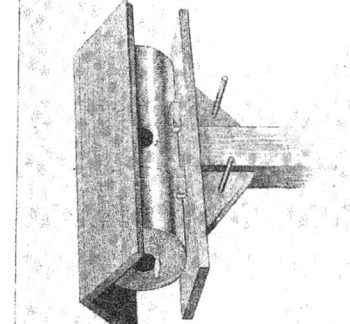

Fig. 485. A Bird Ark.

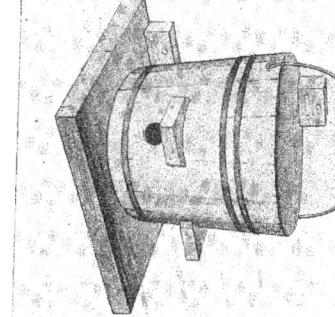

Fig. 486. A House and Swing.

Fig. 483. A Bird Tower.

BIRD-HOUSES

but bend it out as shown in Fig. 488 to form a perch. Then remove the top of one can (*A*, Fig. 489) and the top and bottom of the other two cans (*B* and *C*, Fig. 489). As the ends are generally soldered on, it is only necessary to hold a can over a flame until the solder melts, and then knock them off (Fig. 488). The cans are joined together by means of two circular blocks of wood (*E* and *F*, Fig. 489), which also divide the tower into three compartments

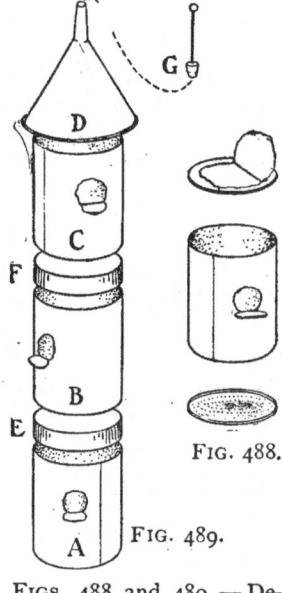

FIG. 488.

FIG. 489.

FIGS. 488 and 489. — Details of the Tin-can Bird Tower shown in Fig. 487.

A 6-inch tin funnel forms the roof (*D*, Fig. 489), and a cork with a piece of a hatpin stuck into it (*G*) fits into the spout of the funnel for a spire.

Tack the edges of the cans to the wooden blocks, and wire the funnel roof to the upper can as shown in Fig. 487, fastening one end of each wire to the funnel rim and the other end to a small staple driven into the upper block. Twist the wires until the funnel is firm. Nail the bottom can to the top of whatever support you provide for the tower. Paint the tin to prevent it from rusting.

The Bird Castle shown in Fig. 484 was designed and built by the author a few years ago for his garden. The corner towers of this are built like the tower in Fig. 487. The castle measures 12 inches long, 7 inches wide, 16 inches high at the highest point, and 11 inches high at the lowest point, and is made out of box boards.

Figure 490 shows an end view of the castle with the tower of the opposite end in position. First cut the two end pieces *H*, and a third piece of the same shape and size for a center partition, then nail the front and back boards *I* and *J* to them. Cut the pieces indicated by the dotted lines *K* to fit between the center partition and the end pieces, for a loft floor. Cut an opening for each compartment in the end pieces (Fig. 490).

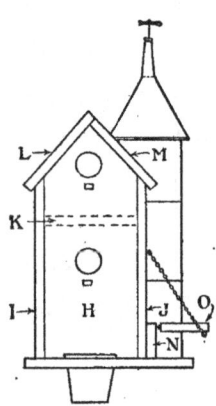

FIG. 490.—End View of Bird Castle shown in Fig. 484, with One Tower in Position.

Nail the roof boards *L* and *M* in place and fasten strip *N* to the base at the front (Fig. 490), then mount the castle upon a platform 11 inches wide and 24 inches long. Build up the towers at the two corners, and nail each can to the corner of the castle as you put it in place.

The drawbridge (*O*, Fig. 490) measures $2\frac{1}{2}$ inches by $3\frac{3}{4}$ inches; hinge one end to the base strip, and suspend the other end by small brass chains fastened to the under side and to the front wall.

Each can of the towers has a circular opening cut in it, but the long narrow windows in the towers and front wall of the castle and the large doorway are painted. The walls should be painted white, and the roof green or red.

The little flag and the weather-vane are mounted upon nails stuck into corks, and the corks are pushed into the spouts of the funnels (Fig. 490). Set a cup in the platform, at each end, for drinking water. The castle may be bracketed upon a wall as shown in Fig. 484, or may be mounted upon a post.

A Bird Ark. For the bird ark shown in Fig. 485, three cans are joined together in the same manner as those of the towers are joined (Figs. 488 and 489). Both ends of the center can are removed, but the bottom is left on the end cans. Cut a $1\frac{3}{4}$-inch hole in the side of the center can and a hole of the same diameter through the bottom of each end can; do not remove the pieces of tin from the openings, but bend them out for perches as shown. Cut the roof boards of the proper size to project over the ends and sides of the cans, nail them together, and then fasten them in place by driving nails through the boards into the connecting blocks between the cans.

Fasten the ark between blocks upon a board platform, then mount the platform upon a post support, and brace the supports with brackets to make it secure. Run several perch sticks through the brackets, as shown.

A Wall Bracket Bird Ark (Fig. 491). This is constructed in the same way as the ark described above, and the shape of the brackets and arrangement of perch sticks is clearly shown in the illustration.

A House and Swing made out of a wooden pail inverted and bracketed to a wall as shown in Fig. 486, so that its

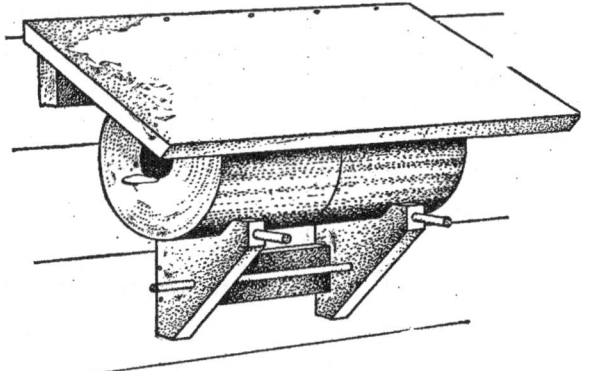

FIG. 491. — A Wall Bracket Bird Ark.

handle hangs down and forms a swing, is an attractive little house for the back yard.

Make the vertical partition to divide the pail into two compartments, and cut a circular piece of board to fit in the top. Nail the roof board to the bottom of the pail, cut an opening into each compartment, and fit a small block of wood beneath each opening for a platform.

Nail a short block of wood to the wall where the house is to go, for the pail to rest on, and nail a longer strip at the proper height above it to nail the roof board to.

The Hanging House shown in Fig. 492 may be made from a 25-pound or a 12½-pound white lead keg, which can be procured from any painter. Cut the square roof board wide enough to project 3 or 4 inches over the sides of the keg, and bore two holes in the proper positions for

BIRD-HOUSES

the wire handles to run through. Each opening should have a perch fastened below it. Suspend the house by means of two cords as shown in the illustration.

Birds seek the protection of trees, roof eaves, and covered ways during storms, and

A Shelter on the plan shown in Fig. 493 will help to make your yard a popular resort at such times. You also will find that the birds will fly to these perches to dry and preen their feathers after taking their morning baths.

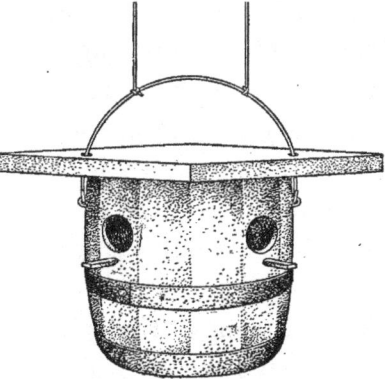

FIG. 492. — A Hanging House.

Figure 494 shows one of the two uprights which support the perches and roof. These may be cut out of strips 3 or 4 inches wide. Miter the top ends as shown, — that is, cut off

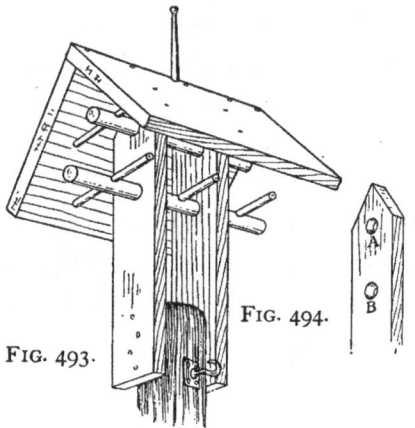

FIGS. 493 and 494. — A Shelter.

the two corners at an angle of 45 degrees; — bore the holes A and B 1 inch in diameter, A about 3 inches below the top and B 6 inches below that again, and then slip a piece of broom-handle through two of the holes to keep them in line, and nail the lower ends to opposite sides of a clothes-post, or to a post set into the ground especially for the purpose.

The long perch sticks are pieces of broom-handle, and the small ones are cabinet-maker's dowel sticks, broken flagstaffs, or sticks whittled round, about $\frac{3}{8}$ inch in diameter. The small perch sticks are run through holes bored through the pieces of broom-handle, after the latter have been slipped through the holes in the uprights.

Cut the roof boards about 18 inches long, one 12 inches in width, and the other as much less as is necessary to allow for the lapping of edges. Nail the face of the wide piece to the edge of the narrow one, and whittle a short wooden spire and stick it into a hole bored in the peak; then set the roof on the end of the uprights, shift it until its projection at the ends is the same, and drive a couple of nails through the roof boards into the uprights to hold it in position.

CHAPTER XXVI
HOUSES FOR PETS

ALTHOUGH the city boy does not have as good an opportunity to keep pets as his country cousin has, he generally manages to own a dog, unless he lives in an apartment building, and often there is space in a woodshed or a barn in which he can keep a few pets such as rabbits, white rats, fancy mice, and pigeons.

The size of a dog-house depends upon the size of the dog, so get your dog and see what he looks like before you build his kennel; but if you get a pup of a large breed, be sure to make the house plenty large enough to allow for his growth, otherwise you will soon have to remodel the house or trade the dog for one that will fit.

A Dog-house may be constructed out of packing-box or may be built up of any boards you can find about the place. Figure 495 shows a well-planned house of medium size, with a feature which is too frequently omitted in building one — provision for ventilation. If the house is set directly upon the ground, the floor is usually damp, for there is little or no chance for it to dry out after a rain, but by raising it a few inches as shown in the illustration by mounting it upon a base, and boring a number of holes through the base, the floor

FIG. 495. — A Dog-house.
(See working-drawings on page 89.)

never comes in contact with the ground, and a constant circulation of air, which will pass in and out of the holes, will keep the ground underneath dry.

Figure 92 on page 89 shows complete working-drawings for this dog-house, it having been taken for an example in explaining the proper method for laying out a sheet of working details. Of course you may alter the dimensions on the drawings to suit your needs.

First construct a frame for the base of the house, then cut the floor boards of the proper size and nail them to the top edge of the base. Next construct the four walls in sections, making the two sides alike and the front and rear wall alike, and fastening the boards together with battens as shown on the working-drawings. Mark out the arched opening on the front wall, and nail a batten across the boards each side of it, as shown, to hold together the ends of the boards which are to be cut. When the sections have been prepared, fasten their ends together and toe-nail their bottom edges to the floor of the base.

The roof may be made of boards alone, or of boards covered with shingles, tin, or some form of composition roofing-paper. If you shingle the roof, lay the boards lengthwise of the house, as shown on the working-drawings; then lay the shingles on in the same way that they are put on any roof, starting at the eaves and laying each succeeding row with 4 or 5 inches of the shingles exposed to the weather. The shingles may be split up into narrow pieces, and the lap may be increased so as to leave 2 or 3 inches exposed, if you want to make them of smaller proportions. Nail a ridge-board along each side of the roof at the peak, to cover the ends of the shingles and make the roof tight at that point.

The dog-house should be given two coats of paint and be repainted once a year to keep it in condition.

The Rabbit-hutch shown in Figs. 496 and 497 may be constructed out of a box or built out of new boards, whichever is the more easily obtained. The box should be about 4 feet long, 14 inches wide, and 20 inches deep.

If you make this box, first prepare the end pieces, then cut the side boards and nail them to the ends, and then

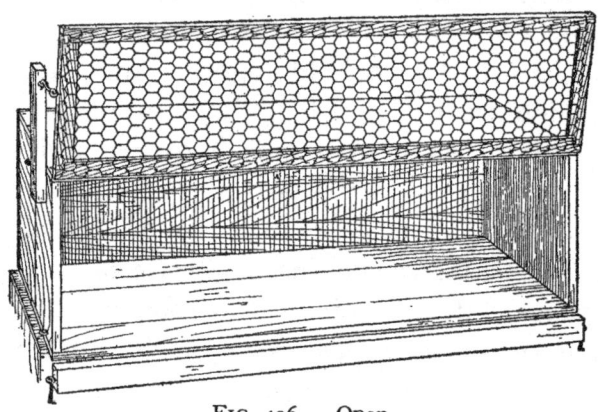

Fig. 496. — Open.

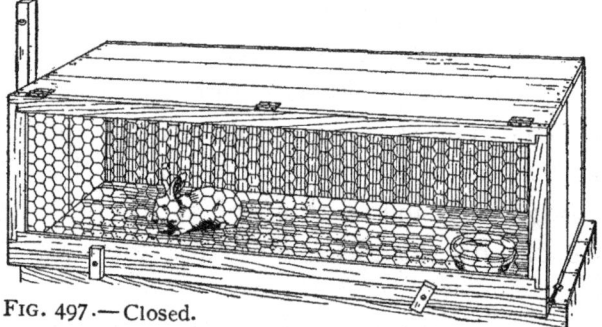

Fig. 497. — Closed.

Figs. 496 and 497. — A Rabbit-hutch.

cut the bottom boards and nail them to the edges of the end and side boards. As shown in the illustration, the box is turned upon its side so the top will form the front of the hutch.

The front is covered with wire netting tacked to a frame, and the frame is hinged in place so that it will also form a door. Make the frame equal to the length of the box and in width about 2 inches less than the width of the box; use strips about 2 inches wide and 1 inch thick. The ends of the strips may be notched and fitted together as shown, or they may be mitered, like the corners of picture-frames.

Galvanized Poultry-netting is the material probably easiest for most boys to procure for covering the open front of the hutch. This is made in widths ranging from 12 inches to 72 inches, and can be had in 1-inch, $1\frac{1}{2}$-inch, and 2-inch mesh (the meshes are the openings formed by the crossed wires). The large mesh is plenty small enough for large rabbits, but the 1-inch size is best for breeding hutches, as the little fellows can crawl through larger openings. Poultry-netting has an hexagonal-shaped mesh.

Twist Wire Cloth is another form of covering which is very good for the purpose. Its meshes are somewhat similar to those of poultry netting, but are 1 inch long and $\frac{1}{2}$ inch wide.

Wire Cloth has a square mesh like the wire used for door and window screens. The heavier grades are suitable for rabbit-hutches and are often used.

Buy small *netting staples* with which to put on the wire netting or cloth.

After covering the frame with the netting or cloth,

hinge it to the top edge of the hutch with three 2-by-2-inch steel butts. Then cut a strip of just the length of the box and 2 inches wide, and hinge it to the bottom directly below the frame with a pair of 2-by-2-inch butts. Screw a hook into each end of the strip, and fasten a screw-eye or nail into each end of the box in the proper place for the hook to catch on to. Cut a couple of wooden buttons, bore a hole through the center of each large enough for a screw to slip through, and screw them to the bottom hinge-strip about 12 inches from the ends for button catches to hold the wire frame closed (Fig. 497). The hinge-strip is provided to keep the sawdust, or other floor covering, from dropping out of the hutch every time the front is opened, and it is hinged in place so it may be dropped as shown in Fig. 496 when cleaning out the hutch, to make easier the work of removing the old sawdust. To hold open the front while cleaning, nail a strip of wood to one end of the hutch, and fasten a hook in the edge of the frame and a screw-eye in the proper position in the stick for it to hook into, as shown in Fig. 496.

The hutch should set up on something high enough to keep it at least 18 inches above the ground or floor, as rabbits are very sensitive to dampness. Brackets may be fastened to a wall at the proper height, or the hutch may be placed upon an overturned packing-box.

If you intend to raise rabbits, you should have

A Breeding Hutch, in addition to this hutch which will

HOUSES FOR PETS

then be used to keep the male rabbit in after the baby rabbits have arrived. The breeding hutch may be constructed out of a box of the same size as that used for the hutch just described, but one end must be partitioned off for a nest, and a doorway 5 inches wide and 6 inches high must be cut through the partition to connect it with the main runway of the hutch. The nest must be kept dark, so, instead of running the wire front along the full length, it must be stopped off upon a line with the partition. In place of the wire, hinge a board over this portion. This provides a doorway by which the nest can be reached from the outside.

The Two-story Rabbit-hutch shown in Fig. 498 is made

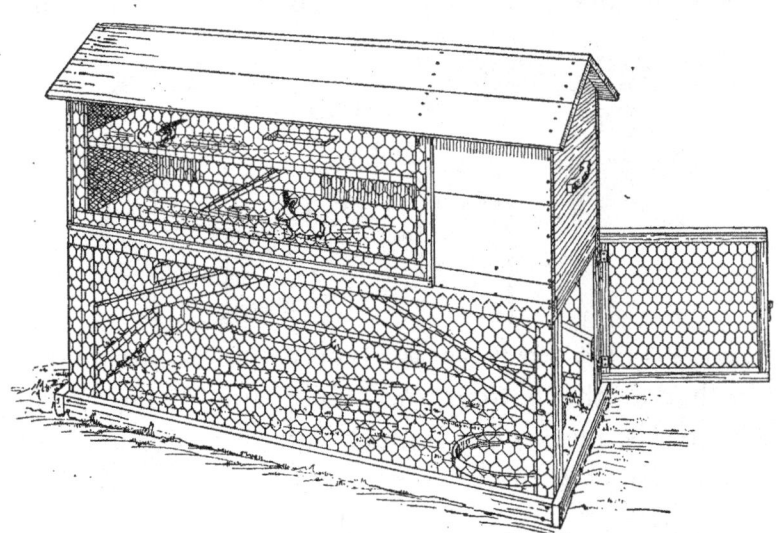

FIG. 498. — A Two-story Rabbit-hutch with Yard Beneath.

portable so it may be taken to a place of shelter during severe weather, and is provided with a handle at either end for convenience in carrying. Then by stretching wire netting or wire cloth around the supports, which should be 18 inches or more high, a good playground is provided in which your "bunnies" can be allowed to run about for a while each day. This yard is also a convenient place to put them in while you clean out the hutch.

If you can find a packing-box 18 inches deep, 18 or 20 inches wide, and 4 feet long, use that for the hutch. Remove the boards from one side of the box (which will be the front of the hutch), then rip up two of the boards removed, into pieces 3 or 4 inches wide, and nail these to the front, one at the top of the box (*A*, Fig. 499) and

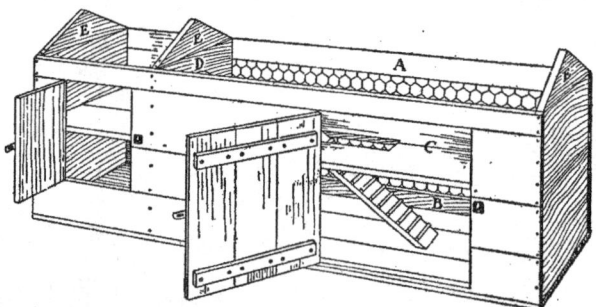

FIG. 499. — The Two-story Rabbit-hutch before the Roof has been put On.

the other at the bottom *B*. Upon the inside of the back boards, mark out a 14-inch square feed and clean-out door 6 inches from one end, and a 6-by-10-inch doorway to the compartments 3 inches from the other end. Before cutting out these openings, nail a vertical batten across the boards each side of the lines to hold the cut ends together.

Cut enough boards of the proper length to make the second-story floor, batten them together upon the under side, and cut a 5-by-10-inch stairway opening about 18 inches from one end, and in the center of the width of the floor; fasten this to the ends and back of the box midway between the top and bottom (*C*, Fig. 499). Then prepare two partitions with an arched doorway about 5 inches wide and 6 inches high cut in each, and fasten one in each story 12 inches away from the compartment end of the hutch (Fig. 499). Cut three triangular pieces and nail one to the top of each end piece of the hutch for gable-ends, and one to the top of partition *D*(*E*, Fig. 499).

Cut a piece of board 5 inches wide and about 18 inches long for stairs, and tack a number of small cross-pieces to it to keep the rabbits from slipping while running up and down. Hinge the stairs to the second floor with a small hinge, or a piece of leather, and leave the lower end loose so it may be raised up out of the way every time you clean out the first story.

Board up the front of the compartments (Fig. 498), and nail a vertical strip of the same width as the top rail *A* and the bottom rail *B* (Fig. 499) to the opposite end of the hutch. Cover the remainder of the front with wire netting or cloth, and tack wooden strips over the edges of the wire to conceal the rough ends (Fig. 498).

Make the door to the compartments out of a single board, and the feed door out of several pieces battened together. Hinge the doors in place, and provide them with hasps and padlocks, if there is any danger of curious ones opening the hutch while you are away. Leather strips may be substituted for iron hinges, and wooden buttons or hooks may be used in place of hasps, if the hutch does not require a padlock.

For breeding purposes the stairway may be omitted; then the doe and her young can be kept by themselves in one story; but it is better to build separate one-story breeding hutches.

The Rabbit Yard. As you must know, if you have had any experience with raising them, rabbits are great burrowers and will dig under the walls of any inclosure you can build for them, unless you provide a floor or carry the walls down below their reach. The best method for keeping them within a small yard is to extend the wire netting with which you cover the framework about 18 inches below the surface of the ground. After laying out the lines of the framework of the yard, dig a trench on all four sides to the required depth, then set up the four corner posts, which should be long enough to stand at least 18 inches above the ground, and nail on the top pieces, the baseboards, and the side braces. Then stretch the wire around the framework and tack it in place; at the gate end cut the wire off at grade and fasten it to the baseboard. Construct the gate as shown, cover it on the

HOUSES FOR PETS

outside with netting, hinge it to one of the corner posts, and provide it with a hook.

If the ground where you build the yard is bare, dig up some sod and plant it inside of the inclosure, so your rabbits will have grass to play in.

The raising of white rats and fancy mice is a profitable business for boys, and it requires very little time and an expenditure of only a dollar for a pair to start with.

A Cage for White Rats or fancy mice should be constructed out of a box about 14 inches deep, 14 inches

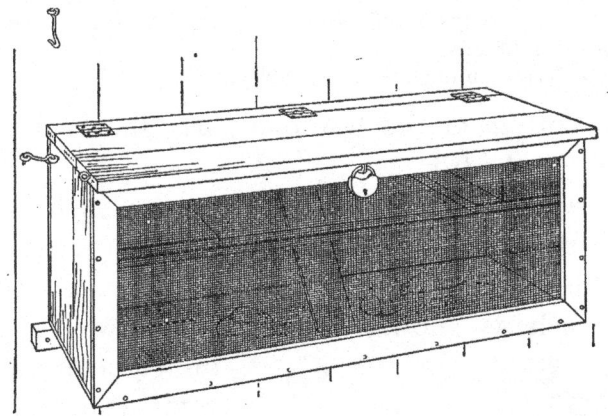

FIG. 500. — Cage for White Rats.

wide, and 3 feet long. A good form of cage is shown in Fig. 500. Remove one side of the box you have procured (this side of the box will be the front of the cage) (Fig. 501), then cut two strips 3 inches wide by the length of the box inside, and fasten them midway between the

WALL
HINGED TOP
BATTEN
STAPLES

FIG. 502.

A
B

FIG. 501.

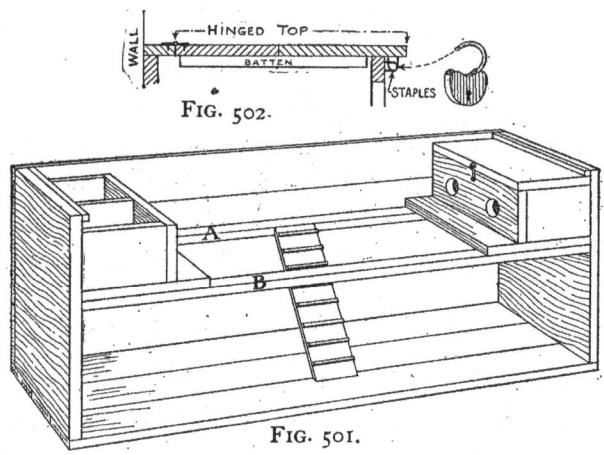

FIG. 501. — View of Inside of White Rat Cage showing Arrangement of Nest Boxes and Stairs.
FIG. 502. — Section through the Hinged Top.

top and bottom of the box, one along the back and the other along the front.

Make a Couple of Nest Boxes as shown in Fig 503, as long as the cage is wide, 5 inches wide (inside), and 4 inches deep (inside); divide them into two compartments each as shown, and cut a doorway $1\frac{1}{2}$ inches in diameter into each compartment. Cut a board to fit the top of each box for a cover, and bend a piece of wire into the shape of a hook (Fig. 503) and fasten it in the proper

(INSIDE OF SCREEN)

FIG. 504.

FIG. 503.

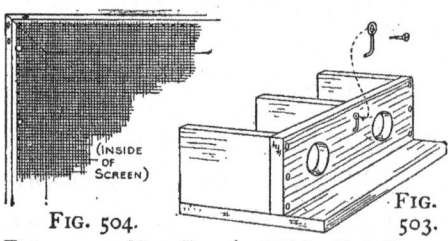

FIG. 503. — Nest Box for White Rat Cage.
FIG. 504. — Corner of Front Screen showing Frame and Attachment of Wire.

position to hook on to a short nail or screw driven into the edge of the cover (Fig. 501). Fasten the nest boxes on top of strips *A* and *B*, and tack a strip to each end of the cage just above the nest box cover to hold down the back edge (Fig. 501). When the cover is unhooked, it can be slipped from under this strip and removed.

Make the stairs out of a piece of board 3 inches wide, tack cross-pieces to it about $1\frac{1}{2}$ inches apart, and fasten it to strip *A* and to the floor, in the center of the cage.

Strips *A* and *B*, together with the platforms in front of the nest boxes, furnish

An Elevated "Race-track" which your rats or mice will make good use of, especially the frisky young ones who love to chase one another about as well as any children do.

Ordinary screen wire cloth is the most satisfactory covering for the front of the cage, and the best method of putting this on is by making a wooden frame out of strips 3 inches wide, with the corners mitered and nailed together (Fig. 504), and tacking the wire to the inside face of this. The frame can be nailed or screwed to the cage (Fig. 500). This is a better method than that of tacking the wire over the edges of the box, as the wire can be stretched tighter and looks neater, and, what is more important, it prevents the wire from bulging out between the tacks and providing the rats with a chance to gnaw away the edge of the box at those points until the space is big enough to escape through.

The top of the cage should project about $\frac{1}{2}$ inch over the ends and 2 inches over the front. First nail a hinge-strip across the top at the back, then batten together the remaining boards, and hinge them to this strip (Fig. 502). By driving a staple into the under side of the cover and another into the screen frame, so the two will come together side by side when the top is closed (Fig. 502), the cage may be padlocked.

Paint your Hutches and Cages on the outside, and whitewash them on the inside.

Floor Covering. Cover the floors with a thick layer of sawdust, which you can get from your grocer; and clean out the hutches and cages twice a week, and replace the old sawdust with fresh, so as to keep conditions sanitary. Place hay in the breeding compartments for the nests.

Drinking Receptacles. Get a small earthenware dish for drinking water. This will stand solidly upon the floor and not be so likely to overturn as a cup, bowl, or other receptacle with a small base. Use a very shallow dish for the rat-cage.

FIG. 505. — A Pigeon-cote.

A Pigeon-cote like the one shown in Fig. 505 may be made out of a packing-box. Divide it into two stories, by fastening a floor midway between the bottom and top, and divide each story into two compartments. Nail the cover boards to the box, fasten a triangular piece to the top edge of each end to form the gables, and then cut and nail the roof boards in place. The space between the box cover and the roof may be divided into two compartments by fastening a triangular piece similar to the gable-ends to the cover boards, before nailing on the roof.

Cut openings through the gable-ends and the sides of the box, into the compartments, and fasten perches below them.

The pigeon-cote may be bracketed to a wall or supported upon a post.

CHAPTER XXVII
A CASTLE CLUB-HOUSE AND HOME-MADE ARMOR

THE castle club-house shown in Fig. 506 is an idea which the author has been holding in reserve for you for a good many years, for he originated it and carried it out on similar lines in his city back yard when a lad. The work is not difficult, and the plan may be simplified or enlarged upon according to how much time you care to spend upon it. A boy's interest in a thing often ceases the moment it is perfected to the point where further improvement is impossible, therefore any piece of work which will suggest alterations and additions from time to time is more acceptable than one which does not. It can be said for the castle club-house that there are many schemes besides those described in this chapter which may be developed by the builders, and which will probably suggest themselves.

Material. As the castle may be built in the corner of the back yard, the material for two walls may be saved, and the lumber required for the rest of the building will cost very little, as you will see by looking at the illustrations. The framework, with the exception of the corner

FIG. 506. THE CASTLE CLUB HOUSE.

post, is buil:
the sides of :
and widths
bought very
torn down c
pose as we'

Before sa
on just wh:
boards yo...
have enoug:
no possibi¹
matter to c..
you will be :

The Frame
ground and
upon which
507). The
two pieces
stand it upo⁻
C, and brac:
fit between :
the inside i.
directly in
horizontal b
corner pos:
F and G a
and I eve⁻
K will be :

post, is built of boards, the corner turrets of barrels, and the sides of box boards and scraps of all sorts of lengths and widths. Second-hand lumber can generally be bought very cheap wherever a frame building is being torn down or remodeled, and this will answer the purpose as well as new material.

Before starting work it is best to do a little figuring on just what you will need, and then sort out all of the boards you have succeeded in getting and see if you will have enough; if you find that you will not, and there is no possibility of procuring more, it will then be an easy matter to cut down the dimensions of the castle so that you will be able to complete the job.

The Framework. Mark out the dimensions upon the ground and lay a board along the end and side for plates upon which to rest the wall framework (*A* and *B*, Fig. 507). Then take a 6-foot piece of 4-by-4-inch stuff, or two pieces of 2-by-4-inch stuff spiked together, and stand it upon the plates at the corner for a corner post *C*, and brace it temporarily. Cut uprights *D* and *E* to fit between the fence rails, if the rails happen to be upon the inside face of the fence, and nail them to the fence directly in line with the corner post. Next, cut the horizontal boards *F*, *G*, *H*, and *I*, and nail them to the corner post *C* and the fence uprights *D* and *E*, placing *F* and *G* about 8 inches above the ground-plates, and *H* and *I* even with the tops of *C*, *D*, and *E*. Boards *J* and *K* will be necessary only in case boards *H* and *I* extend

FIG. 507. The Framework of the Castle, showing how it is built of boards, how the barrel turrets are fastened in place, and how boxes are fastened between the joists for the treasure vaults.

above the top of the fence, as in Fig. 507. Cut uprights *L, M, N, O, P*, and *Q* 7 feet 6 inches long, and nail them to plates *A* and *B*, and to horizontal pieces *F, G, H*, and *I*, 11 inches in from the corners formed by boards *H, I, J,* and *K*. Cut uprights *R* and *S* 7 feet long, and fasten them in the center of the front wall 2 feet apart for the entrance jambs, and set upright *T* in the center of the end wall for an intermediate support.

The Floor Joists, marked *U* in Fig. 507, are 4-inch boards placed on edge, and are fitted between the fence and horizontal piece *G*. If there isn't a rail on the inside face of the fence at the proper height to rest the ends of the joists on, nail a horizontal piece to the fence for the purpose.

Before putting on the wall siding, get three barrels for

The Corner Turrets. Be sure that no hoops are missing from these, and nail each stave to each hoop to keep the barrels from falling apart. Cut a number of pieces of tin about 3 by 5 inches in size, and tack them to the inside edge of the tops of the barrels, about 3 inches apart (Fig. 509), to form the battlements; then set the barrels on boards *H, I, J,* and *K*, between uprights *L, M, N, O, P*, and *Q*, and nail them to these uprights (Fig. 507).

Board up the Walls regardless of the openings, with the exception of the entrance, around which the boards may be fitted, and cut the openings afterwards. Cut the boards so that each end will strike the center of an upright, and use up the short pieces wherever it is possible to do so, in order to save the long pieces for places requiring them. When you are ready

To cut the Openings, mark them out upon the walls and, about $\frac{1}{2}$ inch outside of the lines, nail a vertical strip across the boards which are to be cut to hold them together (Fig. 511). The upper row of openings on the main walls, and those in the turrets, are painted on the wood.

The Roof. To support the upper end of the roof boarding, it will be necessary to nail the horizontal piece V to

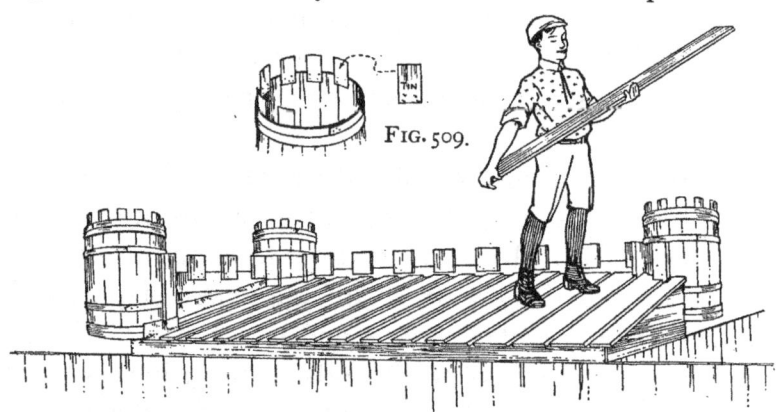

FIG. 508.
FIG. 508. — How the Roof should be put On.
FIG. 509. — Construction of the Turret Battlements.

uprights M, R, S, and N, even with the tops of R and S; at the sides you will have to fasten the diagonal pieces W and X; and around the barrels extra blocking will be required. Figure 508 shows how the roof boarding should be laid. First place one layer of boards about 1

CASTLE CLUB-HOUSE AND HOME-MADE ARMOR 409

inch apart, as shown, then cover the spaces between with another layer. The best way to make water-tight joinings around the barrels and walls is to get some tar paper and tack a strip of it to the roof along the walls, lap it up on to the walls and barrels, and daub it with tar. But if you cannot get the roofing-paper and tar, stuff all the cracks with newspaper, using a pointed stick with which to push the paper in, and then tack pieces of tin over them and lap them up on to the walls and barrels.

If the Roof leaks a little after you have finished it, do not worry; the castle will dry out quickly after a storm, inasmuch as the floor is high off the ground with plenty of space beneath for the air to circulate.

The Battlement. This is made by nailing pieces of board 6 inches square to the walls, above the roof, as shown in Fig. 508. The turret battlements have been described.

The space beneath the floor is plenty large for **Secret Treasure Vaults,** without which, of course, the castle would not be complete. Boxes fastened between the floor joists, as shown in Fig. 507, will make good vaults in which to store the castle's " gold," and the floor boards over these should be battened together in sections so they may be removed to gain access to the vaults.

The Drawbridge should be 1 inch larger all around than the entrance, and its boards should run horizontally and be fastened together with battens (Fig. 511). Cut a piece of broom-handle 8 inches longer than the width of the

A
C
D
B

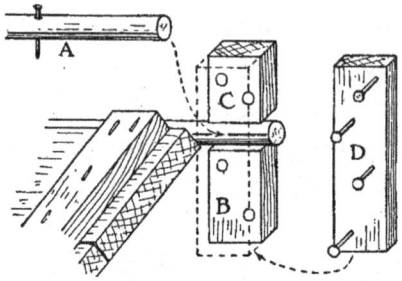

FIG. 510.—Sockets for the Drawbridge.

entrance (*A*, Fig. 510), and nail it to the lower edge of the drawbridge, then make a socket for each end of the broom-handle to set in, by nailing two blocks (*B* and *C*, Fig. 510) to the wall each side of the entrance, and nailing another block (*D*) over these to hold the broom-handle in place.

To counterbalance the Drawbridge, get two clothes-line pulleys, four screw-eyes, and about 18 feet of clothes-line. Bore a hole through each batten of the drawbridge near the end (*A*, Fig. 511), cut two slots in the castle wall above the entrance (*B*, Fig. 511), screw the pulleys into the lower edge

E
C
FIG. 512.
D
V
E
G
B
C
D
A
FIG. 511.

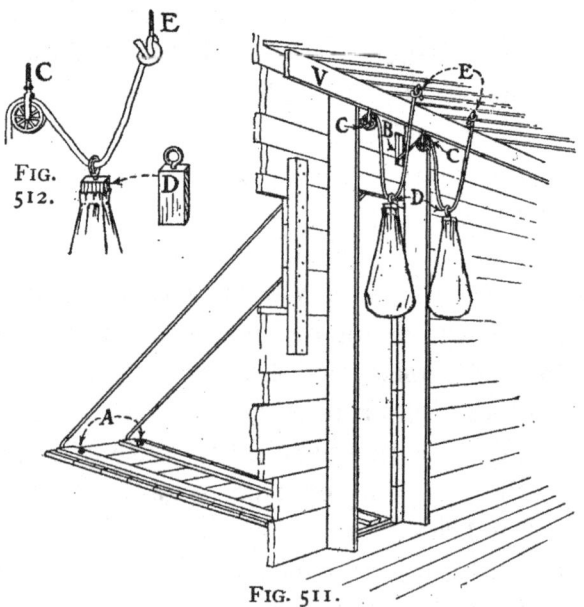

FIG. 511.—How the Drawbridge is Counterbalanced.
FIG. 512.—Details of Counterbalance.

CASTLE CLUB-HOUSE AND HOME-MADE ARMOR

of the horizontal board *V* at *C*, and two screw-eyes into the ceiling at *E*.

For the *counterbalance* take two flour sacks, potato sacks, or two pieces of carpet sewed together in the form of bags; fill them full of sand or gravel, and tack the top of each around a block of wood, in one end of which a screw-eye has been screwed (*D*, Fig. 512). Cut the clothes-line in halves; tie a knot on one end of the pieces; pull them through holes *A* as far as the knotted ends will permit; run them around the ends of the drawbridge, up through slots *B*, over pulleys *C*, through the screw-eyes *D* on the counter-balances, and through screw-eyes *E* (Fig. 511). Then pull up the drawbridge as far as it will go, lower the counterbalances on the ropes until they come within about 6 inches of the floor, and tie the ropes to screw-eyes *E*; cut off the ends of the rope.

A **Windlass** may be substituted for the counter-

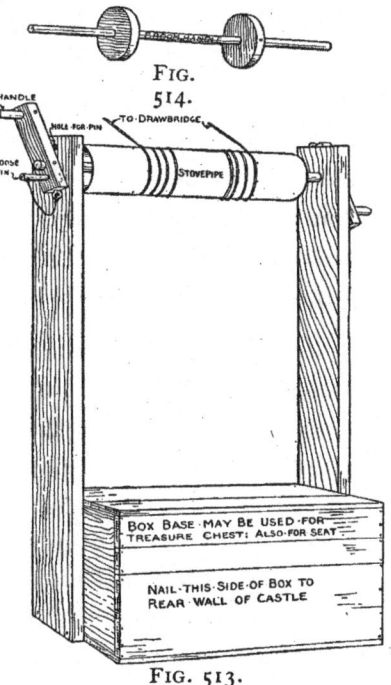

FIG. 513.

FIG. 513. — Windlass for raising the Drawbridge.
(You may make and use one of these instead of the counterbalances shown in Fig. 511.)
FIG. 514. — Shaft for Stovepipe Drum.

balances, if you wish to make one. Figure 513 shows a simple scheme, requiring a section of stovepipe, a broom-handle, a grocery box, and a few boards. Make a shaft for the stovepipe out of the broom-handle; cut two disks equal to the inside diameter of the stovepipe, bore a hole through the center of each large enough for the broom-handle to slip through, and fasten these disks to the shaft (Fig. 514). Slip the shaft through the section of stovepipe, and tack the metal to the wooden disks. Mount the completed drum on two board uprights, and nail the lower ends of the uprights to the ends of the box. Construct a crank for each end of the shaft, fasten them in place as shown, and provide a loose pin to run through a hole bored through each crank and each upright, as a means for locking the windlass; several holes bored through each upright will make it possible to lock the windlass at any point desired. Tie the ends of the ropes leading in from the drawbridge to the drum of the windlass, and fasten them to the metal so they will not slip.

As noted in the illustration, the back of the box base should be nailed to the rear wall of the castle; also connect the upper portions of the uprights to the walls with cross-pieces, to brace them.

A Moat. Dig a trench around the outside of the base for a moat, and your castle will be completed.

Home-made Armor. Of course you will want some armor with which to dress up like a real knight, so I

FIG. 515. A BOY KNIGHT WITH HIS HOME-MADE ARMOR.

CASTLE CLUB–HOUSE AND HOME–MADE ARMOR 413

have invented for you a home-made helmet, a shield, and a sword, which, with the addition of a pair of gauntlets and a sweater (this resembles, somewhat, the texture of coats of chain mail), will make a fairly complete outfit. Figure 515 shows a boy knight equipped with this home-made armor.

The Helmet. Get an old worn-out derby hat (Fig. 516); remove the brim, sweat-band, and ribbon, make slashes 1

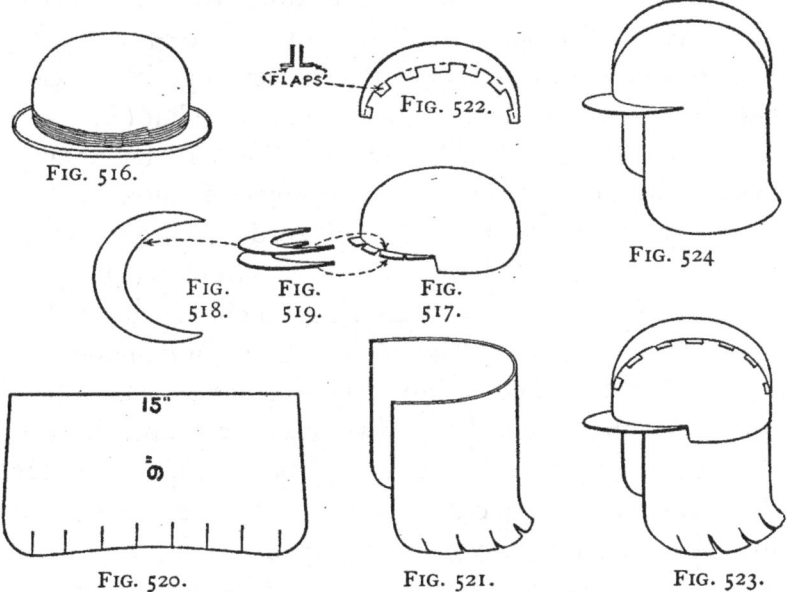

FIGS. 516 to 524. — Details for making the Helmet.

inch in length in the edge of the felt from the center of each side around to the front, and bend up the pieces between the slashes (Fig. 517); cut two vizors out of cardboard (Fig. 518), and glue one of these to the tops of the turned-up felt flaps and one to the under sides (Figs. 517 and 519). For the cape or neck portion of the helmet, cut a piece of cardboard to the shape shown in the diagram, and slash the lower edge (Fig. 520); bend this piece of cardboard as in Fig. 521, and bend out the pieces between the slashes, then coat about 2 inches of the top of the cardboard with glue, place it inside of the hat and press it against the felt until the glue has set (Fig. 523). Prepare the two crown ridge-pieces (Fig. 522) out of cardboard, glue the pieces together back to back, and glue the flaps to the crown of the hat (Fig. 523).

Cover the helmet with tin-foil; this can be obtained from a florist, or from the wrappings of chocolate, etc. Glue the tin-foil to the felt and cardboard, and do not try to smooth out the wrinkles too particularly, for these will give the effect of rich carvings such as you will see on ancient helmets. Figure 524 shows our helmet.

The Shield. Make a bow out of a narrow stick, bending it so there will be a distance of 2 inches between the center of the stick and the bowstring (Fig. 525), then cut the shield out of a piece of heavy cardboard to the dimensions given in Fig. 526 and tack it to the bow. Cut two blocks of wood 4 inches long, and fasten a piece of twisted wire to the ends of each with screws (Fig. 527) for the arm and hand straps; wrap the wire with cord (Fig. 528), and tack the shield to these blocks. Remove the bowstring and cut off the ends of the bow

CASTLE CLUB-HOUSE AND HOME-MADE ARMOR 415

even with the cardboard; then cover the shield with tin-foil or silver paper.

The Sword. Cut this about 3 feet long, with a blade 1½ inches wide, as shown in Fig. 529. First bore a ¼-inch hole through the stick, 6 inches from one end, then whittle the handle round and bevel off the sides of the blade until the edges are sharp. Drive a piece of iron rod of the size marked through the hole in the handle, for the hilt of the sword; then cover the hilt, handle, and the entire blade with tin-foil or silver paper.

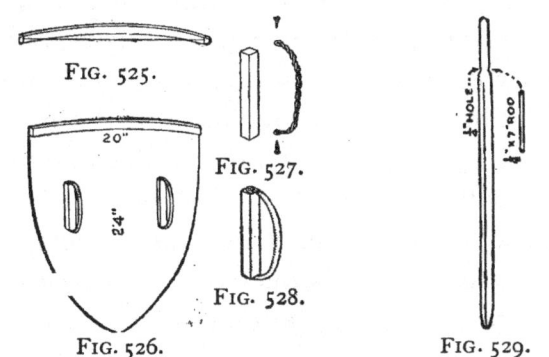

FIG. 525.

FIG. 527.

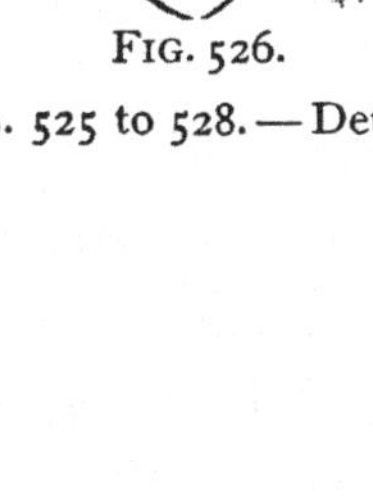

FIG. 528.

FIG. 526.

FIG. 529.

FIGS. 525 to 528.—Details of Shield. FIG. 529.—Sword.

CHAPTER XXVIII
A BOYS' BAND OF HOME-MADE INSTRUMENTS

THE neighborhood parade would be headed by a boys' band, no doubt, were it not for the lack of instruments. This need suggested to the author the idea of devising the home-made cornet, trombone, bass horn, fife, and bass drum shown in the illustrations upon the following pages. They are imitation instruments, to be sure, but they will make plenty of noise, and music, too, if they are properly handled. The notes are produced on the horns by the variation of the voice, and not by the manipulation of keys, so it will be easy for any boy who can carry tunes by ear to play them without having to do very much practicing. If you are not familiar with the tones of the instruments, you can soon become so by listening to the playing of a real band.

The entire band equipment can be completed in a couple of days, if each boy makes his own instrument, and the material should cost but very little, as much of it can be found about the house; most likely something that you will need can be supplied by one of the other boys, in exchange for which you can give him something that he wants.

Fig. 531. The Trombone.

Fig. 532. The Bass Horn.   Fig. 530. The Cornet.
Figs. 530–532. Home-Made Instruments for a Boys' Band.

A BOYS' BAND OF HOME-MADE INSTRUMENTS 417

The Cornet (Fig. 530). Procure a quart-size tin funnel for the bell of the cornet and several feet of round stick ½ inch in diameter for tubing; for this some old flagstaffs can be used, or cabinet-maker's ½-inch dowel sticks can be purchased for a few cents a stick. The curved tubing can be formed of rubber tubing as is shown in the illustration (Fig. 533), or by bending a piece of tree branch

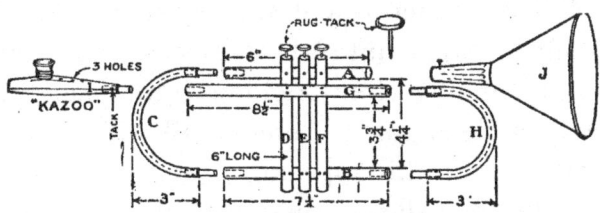

FIG. 533. — Details of Cornet.

to the proper shape (Fig. 538). The lengths of the straight tubing are marked on the diagram, and the pieces are lettered in the order in which they should be assembled. If rubber tubing is used for the ends, run several pieces of heavy wire through it to give it proper stiffness (see dotted lines *C* and *H*, Fig. 533). Bore holes in the ends of the wooden tubing where indicated, and whittle pegs to fit them and the rubber tubing. Fasten the pegs in place with glue, and fasten the other pieces with brads. Drive rug tacks (Fig. 533) into the ends of the key tubes for keys. A "kazoo" is necessary for a mouthpiece. This little instrument, shown in the illustration, will cost a dime, and can be purchased from any music dealer; if he does not carry it in stock, he can procure it for you in a few days' time. Fasten the kazoo in place by means of a wooden peg; then — as you have stopped up its end — it will be necessary to puncture three holes in the top as shown.

When the tubing, keys, bell, and mouthpiece have been put together, procure some tin-foil from empty cigar boxes, buy some from a florist, or get several 5-cent sheets of silver paper at a stationery store. Cut the tin-foil, or silver paper into short pieces, and paste these around the tubing; after sticking it in place, rub each piece with a clean rag to remove all wrinkles. Do the work carefully, as the appearance of the cornet will depend largely upon the neatness with which you cover it.

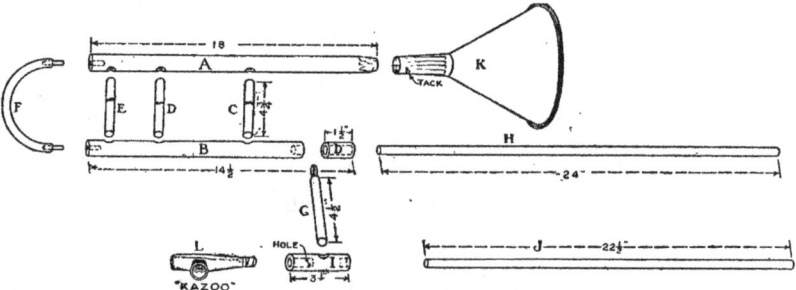

FIG. 534. — Details of the Trombone.

The Trombone (Fig. 531) requires a two-quart tin funnel for its bell and a kazoo for a mouthpiece. Figure 534 shows the details for the main portion of the trombone. The large tubing is made of a broom-handle, the smaller tubing of $\frac{1}{2}$-inch sticks, and the curved ends as described for the *Cornet*.

A BOYS' BAND OF HOME-MADE INSTRUMENTS

The pieces are lettered in the order in which they should be put together, and their lengths are marked. Bore all the holes shown or indicated by dotted lines, of the proper size for the smaller tubing to fit into. Cut *B* and *b* in one piece, and do not separate them until after you have bored a hole in the end 2 inches deep, which will run entirely through *b* and ½ inch into the end of *B*. The idea is to hinge *G* between *b* and *B*. The screw-eye in the end of *G* should be ½ inch in diameter, inside. Cover the end of tube *H* with glue, run it through *b*, through the screw-eye in *G*, and into the hole in *B*. Wrap the end of the kazoo with paper, and glue it in the hole bored in the end of *I*. Make a gimlet hole in *I* as shown, to let out the tone from the kazoo.

Figure 535 shows the completed *trombone slide*, and Fig. 536 the first step in making it. Cut a number

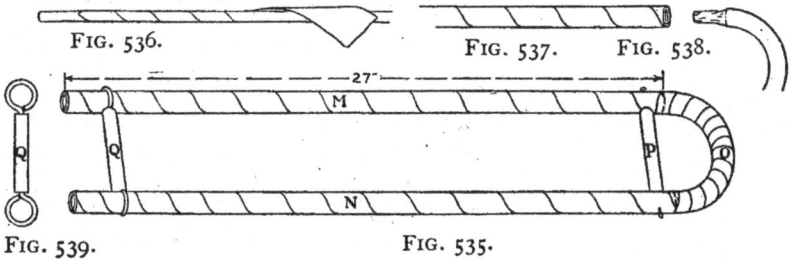

FIGS. 535 to 539.—Details of Trombone Slide.

of strips of newspaper about 3 inches wide and a ½-inch stick about 30 inches long; wrap the stick with a dry strip of paper, then on top of this wrap strips soaked in paste, and gradually build up the tubing until it is as thick as the broom-handle tubing (Fig. 537). Let the tubing dry thoroughly, then pull out the stick and prepare another tube similarly. The curved end O (Fig. 535) may be made out of a tree branch (Fig. 538) or out of rubber tubing (Fig. 533). Fasten P between M and N with brads (Fig. 535). Screw a screw-eye 1 inch in diameter (inside) into each end of Q (Fig. 539), and slip them over the paper tubing (Fig. 535). When all the pieces have been put together properly, cover the tubing with silver paper.

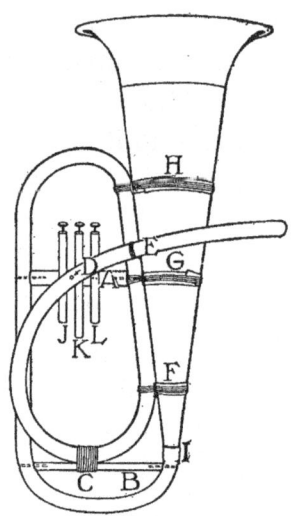

FIG. 540.— Detail of Bass Horn.

The Bass Horn (Fig. 532) is made out of a brass phonograph horn and a piece of an old garden-hose. If you haven't an old phonograph from which you can take the horn, you can probably pick up a horn at a second-hand store for half a dollar. The length of this horn will determine the length of the hose tubing, also that of A and B, but you can follow Fig. 540 in working out the proportions of the instrument. The horn shown in the illustration is 28 inches long, and the garden-hose is 7 feet 6 inches long. The detail shows how the hose should be fastened at C, D, E, F, G, H, and I, and that rug tacks are driven into the ends of tubes J, K, and L. The full tone of the horn can be produced by the voice, as the hose tubing is unobstructed.

A BOYS' BAND OF HOME-MADE INSTRUMENTS

As you probably know, whistling upon the edge of a card makes a pretty fair imitation of

A Fife; we will use this same principle in making our fife shown in Fig. 541. Cut a triangular piece of tin, bend up one corner, and tack it through this corner to a stick 13 inches long, 2 inches from one end. File the edge of the piece of tin blunt and smooth. Bore six "finger holes" in the stick as shown, and cover it with tin-foil or silver paper.

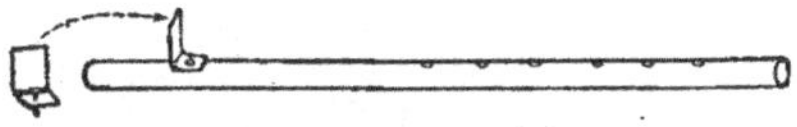

FIG. 541.—The Fife.

FIG. 543.—The Drum Stick.

Figure 542 shows

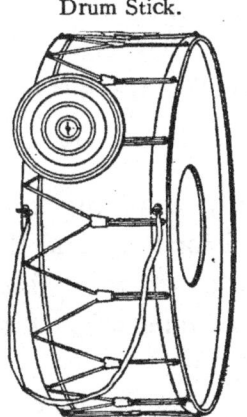

FIG. 542.—The Bass Drum.

The Bass Drum, and Fig. 544 the detail of its framework. Procure eight barrel hoops for the framework; also a small drum. Soak four of the hoops in water, then bend them out and fasten them together so as to make two hoops 30 or 34 inches in diameter. Place the drum in the exact center of one hoop, and fasten strips *A*, *B*, *C*, and *D* around it (Fig. 544). Brace the other hoop with strip *E*, then connect the two hoops with 12-inch strips placed horizontally as shown. Fasten the small drum in place with cords (Fig. 544). Cover the entire framework with wrapping-paper, then cut away the portion covering the head of the small drum (Fig. 542). Nail the four remaining barrel hoops around the bass drum for rims.

Use small staples for the *brace-cord* hooks (Fig. 545); cut the braces out of canvas by the pattern of Fig. 546,

A
B
C
D
E

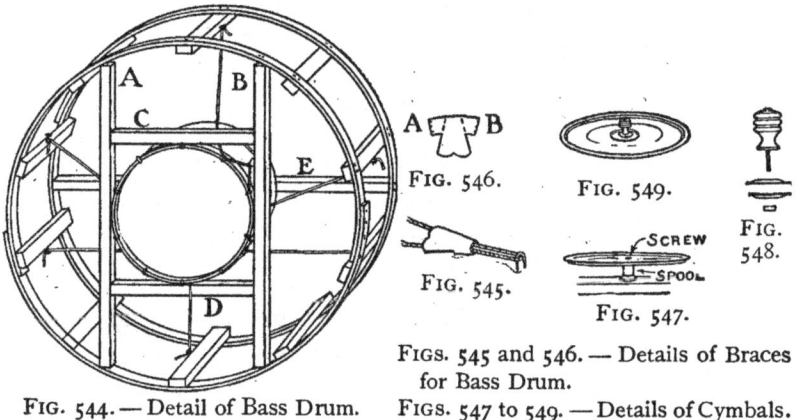

FIG. 544. — Detail of Bass Drum.

A
B

FIG. 546.

FIG. 549.

FIG. 548.

FIG. 545.

SCREW
SPOOL

FIG. 547.

FIGS. 545 and 546. — Details of Braces for Bass Drum.

FIGS. 547 to 549. — Details of Cymbals.

and sew edge *A* to edge *B*. Get heavy wrapping cord for the brace cord, and lace it back and forth around the drum, as shown in Fig. 542. Screw a screw-eye into each rim from which to attach a rope or tape *sling* (Fig. 542).

For Cymbals procure two pot covers; mount one on a spool upon the drum framework (Fig. 547), and fasten a knob (Fig. 548) to the top of the other for a handle (Fig. 549). Pot-cover knobs such as that shown can be bought at any hardware store at 5 cents apiece.

Saw off a 14-inch piece from the end of a broom-handle for

A BOYS' BAND OF HOME-MADE INSTRUMENTS 423

The Drum-stick; cut a hole in an old tennis-ball for it to run through, and drive a nail through the ball into the end of the stick (Fig. 543).

Snare Drums can be easily made by stretching canvas or heavy cloth over cheese boxes, but real drums will help to tone up the band and should be used if you can get them.

The Drum Major (Fig. 550). Choose for your drum-major the boy who can twirl a stick the best.

If an old fur muff can be had, it will make

A Splendid "Bearskin" Cap; sew a piece of elastic to one end of it to go around the chin (Fig. 551). In case

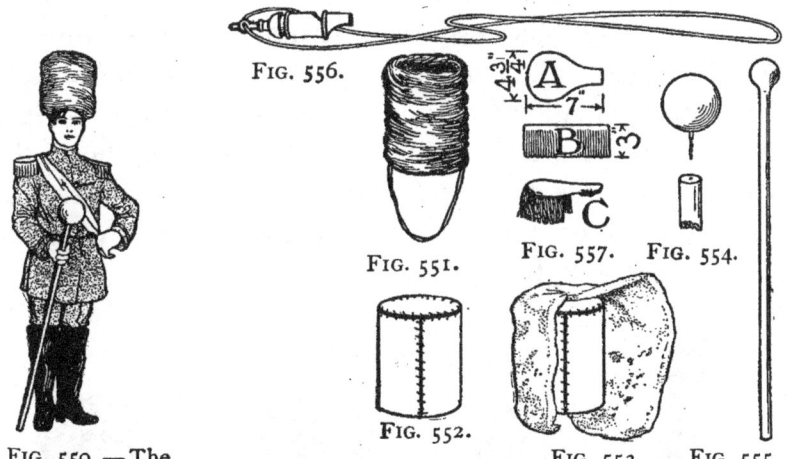

FIG. 550.—The Drum Major.

FIGS. 551 to 557.—Details of Drum Major's Outfit.

you cannot get a muff, make a cardboard cylinder 10 inches in diameter and 12 inches high, and fasten a circular piece of cardboard to the top (Fig. 552); then cover it with cotton (Fig. 553).

Cut a piece of broom-handle 3 feet long for

The Drum Major's Staff, paint it black, and screw to the head a brass ball from a curtain-pole (Fig. 554); then wrap the joint between the ball and piece of broom-handle with cord until it is filled out, as shown in Fig. 555, and cover the cord with a band of tin-foil. Figure 556 shows

The Major's Whistle; with this he signals the band to play. Any toy whistle will do.

Uniforms. The drum major may wear boots if he has a pair, but these are not necessary. He should have a red or blue sash tied across his breast, and red braid stripes pinned down his trousers legs and around his cuffs. Small safety-pins may be sewed to the stripes so they can be attached quickly. Figure 557 shows the way to make the epaulets. Cut a cardboard form similar to *A*, pad it on top with cotton, and cover it with red cloth; then cut fringe out of yellow cloth *B* and sew

A BOYS' BAND OF HOME-MADE INSTRUMENTS 425

it to the edge *C.* Sew a small safety-pin to the under side of *A.*

Figures 530, 531, and 532 will suggest the uniforms for the other band musicians — a soldier cap, a pair of epaulets made similar to the drum major's (see Fig. 557), and red braid stripes for the cuffs and trousers legs.

Now, boys, get to work and organize your band, and after the instruments have been made and you have given a public performance, write and tell me how you succeeded. When your town has a parade on some special occasion, probably you can get permission to head the procession, and when you boys have a vaudeville, a circus, or any kind of a show or entertainment, the band will fill the requirements of an orchestra. If you belong to the "Boy Scouts," organize a Boy Scout Band.

INDEX

A

Admission tickets, 269.
Aërial, a wireless telegraph, 227; form and dimensions of, 227; construction of, 228; insulation of, 229; masts for, 230; grounding of, 230.
Aëro clubs, junior, 300.
Aerogram blanks, 223.
Aeroplanes, model, 297; length of flights, 298, 324; junior aero clubs, 300; meets, 300; glider race, 306; types of machines used, 302; support of models, 302; a cardboard bird glider, 303; a simple monoplane model, 304; a French monoplane model, 309; an Antoinette monoplane model, 314; a more elaborate monoplane model, 316; center-poles, 305, 309, 314, 320; propellers, 306, 310, 315, 321; motors, 307; winding up the motor, 308; planes, 306, 311, 315, 323; warping the planes, 313, 318 (Fig. 399); adjusting the planes, 306, 313, 324; bracing cords, 313, 324; binding material, 320; tails, 316, 325; fins, 316, 325; rudders, 316, 324; running-gears, 311, 321; skids, 311; finish, 324; field for experiments, 326.
Airship, a boy's auto-, 327; framework of balloon, 329; ribs, 330; rib-bands, 331; balloon envelope, 331; stays, 331; car, 332; propeller, 333; starting platform, 334; a push-off platform, 335; rope cable, 335; attachment of car, 335; windlass for pulling airship back to platform, 335; an auto-airship club, 336.
Airships," clockwork "flying, 203.
Amateur wireless telegraph stations, 223.
Ammunition for snow battleship, 285.
Ampere, 252.
Animals for merry-go-round, cardboard, 193, 197.

Annual rings, 44.
Antennæ (same as Aërial).
Antoinette monoplane model, 314.
Ark, a bird, 385; a wall bracket bird, 385.
Armor, home-made, 412; a helmet, 413; a shield, 414; a sword, 415.
Arm rocker, 164.
Attic, a boy's room in an (see Room in an Attic).
Auger-bits, 21.
Auto-airship, a boy's (see Airship).
Auto delivery-wagon, a toy, 180.
Automatic drill, 23.
Automobile moving picture, an, 273.
Auto wagon, 374; steering-gears for, 374, 375; seats for, 376; trip gong for, 376.
Awls, brad-, 22; scratch, 22.
Axles, wagon, 368.

B

Back-saw, 18.
Bag, a sleeping-, 342.
Balloon for auto-airship, framework of, 329; envelope of, 331; stays, 331.
Band of home-made instruments, a boys', 416; a cornet, 417; a trombone, 418; a bass horn, 420; a fife, 421; a bass drum, 421; cymbals, 422; a drum-stick, 423; snare drums, 423; the drum major's "bearskin" cap, 423; his staff, 424; his whistle, 424; uniforms, 424.
Barrel table, 166.
Basket, a waste, 164.
Bass drum, a home-made, 421.
Bass horn, a home-made, 420.
Battens, 69.
Batteries, dry, 247; connections of, 247 and 253.
Battery, a storage, 246.
Battle, rules for a snow naval, 285.
Battlement, a castle club-house, 409.

428 INDEX

Battleship, a snow (see Snow Battleship).
Beaded boards, 49.
Bearings, model aeroplane shaft, 307, 309, 322.
"Bearskin" cap, a drum major's, 423.
Bench, a cabinet-made, 3; a home-made, 3; a chair saw-, 38; a solid work, 4; a work, with tool-drawers, 8; a bedroom or living-room, 117; a camp table, 350; a box, 350.
Bench-hook, 40.
Bench-screw, an iron, 7.
Bench-stop, an adjustable, 12.
Bench-stops, home-made, 11.
Bench-vise, 6.
Bevel, 26, 71.
Biplane type of model aëroplane, faults of the, 302.
Bird glider, a cardboard, 303.
Bird-houses, 379; material for, 379; a box bird-house, 380; another box bird-house, 381; a bird tower, 382; a tin-can bird tower, 382; a bird castle, 383; a bird ark, 385; a wall bracket bird ark, 385; a house and swing, 386; a hanging-house, 386; a shelter, 387.
Bit, expansive-, 21; wood drill, 22; countersink, 22; screw-driver, 23.
Bit-brace, 21.
Bits, auger-, 21.
Blanks, aërogram, 223.
Blocks, single, 329.
Blueprints, working-drawing, 97.
Blunderbuss for "Willie Shute," 268.
Board foot, def. of, 51.
Boards, stock sizes of, 49; undressed, 48; dressed, 48; matched, 49; beaded and matched-and-beaded, 49; rabbeted, 65. (See Lumber.)
Boats, a punt, 351; a sharpie, 356.
Boats," "torpedo, 286.
Bob-sled, 290; runners, 291; seats, 292; check-chains, 293; steering foot-bar, 293; steering lines, 293; handle-bars, 293; seat cushion, 293; painting, 294.
Bolts, 74.
Bonehead, 260.
Book-racks, 107; extension, 108.
Book-shelf, 163.
Bottle-rack, 141.
Box and barrel furniture, 160 (see Furniture).
Boxing-match, moving picture of a, 277.
Boy riders for merry-go-round, 195.

Boy's room in an attic, a (see Room in an Attic).
Brace, ratchet-, 21.
Bracket-saw, 18.
Brad-awls, 22.
Brass craft, 206; tools and materials for, 206; enlarging designs by squares, 207; piercing, 208; polishing, 209; a home-made lacquer, 209; tea-pot stand, 209; calendar board, 211; pen tray, 211; lampshade, 212; candle-shade, 214; fringe for, 214; shade holders, 215; candlestick, 215; "Paul Revere" lantern, 216.
Brushes, 77.
Butt-joint, 60.

C

Cabinet, a tool, 33; a music, 159.
Cabinet-made work benches, 3.
Cabinet-maker's clamps, 29.
Cabin latch, an old-fashioned, 157.
Cable for auto-airship, 335.
Cage, a white rat, 399.
Calendar board, 211.
Call, to receive a "wireless," 249; to make a, 250.
Call list, a "wireless," 223.
Calumet Aero Club, The, 300.
Camp furniture, 349; a chair, 349; a table, 349; a table bench, 350; a box bench, 350; box cupboards, 350.
Camping equipment, 337; cost of "A" and wall tents, 337; how to make an "A" tent, 338; ridge-pole and uprights for a tent, 340; tent stakes, 340; pitching the tent, 340; a tent ground-cloth, 341; a spruce or pine twig mattress, 341; a sleeping-bag, 342; other equipment, 342; an electric flash lamp, 343; packing, 343; a safety match-box, 344; a duffle box, 344; food supplies, 345; learning to cook, 345; an open fire, 345; a backwoodsman's fireplace, 346; pothooks, 347; a sheet-iron camp stove, 347; a Dutch oven, 348; a fireless cooker, 348; building a fire, 348; a camp chair, 349; a camp table, 349; a table bench, 350; a box bench, 350; box cupboards, 350.
Camp stove, a sheet-iron, 347.
Candle-shade, 214; holder for a, 215.
Candle-stick, a brass, 215.

INDEX 429

Can receptacles for nails and screws, 35.
Cap, a drum major's "bearskin," 423.
Captain of snow battleship, duties of, 285.
Car for auto-airship, 332.
Carpenter's horse, 36.
Carpenter's steel square, 26.
Carriage-bolts, 74.
Cars for Ferris wheel, 201; for "flying airships," 205.
Cart, a toy, 180.
Castle, a bird, 383
Castle club-house, a, 404; material, 404; framework, 405; floor joists, 407; corner turrets, 407; walls, 407; openings, 408; roof, 408; battlement, 409; secret treasure vaults, 409; drawbridge, 409; windlass for drawbridge, 411; moat, 412.
Ceiling, def. of boards known as, 49.
Cells (see Batteries).
Center-poles, model aeroplane, 305, 309, 314, 320.
Center-table, a doll's, 182.
Chain fringe for brass craft, 214.
Chair, a Roman, 126; a Mission, 128; an office, 163; a doll's round-seated, 182; a doll's square-seated, 183; a camp, 349.
Chair saw-bench, 38.
Chamfer, 71.
Chamfer bevel, 71.
Chamfer groove, 71.
Check-chain, bob-sled, 293.
Checks in lumber, 47.
Chest, a tool-, 30; a pirate, 159.
Chest-weight, 170.
Chicago Wireless Club, The, 222.
Chiffonier, a box, 167.
Chinning-bar, 175.
Chisels, firmer, 24; framing or mortising, 24; cold-, 25.
Cigar boxes, preparation of, 178; cutting, 179; finish, 179.
Cigar-box toys and gifts, 178 (see Toys; also Furniture).
Clamps, cabinet-maker's, 29; home-made, 29
Cleating boards, 69.
Cleats, 69; porcelain, 229.
Clock-shelf, 105; a corner, 184.
Clockwork motors, 190, 198; to operate, 197; to increase speed of, 205.

Clockwork toys, 189 (see Toys).
Clothes closet for an attic room, 155; trousers hangers for, 155.
Clown and ball moving pictures, 272.
Club-house, a castle (see Castle).
Clubs, workshop, 103, 105; wireless telegraph, 222; vaudeville, 256; junior aero, 300; auto-airship, 336.
Coach-whip pennant, 284.
Coaster, 287; runners for, 287; shoes, 288; seat, 289; handles, 289; foot-bar, 290; painting, 290.
Code card, a "wireless," 223.
Codes, Morse and Continental, 250; a good way to learn the, 251.
Coil, a home-made "wireless" tuning-, 237; an induction- or *spark*-, 245.
Cold-chisel, 25.
Commercial stations, amateur "wireless" 223.
Common-joint, 60.
Common-splice, 60.
Compasses, 92.
Compass-saw, 18.
Condenser, a home-made "wireless," 241.
Contests, model aeroplane, 300, 306, 325.
Continental telegraph code, 251.
Contrivances for the house, handy, 135; a fireless cooker, 136; pot-cover rack, 141; bottle-rack, 141; flat-iron rest, 143; flat-iron rack, 144; sleeve-board, 145; knife-box, 146; scrub-pail platform, 146; towel-roller, 147; ice-pick and ice-chisel rack, 148.
Cooker, a fireless, 136, 348.
Coping-saw, 18.
Cornet, a home-made, 417.
Cote, a pigeon-, 402.
Counterbalance, castle drawbridge, 410.
Countersink-bit, 22.
Countersinking, 73.
Cradle, a doll's, 183.
Crate opener, 17.
Cross-cut saw, 18.
Crosstree, 284.
Cupboards, camp, 350.
Cup-shakes, 47.
Current strength, electrical, 252.
Cutting cigar-box wood, 179.
Cutting large holes, 142.
Cutting pliers, 28.
Cymbals, home-made, 422.

INDEX

D

Dado-plane, 20.
Deck of snow battleship, 283.
Delivery-wagon, a toy auto, 180.
Desk, a Mission writing-, 129; a table, 133; a box writing-, 160.
Detail drawing, 86.
Detectors, home-made "wireless," 233; a microphone, 233; a razor blade microphone, 235; a silicon, 236.
Dickson, Mr. Royal C., 223.
Dimension stuff, sizes of lumber known as, 49.
Dining-table, a doll's, 182.
Dividers, wing-, 27.
Dog-house, 389.
Doll furniture, 182; a round-seated chair, 182; a round center-table, 182; a dining-table, 182; a square-seated chair, 183; a cradle, 183.
Door, a paneled, 124.
Doors for partitions of attic room, 156; transom for, 157; cabin-latch for, 157.
Dot and dash, 226 and 247.
Dovetail half-lap joint, 68.
Dovetailing, 67.
Dovetail-joint, 66.
Doweling, 68.
Dowel-joint, 68.
Dowels, 68.
Drafting table, 91, 133.
Drawbridge, castle, 409.
Drawer-pulls, 32, 288.
Drawers for tools, 10.
Drawing-board, 91.
Drawing outfit, 90.
Drawings, working-, 86; perspective, 88.
Draw-knife, 25.
Dressed stuff, 48.
Drill, an automatic, 23.
Drill bit for wood, 22.
Drop-cord, how to wire up a, 132.
Drum, a home-made bass, 421; a home-made snare, 423.
Drum major, 423; a "bearskin" cap, 423; a staff, 424; a whistle, 424.
Drum-stick, a bass-drum, 423.
Dry batteries (see Batteries).
Duffle box, 344.
Dumb-bell lifting stunt, 258.
Dumb-bell rack, 177.

Dummy assistant to professor with magical mortar, 263.
Dutch oven, 348.

E

Electrical measurements, 252.
Electric fixture, 134.
Electric lamp, 130.
Electromagnetic waves, 226.
Elementary manual training, 42.
Elevations, def. of front, rear, side, right, and left, 87.
Enlarging by squares, 207, 287.
Estimating cost of material, 51.
Exercising machine (see Chest-weight).
Expansive-bit, 21.
Express-wagon, a toy, 180.
Extension book-rack, 108.

F

Falsetto, 263.
Ferris wheel, a clockwork, 198.
Fife, a home-made, 421.
Fighting-tops, 283.
Files, handiest forms of, 25.
Filler, a paste, 82.
Filling woodwork, 82.
Finishing woodwork, 75.
Fins, model aeroplane, 316, 325.
Fire, an open camp, 345; to build a, 348.
Fireless cooker, 136; U. S. Army, 140; a camp, 348.
Fireplace, the backwoodsman's, 346.
Firmer chisels, 24.
Fished-splice, 60.
Fixed condenser, a home-made "wireless," 241.
Flags for snow battleships, 284, 286.
Flash lamp for camping, an electric, 343.
Flat-iron rest, 143.
Flushing Pushmobile Club, The, 365; races of, 365–367.
"Flying airships," clockwork, 203.
Folding rule, a 2-foot, 26.
Food supplies, camp, 345.
Foot-bar for coaster, 290; for bob-sled, 293.
Footstool, 114.
Fore-plane, 20.
Foreshorten, def. of term, 319.
Framing chisel, 24.

INDEX 431

Fringe for brass craft, 214.
Funnels for snow battleships, 284.
Furnishing an attic room, 159.
Furniture, box and barrel, 160; writing-desk, 160; office chair, 163; waste-basket, 164; arm-rocker, 164; barrel table, 166; chiffonier, 167; pirate chest, 159; window seat, 159.
Furniture, camp, 349; a chair, 349; a table, 349; a table bench, 350; a box bench, 350; cupboards, 350.
Furniture, doll, 182; a round-seated chair, 182; a round center-table, 182; a dining table, 182; a square-seated, chair, 183; a cradle, 183.
Furniture, easily made, 103; a whisk-broom holder, 105, 185; a clock-shelf, 105; a corner-clock shelf, 184; a key-board, 183; a match-box, 185; a cottage pipe-rack and match-box, 186; a cottage match-box, 188; a necktie-rack, 107; a towel-rack, 107; book-racks, 107; an extension book-rack, 108; tabourets, 110, 112; a plant stand, 114; a footstool, 114; bench, 117; magazine racks, 120; a music-cabinet, 122; an umbrella-stand, 125; a Roman chair, 126; a Mission chair, 128; a Mission writing-desk, 129; an electric lamp, 130; a drafting table, 133; a desk table, 133.

G

Gauge, a marking-, 26; a mortise-, 27.
Gauging, 52.
Gears, model aëroplane running-, 311, 316, 321.
Gifts, cigar-box, 183 (see Furniture).
Gimlet, a hand, 22.
Girl riders for merry-go-round, 195.
Glider, a cardboard bird, 303; a simple monoplane, 304; a race, 306.
Gong, a trip, 376.
Gothic letters, for working-drawings, 102.
Gouge, 24.
Grindstone, 30.
Groove, 66.
Ground-cloth, a tent, 341.
Grounding an aërial, 230.
Grounds, 116.
Guns for snow battleship, 283, 285.

Gymnasium apparatus, for a boy's room, 170; chest-weight, 170; striking-bag platform, 173; chinning-bar, 175; hitch-and-kick, 175; wand, 176; rack for dumb-bells, Indian clubs, and wand, 177.

H

Half-lap joint, 60.
Halved-joint, 60.
Halved-splice, 60.
Hammer, 17; a tack, 17.
Handle-bars, sled, 293.
Handscrews, 29.
Hanging lamp, a home-made, 158.
Hatchet, 16.
Hay-stove (see Fireless cooker).
Headlights, 373.
Heart-shakes, 47.
Heart-wood, 44.
Heater for attic room, 157.
Hertzian waves, 226.
Hinge-hasp, 31.
Hitch-and-kick, 175.
Holder, a whisk-broom, 105; a shade, 215.
Holes, cutting large, 142.
Home workshop, the, 1.
Hood, a pushmobile, 372.
Hooks, spool, 155.
Horn, a home-made bass, 420.
Horse, a carpenter's, 36.
Horse and hound, moving pictures, 272.
Horses for merry-go-round, 193.
House, a bird- (see Bird-houses); a dog-, 389.
Housed-joint, 66.
Household conveniences, 135 (see Contrivances for the house).
Houses for pets, 389; a dog-house, 389; a rabbit-hutch, 391; a breeding hutch, 394; a two-story rabbit-hutch, 395; a rabbit yard, 398; a cage for white rats, 399; a pigeon-cote, 402.
Hutch, a rabbit-, 391; a breeding, 394; a two-story rabbit-, 395; painting, 402; floor covering, 402; drinking receptacles, 402.

I

Ice-pick and ice-chisel rack, 148.
Indian club rack, 177.
Induction-coil, a "wireless," 245.

432   INDEX

Inkstand, a home-made pencil box and, 96.
Instruments, drawing, 90; "wireless" receiving, 232; "wireless" transmitting, 245; a boys' band of home-made, 416.
Insulation of the "wireless" aërial, 229.
Insulators, porcelain, 229.

J

Jack-in-the-box, 181.
Jack-knife, 15.
Jack-plane, 19.
Joints, 57; common-, 60; butt-, 60; halved-, or *lap*-, 60; mortise-and-tenon, 61; rabbet-, 65; housed-, 66; tongue-and-groove, 66; mitered, 66; dovetail, 66; dovetail half-lap, 68; dowel, 68.
Juggling with "heavy" balls, 260.
Juvenile Manufacturing Co., The, 103.

K

Keel board, an inner, for punt, 353; for sharpie, 361.
Key, a "wireless," 248.
Key-board, 183.
Keyhole-saw, 18.
Kiln drying, 48.
Knife, a jack-, 15; a draw-, 25.
Knife-box, 146.
Knife switch, a double-throw, single-pole, 231; a double-throw, double-pole, 248.
Knobs, spool, 169.
Knots, 47.

L

Lacquer for brass craft, 209.
Lamp, an electric, 130; a home-made hanging-, 158.
Lamp-shade, 212; holder for a, 215.
Lantern hanging-lamp, 158; a "Paul Revere," 216.
Latch, a cabin, 157.
Laying out work, 51; working-drawings, 100.
Lettering working-drawings, 102.
Level, 27; a pocket, 28.
Leveling up uneven legs of furniture, 112.
License number, a pushmobile, 373.
Light for workshop, 3; for attic room, 158.
Lines, dimension, 101; center-, dot-and-dash, dotted, and marginal, 102; plumb-, 153.

Lock, a mortise-, and a half-mortise, 125.
Lockers for a boy's room, 154.
Logs, cutting up, 45.
Lug pole, 346.
Lumber, preparation of, 45; defects in, 47; seasoning of, 48; kiln drying of, 48; stock sizes of, 49; estimating cost of, 51.

M

Machine, a simple moving-picture, 270.
Magazine of snow battleship, 285.
Magazine racks, 120.
Magical mortar, 260; stunts with the, 261.
Main battery of snow battleship, 285.
Mallet, a wooden, 17.
Manual training, elementary, 42.
Marconi, Guglielmo, 219.
Marking-gauge, 26.
Mast for snow battleship, 283.
Masts for aerial, 230.
Match-box, a kitchen, 185; cottage pipe-rack and, 186; a cottage, 188; a safety, 344.
Matched-and-beaded stuff, 49.
Matched stuff, 49.
Material, selection of workshop working-, 43; purchasing, 50; estimating cost of, 51; upholstering, 116; brass craft, 206.
Material boxes, 34.
Mattress, a pine twig, 341.
Medullary rays, 45.
Meets, model aëroplane, 300; pushmobile, 365.
Merry-go-round, a clockwork, 190; horses for, 193; sleighs for, 194; girl and boy riders for, 195; animals for, 197; to operate, 197.
Microphone detector, a home-made, 233; a razor blade, 235.
Mill list, preparation of a, 50.
Mission chair, 128.
Mission writing-desk, 129.
Miter-box, a home-made, 39.
Mitered-joint, 66.
Mitered-splice, 66.
Moat, 412.
Model aeroplanes (see Aëroplanes).
Monoplane model aëroplane, a simple, 304; a French, 309; an Antoinette, 314; a more elaborate, 316. (For parts see Aëroplanes.)
Morse telegraph code, 250.

INDEX 433

Mortar, the magical, 260.
Mortise, 62.
Mortise- and-tenon joints, 61.
Mortise-gauge, 27.
Mortising chisel, 24.
Motors, clockwork, 190, 198; to operate, 197; increasing speed of, 205.
Motors, model aëroplane, 307; winding for flights, 308.
Moving pictures, 270; a simple machine for, 270; the clown and ball, 272; the circus horse and hound, 272; the automobile, 273; the revolving wheels, 276; the boxing match, 277.
Multiple, batteries connected in, 247 and 253.
Music-cabinet, 122.

N

Nail boxes and cans, 34 and 35.
Nailing, 74; toe-, 152 (Fig. 173).
Nails, 74.
Nail-set, 17.
Naval battle, a snow, 285; rules for a, 285.
Necktie-rack, 107.
Nest boxes, rat-cage, 400.
Netting, poultry-, 393.

O

Odd jobs, the, 28.
Office chair, 163.
Ohm, 252.
Oiler, 30.
Oil heater for attic room, 157
Oiling woodwork, 84.
Oil stains, 79.
Oilstone, 30.
Outfit, a tool, 14; a wood finishing, 75; a drawing, 90; a brass craft, 206; a "wireless" receiving, 232; a "wireless" transmitting, 245; a camping, 337.
Oven, a Dutch, 348.

P

Packing a camp outfit, 343.
Paint, 75; mixing, 76.
Painter for punt, 355; for sharpie, 362.
Painting, 77.
Panel door, 124.
Paneling, 124.

Paper for working drawings, 96; for tracing, 97.
Parallel, batteries connected in, 247, 253.
Paring with a chisel, 63.
Partition for attic room, 149.
"Paul Revere" lantern, a brass, 216.
Pencil box, a home-made, 96.
Pencils, drawing, 94.
Pennants for a boy's room, 159; for a snow battleship, 284.
Pens, 95.
Pen tray, 211.
Perspective drawing, def. of a, 88.
Picture-frames, home-made, 159.
Pictures, moving, 270.
Pigeon-cote, 402.
Pins for mortise-and-tenon joints, 65.
Pirate chest, 159.
Pith of a tree, 44.
Plain sawing, 45.
Plan, def. of, 87.
Plane, a jack-, 19; a smoothing-, 20; a fore-, 20; a rabbet-, 20; a dado-, 20.
Planes for model aëroplanes, 306, 311, 315, 323; stability, 303; warping of, 313, 318 (Fig. 399).
Planing exercise, 54.
Planks, sizes of lumber known as, 49.
Plant stand, 110, 114.
Platforms for auto-airship, 334.
Pliers, 28.
Plumb-board, 153.
Plumb-line, 153.
Pocket level, 28.
Polishing, wood, 83; brass, 209.
Pot-cover rack, 141.
Potentiometer, a home-made "wireless," 243.
Pothooks, 347.
Poultry-netting, 393.
Pressure, electrical, 252.
Priming coat, 78.
Printing-frame for blueprints, a home-made, 99.
Professor for a boys' vaudeville show, the, 261; his magical mortar, 260; stunts, 261–263.
Program board for vaudeville show, 268
Propeller, an auto-airship, 333.
Propellers, model aëroplane, 306, 310, 315, 321; shafts and bearings for, 307.
Punching-bag (see Striking-bag).

434 INDEX

Punt, a home-made, 351; dimensions, 351; material, 351; side boards, 352; stem- and stern-pieces, 353; bottom boards, 353; inner keel board, 353; seats, 354; rowlocks, 354; thole-pins, 355; painter, 355; finishing, 355.
Pushmobile, a, 364; a, club, 365, 368; a race, 367; to construct a, 368; axles, 368; wagon-bed, 369; steering-gear, 369; hood, 372; radiator-front, 372; seat, 373; headlights, 373; side lamps, 373; painting, 373; license number, 373; a racing pushmobile, 373.
Push wagon, a simple, 376; wagon-bed, 376; rear wheels, 377; front wheels, 377.
Puttying, 84.
Putty-knife, a home-made, 85.

Q

Quarter sawing, 46.

R.

Rabbet, 65.
Rabbet-joint, 65.
Rabbet-plane, 20.
Rabbit-hutch (see Hutch).
Rabbit yard, 398.
Races, model aeroplane, 300, 306, 325; push- mobile, 365-368.
"Race track," a rat-cage, 401.
Rack, a tool-, 33; a necktie-, 107; a towel-, 107; a book-, 107; an extension book-, 108; a magazine-, 120; a pot-cover, 141; a bottle-, 141; a flat-iron, 144; an ice- pick and ice-chisel, 148; a broom-handle towel-, 158; a dumb-bell, Indian club, and wand, 177.
Radiator-front, a pushmobile, 372.
Ratchet-brace, 21.
Ratchet screw-driver, 23.
Razor blade microphone detector, 235.
Receivers, telephone, 232.
Receiving outfit, a "wireless," 232; aerial, 227; insulating, 229; grounding, 230; telephone receivers, 232; microphone detector, 233; razor blade microphone detector, 235; silicon detector, 236; tuning-coil, 237; fixed condenser, 241; potentiometer, 243; arrangement of in- struments, 248; to receive a call, 249; codes, 250.

Resistance, electrical, 252.
Rest for flat-iron, 143.
Revolving wheels moving picture, 276.
Rib-bands, auto-airship balloon, 331.
Ridge-pole, a tent, 340.
Rip-saw, 18.
Rocker, an arm, 164.
Roller, a towel-, 147.
Roman chair, 126.
Roof, castle, 408.
Room in an attic, a boy's, 149; parti- tions for, 149; lockers for, 154; clothes closet for, 155; heater for, 157; wash- stand for, 158; lighting, 158; furnishing, 159.
Rowlocks, 354.
Rubbing woodwork, 83
Rudder, a model aeroplane, 316, 324; a sharpie, 362.
Rule, a 2-foot folding, 26.
Ruler, a 12-inch, 94
Ruling-pen, 93.
Runners for coaster, 287; for bob-sled, 291; shoes for, 288.
Running-gears, model aeroplane, 311, 316, 321.

S

Sam Dow, the strong man, 256; stunts for, 256-260.
Sandpapering, 84.
Sap-wood, 45.
Saw, cross-cut, 18; rip-, 18; compass-, 18; keyhole-, 18; back-, 18; coping-, 18; bracket-, 18; scroll-, 19.
Saw-bench, a chair, 38.
Sawing, plain, 45; quarter, 46; exercise in, 57.
Scale for mechanical drawing, 94.
Scales to which drawings are made, 88.
Scratch-awl, 22.
Screw-driver, a spiral-ratchet, 23; a hand, 23; a, bit, 23.
Screws, 72; fastening together work with, 73.
Scribing, 51.
Scroll-saw, 19.
Scrub-pail platform, 146.
Seasoning lumber, 48.
Seat, a window, 159; a coaster, 289; a bob-sled, 292.

INDEX   435

Seats, coaster, 289; bob-sled, 292; punt, 354; sharpie, 361; wagon, 373, 376.
Secondary battery of snow battleship, 285.
Section, def. of cross-, and longitudinal, 88.
Series, batteries connected in, 247, 253.
Series-parallel, batteries connected in, 247, 253.
Shade, a lamp-, 212; a candle-, 214.
Shade holders, 215.
Shafts for model aëroplanes, propeller, 307, 310, 322.
Shakes, cup-, 47; heart-, 47.
Sharpie, a home-made, 356; dimensions, 356; side pieces, 357; stem-piece, 358; stern-piece, 358; stretcher, 358; putting the pieces together, 358; bottom boards, 359; skeg, 360; inner keel board, 361; seats, 361; bow, 361; painter, 362; rudder, 362; rowlocks, 363.
Shelf, a clock, 105; a corner clock, 184.
Shellac, 81.
Shellacking, 81.
Shelter, a bird, 387.
Shelves for workshop, 34; for books, 163.
Shoes for sled runners, 288.
Shooting-board, 40.
Shop equipment, work-benches, 3–13; tools, 14–30; tool-chest, 30; tool-cabinet, 33; tool-rack, 33; material boxes, 34–36; horse, 36; chair saw-bench, 38; miter-box, 39; bench-hook, 40; shooting-board, 40.
Show, stunts for a boy's vaudeville (see Vaudeville show).
Side lamp, a bicycle lamp, 373; a clock-case, 373.
Silicon detector, a home-made, 236.
Silver grain in wood, 45.
Skeg, 360.
Skids, model aëroplane, 311.
Sled, a coaster, 287; a bob-, 290.
Sleeping-bag, 342.
Sleeve-board, 145.
Sleighs for merry-go-round, 194.
Smoothing-plane, 20.
Snare drums, home-made, 423.
Snow battleship, 279; central station, 279; hull, 280; torpedo tube, 281; superstructure deck, 283; conning-tower, 283; forward turret, 283; midship turret, 283; mast, 283; fighting-tops, 283; rapid-fire guns, 283; crosstree, 284; coach-whip pennant, 284; signal flags, 284: Union Jack, 284; national ensign, 284; funnels, 284; ventilators, 285; main-battery and secondary battery guns, 285; ammunition stores, 285; duties of the Captain, 285; a naval battle, 285; rules for a naval battle, 285; flag of truce, 286; "torpedo boats," 286; repairs, 286; marksmanship, 286.
Socket and drop-cord for lamp, 131.
Spark-coil, 245.
Spark-gap, 246.
Specifications, 86.
Spiral-ratchet screw-driver, 23.
Spirit level, 27.
Splices, 57; common-, 60; fished-, 60; halved, 60; mitered-, 66.
Spoke-shave, 25.
Spool hooks, 155; knobs, 169.
Spreader for aërial, 229.
Square, a try-, 26; a carpenter's steel, 26.
Squares, enlarging by, 207, 287.
Stability planes, 303.
Staff, a drum-major's, 424.
Staining, 78.
Stains, water, 79; oil, 79.
Stakes, tent, 340.
Stand, a tea-pot, 209.
Steel square, 26.
Steering foot-bar, sled, 293.
Steering-gears, wagon, 369, 374, 375.
Steering lines, sled, 293; wagon, 371, 375.
Steering-wheels, wagon, 369, 374, 375.
Stem-piece, the punt, 353; the sharpie, 358.
Stern-piece, the punt, 353; the sharpie, 358.
Stock, def. of term, 48; sizes of, 49.
Stool, a foot-, 114.
Stop, an adjustable bench-, 12.
Stop chamfer, 71.
Stops, home-made bench-, 11; door, 125.
Storage battery, 246.
Stove, camp, 347.
Stove for attic room, 157.
Striking-bag, 173; platform for, 173.
Structure of wood, 44.
Stuff, def. of term, 48; undressed, 48; dressed, 48; matched, 49; matched-and-beaded, 49.
Swing, a bird, 386.
Switch, a double-throw single-pole knife, 231; a double-throw double-pole knife, 248.

T

Table, a drafting, 91, 133; a desk, 133; a barrel, 166; a doll's round center-, 182; a doll's dining-, 182; a camp, 349.
Tabourets, 110, 112.
Tails, model aeroplane, 316, 325.
Taper, 71.
Targets for Willie Shute's vaudeville stunts, 267.
Tea-pot stand, a brass, 209.
Telephone receivers, 232.
Tenon, 63.
Tent, cost of a, 337; how to make an "A," 338; to pitch a, 340.
Thole-pins, 355.
Thumb-tacks, 96.
Tickets, admission, 269.
Toe-nailing, 152 (Fig. 173).
Tongue-and-groove joint, 66.
Tool-cabinet, 33.
Tool-chest, 30.
Tool drawers, 10.
Tool-rack, 33.
Tools, purchasing, 14; a handy guide for purchasing, 15; the principal, 15; a small outfit of, 15; a chest for, 30; cabinet for, 33; rack for, 33; drawing, 90; brass craft, 206.
Tool tray, 10.
"Torpedo boats" for snow battleship, 286.
Torpedo tube for snow battleship, 281.
Towel-rack, 107; a broom-handle, 158.
Towel-roller, 147.
Tower, a bird, 382; a tin-can bird, 382.
Toys, cigar-box, 178; an express-wagon, 180; a cart, 180; an auto delivery-wagon, 180; a jack-in-the-box, 181; a round-seated chair, 182; a round center-table, 182; a dining-table, 182; a square-seated chair, 183; a doll's cradle, 183.
Toys, clockwork, 189; merry-go-round, 190; miniature Ferris wheel, 198; "flying airships," 203.
Tracing-cloth, 97.
Tracing-paper, 97.
Transmitting outfit, a "wireless," 245; aerial, 227; insulating, 229; grounding, 230; an induction-coil, 245; spark-gap, 246; storage battery, 246; dry batteries, 247; "wireless" key, 248; knife switch, 248; arrangement of instruments, 248; operation of, 249; to make a call, 250; codes, 250; connection of batteries, 253.
Transom for door, 157.
Tray, a tool, 10; a brass pen, 211.
Treasure vaults, castle, 409.
Trestletrees, 283.
Triangles, 92.
Trip gong, 376.
Trombone, a home-made, 418.
Truce, a flag of, 286.
Try-square, 26.
T-square, 91.
Tuner (see Tuning-coil).
Tuning-coil, a home-made "wireless," 237.
Turnbuckles, 174.
Turrets, snow battleship, 283; castle, 407.
Twist wire cloth, 393.

U

Umbrella-stand, 125.
Undercutting, 114.
Undressed stuff, 48.
Uniforms for a boys' band, 424.
Upholstering, and material for, 116.

V

Vanderbilt Pushmobile Cup Race, The, 366.
Varnishing, 83.
Vaudeville show, stunts for a boys', 256; Sam Dow, 256; lifting feats, 256–260; juggling, 260; Bonehead, 260; magical mortar, 260; the professor, 261; the wonderful hat trick, 261; other mortar stunts, 262; the professor's final exhibition, 262; the dummy assistant, 263; Falsetto, 263; the Ventriloquist, 264; his doll, 264; Willie Shute, 266; his targets, 267; his blunderbuss, 268; program board, 268; admission tickets, 269.
Vaults, castle secret treasure, 409.
Ventriloquist, how a boy can be a, 264; doll for the, 264.
Vise, bench-, 6; an iron, 8.
Volt, 252.

ND# INDEX

W

Wagon, a toy express, 180; a toy auto delivery-, 180.
Wagons, pushmobiles and other home-made, 364; a pushmobile, 368; a racing pushmobile, 373; an auto wagon, 374; a simple push wagon, 376.
Wainscoting for attic room, 155.
Wand, a home-made, 176; rack for a, 177.
Warping, cause of wood, 45.
Warping model aëroplane planes, 313, 318 (Fig. 399).
Wash-stand for attic room, 158.
Waste basket, 164.
Water stains, 79.
Waxing, 83.
Wedging mortise-and-tenon joints, 65.
Wheels, the moving-picture revolving, 276.
Wheels, wagon, 364, 368, 377.
Whisk-broom holders, 105, 185.
Whistle, a drum major's, 424.
White rat cage, 399.
Willie Shute's vaudeville stunts, 266; his targets, 267; his blunderbuss, 278.
Winding, testing a board for, 55.
Winding-sticks, 55.
Windlass, a castle drawbridge, 411.
Window seat, 159.
Wind-shakes (same as *Cup-shakes*), 47.
Wing dividers, 27.
Wings, model aëroplane (see Planes).
Wire cloth, 393.
Wireless Club, The Chicago, 222.
Wireless telegraph outfit, a boy's, 219; code card, 223; call list, 223; aërogram blanks, 223; aërial, 227; masts, 230; insulating, 229; grounding, 230; double-throw, single-pole knife switch, 231; telephone receivers, 232; microphone detector, 233; razor blade microphone detector, 235; silicon detector, 236; tuning-coil, 237; fixed condenser, 241; potentiometer, 243; induction-coil, 245; spark-gap, 246; storage battery, 246; dry batteries, 247; wireless key, 248; double-throw, double-pole knife switch, 248; arrangement of instruments, 248; operation of instruments, 249; to receive a call, 249; to make a call, 250; codes, 250.
Wireless telegraphy, development of, 219; amateur commercial stations, 223; fundamental principles of, 224; what some boys have accomplished, 221.
Wiring a socket, plug, and drop-cord, 132.
Wood, structure of, 44; defects in, 47.
Wood drill bit, 22.
Wood-file, a half round, 25.
Wood finishing, 75; paint, 75; mixing paints, 76; painting, 77; brushes, 77; staining, 78; water stains, 79; oil stains, 79; shellacking, 81; filler, and filling, 82; varnishing, 83; waxing, 83; rubbing, 83; polishing, 83; oiling, 84; sandpapering, 84; puttying, 84; home-made putty-knife, 85; caution about oily rags, 85.
Work bench, a cabinet-made, 3; a home-made, 3; a solid, 4; a, with tool drawers, 8.
Working drawings, 86; scales of, 88; preparation of, 100.
Working edge, def. of, 56.
Working face, def. of, 55.
Working material, selection of, 43.
Workshop, the home, 1; location of, 2; light for, 3; equipment for (see Shop equipment).
Wrench, 28.
Writing-desk, a Mission, 129; a box, 160.

Y

Yard, a rabbit, 398.

THE BOY CRAFTSMAN
Practical and Profitable Ideas for a Boy's Leisure Hours
By A. NEELY HALL

Illustrated with over 400 diagrams and working drawings 8vo Price, $2.00

EVERY real boy wishes to design and make things, but the questions of materials and tools are often hard to get around. In this book a number of chapters give suggestions for carrying on a small business that will bring a boy in money with which to buy tools and materials necessary for making apparatus and articles described in other chapters. No work of its class is so completely up-to-date, the drawings are profuse and excellent, and every feature of the book is first-class. It tells how to make a boy's workshop, how to handle tools, and what can be made with them; how to start a printing shop and conduct an amateur newspaper, to fit up a dark-room, build a log cabin, a canvas canoe, a gymnasium, a miniature theatre, and many other things dear to the soul of youth.

We cannot imagine a more delightful present for a boy than this book. — *Churchman, N. Y.*

Every boy should have this book. It's a practical book — it gets right next to the boy's heart and stays there. He will have it near him all the time, and on every page there is a lesson or something that will stand the boy in good need. Beyond a doubt in its line this is one of the cleverest books on the market. — *Providence News.*

If a boy has any sort of a mechanical turn of mind, his parents should see that he has this book. — *Boston Journal.*

This is a book that will do boys good. — *Buffalo Express.*

The boy who will not find this book a mine of joy and profit must be queerly constituted. — *Pittsburgh Gazette.*

Will be a delight to the boy mechanic. — *Watchman, Boston.*

An admirable book to give a boy. — *Newark News.*

This book is the best yet offered for its large number of practical and profitable ideas. — *Milwaukee Free Press.*

Parents ought to know of this book. — *New York Globe.*

For sale by all booksellers or sent postpaid on receipt of price by the publishers,

LOTHROP, LEE & SHEPARD CO., BOSTON

Made in the USA
Columbia, SC
27 October 2023